HO

℣. Christus factus est
pro nobis obédiens us-
que ad mortem.

HOLY WEEK

THE COMPLETE OFFICES
OF HOLY WEEK
IN LATIN AND ENGLISH

A NEW EXPLANATORY EDITION

BY

THE RIGHT REVEREND

ABBOT CABROL, O. S. B.

Third edition

Norfolk, Virginia ✷ MMXIII

NOTA TOMUS
GREGORIANA
An Imprint of IHS Press

Holy Week. The Complete Offices of Holy Week in Latin and English. New Matter
Copyright © 2013 IHS Press. All rights reserved.

Holy Week, by the Right Rev. Abbot Fernand Cabrol, was first published in Latin and English, on the basis of the Pio-Benedictine Roman Missal and Breviary, as early as 1926 by various publishers such as B. Herder and A. Mame (London), P. J. Kennedy and Sons (New York), Diedrich-Schaefer (Milwaukee), and J. W. Winterich (Cleveland). The latter's third printing, dated August 1927, forms the basis for the images contained in this facsimilie edition. Cabrol's text here reproduced bore the imprimatur of the Most Rev. William T. Cotter, bishop of Portsmouth, England (1910–1940). Abbot Cabrol (1855–1937) made his vows as a Benedictine in 1877 at Solesmes, was ordained a priest in 1882, and served as Prior there beginning in 1890. In 1896 he became the first Prior of St. Michael's in Farnborough, England, a daughter house of the Solesmes Abbey, and, when the former was raised to an Abbey in 1903, Cabrol became its first Abbot. He authored some dozen books on the liturgy and liturgical history, and his research and study in France, Italy, Switzerland, and Germany contributed to *La Paleógraphie Musicale*. He was awarded the Order of the British Empire in 1920 for his services to the Red Cross in World War I.

ISBN-13: 978-1-60570-093-9

Library of Congress Cataloging-in-Publication Data pending

IHS Press is the only publisher dedicated exclusively to the Social Teachings of the Catholic Church. Contact us as info@ihspress.com or 877-1HS-PRES (447.7737).

The aim of our liturgical imprint, *Nota Tomus Gregoriana* ("Gregorian Note Books"), is to make available to both clerical and lay audiences, for practical, historical, and academic purposes, liturgical and related books antedating the so-called reforms of the second half of the 20th century. These works are offered in the spirit both of liturgist Klaus Gamber's remark that "[i]t most certainly is not the function of the Holy See to introduce Church reforms," but rather to "watch over [her] traditions" (*The Reform of the Roman Liturgy*, trans. Klaus D. Grimm [San Juan Capistrano, Calif.: Una Voce Press, 1993], 38), and, more emphatically, of St. Gregory the Great's rebuke to Emperor Maurice, that one must not "raise his neck against the statutes of the Fathers" (*Registr.* v. 37, cited in St. Pius x's *Iucunda Sane* of 1904).

"Long before the rationalism of the sixteenth century . . . , people had ceased to unite themselves exteriorly with the prayer of the Church, except on Sundays and festivals. During the rest of the year, . . . the people took no share in it. Each new generation increased in indifference . . . . Social prayer was made to give way to individual devotion . . . . That was the first sad revolution in the Christian world."
—Dom Prosper Gueranger, *The Liturgical Year*

CONTENTS

INDEX TO CERTAIN HYMNS, PSALMS ETC.

INTRODUCTION

I. THE ORIGIN OF HOLY WEEK

As, historically speaking, Holy Week was the nucleus from which the whole cycle developed, so also from a liturgical point of view it is the very centre of the liturgical year.

In the early days of the Church there was as yet no liturgical year ; it developed gradually, by successive stages, the formation of the liturgical week in all probability preceeding that of the liturgical year.

The one great absorbing fact which filled the minds of the primitive Christians was the Passion of Our Lord, his Death and Resurrection. The Mass, or the breaking of bread, which took place in private houses from the very earliest days, as we learn from the Acts of the Apostles, was a commemoration, or rather renewal of these sacred events. The institution of the Holy Eucharist on Maundy Thursday was but the prelude to the great drama of Calvary, the Resurrection its triumphant sequel. These three events are so intimately connected that they cannot be considered separately ; each one completes and explains the others, and they form the basis of Christianity.

As we have just seen, these three events are commemorated in the Mass, not in a symbolical form, but in the great reality of the Holy Sacrifice, which is to the Christian the reproduction of the tragedy of the Cross and of the last days of Holy Week. This is found in all the liturgies, though under various forms : *Qui pridie quam pateretur ; hoc facite in meam commemorationem ; unde et memores nos... tam beatæ passionis, nec non et ab inferis resurrectionis, sed et in cælos gloriosæ Ascensionis*. (Who the day before he suffered ; Do this in remembrance of me ; wherefore we thy servants... the blessed passion, his rising up from hell, and glorious ascension into heaven.)

Thus the Mass is the commemoration of the Passion, the Death and the Resurrection of Our Saviour, and even of the last act of his mortal life, his Ascension.

a — The Office of Holy Week.

The Christians attached such importance to the Mass that all religious worship seemed centred in it and dependent on it. In the primitive Church of Jerusalem, which was the type and ideal of religious fervour, we learn from the Acts that the breaking of bread took place daily. The memory of the sufferings and triumph of Christ, and his own coming to them in communion filled the lives of these Christians. These mysteries were complete in themselves, nothing essential could be added to them. Their different aspects and various points might indeed be analysed, but they still remained the keystone of the liturgical system. Every day was therefore in one sense a complete liturgical year, a feast containing substantially all the other feasts. Moreover there was at that time no other liturgical distinction between the days, weeks or years. The idea developed later on by Clement of Alexandria, Origen and others, that to the Christian every day should seem a feast day, was but founded on fact, the proof of which is found in the Epistles of St. Paul, the Acts of the Apostles, and even the Didache [1].

The Institution of Sunday.

If this was the state of things in the primitive Church of Jerusalem, where every day was sanctified by the breaking of bread, and spent in prayer and meditation on the Passion of Our Lord, it is obvious that it could not continue when the faith began to spread outside Jerusalem. New centres sprang up at Cæsarea, Antioch, Ephesus, Smyrna, Corinth, Thessalonica, where the exigencies of life made it impossible for these churches to imitate the retired, contemplative life of the apostolic Church of Jerusalem. The majority of the Christians belonged to the lower classes, slaves, cobblers, tanners, people who had to earn their living, and for whom the *quotidie* (every day) of the Acts, the daily Mass, was an impossibility. It naturally followed that one special day in the week was set apart for the synaxis [2], when they could all meet together. Everything pointed to the sabbath being

---

[1] The *Didache* or the *Doctrine of the Apostles* is a work of the end of the first century.

[2] *Synaxis* means meeting, assembly.

chosen for this day, the day kept sacred by the Jews, the day on which God himself rested after the creation. Here however occurs a break with tradition, a fact of the highest importance, as only the Apostles could have taken the initiative in this case. The sabbath was not the day chosen for the liturgical synaxis but the day after, the *prima sabbati*, the day we call *Sunday*, or *dies Dominica*, the *Lord's Day*, the day of Our Lord's Resurrection, Easter Day. It was the first day of the Hexameron, when God began creation by saying : " Let there be light. " From the very beginning this day had been rich in symbolical meaning. This was a liturgical revolution, a decision full of import for the future, marking the separation of Christianity from Judaism.

Although Christianity owed its origin to the Mosaic religion, yet the mission of the latter was but to prepare the way for that of the Messias. The Church kept as a precious treasure the Sacred Scriptures, she embodied many Jewish rites in her own ceremonies, but she plainly showed to those who lagged behind in Judaism that she had definitely broken with it. St. Paul brings this out strongly in his Epistles. The substitution of the Sunday for the Sabbath must have been a cruel blow to the converted Jews, all the harder to bear as it was repeated every week, a striking proof of the new order of things, *et antiquum documentum novo cedat ritui*. (Let types of former days give way to the new rite.) Some witnessed it with regret, others clung to the Sabbath and left the Church. The Judaising Christians used it as a fresh cause of complaint against the Church, whom they accused of throwing aside too lightly the Mosaic customs.

The institution of the Sunday, mentioned in the Acts and the Apocalypse, was thus a very instructive lesson for the Christians of those days.

The Institution of the Christian Week.

It also marked the first step in the institution of a liturgical week and year. The Sunday commemorated in a very special way the Resurrection, being as it were the Easter Day of every week ; but Easter does not commemorate as an isolated fact the Resurrec-

tion only, but also the Passion and Death of Our Saviour. In the primitive Church it was spoken of as *pascha staurosimon, pascha anastasimon*, the pasch of the Crucifixion, the pasch of the Resurrection ; from which comes the keeping of the Friday as a holy day, and possibly also the Wednesday, as it was the day on which Judas betrayed Our Lord. Towards the close of the first century these two days are spoken of as being days for the *station*. Thus the liturgical week was founded on the memory of Our Lord's last days, the Sunday, Wednesday and Friday being specially honoured, but Saturday was passed over, as also the Thursday, a Jewish fast-day.

The Date of Easter.

This led to further developments. Although chronologically speaking the liturgical week preceded the liturgical year, and the Christians commemorated the Resurrection every Sunday, yet the fixing of a date for the special keeping of this feast every year had to be considered. This was a difficult problem. The Christians of those days thought that it should be March 25th; a memorable day for them, as they liked to think that the work of creation was started on that day. It was also held to be the day of the Annunciation, which inevitably settled that of the Nativity of Our Lord nine months later.

Easter is the pivot on which turns the whole liturgical cycle, but from the beginning this date was the subject of much controversy. Was the Sunday to give up its privilege, and the feast be kept on any day of the week, which would be the result of keeping to March 25? This still remains the difficulty in the question of the reform of the calendar.

Some kept Easter on March 25th, others on the fourteenth day of the March moon which was the date of the Jewish pasch ; in either case the idea of Sunday being abandoned, as these dates would fall on the various days of the week successively. In the end the Sunday kept its privilege, for after endless discussions the Holy See by an act of supreme authority decided that the feast of Easter should be kept on the Sunday after the fourteenth day of the March moon. The Church thus attained a double

end, she maintained the privilege belonging to the Sunday, and she showed once more her determination to throw off the yoke of Jewish customs. Those who refused to accept this ruling vere very few. They left the Church and were known as the *quartodecimans*, or those who kept the fourteenth day.

Holy Week.

This from an historical point of view is the origin both of Holy Week and of the liturgical year. The Mass renews the memory of the different events in the work of our Redemption, every Sunday commemorates the Resurrection and the yearly cycle of the liturgy brings back Maundy Thursday and Good Friday. This in itself proves .the importance of Holy Week but only from the historical point of view, which is the least essential side of the question.

To the Christian, from a liturgical point of view this week sums up the whole Christian teaching, as will be shown later on. The Holy Week of to day marks a more advanced stage in the development of the liturgy but in its essentials it has not changed. Thursday, Friday and Sunday are still the most important days, but it was necessary to embrace all the events of Our Lord's last days more fully, so the preceding Sunday, known as Palm Sunday, was included, a custom which dates from the fourth century.

*   *   *

In the course of this work we shall quote frequently from a very interesting document published in the nineteenth century, the *Peregrinatio Silviæ* (Pilgrimage of Sylvia). It is the impressions of a Spanish abbess *Sylvia*, or rather *Etheria*, who in the fourth century assisted at the Holy Week ceremonies in Jerusalem. Many of our present day rites were in use then, and they probably originated .in the very city where Christ was condemned, suffered, died, was buried and rose again, and were not invented during the " detestable " Middle Ages as some Protestant critics of the sixteenth and seventeenth centuries asserted.

In consideration then of all these facts one is justified in saying that Holy Week in the beginning was of apostolic origin and was finally developed and per-

fected in Jerusalem in the fourth century, until it became the magnificent ceremonial which we shall now proceed to study.

II. OUR LORD'S LAST WEEK UPON EARTH

As the purpose of Holy Week is but to recall the memory of Our Lord's last days, let us first go over the events of these days.

On the Saturday before Palm Sunday Our Lord was at Bethania, the home of Lazarus, Martha and Mary Magdalen. After supper Mary Magdalen anointed the feet of Our Lord, as we read in the Gospel according to St. John on Monday in Holy Week. It was not read on the Saturday, as in Rome this day was considered a day of rest, *vacat,* on account of Palm Sunday following, and it had no station. This same event is mentioned in the reading of the Passion according to St. Matthew on Palm Sunday, and from St. Mark on Tuesday in Holy Week.

On Sunday morning Our Lord went up to Jerusalem with his disciples ; when they reached Bethphage on Mount Olivet, two of the disciples were sent to fetch the ass and her colt on which Our Lord was to make this triumphal entry into Jerusalem. The account of this is given in the Gospel for the blessing of the palms, and in the antiphons and responsories which follow. It is also in the Gospel according to St. John for the Saturday before Palm Sunday. Some commentators think that it was on this Sunday that Our Lord wept over Jerusalem and drove the buyers and sellers out of the temple (Luke XIX. 41-45). That same night he returned to Bethania (Math xx. 17).

Our Lord returned to Jerusalem early on Monday in Holy Week ; on his way he cursed the barren fig tree (Math. XXI. 18). That day he spent in the temple, teaching (Math. XXI-XXIII). According to some commentators Our Lord stopped on Mount Olivet on his way back to Bethania, and looking at the walls of Jerusalem and the temple which rose before him on the other side of the valley, he uttered the prophecy of the destruction of the temple and of the end of the world (Math. XXIV. 34).

On the Tuesday he again went from Bethania to Jerusalem, finding the fig tree withered by the wayside, and went up to the temple. (Mark. XI. 17-18.) In the evening he returned to Bethania.

Meanwhile the chief priests and ancients of the people alarmed at Our Lord's popularity and enraged by his triumphal entry into Jerusalem on the preceding Sunday, sought to make away with him. Whilst they were consulting together on the Wednesday in the temple, Judas Iscariot who was well aware of what was going on, came in offering to betray Jesus and made his infamous bargain. The account of this comes at the beginning of the Passion according to the three synoptic writers; St. John's famous passage on this event forms the text of the responsory *Collegerunt* for the blessing of the palms.

On Maundy Thursday Our Lord was again at Bethania, having returned the evening before. This day was the first day of the azymes, and in the evening the Jews would eat the pasch in Jerusalem. Jesus sent two of his best loved disciples, Peter and John, to make all things ready for the supper in the house of a wealthy Jew. This was the last meal Our Lord was to take with his disciples, and so great an event was to take place during it that it was fitting that all should be done with as much solemnity as possible. The Cenacle was a large room, becomingly decorated for a feast. Before the institution of the Holy Eucharist Our Lord washed the feet of his apostles; the account of this in St. John's Gospel is read during a ceremony which takes place on Maundy Thursday, and which will be treated of later. The account of the Last Supper comes in the Passion according to the three synoptic writers. It was at this moment that there was strife amongst the apostles as to who should seem to be the greater, followed by the promise made to St. Peter that he should confirm his brethren, and the warning of his betrayal (Luke XXII. 26-27; John XIII. 33-38).

When Judas left the Cenacle night had fallen, and the Passion had begun. Our Lord's last discourse to the apostles and the hymn of thanksgiving after the supper are found in St. John, ch. XIV. After the hymn was over Our Lord set out with the eleven

towards Mount Olivet. As they were passing some vineyards Our Lord spoke to them the parable of the vine, which is the most beautiful commentary on the mystery of the Holy Eucharist (John xv). The discourse to his disciples and Our Lord's prayer to his Heavenly Father are found in St. John, ch. XVI-XVII. The agony in the garden, the arrival of Judas and seizing of Jesus, the trial and condemnation, all these events which happened between Thursday night and Friday morning are recounted in all the four Gospels, as also the account of the death and burial of Our Lord. On this tragic Friday night all seems lost from the human point of view. The apostles, completely demoralized, have scattered and hidden themselves. Nothing is heard of their doings on the following sabbath day, only the placing of the guard round the sepulchre by the chief priests and Pharisees is mentioned. It was on the day following the Sabbath, our Sunday, that the sudden glory of the Resurrection shone out with the dawn.

III. THE LITURGY OF HOLY WEEK

Originally Holy Week formed part of Lent, or rather was itself Lent. These few days of preparation for the feast of Easter were later extended to a period of six weeks in the Western Church and of eight in the Eastern Church. These weeks of Lent, and even the three weeks of Septuagesima may be considered in the light of a preparation for, or prelude to Holy Week. These long weeks of penance, mortification and prayer are meant to lead us on to higher things step by step until at length we reach the heights from which we are to contemplate the mystery of the Passion.

The last two weeks of Lent have a special liturgical character of their own, and are known as Passiontide. Passion Week, however, or the fifth week of Lent, does not differ very much from the preceding weeks, and so we refer the faithful to our Roman missal, for the liturgy of this week except for that of the Saturday before Palm Sunday which was, according to St. John, the sixth day before the pasch, famous in the primitive liturgy as the *Saturday of Lazarus*.

The Saturday of Lazarus.

The ceremony which used to take place at Bethania on that day is described in the *Peregrinatio Silviæ* mentioned in our last chapter [1].

As we have already remarked, in the Roman liturgy there was no *station* on this Saturday and so the Gospel of the anointing of Our Lord's feet by Mary Magdalen which should have been read on this day was transfered to the Monday in Holy Week. The Pope however on that day sent a fragment of the consecrated Host to each priest, or presbyter, of the parish churches in Rome, as was the custom on Sundays; the reason for this ceremony being performed in advance probably being on account of the very long ceremonies of Palm Sunday. Each priest placed a particle of this consecrated Host in the chalice before communicating, as a sign of union with the Pope. The Sovereign Pontiff also distributed alms on this day. After the twelfth century there was a stational Mass at the church of St. John before the Latin Gate.

Palm Sunday and the Other Days of Holy Week.

A description of the ceremonies of Palm Sunday will be given in a special chapter. The Monday and Tuesday of Holy Week have also a proper Mass for each day.

On Wednesday in Holy Week was held the sixth scrutiny or examination of the catechumens, and therefore two lessons are read as on the Wednesday of the fourth week in Lent, which was the day of the great scrutiny. On Wednesday evening the office of Tenebræ for the following day is recited, which will be treated of later.

From the liturgical point of view the last three days of Holy Week are the most important of the whole year. Each has its special liturgy and ceremonies; Maundy Thursday, the institution of the Eucharist, the blessing of the holy oils and the *Mandatum* or washing of the feet; Good Friday has a series of cere-

---

[1] We refer our readers to our work : Etude sur la *Peregrinati Silviæ*. (Etheriæ), *La discipline et la liturgie au* VIe *siècle* Paris, 1895.

monies to be treated of later ; the office formerly said during the night of Saturday to Sunday is now anticipated and celebrated on the Saturday morning.

Maundy Thursday and Good Friday are, liturgically speaking, one, being so intimately connected, as Holy Saturday is with Easter Day. This division simplifies the explanation of the ceremonies taken as a whole. When the office of Holy Saturday was celebrated during the night, it ended at dawn with a Mass which was that of Easter Day. To-day though the Mass of Easter Day is different to that of Holy Saturday, yet in some ways it is very similar.

To understand fully the meaning of the liturgy it must be remembered that Holy Week ends on Saturday evening before the night office begins because this latter belongs to another part of the liturgy, that of Paschal Time which lasts till the Ascension, or rather until Pentecost. It is the sacred number of fifty days corresponding to the season of Lent, a season all of joy and triumph setting off one of penance and mortification.

Tenebræ of the Last Three Days of Holy Week.

The night office of these three days has been given the name of Tenebræ and is said earlier so as to enable a greater number of the faithful to assist. During the first few centuries the synaxis or assembly was celebrated at night ; a reference to this is made in the Acts (ch. xx). Pliny in his letter to Trajan written early in the second century, states that the Christians assemble during the night to sing hymns to Christ and to celebrate their mysteries. Lucian about the same time mocks at the Christians, pitying them as poor wretches who spend the night singing hymns. The Vigil, or night office during Holy Week was celebrated with greater solemnity as we learn from the Acts of the Martyrs, the Apostolic Constitutions, Tertullian, and from several of the Fathers of the Church of the fourth and fifth centuries. These references will be given in our bibliographical index.

Matins or Tenebræ for these three days have three nocturns as on feast days, each consisting of three psalms with antiphons and three lessons with responsories. Each day will be treated of in detail in its

proper place, but a few general remarks may be made here. Most of the psalms used are *Messianic* psalms referring particularly to Our Lord and his Passion. The first nocturn lessons are always from Jeremias and the Lamentations. This choice is obvious; by the mouth of Jeremias the Church expresses her grief at the sufferings and death of the Just One. The Fathers see in Jeremias a type of the persecuted and suffering Messias. The second nocturn lessons are taken from St. Augustine's commentaries on the Psalms. According to an ancient custom, second nocturn lessons usually consist of explanations or commentaries on the psalms or lessons recited during the office. The third nocturn lessons are taken from St. Paul. The ancient and almost universal custom is that first nocturn lessons are taken from the Old Testament, second nocturn lessons from the works of the Fathers and Doctors of the Church, and third nocturn lessons from the New Testament.

Lauds.

This office was usually recited towards daybreak; like Matins it consists mostly of psalms but it is a shorter office, there being only four psalms with antiphons and a canticle from the Old Testament. The Benedictus canticle from the Gospel is said every day at the end of Lauds. Lauds is a morning office corresponding to Vespers, the evening office which has five psalms and ends also with a canticle from the Gospel, the Magnificat. There is a proper office for Lauds each day during Holy Week, psalms and antiphons all having reference to the Passion.

A special ending for all the canonical Hours for the last three days of Holy Week, is the antiphon: *Christus factus est* (Christ became) and Psalm 50. This was a subsequent addition, whereas Matins and Lauds are a faithful reproduction in their simplicity of the Roman *cursus* from the fifth to the seventh century.

* * *

In conclusion we may say that Holy Week is the culminating point of the liturgical year, the great week during which we spend those last days of Our Lord's life on earth in close union with him. The Church shows the trend of her thoughts by deeply moving ceremonies full of profound meaning, which

do far more than any other exercise could to teach the
Christian the reality of the mysteries of faith and fill
his heart with grateful love for Our Saviour. Moreover to the liturgical student as also to all the faithful, who in daily increasing numbers are taking an
interest in the liturgy of the Church, Holy Week is
the most important of all the liturgical seasons, and
this not only because the Church desires her children
to spend these days in recollection and prayer, but
because these very prayers and rites have been pre-
served with such loving veneration that they are the
most ancient portion of the liturgy, and most truly
representative of the primitive spirit and character.
This is the reason why archeologists, historians and
liturgists have studied this part of the liturgy so carefully. Their works are of the greatest interest to those
who study the historical origin of our ceremonies [1]

For this reason we have thought it more convenient to publish our Holy Week Book separately,
giving a full explanation of the various ceremonies
with their mystical meaning. In this way a fuller
description can be given than would have been possible within the limits of an ordinary missal, and also
one volume contains the entire office for this week.

IV. THE THEOLOGY OF HOLY WEEK

The Death and Resurrection of our Lord.

The prayers and ceremonies of Holy Week are a
summary of Christian theology, at least of its elements. St. Paul brings out strongly these great
truths, that Christ came down on earth to redeem us
by his own death, to restore the primitive order of
things so grievously disordered by sin, to make us
partakers of his divine life and to open Heaven to us.
St. Paul makes the Passion, Death and Resurrection
of Our Lord the foundation of his teaching, and they
are indeed the fundamental principles of Christian
doctrine.

Our Redemption was accomplished during this
most sacred week. Our Lord foretold to the disciples
that he must go up to Jerusalem and suffer many

---

[1] The principal works on this subject will be found in the
bibliographical index.

things from the ancients and scribes and chief priests, that he would be put to death and that on the third day he would rise again (Matth. XVI. 21). After the Resurrection he said to the disciples on the way to Emmaus : " Ought not Christ to have suffered these things and so to enter into his glory? " (Luke XXIV. 26). On Palm Sunday all the prophecies concerning his Passion began to be fulfilled.

The Jewish Pasch and the Christian Pasch.

That the Christian and the Jewish pasch should coincide is in itself a fact full of significance. The pasch was the greatest feast of the Jews, the first to be instituted, set as a seal on their independant nationality at the time of their liberation from Egyptian oppression. It was their great national feast ; every Jew went up to Jerusalem to keep the pasch which commemorated the immolation of the lamb, the passing of the destroying angel, the miraculous passage through the Red Sea and the pillar of fire which guided the Israelites in the desert. The passages from the Old Testament which describe these events are read on Good Friday as the second lesson at Mass, and as the ninth prophecy on Holy Saturday. The fourth prophecy refers to these events also, and, in a mystical and lyrical setting, the connection between the Christian and Jewish pasch is brought forward in the *Exsultet*.

The Christian pasch supplants the Jewish pasch, which becomes as it were its shadow. Jesus is the Lamb who takes away the sins of the world ; already Isaias and Jeremias had seen in the lamb a type of the Messias (Isaias XVI. I ; LIII. 7 ; Jer. XI. 19) ; St. John the Baptist pointed out Our Lord as the Lamb of God ; St. Paul speaks of him as the pasch immolated for us ; St. John in the Apocalypse sees the Lamb in Heaven, and St. Peter speaks of our having been redeemed by the precious blood of Christ, as of a lamb unspotted and undefiled (I Pet. I. 19). This is an essential point of apostolic theology and is clearly brought out in the liturgy of Holy Week.

Jesus, Messias and King.

The triumphal entry of Our Lord into Jerusalem was to the disciples but a momentary illusion, quickly

dispelled. He had been received as the Son of David in his own city of Sion by the acclamations of the people ; was not this at last the coming of the Messias, the promised King of Israel? This triumph however only served to rouse the fury of his enemies, who fearing the result of the enthusiasm of the crowd plotted his death. Judas with far-seeing hatred followed up the course of events and knew when the decisive moment had come to make his shameful bargain with the chief priests. Whatever may have been his motives, his treacherous act was only too well calculated, to his eternal undoing.

Each of these events has its own special lesson ; Our Lord's triumph confirmed St. Peter's confession of faith made so shortly before : *Thou art Christ, the son of the living God,* for the people hailed him as Christ, as Messias, as Son of David and King of Israel, and on that day the prophecies were fulfilled. He was greater than Elias, greater than John the Baptist, more than a prophet, he was the Messias, Son of the living God, and Peter who had confessed this before the others deserved to be the stone upon which the Church was to be built ; but on Palm Sunday the whole populace joined with Peter in proclaiming him the Messias, crying : *Hosannah filio David, Benedictus qui venit in nomine Domini.* (Hosanna to the Son of David, Blessed he that cometh in the name of the Lord.)

From now onwards the Church in her offices emphasizes this truth, that Jesus is the Messias promised to the Jewish people all through the centuries, of whom each prophet had described some particular characteristic. He has nothing of the warrior, of the conquering hero ; he is a king, meek and gentle, who makes his entry into his own city seated upon an ass ; his kingdom is not of this world. In the passages from Isaias and Jeremias in the liturgy of Holy Week a suffering Christ is portrayed. The apologetics of the Acts, the Epistles and all early Christian writings consisted in placing the prophecy beside its fulfilment, like twin pages of a diptych each completing and explaining the other. The Church has adopted this method in her liturgy of Holy Week and embodies this thought in the collect which follows the twelfth prophecy on Holy Saturday, *Deus...*

qui prophetarum tuorum præconio, præsentium temporum declarasti mysteria. (God...; who, by the proclamations of thy prophets, didst declare the mysteries of these present times.) This is the key to the choice of most of the passages from Scripture used in the Lenten liturgy and more especially during Holy Week. In the lessons, antiphons and responsories the Old and the New Testament bear mutual testimony that every detail of the Passion had been foretold by the prophets. This was one of the most convincing arguments used against the Jews by St. Peter and St. Stephen in the Acts, by St. Paul, St. Barnabas, St. Justin and many others.

The Institution of the Holy Eucharist.

At the Last Supper on Maundy Thursday a new mystery is revealed, the *mysterium fidei* (mystery of Faith) ; the ceremonies commemorating this institution will be treated of later. Jesus gives himself to his disciples under the form of bread and wine — the multiplication of the loaves prefigured the Eucharistic banquet — showing the tender mercy of Our Lord who would not let the multitude go away hungry, *misereor super turbam.* (I have compassion on the multitude.) He multiplies the loaves and fishes to feed them. But man does not live by bread alone, and it is a spiritual food that Jesus is about to give his disciples, the bread of angels, the bread of eternal life. By the multiplication of the loaves and fishes Our Lord appeased mere physical hunger, but in Holy Communion he feeds our souls who hunger and thirst after spiritual food.

The office of Maundy Thursday develops this idea. Christianity itself seems but to lead up to this sacrament, which is its consummation. Although in manner and in style St. Paul and St. John are as the poles apart, yet their teaching on this point is identical, that we must become one with Christ. He is the Head, we the members ; he is the Vine, and we are the branches ; he is the Light that lights us on our way, the Good Shepherd who keeps his sheep ; he abides in us and becomes one with us, we therefore must live in him. We die and are buried with him, and he raises us up also in his resurrection.

Our Lord came into this world to give us eternal

life, his own life, and this sublime reality is accomplished in the Holy Eucharist, as Christ himself taught his disciples saying : *He that eateth my flesh and drinketh my blood, abideth in me and I in him.* This explains the important part the institution of the Holy Eucharist takes in the liturgy of Holy Week ; Maundy Thursday is the true feast of the Blessed Sacrament, and was for centuries the only one. The feast of Corpus Christi was instituted in the thirteenth century as a protest against the errors of Berengarius, of the Albigenses, Cathari and other heretics. It was kept on the Thursday after Trinity Sunday, but did not take away from the importance of the feast of the institution of the Blessed Sacrament ; it only completed it. The Mass of Maundy Thursday enjoys a privilege belonging only to great feasts, that of a proper *communicantes*, and moreover on this one day in the year there is a modification in the formula of consecration. After Mass the Blessed Sacrament is carried solemnly in procession to the altar of repose, where it remains exposed for adoration until the following day.

The *Mandatum* or washing of the feet which takes place on maundy Thursday is also a part of the commemoration of the institution of the Holy Eucharist, as this act of charity formed part of Our Lord's teaching on the Sacrament. But there are still more lessons to be learnt from the liturgy of these days ; the sacraments of Baptism and Confirmation are closely connected with the Holy Eucharist and have their place in the liturgy, as also has the sacrament of Penance.

Penance - Baptism - Confirmation.

As regards the latter, the teaching of Lent is chiefly concerned with the bringing back of sinners to repentance. The Gospel of the prodigal son and of the resurrection of Lazarus and other portions of the Mass are intended to excite sorrow for sin and desire of conversion. The reconciliation of public penitents took place on Maundy Thursday, and this ceremony is still in the Pontifical [1].

Although the Church addresses herself to the

---

[1] For an account of this ceremony, see Dom Guéranger's *Liturgical Year*, *Maundy Thursday*, p. 353.

public penitents, yet as the ashes were distributed to all the faithful at the beginning of Lent and not to the public penitents only as formerly, every Christian can apply these appeals for conversion to himself. These formulæ show that the Church has received power to forgive sins from her divine Head.

Baptism and Confirmation are even more closely connected with the Lenten liturgy than is the sacrament of Penance. In our Missal we have pointed out the various places in the Proper of the Mass where reference to these sacraments is made. The sixth scrutiny took place on Wednesday in Holy Week, the seventh and last on Holy Saturday. The night office of Saturday, now celebrated during the day, is almost exclusively concerned with the sacrament of Baptism, its symbolism and effect, ending up with the blessing of the font and Mass, all showing that the neophyte dead to sin is buried with Christ and rises together with him a new man, to live henceforward the life of Christ.

The blessing of the holy oils on Maundy Thursday and that of the new fire and of the font on Holy Saturday are full of doctrine and have a deep spiritual meaning. In each there is the same intention, that of sanctifying material elements which play such a large part in the economy of our human life, oil, fire and water, for a supernatural end. By water man is regenerated in Baptism; oil is used in Baptism, Confirmation, Extreme Unction, Holy Orders, and in several sacramentals. The fire blessed on Holy Saturday is a symbol of that light which Christ came to bring into the world. To understand the spirit of the Church the text of the prayers she uses should be studied attentively. These material elements created by God for the good of man, fell after the Fall together with the rest of nature into the power of the prince of this world, as he is called in the Gospel. This is why these rites are usually accompanied by exorcisms which drive away the devil, whilst the blessings and signs of the cross sanctify the various objects for a spiritual use.

The Mystery of the Passion.

When at the Last Supper Our Lord pronounced the words of consecration *sanguis... qui pro vobis*

effundetur (my blood... which shall be shed for you) it was the announcement of the great sacrifice of the morrow. There were only three witnesses of the agony in the garden, and even these were overcome by sleep, but the angels realised what it all meant when they saw the Son of Man prostrate on the ground, crushed by the weight of our sins. This was that supreme moment in the great drama of the Passion when Our Lord accepted the mission given him by his Heavenly Father to save mankind, offering himself as a victim to the divine justice in expiation for all our sins.

This surrender once made, the willing victim gave himself up to the cruel sufferings that followed on immediately. Dragged from Annas to Caiphas, from Pilate to Herod, his trial was a hideous mockery. Scourged, insulted, he carried his own cross to the place where it was set up as an infamous gibbet on which he hung for three long hours in indescribable torment, exposed to the gaze of the crowd. At last all was consummated, the sacrifice completed, and at three o'clock Our Lord gave up his soul into the hands of his Heavenly Father. The account of the Passion from all four evangelists is read in Holy Week.

The passage from Ps. 139, the Passion according to St. John, the adoration of the Cross, the improperia and the hymn *Pange lingua gloriosi lauream certaminis* (Sing my tongue the victor's praise) during the office of Friday morning, as well as the psalms, responsories and lessons of Tenebræ are an eloquent commentary on these events.

There are certain pious practices kept up in some churches with this same intention of impressing on the minds of the faithful the great facts of our Redemption, such as sermons on the Passion and on the seven last words spoken by Our Lord on the cross, and various other exercises.

The Priesthood of Our Lord.

The office of Holy Saturday is full of doctrine, under a symbolical form. Formerly the taking down of Our Lord's body from the cross occupied a much more prominent place in the liturgy than it does now. The body of Our Saviour remained united to

is divinity whilst in the tomb, but his soul went own to that place where the souls of the just awaited their liberation. The ancient liturgy delighted to dwell on the thought of what Our Lord's coming was to t hese souls, and theology has pronounced on this point.

The third nocturn lessons of Holy Saturday, taken from the Epistle to the Hebrews, introduce a new element of doctrine. In most of the lessons and responsories the Messias has been considered in the light of a victim, as the Lamb immolated for the sins of the world, as the Man of sorrows, but he is also the great High Priest of the new covenant, as the Epistle teaches. The priests of the Old Law were all of the race of Aaron, but Jesus, son of David according to the flesh through Mary, belonged to the tribe of Juda. If he is the priest of the new alliance, then the old priesthood is abolished and the new established. But in virtue of what right does Jesus become our High Priest? Because he is the Messias, and God himself speaking by the prophet said : *Thou art a priest for ever according to the order of Melchisedech* (and not according to the order of Aaron).

The Symbolism of the Fire.

The office of Saturday morning, which is in reality the night office, begins by the blessing of the new fire and the paschal candle, and is practically the same as the *Lucernarium*, which was the night office and which also included the blessing of the new fire. The *Exusltet* explains in mystical and inspired language the symbolism of this fire, image of Christ the Light of the world. This is the teaching of St. John, that the Word was God, and that he was the Light shining in the darkness of this world.

CONCLUSION

The limited scope of this work does not allow us to enlarge on the profound teaching contained in all the ceremonies and prayers of Holy Week, we have only briefly touched on a few points. In thinking and meditating on the liturgy, the force of the argument drawn from a comparison of the prophecies and their fulfilment in the life of Our Lord comes out strongly. But there is yet another impression still deeper, made on the minds of those who have fol-

lowed the liturgy of this week. Overcome by its
sublime beauty and pathos, they are moved to cry
out with Rousseau : " If the life and death of So-
crates were those of a just man, then the life and
death of Jesus Christ were those of a God ! " By
making light of prophecies and miracles as evidence in favour of the Catholic faith, and insisting
only on an interior adherence to the truth, the
modernists have by their errors unwillingly done
harm to the interior attitude they advocated, though
it would be unjust to rule it out too arbitrarily.
There is a mysterious force in the teaching of the
Church and especially in her liturgy, which moves the
heart and wins its assent.

Without dwelling any longer on this subject,
enough has been said to show that this week contains
many great lessons for the Christian. Meditation
on the prayers of the liturgy is not only an aid to devotion, but it gives such light to the soul that it is
not surprising that St. Thomas Aquinas always found
the solution to his difficulties at the foot of the crucifix.

If Holy Week means so much to the average
Christian, even if he be somewhat indifferent, what
must it not mean to those holy souls who live to the
full the Christian life, to the mystics throughout the
ages? Hermits, solitaries of the desert, monks and
nuns of the East and of the West, religious of every
order, converted sinners and pure, unsullied souls,
all made the Cross their hope, and from it drew their
ardent charity. Who could count the tears shed at
the foot of the crucifix, and tell of the heroic strength
gained there by countless Christians, of the burning
love and zeal awakened by the sight of our crucified
Saviour? How many have not repeated those words
of St. Paul : With Christ I am nailed to the cross, I
will not glory save in the cross of the Lord Jesus
Christ ! What miracles of grace have not these mysteries of our Redemption commemorated during this
week achieved in the way of conversions, transform-
ing and sanctifying souls. With good reason is it called *Holy Week*, and the *Great Week.*

Let it be in a spirit of deep faith and love that the
Christian makes use of this book to follow the myste-
ries of the Passion, Death and Resurrection of Our
Lord Jesus Christ.

BIBLIOGRAPHY

On the Holy Week see

Dom GUÉRANGER, **Passiontide and Holy Week**, in-12. Stanbrook Abbey, 1901 ;

Herbert THURSTON, S. J., **Lent and Holy Week**, in-12, London, 1904 ;

WISEMAN, **Four lectures on the Offices and the Ceremonies of Holy Week**, 1837, Rome ;

FEASEY, **Ancient English Holy Week Ceremonial**, London, 1897 ;

MARTINDALE S. J., **Palm Sunday, Tenebræ, Maundy Thursday, Good Friday, Holy Saturday**, in *Catholic Truth Society ;*

Canon KEATINGE, **The Cœremonies of Holy Week explained**, in *Catholic Truth Society ;*

Franc. CANCELLIÉRI, **Descrizione delle Funzioni della settimana santa**, 4ª ediz., Roma, 1818 ;

L'abbé HOUSSAYE, **Les cérémonies de la semaine sainte, leur antiquité, leur histoire** dans la *Revue des questions historiques*, 1878, t. XXIII, p. 447-487 ;

Dom. F. CABROL, **Étude sur la Peregrinatio Silviæ, les églises de Jérusalem, la discipline et la liturgie au IV**e **siècle**, Paris, 1895.

ECCE · LIGNVM · CRVCIS, IN · QVO · SA·
LVS · MVNDI · PEPENDIT

THE ASPERGES

ON PALM SUNDAY

Before the mass the priest goes to the foot of the altar and sprinkles the altar thrice with holy water, and then himself, intoning the antiphon Aspérges me, *as below. This is continued by the choir. Then the priest sprinkles the clergy and laity, saying in a low voice the Psalm,* Miserére mei Deus.

ASPERGES me, Dómine, hyssópo, et mundábor ; lavábis me, et super nivem dealbábor. *Ps.* 50. Miserére mei, Deus, secúndum magnam misericórdiam tuam.

THOU shalt sprinkle me with hyssop, O Lord, and I shall be cleansed; thou shalt wash me, and I shall be made whiter than snow. *Ps.* 50. Have mercy on me, O God, according to thy great mercy.

Then the antiphon Aspérges me *is repeated.*

℣. Osténde nobis, Dómine, misericórdiam tuam. ℟. Et salutáre tuum da nobis.

℣. Show us, O Lord, thy mercy. ℟. And grant us thy salvation.

℣. Dómine, exáudi oratiónem meam. ℟. Et clamor meus ad te véniat.

℣. O Lord, hear my prayer. ℟. And let my cry come unto thee.

℣. Dóminus vobíscum. ℟. Et cum spíritu tuo.

℣ The Lord be with you. ℟. And with thy spirit.

Orémus.

EXAUDI nos, Dómine sancte, Pater omnípotens, ætérne Deus : et míttere dignéris sanctum Angelum tuum de cælis, qui custódiat, fóveat, prótegat, vísitet, atque deféndat omnes habitántes in hoc habitáculo. Per Christum Dóminum nostrum. ℟. Amen.

Let us pray.

HEAR us, O holy Lord, almighty Father, eternal God ; and vouchsafe to send thy holy angel from heaven, to guard, cherish, protect, visit, and defend all that dwell in this house. Through Christ our Lord. ℟. Amen.

ON EASTER SUNDAY

VIDI aquam egrediéntem de templo a látere dextro, allelúia ; et omnes ad quos pervénit aqua ista salvi facti sunt, et dicent : Allelúia, allelúia. *Ps.* 117. Confitémini Dómino, quóniam bonus ; quóniam in sæculum misericórdia ejus.

℣. Glória Patri, et Fílio, et Spirítui Sancto. Sicut erat in princípio, et nunc, et semper, et in sæcula sæculórum. Amen.

I SAW water flowing from the right side of the temple, alleluia ; and all to whom that water came were saved, and they shall say : Alleluia, allelúia. Ps. 117. Praise the Lord, for he is good : for his mercy endureth for ever.

℣. Glory be to the Father, and to the Son, and to the Holy Ghost. As it was in the beginning, is now and ever shall be, world without end. Amen.

The antiphon Vidi aquam *is repeated.*

℣. Osténde nobis, Dómine, misericórdiam tuam, allelúia. ℟. Et salutáre tuum da nobis, allelúia.

℣. Dómine, exáudi oratiónem meam. ℟. Et clamor meus ad te véniat.

℣. Dóminus vobíscum. ℟. Et cum spíritu tuo.

℣. Show us, O Lord, thy mercy, alleluia. ℟. And grant us thy salvation, alleluia.

℣ O Lord, hear my prayer ℟. And let my cry come unto thee.

℣. The Lord be with you. ℟. And with thy spirit.

Oremus Exaudi, *etc.* (*See page* 1).

THE ORDINARY OF THE MASS

When the priest has vested, he goes to the altar, bows or genuflects before it, makes the sign of the cross, and says aloud :

IN nómine Patris, et Fílii, et Spíritus Sancti. Amen.	IN the name of the Father, and of the Son, and of the Holy Ghost. Amen.

Then he joins his hands before his breast and begins the Antiphon.

Introíbo ad altáreDei.	I will go in unto the altar of God.
℟. Ad Deum qui lætíficat juventútem meam.	℟. Unto God, who giveth joy to my youth.

Then he says the following Psalm 42 alternately with the servers :

P. JUDICA me, Deus, et discérne causam meam de gente non sancta ; ab hómine iníquo et dolóso érue me.	JUDGE me, O God, and distinguish my cause from the nation that is not holy ; deliver me from the unjust and deceitful man.
M. Quia tu es, Deus, fortitúdo mea : quare me repulísti, et quare tristis incédo, dum affligit me inimícus?	For thou, O God, art my strength, why hast thou cast me off? and why go I sorrowful whilst the enemy afflicteth me?
P. Emítte lucem tuam et veritátem tuam ; ipsa me deduxérunt et adduxérunt in montem sanctum tuum, et in tabernácula tua.	Send forth thy light and thy truth : they have led me and brought me unto thy holy hill, and into thy tabernacles.
M. Et introíbo ad altáre Dei : ad Deum qui lætíficat juventútem meam.	And I will go in unto the altar of God : unto God,who giveth joy to my youth.
P. Confitébor tibi in cíthara, Deus, Deus meus : quare tristis es, ánima mea, et quare contúrbas me?	I will praise thee upon the harp, O God, my God : why art thou sad, O my soul? and why dost thou disquiet me?
M. Spera in Deo, quóniam adhuc confitébor illi : salutáre vultus mei, et Deus meus.	Hope in God, for I will yet praise him : who is the salvation of my countenance, and my God.

P. Glória Patri, et Fílio, et Spirítui Sancto.

Glory be to the Father, and to the Son, and to the Holy Ghost.

M. Sicut erat in princípio, et nunc, et semper: et in sǽcula sæculórum. Amen.

As it was in the beginning, is now, and ever shall be, world without end. Amen.

Aña. Introíbo ad altáre Dei.

Ant. I will go in unto the altar of God.

℞. Ad Deum qui lætíficat juventútem meam.

℞. Unto God, who giveth joy to my youth.

He makes the sign of the cross, saying :

℣. Adjutórium nostrum in nómine Dómini.

℣. Our help is in the name of the Lord.

℞. Qui fecit cælum et terram.

℞. Who made heaven and earth.

Then with his hands joined together he bows low and makes the Confession. At all masses of the season from Passion Sunday to Holy Saturday exclusively, Psalm 42 and Glória Patri are not said, and the Antiphon is not repeated ; but when In nómine Patris, Introíbo *and* Adjutórium *have been said, the Confession is made as follows :*

CONFITEOR Deo omnipoténti, beátæ Maríæ semper Vírgini, beáto Michaéli Archángelo, beáto Joánni Baptístæ, sanctis Apóstolis Petro et Paulo, ómnibus Sanctis, et vobis, fratres: quia peccávi nimis cogitatióne, verbo, et ópere (*percutit sibi pectus ter, dicens*) : mea culpa, mea culpa, mea máxima culpa. Ideo precor beátam Maríam semper Vírginem, beátum Michaélem Archángelum, beátum Joánnem Baptístam, sanctos Apóstolos Petrum et Paulum, omnes Sanctos, et vos, fratres, oráre pro me ad Dóminum Deum nostrum.

I CONFESS to almighty God, to blessed Mary ever virgin, to blessed Michael the Archangel, to blessed John the Baptist, to the holy Apostles Peter and Paul, to all the saints, and to you, brethren, that I have sinned exceedingly, in thought, word, and deed (*he strikes his breast three times, saying*), through my fault, through my fault, through my most grievous fault. Therefore I beseech the blessed Mary ever virgin, blessed Michael the Archangel, blessed John the Baptist, the holy Apostles Peter and Paul, all the saints, and you, brethren, to pray to the Lord our God for me.

The servers answer :

MISEREATUR tui omnípotens Deus, et, dimíssis peccátis tuis, perdúcat te ad vitam ætérnam.

MAY almighty God have mercy upon thee, forgive thee thy sins, and bring thee to life everlasting.

The priest says Amen *and stands upright. Then the servers repeat the Confession, and where the priest has said* vobis fratres, *and* vos fratres, you, brethren, *the servers say* tibi pater, *and* te pater, thee, father. *Then the priest with his hands joined gives the absolution, saying :*

MISEREATUR vestri omnípotens Deus, et, dimíssis peccátis vestris, perdúcat vos ad vitam ætérnam. ℞. Amen.

MAY almighty God have mercy upon you, forgive you your sins, and bring you to life everlasting. ℞. Amen.

The priest makes the sign of the cross, saying :

INDULGENTIAM, absolutiónem, et remissiónem peccatórum nostrórum, tríbuat nobis omnípotens et miséricors Dóminus. ℞. Amen.

MAY the almighty and merciful Lord grant us pardon, absolution, and remission of our sins. ℞. Amen.

Ard bowing, he continues :

℣. Deus, tu convérsus vivificábis nos. ℞. Et plebs tua lætábitur in te.

℣. Thou shalt turn again, O God, and quicken us. ℞. And thy people shall rejoice in thee.

℣. Osténde nobis, Dómine, misericórdiam tuam. ℞. Et salutáre tuum da nobis.

℣. Show us, O Lord, thy mercy. ℞. And grant us thy salvation.

℣. Dómine, exáudi oratiónem meam. ℞. Et clamor meus ad te véniat.

℣. O Lord, hear my prayer. ℞. And let my cry come unto thee.

℣. Dóminus vobíscum. ℞. Et cum spíritu tuo.

℣. The Lord be with you. ℞. And with thy spirit.

Extending and then joining his hands, the priest says aloud: Orémus, Let us pray ; *and going up to the altar he says silently :*

AUFER a nobis, quǽsumus, Dómine, iniquitátes nostras : ut ad

TAKE away from us our iniquities, we beseech thee, O Lord : that we may

Sancta sanctórum puris mereámur méntibus intoíre. Per Christum Dóminum nostrum. Amen.

be worthy to enter with pure minds into the Holy of Holies. Through Christ our Lord. Amen.

Bowing, with his hands joined above the altar, he says :

ORAMUS te, Dómine, per mérita Sanctórum tuórum, (*osculatur altare in medio*) quorum relíquiæ hic sunt, et ómnium Sanctórum : ut indulgére dignéris ómnia peccáta mea. Amen.

WE beseech thee, O Lord, by the merits of thy saints (*he kisses the altar in the middle*) whose relics are here, and of all the saints, that thou wouldst vouchsafe to forgive me all my sins. Amen.

At high mass the priest, before reading the Introit, blesses incense, saying :

AB illo bene✠dicáris, in cujus honóre cremáberis. Amen.

BE thou ✠ blessed by him in whose honour thou shalt burn. Amen.

INTROIT, KYRIE AND GLORIA

And receiving the thurible from the deacon, he incenses the altar in silence. Then the deacon, taking the thurible from the celebrant, incenses him alone. The celebrant, making the sign of the cross, begins the Introit. When it is finished, he says alternately with the servers :

KYRIE, eléison. Kýrie, eléison. Kýrie, eléison. Christe, eléison. Christe, eléison. Christe, eléison. Kýrie, eléison. Kýrie, eléison. Kýrie, eléison.

LORD, have mercy. Lord, have mercy. Lord, have mercy. Christ, have mercy. Christ, have mercy. Christ, have mercy. Lord, have mercy. Lord, have mercy. Lord, have mercy.

Then at the middle of the altar, extending and then joining his hands, and slightly bowing his head, he says the Glória in excélsis Deo, *if it is to be said. He bows his head when he says,* Adorámus te, Grátias ágimus tibi, Jesu Christe, *and* Súscipe deprecatiónem. *He makes the sign of the cross at the end when he says,* Cum sancto Spíritu.

GLORIA in excélsis Deo. Et in terra pax homínibus bonæ voluntátis. Laudámus te. Benedícimus te. Adorámus te. Glorificámus te. Grátias ágimus tibi propter magnam glóriam

GLORY be to God on high, and on earth peace to men of good will. We praise thee ; we bless thee ; we adore thee ; we glorify thee. We give thee thanks for thy great glory. O Lord God, heavenly King,

tuam. Dómine Deus Rex cæléstis, Deus Pater omnípotens. Dómine Fili unigénite, Jesu Christe, Dómine Deus, Agnus Dei, Fílius Patris. Qui tollis peccáta mundi, miserére nobis. Qui tollis peccáta mundi, súscipe deprecatiónem nostram. Qui sedes ad déxteram Patris, miserére nobis. Quóniam tu solus sanctus. Tu solus Dóminus. Tu solus altíssimus, Jesu Christe. Cum sancto Spíritu, in glória Dei Patris. Amen.

God the Father almighty. O Lord Jesus Christ, the only-begotten Son : O Lord God, Lamb of God, Son of the Father, who takest away the sins of the world, have mercy on us : who takest away the sins of the world, receive our prayer : who sittest at the right hand of the Father, have mercy on us. For thou only art holy : thou only art Lord : thou only, O Jesus Christ, art most high, together with the Holy Ghost, in the glory of God the Father. Amen.

The priest kisses the altar at the middle, and turning towards the people, says :

℣. Dóminus vobíscum.
℟. Et cum spíritu tuo.

℣. The Lord be with you.
℟. And with thy spirit.

COLLECT, EPISTLE, GRADUEL, ALLELUIA, TRACT, SEQUENCE

He then says, Orémus, Let us pray, *and one or more Collects as required by the order of the office. The Epistle, Gradual, Tract or Alleluia with verse or Sequence follow, as the season requires.*

GOSPEL

At high mass the deacon then puts the book of the Gospels on the middle of the altar, and the celebrant blesses incense, as above. The deacon kneels before the altar, and with joined hands says :

MUNDA cor meum, ac lábia mea, omnípotens Deus, qui lábia Isaíæ Prophétæ cálculo mundásti igníto : ita me tua grata miseratióne dignáre mundáre, ut sanctum Evangélium tuum digne váleam nuntiáre. Per Christum Dóminum nostrum. Amen.

CLEANSE my heart and my lips, O God almighty, who didst cleanse the lips of the prophet Isaias with a live coal : vouchsafe, of thy gracious mercy, so to cleanse me, that I may worthily proclaim thy holy Gospel. Through Christ our Lord. Amen.

He takes the book from the altar, kneels again, and asks the priest for his blessing.

Jube, domne, benedí- | Pray, sir, a blessing.
cere.

The priest answers :

DOMINUS sit in corde tuo et in lábiis tuis, ut digne et competénter annúnties Evangélium suum. In nómine Patris, et Fílii, ✠ et Spíritus Sancti. Amen.

THE Lord be in thy heart and on thy lips, that thou mayest worthily, and in a becoming manner, announce his holy Gospel. In the name of the Father, and of the Son ✠ and of the Holy Ghost. Amen.

Having received the blessing he kisses the celebrant's hand, and with the other servers, incense, and candles goes to the place of the Gospel, where he stands with hands joined together, and sings :

℣. Dóminus vobíscum. | ℣. The Lord be with you.
℟. Et cum spíritu tuo. | ℟. And with thy spirit.
Sequéntia (*sive* Inítium) sancti Evangélii secúndum N. | The continuation (*or* beginning) of the holy Gospel according to N.

With the thumb of his right hand he makes the sign of the cross on the book at the beginning of the Gospel he is about to read, then on his own forehead, mouth, and breast while the servers answer :

℟. Glória tibi, Dómine. | ℟. Glory be to thee, O Lord.

He incenses the book three times and sings the Gospel with joined hands. When it is finished, the subdeacon takes the book to the priest, who kisses the Gospel and says :

PER evangélica dicta deleántur nostra delícta.

BY the words of the Gospel may our sins be blotted out.

The priest is then incensed by the deacon.

If the priest celebrates without deacon and subdeacon, when the book is taken to the other side of the altar, he bows in the middle and, joining his hands together, says : Munda cor meum, *as above,* and :

JUBE, Dómine, benedícere. Dóminus sit in corde meo et in lábiis meis, ut digne et competénter annúntiem Evangélium suum. Amen.

PRAY, Lord, a blessing. The Lord be in my heart and on my lips, that I may worthily and in a becoming manner announce his holy Gospel. Amen.

Then, turning towards the book, with hands joined together, he says :

℣. Dóminus vobíscum. | ℣. The Lord be with you.
℟. Et cum spíritu tuo. | ℟. And with thy spirit.
Inítium, *sive* sequén- | The beginning *or* conti-

tia sancti Evangélii se-cúndum *N*.

nuation of the holy Gospel according to N.

He makes the sign of the cross on the book and on his forehead, mouth, and breast, and reads the Gospel as said above. When it is finished, the server answers :

Laus tibi, Christe.

Praise be to thee, O Christ.

The priest kisses the Gospel, saying: Per evangélica dicta as above.

THE CREED

Then at the middle of the altar, extending, lifting up, and joining his hands, he says, on days when it is to be said : Credo in unum Deum, and continues it with his hands joined together. When he says Deum, he bows his head to the cross, also when he says, Jesum Christum, and simul adorátur. At the words Et incarnátus est, he kneels until the words, Et homo factus est. At the end, when he says, Et vitam ventúri sæculi, he makes the sign of the cross from his forehead to his breast.

CREDO in unum Deum, Patrem omnipoténtem, factórem cæli et terræ, visibílium ómnium, et invisibílium. Et in unum Dóminum Jesum Christum, Fílium Dei unigénitum : et ex Patre natum ante ómnia sæcula ; Deum de Deo, lumen de lúmine, Deum verum de Deo vero ; génitum, non factum, consubstantiálem Patri ; per quem omnia facta sunt. Qui propter nos hómines et propter nostram salútem, descéndit de cælis (*hic genuflectitur*). Et incarnátus est de Spíritu Sancto ex María Vírgine ; ET HOMO FACTUS EST. Crucifíxus étiam pro nobis : sub Póntio Piláto passus, et sepúltus est. Et resurréxit tértia die, secúndum Scriptúras. Et ascéndit in cælum, sedet

I BELIEVE in one God, the Father almighty, maker of heaven and earth, and of all things visible and invisible. And in one Lord Jesus Christ, the only-begotten Son of God, born of the Father before all ages ; God of God, light of light, true God of true God ; begotten not made ; consubstantial with the Father ; by whom all things were made. Who for us men, and for our salvation, came down from heaven (*here all kneel*) ; and was incarnate by the Holy Ghost, of the Virgin Mary ; and was made man. He was crucified also for us, suffered under Pontius Pilate, and was buried. And the third day he rose again according to the scriptures; and ascended into heaven. He sitteth at the right hand of the Father ; and he shall come again with glory to

ad déxteram Patris. Et íterum ventúrus est cum glória judicáre vivos et mórtuos: cujus regni non erit finis. Et in Spíritum Sanctum Dóminum et vivificántem, qui ex Patre Filióque procédit. Qui cum Patre et Fílio simul adorátur et conglorificátur; qui locútus est per Prophétas. Et unam, sanctam, cathólicam et apostólicam Ecclésiam. Confíteor unum báptisma in remissiónem peccatórum. Et exspécto resurrectiónem mortuórum, et vitam ventúri sǽculi.   Amen.

judge the living and the dead; and his kingdom shall have no end.   And in the Holy Ghost, the Lord and giver of life, who proceedeth from the Father and the Son, who together with the Father and the Son is adored and glorified ;who spoke by the prophets. And one holy Catholic and Apostolic Church.   I confess one baptism for the remission of sins.   And I await the resurrection of the dead, and the life of the world to come.   Amen.

THE OFFERTORY

He kisses the altar, and turning towards the people says :

℣. Dóminus vobíscum.
℟. Et cum spíritu tuo.

℣. The Lord be with you.
℟. And with thy spirit.

Then he says : Orémus, Let us pray, *and the Offertory.*
At high mass the deacon then hands the paten with the host to the celebrant.   If it is low mass the priest himself takes the paten with the host, and offering it up says :

SUSCIPE, sancte Pater, omnípotens ætérne Deus, hanc immaculátam hóstiam, quam ego, indígnus fámulus tuus, óffero tibi Deo meo vivo et vero, pro innumerabílibus peccátis, et offensiónibus et negligéntiis meis, et pro ómnibus circumstántibus, sed et pro ómnibus fidélibus christiánis vivis atque defúnctis, ut mihi et illis profíciat ad salútem in vitam ætérnam. Amen.

RECEIVE, O holy Father almighty, eternal God, this spotless host, which I, thy unworthy servant, do offer unto thee, my living and true God, for mine own countless sins, offences, and negligences, and for all here present ; as also for all faithful Christians, living or dead that it may avail for my own and for their salvation unto life eternal. Amen.

Then, making a cross with the paten, he puts the host on the corporal. The deacon pours wine and the subdeacon water into the chalice ; but if it is a low mass, the priest pours in both himself. He blesses the water to be mixed in the chalice, saying :

DEUS, qui humánæ substántiæ dignitátem mirabíliter condidísti, et mirabílius reformásti : da nobis per hujus aquæ et vini mystérium, ejus divinitátis esse consórtes, qui humanitátis nostræ fíeri dignátus est párticeps, Jesus Christus Fílius tuus Dóminus noster. Qui tecum vivit et regnat in unitáte Spíritus Sancti Deus : per ómnia sǽcula sæculórum. Amen.

O GOD, who, in creating human nature, didst marvellously ennoble it, and hast still more marvellously renewed it ; grant that, by the mystery of this water and wine, we may be made partakers of his divinity who vouchsafed to become partaker of our humanity, Jesus Christ, thy Son, our Lord ; who liveth and reigneth with thee in the unity of the Holy Ghost, one God, world without end. Amen.

He then takes the chalice, and offers it up, saying :

OFFERIMUS tibi, Dómine, cálicem salutáris, tuam deprecántes cleméntiam : ut in conspéctu divínæ majestátis tuæ, pro nostra et tótius mundi salúte, cum odóre suavitátis ascéndat. Amen.

WE offer unto thee, O Lord, the chalice of salvation, beseeching thy clemency, that it may rise up in the sight of thy divine majesty, as a savour of sweetness, for our salvation, and for that of the whole world. Amen.

He makes the sign of the cross with the chalice, and puts it on the corporal and covers it with the pall. With his hands joined over the altar he bows a little, and says :

IN spíritu humilitátis, et in ánimo contríto suscipiámur a te, Dómine, et sic fiat sacrificium nostrum in conspéctu tuo hódie, ut pláceat tibi, Dómine Deus.

IN an humble spirit, and a contrite heart, may we be received by thee, O Lord ; and may our sacrifice so be offered up in thy sight this day that it may be pleasing to thee, O Lord God.

Rising up, he stretches out his hands, lifts them up, and joins them. He lifts his eyes upwards, and lowering them immediately, says:

VENI sanctificátor, omnípotens ætérne Deus (*benedicit oblata,*

COME, O thou who makest holy, almighty, eternal God (*he blesses the*

prosequendo), et béne ✠ dic hoc sacrifícium tuo sancto nómini' præparátum.

offerings), and bless ✠ this sacrifice, prepared for thy holy name.

If it is high mass, he blesses incense, saying :

PER intercessiónem beáti Michaélis Archángeli stantis a dextris altáris incénsi, et ómnium electórum suórum, incénsum istud dignétur Dóminus bene✠dícere, et in odórem suavitátis accípere. Per Christum Dóminum nostrum. Amen.

THROUGH the intercession of blessed Michael the archangel standing at the right of the altar of incense, and of all his elect, may the Lord vouchsafe to bless ✠ this incense, and to receive it for a sweet savour. Through Christ our Lord. Amen.

Taking the thurible from the deacon, he incenses the offerings, saying :

INCENSUM istud a te benedíctum, ascéndat ad te, Dómine, et descéndat super nos misericórdia tua.

MAY this incense which thou hast blessed, O Lord, rise up before thee, and may thy mercy come down upon us.

He incenses the altar, saying (Ps. 140) :

DIRIGATUR, Dómine, orátio mea sicut incénsum in conspéctu tuo : elevátio mánuum meárum sacrifícium vespertínum. Pone, Dómine, custódiam ori meo, et óstium circumstántiæ lábiis meis : ut non declínet cor meum in verba malítiæ, ad excusándas excusatiónes in peccátis.

LET my prayer, O Lord, be directed as incense in thy sight : the lifting up of my hands as the evening sacrifice. Set a watch, O Lord, before my mouth, and a door round about my lips, lest my heart incline to evil words, to seek excuses in sins.

He returns the thurible to the deacon, saying :

ACCENDAT in nobis Dóminus ígnem sui amóris, et flammam ætérnæ caritátis. Amen.

MAY the Lord enkindle within us the fire of his love, and the flame of everlasting charity. Amen

Then the priest is incensed by the deacon, and afterwards the rest in order. Meanwhile the priest washes his hands, saying (Ps. 25) :

LAVABO inter inno-céntes manus me-as : et circúmdabo al-táre tuum, Dómine.

Ut áudiam vocem lau-dis : et enárrem univérsa mirabília tua.

Dómine, diléxi decó-rem domus tuæ : et lo-cum habitatiónis glóriæ tuæ.

Ne perdas cum ímpiis, Deus, ánimam meam : et cum viris sánguinum vi-tam meam.

In quorum mánibus iniquitátes sunt : déxte-ra eórum repléta est mu-néribus.

Ego autem in inno-céntia mea ingréssus sum : rédime me, et mi-serére mei.

Pes meus stetit in di-récto ; in ecclésiis bene-dícam te, Dómine.

Glória Patri.

I WILL wash my hands among the innocent : and compass thine altar : O Lord.

That I may hear the voice of thy praise : and tell of all thy wondrous works.

O Lord, I have loved the beauty of thy house : and the place where thy glory dwelleth.

Destroy not my soul with the wicked, O God : nor my life with men of blood.

In whose hands are ini-quities : their right hand is filled with gifts.

But I have walked in mine innocence : redeem me, and have mercy on me.

My foot hath stood in the straight way : in the chur-ches I will bless thee, O Lord.

Glory.

During Passiontide Glória Patri *is not said. Then, bowing a little at the middle of the altar, with his hands joined above it, the priest says :*

SUSCIPE, sancta Trí-nitas, hanc obla-tiónem quam tibi offéri-mus ob memóriam pas-siónis resurrectiónis et ascensiónis Jesu Christi Dómini nostri, et in ho-nórem beátæ Maríæ sem-per Vírginis, et beáti Joánnis Baptístæ, et san-ctórum Apostolórum Pe-tri et Pauli, et istórum, et ómnium sanctórum ; ut illis profíciat ad honó-

RECEIVE, O Holy Tri-nity, this offering, which we make to thee, in remem-brance of the Passion, Re-surrection, and Ascension of our Lord Jesus Christ, and in honour of blessed Mary ever virgin, of blessed John the Baptist, of the holy apostles Peter and Paul, of these and of all the saints : that it may avail to their honour and our salva-tion : and may they vouch-

1*

rem, nobis autem ad sa-
lútem ; et illi pro nobis
intercédere dignéntur in
cælis, quorum memó-
riam ágimus in terris. Per
eúmdem Christum Dó-
minum nostrum. Amen.

safe to intercede for us in
heaven, whose memory we
celebrate on earth. Through
the same Christ our Lord.
Amen.

He kisses the altar, turns towards the people, extends and then joins his hands, and says with his voice a little raised :

ORATE, fratres, ut
meum ac vestrum
sacrifícium acceptábile
fiat apud Deum Patrem
omnipoténtem.

BRETHREN, pray that
my sacrifice and yours
may be acceptable to God
the Father almighty.

The server or those around answer ; or if not, the priest himself says :

SUSCIPIAT Dóminus
sacrifícium de máni-
bus tuis (*vel* meis), ad laudem et glóriam nóminis
sui, ad utilitátem quo-
que nostram, totiúsque
Ecclésiæ suæ sanctæ.

MAY the Lord receive the
sacrifice at thy (*or* my)
hands, to the praise and
glory of his name, to our
benefit, and to that of all
his holy Church.

The priest says Amen *in a low voice. Immediately, with his hands extended, without* Orémus, *he says the Secret prayers. At the end he says aloud :*

Per ómnia sǽcula sæ-
culórum.

World without end.

PREFACE AND SANCTUS

Then follows the Preface, which he begins with both his hands extended. He raises them a little when he says, Sursum corda. *He joins them before his breast, and bows his head, when he says :* Grátias agámus ; *then he holds them apart till the end of the Preface, when with his hands again joined and his head bowed, he says :* Sanctus. *When he says* Benedíctus qui venit, *he makes the sign of the cross on himself.*

℣. Dóminus vobíscum.
℞. Et cum spíritu tuo.
℣. Sursum corda. ℞.
Habémus ad Dóminum.

℣. Grátias agámus Dó-
mino Deo nostro. ℞. Di-
gnum et justum est.

℣. The Lord be with you.
℞. And with thy spirit.
℣. Lift up your hearts.
℞. We have lifted them up unto the Lord.
℣. Let us give thanks to the Lord our God. ℞. It is meet and just.

AT MASSES OF THE PASSION OR OF THE CROSS

The following Preface is said from Passion Sunday till Maundy Thursday, except on any feast having a proper Preface, and also at masses of the Passion and of the Cross.

VERE dignum et justum est, æquum et salutáre, nos tibi semper et ubíque grátias ágere, Dómine sancte, Pater omnípotens, ætérne Deus : qui salútem humáni géneris in ligno crucis constituísti : ut unde mors oriebátur, inde vita resúrgeret, et qui in ligno vincébat, in ligno quoque vincerétur: per Christum Dóminum nostrum. Per quem majestátem tuam laudant Angeli, adórant Dominatiónes, tremunt Potestátes. Cæli cælorúmque Virtútes, ac beáta Séraphim, sócia exsultatióne concélebrant. Cum quibus et nostras voces, ut admítti júbeas, deprecámur, súpplici confessióne dicéntes :

Sanctus, sanctus, sanctus Dóminus Deus sábaoth. Pleni sunt cæli et terra glória tua : Hosánna in excélsis. Benedíctus qui venit in nómine Dómini : Hosánna in excélsis.

IT is truly meet and just, right and availing unto salvation, that we should always and in all places give thanks unto thee, holy Lord, Father almighty, everlasting God ; who didst set the salvation of mankind upon the tree of the cross, so that whence came death, thence also life might rise again, and he that overcame by the tree, on the tree also might be overcome : through Christ our Lord. Through whom the angels praise thy majesty, the dominions worship it, and the powers are in awe. The heavens and the heavenly hosts, and the blessed seraphim join together in celebrating their joy. With these we pray thee join our own voices also, while we say with lowly praise :

Holy, holy, holy, Lord God of hosts. Heaven and earth are full of thy glory. Hosanna in the highest. Blessed is he that cometh in the name of the Lord. Hosanna in the highest.

AT EASTERTIDE

From Holy Saturday until Ascension day, except on feasts which have a proper Preface.

On Holy Saturday is said : in hac potíssimum nocte ; especially in this night ; *from Easter day till the following Saturday :* in hac potíssimum die ; especially on this day.

VERE dignum et justum est, æquum et salutáre : Te quidem, Dómine, omni témpore, sed in hac potíssimum nocte (*vel* in hac potíssimum die, *vel* in hoc potíssimum) gloriósius prædicáre, cum Pascha nostrum immolátus est Christus. Ipse enim verus est Agnus qui ábstulit peccáta mundi. Qui mórtem nostram moriéndo destrúxit, et vitam resurgéndo reparávit. Et ídeo cum Angelis et Archángelis, cum Thronis et Dominatiónibus, cumque omni milítia cæléstis exércitus, hymnum glóriæ tuæ cánimus, sine fine dicéntes : Sanctus, sanctus, sanctus.

IT is truly meet and just right and availing unto salvation, that at all times, but more especially in this night (*or* on this day, *or* at this season) we should extol thy glory, when Christ our pasch was sacrificed. For he is the true lamb that hath taken away the sins of the world ; who by dying hath overcome our death, and by rising again hath restored our life. And therefore with the angels and archangels, the thrones and dominions, and the whole host of the heavenly army we sing a hymn to thy glory, saying again and again : Holy, holy, holy.

Infra actionem.

COMMUNICANTES, et diem sacratíssimum celebrántes, Resurrectiónis Dómini nostri Jesu Christi secúndum carnem : sed et memóriam venerántes, in primis gloriósæ semper Vírginis Maríæ, genitrícis ejúsdem Dei et Dó-

Within the action.

COMMUNICATING, and keeping the most holy day of the resurrection of our Lord Jesus Christ according to the flesh ; and also reverencing the memory, first, of the glorious Mary, ever a virgin, Mother of the same our God and Lord Jesus Christ ; like-

mini nostri Jesu Christi : sed et beatórum Apostolórum ac Mártyrum tuórum, Petri et Pauli, Andréæ, Jacóbi, Joánnis, Thomæ, Jacóbi, Philíppi, Bartholomæi, Matthæi, Simónis et Thaddæi : Lini, Cleti, Cleméntis, Xysti, Cornélii, Cypriáni, Lauréntii, Chrysógoni, Joánnis et Pauli, Cosmæ et Damiáni, et ómnium Sanctórum tuórum : quorum méritis precibúsque concédas, ut in ómnibus protectiónis tuæ muniámur auxílio. (*Jungit manus.*) Per eúmdem Christum Dóminum nostrum. Amen.

HANC ígitur oblatiónem servitútis nostræ, sed et cunctæ famíliæ tuæ, quam tibi offérimus pro his quoque, quos regeneráre dignátus es ex aqua et Spíritu sancto, tríbuens eis remissiónem ómnium peccatórum, quæsumus Dómine, ut placátus accípias, diésque nostros in tua pace dispónas, atque ab ætérna damnatióne nos éripi, et in electórum tuórum júbeas grege numerári. (*Jungit manus.*) Per Christum Dóminum nostrum. Amen.

wise of thy blessed apostles and martyrs, Peter and Paul, Andrew, James, John, Thomas, James, Philip, Bartholomew, Matthew, Simon and Thaddæus ; of Linus, Cletus, Clement, Sixtus, Cornelius, Cyprian, Lawrence, Chrysogonus, John and Paul, Cosmas and Damian, and of all thy saints ; for the sake of their merits and prayers grant that we may in all things be guarded by thy protecting help. (*He joins his hands together.*) Through the same Christ our Lord. Amen.

WE therefore beseech thee, O Lord, to be appeased and to accept this offering of our bounden duty, as also of thy whole household, which we make unto thee on behalf of these too whom thou hast vouchsafed to bring to a new birth by water and the Holy Ghost, giving them remission of all their sins ; order our days in thy peace ; grant that we be rescued from everlasting damnation and counted within the fold of thine elect. (*He joins his hands together.*) Through Christ our Lord. Amen.

THE CANON OF THE MASS

TE ígitur, clementíssime Pater, per Jesum Christum Fílium tuum Dóminum nostrum súpplices rogámus ac pétimus (*osculatur altare*), uti accépta hábeas, et benedícas (*jungit manus, deinde signat ter super oblata*), hæc ✠ dona, hæc ✠ múnera, hæc ✠ sancta sacrifícia illibáta (*extensis manibus prosequitur*) : in primis quæ tibi offérimus pro Ecclésia tua sancta cathólica : quam pacificáre, custodíre, adunáre, et régere dignéris toto ʾorbe terrárum, una cum famulo tuo Papa nostro *N.* et Antístite nostro *N.* et ómnibus orthodóxis, atque cathólicæ et apostólicæ fídei cultóribus.

WHEREFORE, O most merciful Father, we humbly pray and beseech thee, through Jesus Christ thy Son, our Lord (*he kisses the altar*), that thou wouldst vouchsafe to receive and bless (*he joins his hands together, and then makes the sign of the cross thrice over the offerings*) these ✠ gifts, these ✠ offerings, this ✠ holy and unblemished sacrifice (*he extends his hands and continues*), which in the first place we offer thee for thy holy Catholic Church, that it may please thee to grant her peace : as also to protect, unite, and govern her throughout the world, together with thy servant *N.*, our Pope *N.*, our Bishop, as also all orthodox believers who keep the Catholic and Apostolic faith.

The Commemoration for the living.

MEMENTO, Dómine, famulórum famularúmque tuárum *N.* et *N.*

BE mindful, O Lord, of thy servants and handmaids, *N.* and *N.*

He joins his hands, prays a little while for those he wishes to pray for, then with his hands stretched out he continues :

et ómnium circumstántium, quorum tibi fides cógnita est, et nota devótio ; pro quibus tibi offérimus, vel qui tibi ófferunt hoc sacrifícium laudis, pro se,

and of all here present, whose faith and devotion are known unto thee ; for whom we offer, or who offer up to thee, this sacrifice of praise for themselves and theirs, for the redee-

suísque ómnibus, pro redemptióne animárum suárum, pro spe salútis et incolumitátis suæ ; tibíque reddunt vota sua ætérno Deo, vivo et vero.

ing of their souls, for the hope of their safety and salvation, and who pay their vows to thee, the eternal, living, and true God.

Infra actionem.

COMMUNICANTES, et memóriam venerántes, in primis gloriósæ semper Vírginis Maríæ, genitrícis Dei et Dómini nostri Jesu Christi : sed et beatórum Apostolórum ac Mártyrum tuórum, Petri et Pauli, Andréæ, Jacóbi, Joánnis, Thomæ, Jacóbi, Philíppi, Bartholomǽi, Matthǽi, Simónis et Thaddǽi : Lini, Cleti, Cleméntis, Xysti, Cornélii, Cypriáni, Lauréntii, Chrysógoni, Joánnis et Pauli, Cosmæ et Damiáni, et ómnium sanctórum tuórum : quorum méritis precibúsque concédas, ut in ómnibus protectiónis tuæ muniámur auxílio. (*Jungit manus.*) Per eúmdem Christum Dóminum nostrum. Amen.

Within the action.

COMMUNICATING, and reverencing the memory first of the glorious Mary, ever a virgin, Mother of our God and Lord Jesus Christ ; likewise of thy blessed apostles and martyrs, Peter and Paul, Andrew, James, John, Thomas, James, Philip, Bartholomew, Matthew, Simon and Thaddeus ; of Linus, Cletus, Clement, Xystus, Cornelius, Cyprian, Lawrence, Chrysogonus, John and Paul, Cosmas and Damian, and of all thy saints ; by whose merits and prayers grant that in all things we may be guarded by thy protecting help. (*He joins his hands together.*) Through the same Christ our Lord. Amen.

With his hands spread over the offerings, he says :

HANC ígitur oblatiónem servitútis nostræ, sed et cunctæ famíliæ tuæ, quǽsumus, Dómine, ut placátus accípias, diésque nostros in tua pace dispónas, atque ab ætérna damnatióne

WE therefore beseech thee, O Lord, to be appeased, and to receive this offering of our bounden duty, as also of thy whole household ; order our days in thy peace ; grant that we be rescued from eternal

nos éripi, et in electórum tuórum júbeas grege numerári. (*Jungit manus.*) Per Christum Dóminum nostrum. Amen.

damnation and counted within the fold of thine elect. (*He joins his hands together.*) Through Christ our Lord. Amen.

QUAM oblatiónem tu, Deus, in ómnibus, quæsumus,

WHICH offering do thou, O God, vouchsafe in all things,

He makes the sign of the cross three times over the offerings.

bene✠díctam, adscrí✠ptam, ra✠tam, rationábilem, acceptabilémque fécere dignéris :

to bless ✠, consecrate ✠, approve ✠, make reasonable and acceptable :

He makes the sign of the cross once over the host and once over the chalice.

ut nobis Cor✠pus et San✠guis fiat dilectíssimi Fílii tui Dómini nostri Jesu Christi.

that it may become for us the Body ✠ and ✠ Blood of thy most beloved Son our Lord Jesus Christ.

QUI prídie quam paterétur (*accipit hostiam*), accépit panem in sanctas ac venerábiles manus suas (*elevat oculos ad cælum*), et elevátis óculis in cælum, ad te Deum Patrem suum omnipoténtem, tibi grátias agens,

WHO the day before he suffered took bread (*he takes the host*) into his holy and venerable hands (*he raises his eyes to heaven*), and with his eyes lifted up to heaven, unto thee, God, his almighty Father, giving thanks to thee,

He makes the sign of the cross over the host.

bene✠díxit, fregit, dedítque discípulis suis, dicens : Accípite, et manducáte ex hoc omnes.

he blessed ✠, brake, and gave to his disciples, saying, Take and eat ye all of this:

Holding the host between the first fingers and thumbs of both hands, he says the words of consecration, silently with clearness and attention, over the host, and at the same time over all the other hosts, if several are to be consecrated.

Hoc est enim Corpus meum.

For this is my Body.

As soon as the words of consecration have been said, he kneels and adores the consecrated host. He rises, shows it to the people,

puts it on the corporal, and again adores. Then, uncovering the chalice, he says :

SIMILI modo post-quam cœnátum est,

IN like manner, after he had supped,

He takes the chalice with both hands.

accípiens et hunc præclárum Cálicem in sanctas ac venerábiles manus suas, item tibi grátias agens,

taking also this excellent chalice into his holy and adorable hands ; also giving thanks to thee,

Holding the chalice with his left hand, he makes the sign of the cross over it with his right.

bene✠díxit, dedítque discípulis suis, dicens : Accípite, et bíbite ex eo omnes :

he blessed ✠, and gave it to his disciples, saying : Take, and drink ye all of this ;

He utters the words of consecration over the chalice silently, attentively, carefully, and without pausing, holding it slightly raised.

Hic est enim Calix Sánguinis mei, novi et ætérni testaménti; mystérium fîdei : qui pro vobis et pro multis effundétur in remissiónem peccatórum.

For this is the Chalice of my Blood, of the new and eternal testament ; the mystery of faith : which shall be shed for you and for many unto the remission of sins.

As soon as the words of consecration have been said, he puts the chalice on the corporal, and says silently :

Hæc quotiescúmque fecéritis, in mei memóriam faciétis.

As often as ye shall do these things, ye shall do them in memory of me.

He kneels and adores ; then rises, shows it to the people, puts it down, covers it, and again adores. Then holding his hands apart, he says :

UNDE et mémores, Dómine, nos servi tui, sed et plebs tua sancta, ejúsdem Christi Fílii tui Dómini nostri, tam beátæ passiónis,

WHEREFORE, O Lord, we thy servants, as also thy holy people, calling to mind the blessed passion of the same Christ thy Son our Lord, and also his rising

necnon et ab ínferis resurrectiónis, sed et in cælos gloriósæ ascensiónis : offérimus præcláræ majestáti tuæ de tuis donis ac datis,

up from hell, and his glorious ascension into heaven, do offer unto thy most excellent majesty, of thine own gifts bestowed upon us,

He joins his hands and makes the sign of the cross three times over the host and chalice together.

hóstiam ✠ puram, hóstiam ✠ sanctam, hóstiam ✠ immaculátam,

a pure ✠ victim, a holy ✠ victim, a spotless ✠ victim,

He makes the sign of the cross once over the host and once over the chalice.

Panem ✠ sanctum vitæ ætérnæ, et Cálicem ✠ salútis perpétuæ.

the holy ✠ Bread of eternal life, and the Chalice ✠ of everlasting salvation.

He continues with his hands stretched out :

SUPRA quæ propítio ac seréno vultu respícere dignéris ; et accépta habére, sícuti accépta habére dignátus es múnera púeri tui justi Abel, et sacrifícium patriárchæ nostri Abrahæ, et quod tibi óbtulit summus sacérdos tuus Melchísedech sanctum sacrifícium, immaculátam hóstiam.

UPON which do thou vouchsafe to look with a propitious and serene countenance, and to accept them as thou wert graciously pleased to accept the gifts of thy just servant Abel, and the sacrifice of our patriarch Abraham, and that which thy high priest Melchisedech offered to thee, a holy sacrifice, a spotless victim.

Bowing low with his hands joined together and then laid on the altar, he says :

SUPPLICES te rogámus, omnípotens Deus : jube hæc perférri per manus sancti Angeli tui in sublíme altáre tuum, in conspéctu divínæ majestátis tuæ : ut quotquot (*osculatur altare*), ex hac altáris participatióne, sacrosánctum Fílii tui,

WE most humbly beseech thee, almighty God, to command that these things be borne by the hands of thy holy angel to thine altar on high, in the sight of thy divine majesty, that as many of us (*he kisses the altar*) as, at this altar, shall partake of and receive the

He joins his hands together and makes the sign of the cross over the host and once over the chalice.

Cor✠pus et Sán✠guinem sumpsérimus (*seipsum signat*), omni benedictióne cælésti, et grátia repleámur (*jungit manus*). Per eúmdem Christum Dóminum nostrum. Amen.

most holy Body ✠ and ✠ Blood of thy Son (*he makes the sign of the cross on himself*), may be filled with every heavenly blessing and grace (*he joins his hands together*). Through the same Christ our Lord. Amen.

The Commemoration for the dead.

MEMENTO étiam, Dómine, famulórum famularúmque tuárum N. et N. qui nos præcessérunt cum signo fídei, et dormiunt in somno pacis.

BE mindful, O Lord, of thy servants and handmaids N. and N., who are gone before us, with the sign of faith, and sleep in the sleep of peace.

He joins his hands, prays a little while for those dead whom he means to pray for, then with his hands stretched out, continues :

Ipsis, Dómine, et ómnibus in Christo quiescéntibus, locum refrigérii, lucis et pacis, ut indúlgeas, deprecámur.

To these, O Lord, and to all that rest in Christ, we beseech thee, grant a place of refreshment, light, and peace.

He joins his hands together, and bows his head.

Per eúmdem Christum Dóminum. nostrum. Amen.

Through the same Christ our Lord. Amen.

He strikes his breast with his right hand, and slightly raising his voice, says :

NOBIS quoque peccatóribus, fámulis tuis, de multitúdine miseratiónum tuarum sperántibus, partem áliquam et societátem donáre dignéris, cum tuis sanctis Apóstolis et Martýribus : cum Joánne, Stéphano,Mathía,Bárnaba, Ignátio, Alexándro, Marcellíno, Petro, Felicitáte, Perpétua, Agatha, Lúcia, Agnéte, Cæcília, Anastásia, et ómnibus

TO us sinners, also, thy servants, hoping in the multitude of thy mercies, vouchsafe to grant some part and fellowship with thy holy apostles and martyrs : with John, Stephen, Matthias Barnabas, Ignatius, Alexander, Marcellinus, Peter, Felicity, Perpetua, Agatha, Lucy, Agnes, Cecily, Anastasia, and with all thy saints, into whose company we pray thee admit us, not

sanctis tuis ; intra quorum nos consórtium, non æstimátor mériti, sed véniæ, quæsumus, largítor admítte. Per Christum Dóminum nostrum.

PER quem hæc ómnia, Dómine, semper bona creas, sanctí✠ficas, viví✠ficas, bene✠dícis, et præstas nobis.

considering our merit, but of thine own free pardon. Through Christ our Lord ;

THROUGH whom, O Lord, thou dost always create, hallow, ✠ quicken, ✠ and bless ✠ these thine everbountiful gifts and give them to us.

He uncovers the chalice, kneels, takes the blessed sacrament in his right hand, and holding the chalice in his left, makes the sign of the cross three times over it from lip to lip, saying :

Per ip✠sum, et cum ip✠so, et in ip✠so,

By ✠ him, and with ✠ him, and in ✠ him,

He makes the sign of the cross twice between the chalice and his breast.

est tibi Deo Patri ✠ omnipoténti, in unitáte Spíritus ✠ Sancti,

is to thee, Gòd the Fathèr✠ almighty, in the unity of the Holy ✠ Ghost,

Lifting up the chalice a little with the host, he says :

omnis honor et glória.

all honour and glory.

He puts back the host, covers the chalice, kneels, rises, and sings or reads :

Per ómnia sǽcula sæculórum. ℞. Amen.

For ever and ever. ℞. Amen.

PATER NOSTER AND FRACTION

Orémus. Præcéptis salutáribus móniti, et divína institutióne formáti, audémus dícere :

Let us pray. Taught by the precepts of salvation, and following the divine commandment, we make bold to say :

He stretches out his hands.

PATER noster, qui es in cælis, sanctificétur nomen tuum : advéniat regnum tuum : fiat volúntas tua, sicut in cælo et in terra : panem nostrum quotidiánum da nobis hódie ; et dimítte nobis débita no-

OUR Father, who art in heaven, hallowed be thy name : thy kingdom come ; thy will be done on earth as it is in heaven. Give us this day our daily bread : and forgive us our trespasses, as we forgive

stra sicut et nos dimítti- | them that trespass against
mus debitóribus nostris : | us. And lead us not into
et ne nos indúcas in ten- | temptation.
tatiónem.

℞. Sed líbera nos a | ℞. But deliver us from
malo. | evil.

*The priest says, Amen. He takes the paten between his first
and middle finger, and says :*

LIBERA nos, quǽsu- | DELIVER us, we beseech
mus, Dómine, ab óm- | thee, O Lord, from all
nibus malis prætéritis, | evils, past, present, and to
præséntibus, et futúris, | come ; and by the interces-
et intercedénte beáta et | sion of the blessed and glo-
gloriósa semper Vírgine | rious Mary ever virgin, Mo-
Dei genítrice María, cum | ther of God, together with
beátis Apóstolis tuis Pe- | thy blessed apostles Peter
tro et Paulo, atque An- | and Paul, and Andrew, and
dréa, et ómnibus san- | all the saints,
ctis,

*He makes the sign of the cross with the paten from his forehead to
his breast and kisses it.*

da propítius pacem in | mercifully grant peace in
diébus nostris : ut ope | our days : that through the
misericórdiæ tuæ adjúti, | help of thy mercy we may
et a peccáto simus sem- | always be free from sin, and
per líberi, et ab omni | safe from all trouble.
perturbatióne secúri.

*He puts the paten under the host, uncovers the chalice, kneels,
rises, takes the host and breaks it in half over the chalice, saying :*

Per eúmdem Dóminum | Through the same Jesus
nostrum Jesum Chri- | Christ thy Son our Lord.
stum Fílium tuum,

*He puts the portion that is in his right hand on to the paten ; he
then breaks off a small piece from the portion which is in his left
hand, saying :*

qui tecum vivit et regnat | who liveth and reigneth
in unitáte Spíritus San- | with thee in the unity of the
cti Deus. | Holy Ghost, one God.

*He puts the other half with his left hand on to the paten, and hold-
ing the particle over the chalice in his right hand, and the chalice
with his left, he says :*

Per ómnia sǽcula sæcu- | For ever and ever. ℞. A-
lórum. ℞. Amen. | men.

AGNUS DEI, KISS OF PEACE
COMMUNION AND POSTCOMMUNION

He makes the sign of the cross three times over the chalice with the article of the host, saying :

Pax ✠ Dómini sit ✠ semper vobís✠cum.
℟. Et cum spíritu tuo.

The peace ✠ of the Lord be ✠ always with ✠ you.
℟. And with thy spirit.

He puts the particle into the chalice, saying silently :

HÆC commíxtio et consecrátio Córporis et Sánguinis Dómini nostri Jesu Christi, fiat accipiéntibus nobis in vitam ætérnam. Amen.

MAY this mingling and hallowing of the Body and Blood of our Lord Jesus Christ avail us that receive it unto life everlasting. Amen.

He covers the chalice, kneels, rises, and bowing before the blessed Sacrament with his hands joined together and striking his breast three times, says :

AGNUS Dei, qui tollis peccáta mundi, miserére nobis.
Agnus Dei, qui tollis peccáta mundi, miserére nobis.
Agnus Dei, qui tollis peccáta mundi, dona nobis pacem.

LAMB of God, who takest away the sins of the world, have mercy on us.
Lamb of God, who takest away the sins of the world, have mercy on us.
Lamb of God, who takest away the sins of the world, grant us peace.

Then with his hands joined together above the altar he bows down and says the following prayers :

DOMINE Jesu Christe, qui dixísti Apóstolis tuis : Pacem relínquo vobis, pacem meam do vobis : ne respícias peccáta mea, sed fidem Ecclésiæ tuæ : eámque secúndum voluntátem tuam pacificáre et coadunáre dignéris. Qui vivis et regnas Deus, per ómnia sǽcula sæculórum. Amen.

O LORD Jesus Christ, who didst say to thy apostles, Peace I leave with you, my peace I give unto you ; look not upon my sins, but upon the faith of thy Church ; and vouchsafe to her that peace and unity which is agreeable to thy will ; who livest and reignest God for ever and ever. Amen.

If the kiss of peace is to be given, the priest kisses the altar, and giving the kiss of peace, says :

Pax tecum.
℟. Et cum spíritu tuo.

DOMINE Jesu Christe, Fili Dei vivi, qui ex voluntáte Patris, cooperánte Spíritu Sancto, per mortem tuam mundum vivificásti : líbera me per hoc sacrosánctum Corpus et Sánguinem tuum, ab ómnibus iniquitátibus meis, et univérsis malis, et fac me tuis semper inhærére mandátis, et a te numquam separári permíttas, Qui cum eódem Deo Patre et Spíritu Sancto vivis et regnas Deus in sǽcula sæculórum. Amen.

PERCEPTIO Córporis tui, Dómine Jesu Christe, quod ego indígnus súmere præsúmo, non mihi provéniat in judícium et condemnatiónem : sed pro tua pietáte prosit mihi ad tutaméntum mentis et córporis, et ad medélam percipiéndam. Qui vivis et regnas cum Deo Patre in unitáte Spíritus Sancti Deus, per ómnia sǽcula sæculórum. Amen.

Peace be with you.
℟. And with thy spirit.

O LORD Jesu Christ, Son of the living, who, according to the will of thy Father, through the co-operation of the Holy Ghost, hast by thy death given life to the world, deliver me by this, thy most holy Body and Blood, from all my iniquities and from every evil ; and make me always cleave to thy commandments, and never suffer me to be separated from thee ; who with the same God the Father and Holy Ghost livest and reignest God for ever and ever. Amen.

LET not the receiving of thy Body, O Lord Jesus Christ, which I, all unworthy presume to take, turn to my judgment and damnation : but through thy loving-kindness may it avail me for a safeguard and remedy, both of soul and body. Who with God the Father, in the unity of the Holy Ghost, livest and reignest God for ever and ever. Amen.

The priest kneels down, rises, and says :

PANEM cæléstem accípiam, et nomen Dómini invocábo.

I WILL take the Bread of heaven, and call upon the name of the Lord.

Then, bowing a little, ke takes both parts of the host with the thumb and first finger of his left hand, and the paten between his first and middle finger. He strikes his breast with his right hand, and, slightly raising his voice, says three times reverently and humbly :

DOMINE, non sum dignus, ut intres sub tectum meum : sed tantum dic verbo, et sanábitur ánima mea.

LORD, I am not worthy that thou shouldst enter under my roof ; say but the word, and my soul shall be healed.

He makes the sign of the cross with the host in his right hand over the paten, and says :

CORPUS Dómini nostri Jesu Christi custódiat ánimam meam in vitam ætérnam. A-men.

MAY the Body of our Lord Jesus Christ preserve my soul unto life everlasting. Amen.

He receives both portions of the host reverently, joins his hands together, and remains for a little while quietly meditating on the most holy Sacrament. Then he uncovers the chalice, kneels, gathers up the crumbs, if there are any, and wipes the paten above the chalice, whilst he says :

QUID retríbuam Dómino pro ómnibus, quæ retríbuit mihi? Cálicem salutáris accípiam, et nomen Dómini invocábo. Laudans invocábo Dóminum, et ab inimícis meis salvus ero.

WHAT return shall I make to the Lord for all he hath given unto me? I will take the Chalice of salvation, and call upon the name of the Lord. Praising I will call upon the Lord, and I shall be saved from my enemies.

He takes the chalice into his right hand, and making the sign of the cross on himself with it, he says :

SANGUIS Dómini nostri Jesu Christi custódiat ánimam meam in vitam ætérnam. A-men.

MAY the Blood of our Lord Jesus Christ keep my soul unto life everlasting. Amen.

He receives the precious blood with the particle. Then, if there are any communicants, he should give them communion before purifying. Afterwards he says :

QUOD ore súmpsimus, Dómine, pura mente capiámus ; et de múnere temporáli fiat nobis remédium sempitérnum.

GRANT, Lord, that what we have taken with our mouth we may receive with a pure mind ; and that from a temporal gift it may become for us an eternal remedy.

Meanwhile he passes the chalice to the server, who pours into it a little wine, with which he cleanses his fingers ; then he continues :

CORPUS tuum, Dómine, quod sumpsi, et Sanguis quem potávi, adhǽreat viscéribus meis : et præsta ; ut in me non remáneat scélerum mácula, quem pura et sancta refecérunt sacraménta. Qui vivis et regnas in sǽcula sæculórum. Amen.

MAY thy Body, O Lord, which I have received, and thy Blood which I have drunk, cleave to my bowels; and grant that no stain of sin may remain in me, whom thy pure and holy sacraments have refreshed ; who livest and reignest world without end. Amen.

He washes his fingers, wipes them, and takes the ablution ; he wipes his mouth and the chalice, which he covers, and after folding up the corporal, arranges it on the altar as before. Then he continues mass. After the last Postcommunion the priest says :

FINAL PRAYERS AND DISMISSAL

Dóminus vobíscum.
℟. Et cum spíritu tuo.

The Lord be with you.
℟. And with thy spirit.

Then either :

Ite, missa est.

Go, you are dismissed.

or, according to what mass is being said :

Benedicámus Dómino.
℟. Deo grátias.

Let us bless the Lord.
℟. Thanks be to God.

After saying, Ite missa est *or* Benedicámus Dómino, *the priest bows down at the middle of the altar, and with his hands joined above it, says :*

PLACEAT tibi, sancta Trínitas, obséquium servitútis meæ : et præsta ; ut sacrificium quod óculis tuæ majestátis indígnus óbtuli, tibi sit acceptábile, mihíque, et ómnibus pro quibus illud óbtuli, sit, te miseránte, propitiábile. Per Christum Dóminum nostrum. Amen.

MAY the homage of my service be pleasing to thee, O holy Trinity ; and grant that the sacrifice which I, though unworthy, have offered in the sight of thy majesty, may be acceptable to thee : and through thy mercy win forgiveness for me and for all those for whom I have offered it. Through Christ our Lord. Amen.

Then he kisses the altar, and raising his eyes upward, stretching out, lifting up, and joining his hands, bowing his head before the cross, he says :

Benedícat vos omnípotens Deus,

May God almighty bless you,

and turning towards the people, he blesses them once only, even at high mass, and continues :

Pater, et Fílius ✠ et Spíritus Sanctus. ℟. Amen

Father, and Son ✠ and Ho-
ly Ghost. ℟. Amen.

At a bishop's mass a triple blessing is given.

THE LAST GOSPEL

Then at the Gospel corner, after saying Dóminus vobíscum, *and* Inítium *or* Sequéntia sancti Evangélii, *and making the sign of the cross on the altar, or on the book and on himself as at the Gospel in the mass, he reads the Gospel of St. John, as below, or another Gospel as appointed.*

✠ Inítium sancti Ev-
angélii secúndum Joán-
nem. ℟. Glória tibi, Dó-
mine.

IN princípio erat Ver-
bum, et Verbum erat
apud Deum, et Deus
erat Verbum. Hoc erat
in princípio apud Deum.
Omnia per ipsum facta
sunt, et sine ipso factum
est nihil quod factum
est. In ipso vita erat,
et vita erat lux hómi-
num, et lux in ténebris
lucet, et ténebræ eam
non comprehendérunt.
Fuit homo missus a Deo,
cui nomen erat Joánnes.
Hic venit in testimó-
nium, ut testimónium
perhibéret de lúmine, ut
omnes créderent per il-
lum. Non erat ille lux,
sed ut testimónium per-
hibéret de lúmine. Erat
lux vera quæ illúminat
omnem hóminem veni-
éntem in hunc mundum.
In mundo erat, et mun-
dus per ipsum factus est,
et mundus eum non co-
gnóvit. In própria ve-
nit, et sui eum non rece-

✠ The beginning of the
holy Gospel according to St.
John. ℟. Glory be to thee,
O Lord.

IN the beginning was the
Word, and the Word
was with God, and theWord
was God : the same was in
the beginning with God. All
things were made by him,
and without him was made
nothing that was made : in
him was life, and the life
was the light of men ; and
the light shineth in darkness
and the darkness did not
comprehend it. There was a
man sent from God, whose
name was John. This man
came for a witness to give
testimony of the light, that
all men might believe
through him. He was not
the light, but was to give
testimony of the light, that
was the true light which en-
lighteneth every man that
cometh into this world. He
was in the world, and the
world was made by him, and
the world knew him not. He
came unto his own, and his
own received him not. But
as many as received him, he

pérunt ; quotquot autem recepérunt eum, dedit eis potestátem fílios Dei fíeri ; his qui credunt in nómine ejus, qui non ex sanguínibus, neque ex voluntáte carnis, neque ex voluntáte viri, sed ex Deo nati sunt. (*Hic genuflectitur.*) ET VERBUM CARO FACTUM EST, et habitávit in nobis : et vídimus glóriam ejus, glóriam quasi Unigéniti a Patre, plenum grátiæ et veritátis.

℟. Deo grátias.

gave them power to become the sons of God : to them that believe in his name, who are born not of blood, nor of the will of the flesh, nor of the will of man, but of God. AND THE WORD WAS MADE FLESH (*here the people kneel down*), and dwelt among us ; and we saw his glory, the glory as it were of the only-begotten of the Father, full of grace and truth.

℟. Thanks be to God.

PRAYER TO BE SAID BEFORE A CRUCIFIX

EN ego, o bone et dulcissime Jesu, ante conspéctum tuum génibus me provólvo, ac máximo ánimi ardóre te oro atque obtéstor, ut meum in cor vívidos fidei, spei et caritátis sensus, atque veram peccatórum meórum pœniténtiam, éaque emendándi firmíssimam voluntátem velis imprímere, dum magno ánimi afféctu et dolóre, tua quinque vúlnera mecum ipse cónsidero, ac mente contémplor, illud præ óculis habens, quod jam in ore ponébat suo David Prophéta de te, o bone Jesu : Fodérunt manus meas et pedes meos : dinumeravérunt ómnia ossa mea.

BEHOLD, O kind and most sweet Jesus, I cast myself upon my knees in thy sight, and with the most fervent desire of my soul, I pray and beseech thee that thou wouldst impress upon my heart lively sentiments of faith, hope and charity, with true contrition for my sins and a firm purpose of amendment ; whilst with deep affection and grief of soul I ponder within myself and mentally contemplate thy five wounds, having before my eyes that which David the prophet spake of thee : They have pierced my hands and my feet, they have numbered all my bones.

IN PALMIS

PALM SUNDAY

Before Mass there is a ceremony which commemorates the entry of Our Lord into Jerusalem when he was received by the acclamations of the people, as we have described above.

The blessing of the palms like that of the candles on the feast of the Purification and the ashes at the beginning of Lent, is one of the principal blessings in the Roman liturgy. It belongs more or less to the same category as these two latter, but is far more solemn. It has all the liturgical setting of a synaxis [1] at which the Holy Sacrifice is not offered up. We see this again on Good Friday and Holy Saturday, and indeed every day as the first part of the Mass, or Mass of the catechumens. (The Mass strictly speaking begins at the Offertory and is known as the Mass of the faithful.) This ceremony consists of psalms, Collects, an Epistle and Gospel, and sometimes even a Preface as is the case on Palm Sunday, and ends with the blessing. The blessing of the palms has in addition to this a procession. The other three blessings which take place during Holy Week, that of the holy oils, the paschal candle and the font have a very different setting.

The antiphons recall the hosannas of the crowd when Our Lord and his disciples entered Jerusalem. The lesson from the book of Exodus was chosen because of the palm trees of Elim mentioned in this passage. Further on it speaks of the miracle of the manna, a figure of the Holy Eucharist which is to be instituted on Maundy Thursday. The responsory *Collegerunt*, one of the gems of Gregorian chant, shows how Our Lord's miracles, and in particular that of the raising of Lazarus, were the chief cause of his death. The Gospel is St. Matthew's account of the entry into Jerusalem.

See note 2, page ii of the *Introduction*.

2 — The Office of Holy Week.

The prelude to the blessing being ended the palms are then blessed, the Collects explaining most beautifully their symbolical meaning. The palms typify Christ's triumph, the olive branches, symbol of peace, remind us of the oil used in several sacred rites.

The Preface is an invitation to praise God in his Saints, every creature following the example of the Jews on this day and giving glory to him. The antiphons sung during the procession take up the narrative of the Gospel, interpolating and modifying the text according to a familiar custom in Gregorian chant. The other antiphons composed by the Church have also a beautiful and striking melody. The *Gloria, laus et honor* is taken from a hymn composed by Theodulph, Bishop of Orleans in the ninth century. He is said to have composed it in prison, where he was by order of Louis the Debonnaire, who was so touched by the beauty of this hymn that he had him released. It is usually the custom to sing litanies at processions, but this one is meant to reproduce Our Lord's entry into Jerusalem. An eye witness who wrote in the fourth century (Peregrinatio Silviæ) describes the procession as leaving Mount Olivet and going up to Jerusalem, the crowd bearing palm branches and singing antiphons. The bishop riding on an ass and leading the procession added a realistic touch to the ceremony. The night office, or Lucernarium was then celebrated.

It is to commemorate the entry into Jerusalem that the doors of the church are kept shut during the singing of the *Gloria, laus*. The sub-deacon knocks with the foot of the croos to obtain admission and the procession re-enters the church singing the responsory *Ingrediente Domino*.

THE BLESSING OF THE PALMS

When Terce has been sung, and the Asperges given in the usual manner, the priest vested in purple cope, with his ministers also vested in purple, proceeds to the blessing of the palms, or branches of olive or of other trees, which are placed either in the middle, before the altar or at the Epistle side. In the first place the choir sings the following antiphon :

Matth. 21.

HOSANNA fílio David : benedíctus qui venit in nómine Dómini. O Rex Israël : Hosánna in excélsis.

Matth. 21.

HOSANNA to the Son of David ; blessed is he that cometh in the name of the Lord. O King of Israel : Hosanna in the highest.

Then, standing at the Epistle corner of the altar, the priest sings :

℣. Dóminus vobíscum.

℟. Et cum spíritu tuo.

Oratio.

DEUS, quem dilígere et amáre, justítia est : ineffábilis grátiæ tuæ in nobis dona multíplica : et qui fecísti nos in morte Fílii tui speráre quæ crédimus ; fac nos, eódem resurgénte, perveníre quo tendimus. Qui tecum vivit.

℣. The Lord be with you.

℟. And with thy spirit.

Collect.

O GOD, whom to love above all is righteousness, multiply in us the gifts of thy ineffable grace : and since thou hast given us, in the death of thy Son, to hope for those things which we believe, grant us in the resurrection of the same, to attain the end to which we aspire. Who liveth and reigneth.

The subdeacon then sings the following Lesson :

Léctio Libri Exodi, *c.* 15 & 16.

IN diébus illis : Venérunt fílii Israël in Elim, ubi erant duódecim fontes aquárum, et septuagínta palmæ ; et castrametáti sunt juxta aquas. Profectíque sunt de Elim, et venit omnis multitúdo filiórum Israël in desértum Sin, quod est inter Elim et Sínaï, quinto décimo die mensis secúndi, postquam egréssi sunt de terra Ægýpti. Et murmurávit omnis congregátio filiórum Israël contra Móysen et Aaron in solitúdine. Dixerúntque fílii Israël ad eos : Utinam mórtui essémus per manum Dómini in terra Ægýpti, quando sedebámus super ollas cárnium et co-

Lesson from the Book of Exodus, *c.* 15 & 16.

IN those days : The children of Israel came into Elim, where there were twelve fountains of water, and seventy palm trees ; and they encamped by the waters. And they set forward from Elim, and all the multitude of the children of Israel came into the desert of Sin, which is between Elim and Sinai, the fifteenth day of the second month, after they came out of the land of Egypt. And all the congregation of the children of Israel murmured against Moses and Aaron in the wilderness. And the children of Israel said to them : Would to God we had died by the hand of the Lord in the land of Egypt, when we sat over the flesh-pots and ate bread to the full : Why have you

medebámus panem in saturitáte : cur eduxísti nos in desértum istud, ut occiderétis omnem multitúdinem fame? Dixit autem Dóminus ad Móysen : Ecce, ego pluam vobis panes de cælo ; egrediátur pópulus, et cólligat quæ suffíciunt per síngulos dies, ut tentem eum, utrum ámbulet in lege mea, an non. Die autem sexto parent quod ínferant : et sit duplum quam collígere solébant per síngulos dies. Dixerúntque Móyses et Aaron ad omnes fílios Israël : Véspere sciétis quod Dóminus edúxerit vos de terra Ægýpti : et mane vidébitis glóriam Dómini.

brought us into this desert, that you might destroy all the multitude with famine? And the Lord said to Moses : Behold I will rain bread from heaven for you : let the people go forth, and gather what is sufficient for every day : that I may prove them whether they will walk in my law or not. But the sixth day let them provide for to bring in ; and let it be double to that they were wont to gather every day. And Moses and Aaron said to the children of Israel : In the evening you shall know that the Lord hath brought you forth out of the land of Egypt : And in the morning you shall see the glory of the Lord.

In place of the Gradual the choir sings one or other of the following Responsories :

℟. 1. *Joan.* 11.

COLLEGERUNT Pontífices et Pharísæi concílium, et dixérunt : Quid fácimus quia hic homo multa signa facit? Si dimíttimus eum sic, omnes credent in eum : * Et vénient Románi, et tollent nostrum locum et gentem. ℣. Unus autem ex illis, Cáiphas nómine, cum esset Póntifex anni illíus, prophetávit dicens : Expedit vobis, ut unus moriátur homo pro pópulo, et non tota gens

℟. 1. *John* 11.

THE chief priests and the pharisees gathered a council, and said : What do we, for this man doth many miracles? If we let him alone so, all will believe in him : *And the Romans will come, and take away our place and nation. ℣. But one of them named Caiphas, being the high priest that year, prophesied, saying : It is expedient for you, that one man should die for the people, and that the whole nation perish not. From that day, therefore, they devised to

péreat. Ab illo ergo die, cogitavérunt interfícere eum, dicéntes : * Et vénient.

℞. 2. *Matth.* 26.

IN monte Olivéti orávit ad Patrem : Pater, si fíeri potest, tránseat a me calix iste. * Spíritus quidem promptus est, caro autem infírma : fiat volúntas tua. ℣. Vigiláte, et oráte, ut non intrétis in tentatiónem. * Spíritus quidem.

put him to death, saying : *And the Romans.

℞. 2. *Matth.* 26.

ON Mount Olivet he prayed to his Father : Father, if it be possible, let this chalice pass from me. *The spirit indeed is willing, but the flesh is weak : thy will be done. ℣. Watch and pray, that ye enter not into temptation. *The spirit.

After this, the Gospel is sung by the deacon with all the ceremonies usual at High Mass.

✠ Sequéntia sancti Evangélii secúndum Matthǽum,

c. 21.

IN illo témpore : Cum appropinquásset Jesus Jerosólymis, et venísset Béthphage ad montem Olivéti : tunc misit duos discípulos suos, dicens eis : Ite in castéllum, quod contra vos est, et statim veniétis ásinam alligátam, et pullum cum ea : sólvite et addúcite mihi : et si quis vobis áliquid díxerit, dícite quia Dóminus his opus habet ; et conféstim dimíttet eos. Hoc autem totum factum est, ut adimplerétur quod dictum est per Prophétam, dicéntem : Dícite fíliæ Sion : Ecce Rex tuus venit tibi mansuétus, sedens su-

✠ Continuation of the holy Gospel according to St. Matthew,

c. 21.

AT that time : When Jesus drew nigh to Jerusalem, and was come to Bethphage, unto Mount Olivet, then he sent two disciples, saying to them : Go ye into the village that is over against you, and immediately you shall find an ass tied, and a colt with her : loose them and bring them to me : and if any man shall say any thing to you, say ye that the Lord hath need of them : and forthwith he will let them go. Now, all this was done that it might be fulfilled, which was spoken by the prophets, saying : Tell ye the daughter of Sion: Behold thy King cometh to thee, meek, and sitting upon an ass, and a colt the foal of

per ásinam, et pullum fílium subjugális. Euntes autem discípuli fecérunt sicut præcépit illis Jesus. Et adduxérunt ásinam et pullum : et imposuérunt super eos vestiménta sua, et eum désuper sedére fecérunt. Plúrima autem turba stravérunt vestiménta sua in via : álii autem cædébant ramos de arbóribus, et sternébant in via : turbæ autem quæ præcedébant et quæ sequebántur clamábant, dicéntes : Hosánna Fílio David : benedíctus qui venit in nómine Dómini.

her that is used to the yoke. And the disciples going did as Jesus commanded them. And they brought the ass and the colt : and laid their garments upon them, and made him sit thereon. And a very great multitude spread their garments in the way : and others cut boughs from the trees, and strewed them in the way ; and the multitudes that went before and that followed, cried, saying : Hosanna to the Son of David : Blessed is he that cometh in the name of the Lord.

The palms are then blessed. The priest, still standing at the Epistle corner, sings :

℣. Dóminus vobíscum.
℞. Et cum spíritu tuo.
Orémus.

℣. The Lord be with you.
℞. And with thy spirit.
Let us pray.

AUGE fidem in te sperántium, Deus, et súpplicum preces cleménter exáudi : véniat super nos múltiplex misericórdia tua : bene☩dicántur et hi pálmites palmárum seu olivárum: et sicut in figúra Ecclésiæ multiplicásti Noe egrediéntem de arca, et Móysen exeúntem de Ægýpto cum fíliis Israël, ita nos portántes palmas et ramos olivárum, bonis áctibus occurrámus óbviam Christo : et per ipsum in gáudium introeámus ætér-

INCREASE, O God, the faith of those that hope in thee, and in thy mercy hear the prayers of thy suppliants : let thy manifold mercy descend upon us. Bless ☩ also these branches of palm or olive : and as in a figure of thy Church thou didst multiply Noe going out from the ark, and Moses going forth out of Egypt with the children of Israel, so may we go forth with good deeds to meet Christ, bearing palms and branches of olive : and through him may we enter into eternal joy : who liveth and reigneth

num : qui tecum vivit et regnat in unitáte Spíritus Sancti Deus, per ómnia sǽcula sæculórum

℞. Amen.

℣. Dóminus vobíscum.

℞. Et cum spíritu tuo.

℣. Sursum corda.

℞. Habémus ad Dóminum.

℣. Grátias agámus Dómino Deo nostro.

℞. Dignum et justum est.

Vere dignum et justum est, æquum et salutáre, nos tibi semper et ubíque grátias ágere, Dómine sancte, Pater omnípotens, ætérne Deus : qui gloriáris in consílio sanctórum tuórum. Tibi enim sérviunt creatúræ tuæ, quia te solum auctórem et Deum cognóscunt. Et omnis factúra tua te colláudat, et benedícunt te sancti tui : quia illud magnum Unigéniti tui nomen coram régibus et potestátibus hujus sæculi líbera voce confiténtur. Cui assístunt Angeli et Archángeli, Throni et Dominatiónes, cumque omni milítia cæléstis exércitus, hymnum glóriæ tuæ cóncinunt, sine fine dicéntes :

with thee, in the unity of the Holy Ghost, God, world without end.

℞. Amen.

℣. The Lord be with you.

℞. And with thy spirit.

℣. Lift up your hearts.

℞. We have lifted them up to the Lord.

℣. Let us give thanks to the Lord our God.

℞. It is meet and just.

It is truly meet and just, right and available to salvation, always and everywhere to give thee thanks, O holy Lord, almighty Father, eternal God ; who art glorious in the assembly of thy saints. For thy creatures serve thee, because they acknowledge thee for their only Creator and God. All that thou hast made praise thee, and thy saints bless thee ; because they confess with freedom, before the kings and powers of this world, the great name of thy only-begotten Son. The angels and archangels, the thrones and dominions stand before thee, and with all the hosts of the heavenly army sing the hymn of thy glory, saying without end :

The choir here sings :

Sanctus, sanctus, sanctus, Dóminus Deus Sábaoth. Pleni sunt cæli

Holy, holy, holy, Lord God of hosts ! The heavens and the earth are full of thy

et terra glória tua. Hosánna in excélsis. Benedíctus qui venit in nómine Dómini : Hosánna in excélsis.

glory. Hosanna in the highest. Blessed is he that cometh in the name of the Lord : Hosanna in the highest.

The priest continues :

℣. Dóminus vobíscum.
℞. Et cum spíritu tuo.
Orémus.

℣. The Lord be with you.
℞. And with thy spirit.
Let us pray.

PETIMUS, Dómine sancte, Pater omnípotens, ætérne Deus ; ut hanc creatúram olívæ, quam ex ligni matéria prodíre jussísti, quamque colúmba rédiens ad arcam próprio pértulit ore, bene✠dícere et sancti✠ficáre dignéris : ut quicúmque ex ea recéperint, accípiant sibi protectiónem ánimæ et córporis ': fiátque, Dómine, nostræ salútis remédium, et tuæ grátiæ sacraméntum. Per Dóminum. ℞. Amen.

WE beseech thee, O holy Lord, Father almighty, eternal God, that thou wouldst vouchsafe to bless✠ and sanctify✠this creature of the olive tree which thou didst cause to spring forth from the substance of the wood, and which the dove, returning to the ark, brought in its mouth : that all who receive it may find protection of soul and body ; and may it be to us, O Lord, a saving remedy, and a sacred sign of thy grace. Through our Lord. ℞. Amen.

Orémus.

Let us pray.

DEUS, qui dispérsa cóngregas, et congregáta consérvas ; qui pópulis óbviam Jesu ramos portántibus benedixísti : béne✠dic étiam hos ramos palmæ et olívæ, quos tui fámuli ad honórem nóminis tui fidéliter suscípiunt : ut in quemcúmque locum introdúcti fúerint, tuam benedictiónem habitatóres loci illíus consequántur : et omni adversitáte effugáta, déxtera tua prótegat quos redémit

O GOD, who dost gather together what is scattered, and preserve what is gathered together: who didst bless the people that went forth to meet Jesus bearing branches of palms : bless✠ likewise these branches of palm and olive which thy servants receive with faith to the honour of thy name : that wheresoever they shall be brought, they who dwell in that place may receive thy blessing ; and all adversity being removed, thy right hand may protect

Jesus Christus, Fílius tuus, Dóminus noster. Qui tecum vivit et regnat. ℞. Amen.

Orémus.

DEUS qui miro dispositiónis órdine, ex rebus étiam insensibílibus dispensatiónem nostræ salútis osténdere voluísti : da, quǽsumus, ut devóta tuórum corda fidélium salúbriter intélligant quid mýstice designet in facto, quod hódie cælésti lúmine affláta, Redemptóri óbviam procédens, palmárum atque olivárum ramos vestígiis ejus turba substrávit : palmárum ígitur rami de mortis príncipe triúmphos exspéctant : súrculi vero olivárum, spirituálem unctiónem advenísse quodam modo clamant. Intelléxit enim jam tunc illa hóminum beáta multitúdo præfigurári : quia Redémptor noster humánis cóndolens misériis, pro totíus mundi vita cum mortis príncipe esset pugnatúrus ac moriéndo triumphatúrus. Et ídeo tália óbsequens administrávit, quæ in illo et triúmphos victóriæ et misericórdiæ pinguédinem declarárent. Quod nos quoque plena fide, et factum et significátum retinéntes, te, Dómine sancte, Pater

those who have been redeemed by Jesus Christ thy Son our Lord : who liveth and reigneth. ℞. Amen.

Let us pray.

O GOD, who by the wonderful order of thy providence wouldst even in insensible things show us the manner of our salvation ; grant, we beseech thee, that the devout hearts of the faithful may understand to their benefit the mystical meaning of that ceremony, when the multitude, by direction from heaven, going this day to meet our Redeemer, strewed under his feet palms and olive branches : the palms represent his triumph over the prince of death, and the olive branches proclaim in a manner the coming of a spiritual unction. For that pious multitude knew that by them was signified, that our Redeemer, compassionating the misery of mankind, was to fight for the life of the whole world with the prince of death, and to triumph over him by his own death. And, therefore, in that action they made use of such things as might declare, both the triumph of his victory, and the riches of his mercy. We also with a firm faith, retaining both the ceremony and its signification, humbly beseech thee, O holy Lord, almighty Father, eternal God, through

omnípotens, ætérne De-
us, per eúmdem Dómi-
num nostrum Jesum
Christum supplíciter ex-
orámus : ut in ipso, at-
que per ipsum, cujus
nos membra fíeri volu-
ísti, de mortis império
victóriam reportántes,
ipsíus gloriósæ resurre-
ctiónis partícipes esse
mereámur. Qui tecum
vivit et regnat.   ℟. A-
men.

the same Lord Jesus Christ,
that we, whom thou hast
made his members, gaining
by him and in him a victory
over the empire of death,
may deserve to be partakers
of his glorious resurrection.
Who liveth and reigneth.
℟. Amen.

Orémus.

Let us pray.

DEUS, qui per olívæ
ramum, pacem ter-
ris colúmbam nuntiáre
jussísti : præsta, quǽsu-
mus, ut hos olívæ, cete-
rarúmque árborum ra-
mos, cælésti bene✠di-
ctióne sanctífices : ut
cuncto pópulo tuo pro-
fíciant ad salútem.   Per
Christum Dóminum no-
strum.   ℟. Amen.

O GOD, who didst bid
the dove proclaim
peace to the earth by an
olive branch : grant, we beseech thee, that these branches of the olive and other
trees may be hallowed by
thy heavenly ✠ benediction,
and so profit all thy people
unto salvation.   Through
Christ our Lord.   ℟. Amen.

Orémus.

Let us pray.

BENE✠DIC, quǽsu-
mus, Dómine, hos
palmárum, seu olivárum
ramos : et præsta, ut
quod pópulus tuus in tui
veneratiónem hodiérna
die corporáliter agit, hoc
spirituáliter summa de-
votióne perfíciat, de ho-
ste victóriam reportándo
et   opus   misericórdiæ
summópere   dilígéndo.
Per Dóminum.   ℟. A-
men.

BLESS,✠ we beseech thee,
O Lord, these branches
of palm and olive : and
grant that the bodily service
with which thy people ho-
nour thee to-day may be
perfected spiritually by the
utmost devotion, by victory
over the enemy, and by the
ardent love of works of
mercy.   Through our Lord.
℟. Amen.

*Here the priest sprinkles the palms with holy water, and incenses
them thrice.   Then he says :*

℣. Dóminus vobíscum.
℟. Et cum spíritu tuo.

Orémus.

DEUS, qui Fílium tu- um Jesum Christ- tum Dóminum nostrum, pro salúte nostra in hunc mundum misísti, ut se humiliáret ad nos, et nos revocáret ad te : cui étiam, dum Jerúsalem veníret, ut adimpléret Scriptúras, credéntium populórum turba, fidelís- sima devotióne, vesti- ménta sua cum ramis palmárum in via sterné- bant ; præsta, quǽsu- mus, ut illi fídei viam præparémus, de qua, re- móto lápide offensiónis, et petra scándali, flo- reant apud te ópera no- stra justítiæ ramis ; ut ejus vestígia sequi me- reámur. Qui tecum vi- vit et regnat.
℟. Amen.

℣. The Lord be with you.
℟. And with thy spirit.

Let us pray.

O GOD, who for our sal- vation didst send thy Son Jesus Christ our Lord into this world that he might humble himself be- fore us and might call us back to thee : before whom also, when he came to Jeru- salem that he might fulfil the Scriptures, a multitude of believers with devotion full of faith strewed their garments and branches of palms in the way : grant, we beseech thee, that we may prepare for him the way of faith ; that, the stone of offence and rock of scan- dal being removed, our works may flourish before thee with branches of jus- tice, that so we may be found worthy to follow his footsteps. Who liveth and reigneth. ℟. Amen.

After the blessing the priest distributes the palms to the clergy and laity ; each one, as he receives it, kisses first the palm and then the priest's hand. Meanwhile the choir sings the following anti- phons :

Aña. Púeri Hebræ- órum, portántes ramos olivárum, obviavérunt Dómino, clamántes et dicéntes : Hosánna in excélsis.

Aña. Púeri Hebræ- órum vestiménta pro- sternébant in via, et cla- mábant, dicéntes : Ho- sánna Fílio David ; be- nedíctus qui venit in nó- mine Dómini.

Ant. The Hebrew children carrying olive branches, met our Lord, crying out, and saying : Hosanna in the highest.

Ant. The Hebrew children spread their garments in the way, and cried out saying : Hosanna to the Son of Da- vid : blessed is he that co- meth in the name of the Lord.

Returning to the altar the priest sings :

℣. Dóminus vobíscum.

℟. Et cum spíritu tuo.

Orémus.

OMNIPOTENS sempitérne Deus, qui Dóminum nostrum Jesum Christum super pullum ásinæ sedére fecísti, et turbas populórum vestiménta, vel ramos árborum in via stérnere, et Hosánna decantáre in laudem ipsíus docuísti : da, quǽsumus ; ut illórum innocéntiam imitári possímus, et eórum méritum cónsequi mereámur. Per eúmdem Christum Dóminum nostrum. ℟: Amen.

℣. The Lord be with you.

℟. And with thy spirit.

Let us pray.

ALMIGHTY and eternal God, who wouldst have our Lord Jesus Christ to ride on the colt of an ass, and didst inspire the multitudes of people to spread their garments or branches of trees in the way, and to sing Hosanna in his praise : grant, we beseech thee, that we may imitate their innocence, and deserve to partake of their merit. Through the same Christ our Lord. ℟. Amen.

***

The procession now takes place. When the priest has put incense into the thurible, the deacon turns towards the people and sings :

Procedámus in pace.

Let us go forth in peace.

The choir responds :

In nómine Christi. Amen.

In the name of Christ. Amen.

During the procession the following antiphons are sung, or as many of them as are required.

Aña. Cum appropinquáret Dóminus Jerosólymam, misit duos ex discípulis suis, dicens : Ite in castéllum quod contra vos est, et inveniétis pullum ásinæ alligátum, super quem nullus hóminum sedit ; sólvite, et addúcite mihi. Si quis vos interrogáverit, dícite : Opus Dómino est. Solvéntes adduxé-

Ant. When our Lord drew nigh to Jerusalem, he sent two of his disciples, saying : Go ye into the village that is over against you, and you will find an ass's colt tied, on which no man hath ever sat : loose it, and bring it to me. If any man shall question you, say : Our Lord hath need of it. They loosed it and brought it to Jesus, and put their gar-

runt ad Jesum : et impo-
suérunt illi vestiménta
sua, et sedit super eum :
álii expandébant vesti-
ménta sua in via : álii
ramos de arbóribus ster-
nébant : et qui seque-
bántur clamábant : Ho-
sánna, benedíctus qui
venit in nómine Dómini:
benedíctum regnum pa-
tris nostri David : Ho-
sánna in excélsis : mise-
rére nobis, Fíli David.

Aña. Cum audísset
pópulus, quia Jesus ve-
nit Jerosólymam, acce-
pérunt ramos palmárum,
et exiérunt ei óbviam, et
clamábant púeri, dicén-
tes : Hic est qui ventú-
rus est in salútem pó-
puli. Hic est salus no-
stra, et redémptio Israël.
Quantus est iste, cui
Throni et Dominatiónes
occúrrunt ! Noli timére,
fília Sion ; ecce Rex tuus
venit tibi, sedens super
pullum ásinæ ; sicut scriptum est : Salve, Rex,
fabricátor mundi, qui
venísti redímere nos.

Aña. Ante sex dies sol-
lémnis Paschæ, quando
venit Dóminus in civi-
tátem Jerúsalem, occur-
rérunt ei púeri ; et in mánibus portábant ramos
palmárum : et clamá-
bant voce magna, dicén-
tes : Hosánna in excél-
sis ; benedíctus qui ve-
nísti in multitúdine mi-

ments upon it, and he sat
thereon : some spread their
garments in the way : some
strewed branches cut from
trees ; and they that followed cried out : Hosanna,
blessed is he that cometh in
the name of the Lord : blessed is the kingdom of our
father David : Hosanna in
the highest : have mercy on
us, O Son of David.

Ant. When the people
heard that Jesus was com-
ing to Jerusalem, they
took palm branches, and
went out to meet him, and
the children cried out,
saying : This is he that is to
come for the salvation of
the people. He is our salvation, and the redemption
of Israel. How great is he
whom the thrones and do-
minions go out to meet !
Fear not, O daughter of
Sion, be hold thy King comes to thee sitting on an
ass's colt ; as it is written :
Hail, O King, Creator of the
world, who hast come to
redeem us.

Ant. Six days before the
solemnity of the Passover,
when our Lord was coming
into the city of Jerusalem,
the children met him, and
carried palm branches in
their hands ; and they cried
with a loud voice, saying :
Hosanna in the highest ;
blessed art thou who hast
come in the multitude of thy

sericórdiæ tuæ : Hosánna in excélsis.

Aña. Occúrrunt turbæ cum flóribus et palmis Redemptóri óbviam, et victóri triumphánti digna dant obséquia : Fílium Dei ore gentes prædícant ; et in laudem Christi voces tonant per núbila : Hosánna in excélsis.

Aña. Cum Angelis et púeris fidéles inveniámur, triumphatóri mortis clamántes : Hosánna in excélsis.

Aña. Turba multa quæ convénerat ad diem festum, clamábat Dómino : Benedíctus qui venit in nómine Dómini: Hósanna in excélsis.

mercy : Hosanna in the highest.

Ant. The multitude go out to meet our Redeemer with flowers and palms, and pay the homage due to a triumphant conqueror : nations proclaim the Son of God ; and their voices rend the skies in the praise of Christ : Hosanna in the highest.

Ant. Let us join in faith with the angels and children singing to the conqueror of death : Hosanna in the highest.

Ant. A great multitude that was met together at the festival, cried out to the Lord : Blessed is he that cometh in the name of the Lord : Hosanna in the highest.

On the return of the procession two or four cantors enter the church, and, closing the door, stand with their faces towards the procession singing the hymn Glória laus, *after each stanza of which the choir outside repeats the first stanza as a refrain.*

GLORIA, laus, et honor, tibi sit, Rex Christe, Redémptor :
Cui pueríle decus prompsit Hosánna pium.
℟. Glória, laus.

ALL glory, praise, and honour be,
O Christ, Redeemer King, to thee,
Whom children hailed with joyous song
' Hosanna ' in sweet melody.
℟. All Glory.

Israël es tu Rex, Davídis et ínclyta proles :
Nómine qui in Dómini, Rex benedícte, venis.
℟. Glória, laus.

Thou David's Son of royal fame,
Who in the God of Israel's name
Art come our praise and love to claim.
℟. All glory.

Cœtus in excélsis te lau-
dat cǽlicus omnis,
Et mortális homo, et
cuncta creáta simul.
℟. Glória, laus.

The angel host laud thee on
high,
All creatures too in earth
and sky,
And mortal man takes up
the cry.
℟. All glory.

Plebs Hebrǽa tibi cum
palmis óbvia venit ;
Cum prece, voto, hym-
nis ádsumus ecce tibi.
℟. Glória, laus.

The Hebrews came with
branches fair,
And we with hymns and
suppliant prayer
Would in thy gracious
triumph share.
℟. All glory.

Hi tibi passúro solvé-
bant múnia laudis :
Nos tibi regnánti pángi-
mus ecce melos.
℟. Glória, laus.

Thee on thy way to death
they praise,
To thee exultant psalms we
raise,
Who reignest unto endless
days.
℟. All glory.

Hi placuére tibi, pláceat
devótio nostra :
Rex bone, Rex clemens,
cui bona cuncta pla-
cent.
℟. Glória, laus.

To thee this day, O gracious
King,
Whom their devotion pleas-
ed, we sing,
Do thou accept the praise
we bring.
℟. All glory.

*After this the subdeacon knocks at the door with the foot of the cross ;
which being opened, the procession enters the church, singing :*

INGREDIENTE Dó-
mino in sanctam ci-
vitátem, Hebrǽórum
púeri resurrectiónem vi-
tæ pronuntiántes : * cum
ramis palmárum Ho-
sánna clamábant in ex-
célsis. ℣. Cum audísset
pópulus quod Jesus ve-
níret Jerosólymam, ex-
iérunt óbviam ei : * cum
ramis.

AS our Lord entered the
holy city, the Hebrew
children declaring the resurrection of life : * with palm
branches, cried out : Hosan
na in the highest. ℣. When
the people heard that Jesus
was to come to Jerusalem,
they went out to meet him :
* with palm branches.

*At Mass all hold the palms in their hands while the Passion and
Gospel are being sung.*

THE MASS

Our Lord's entry into Jerusalem having been fully commemorated by the procession, the Mass is entirely consecrated to the memory of the Passion. The Introit, Collect, Epistle, Gospel, Offertory and Communion all recall the Passion, and one very striking feature is the Tract taken from Psalm 21, a Messianic psalm which foretold centuries in advance every detail of the Passion.

The choice of the psalms and the plaintive melody of the chant go to make this Mass one of the most beautiful of the year. The stational church is St. John Lateran as is usual for Solemn functions, although in these days the papal ceremony takes place at St. Peter's.

STATION AT ST. JOHN LATERAN

Introitus. Ps. 21.

DOMINE, ne longe fácias auxílium tuum a me, ad defensiónem meam áspice : líbera me de ore leónis, et a córnibus unicórnium humilitátem meam. *Ps.* Deus, Deus meus, réspice in me ; quare me dereliquísti? longe a salúte mea verba delictórum meórum. Dómine, ne longe.

Oratio.

OMNIPOTENS sempitérne Deus, qui humáno géneri ad imitándum humilitátis exémplum, Salvatórem nostrum carnem súmere, et crucem subíre fecísti : concéde propítius ; ut et patiéntiæ ipsíus habére documénta, et resurrectiónis consórtia mereámur. Per eúmdem Dóminum nostrum.

Introït. Ps. 21

O LORD, remove not thy help to a distance from me, look towards my defence ; deliver me from the lion's mouth, and my lowness from the horns of the unicorns. *Ps.* O God, my God, look upon me : why hast thou forsaken me? far from my salvation are the words of my sins. O Lord.

Collect.

ALMIGHTY and eternal God, who didst cause our Saviour to take upon him our flesh and to suffer death upon the cross, that all mankind might imitate the example of his humility : mercifully grant that treasuring the lessons of his patience, we may deserve to have fellowship in his resurrection. Through the same Lord.

No other Collect is said.

Léctio Epístolæ beáti Pauli Apóstoli ad Philippénses, *c.* 2.

FRATRES : Hoc enim sentíte in vobis, quod et in Christo Jesu, qui cum in forma Dei esset, non rapínam arbitrátus est esse se æquálem Deo : sed semetípsum exinanívit, formam servi accípiens, in similitúdinem hóminum factus, et hábitu invéntus ut homo. Humiliávit semetípsum factus obédiens usque ad mortem, mortem autem crucis. Propter quod et Deus exaltávit illum, et donávit illi nomen, quod est super omne nomen ; (*hic genuflectitur*) ut in nómine Jesu omne genu flectátur cæléstium, terréstrium, et infernórum : et omnis lingua confiteátur, quia Dóminus Jesus Christus in glória est Dei Patris.

Graduale. Ps. 72.
TENUISTI manum déxteram meam : et in voluntáte tua deduxísti me : et cum glória assumpsísti me. ℣. Quam bonus Israël Deus rectis corde ; mei autem pene moti sunt pedes, pene effúsi sunt gressus mei : quia zelávi in peccatóribus, pacem peccatórum videns.

Lesson from the Epistle of St. Paul the Apostle to the Philippians, *c.* 2.

BRETHREN : Let this mind be in you, which was also in Christ Jesus ; who being in the form of God, thought it not robbery to be equal with God ; but emptied himself, taking the form of a servant, being made in the likeness of men, and in habit found as a man. He humbled himself, becoming obedient unto death, even the death of the cross. For which cause God also hath exalted him, and hath given him a name which is above all names : (*here. all kneel*) that in the name of Jesus every knee should bow, of those that are in heaven, on earth, and under the earth ; and that every tongue should confess that the Lord Jesus Christ is in the glory of God the Father.

Gradual. Ps. 72
THOU hast held me by my right hand, and by thy will thou hast conducted me ; and with glory thou hast assumed me. ℣. How good is God to Israel, to them that are of right heart ; but my feet were almost moved, my steps had well nigh slipped ; because I had a zeal on occasion of sinners, seeing the peace of sinners.

Tractus. Ps. 21.

DEUS, Deus meus, réspice in me : quare me dereliquísti? ℣. Longe a salúte mea verba delictórum meórum. ℣. Deus meus clamábo per diem, nec exáudies : in nocte, et non ad insipiéntiam mihi. ℣. Tu autem in sancto hábitas, laus Israël. ℣. In te speravérunt patres nostri : speravérunt, et liberásti eos. ℣. Ad te clamavérunt, et salvi facti sunt : in te speravérunt, et non sunt confúsi. ℣. Ego autem sum vermis, et non homo : oppróbrium hóminum, et abjéctio plebis. ℣. Omnes qui vidébant me, aspernabántur me : locúti sunt lábiis, et movérunt caput. ℣. Sperávit in Dómino, erípiat eum : salvum fáciat eum quóniam vult eum. ℣. Ipsi vero consideravérunt, et conspexérunt me : divisérunt sibi vestiménta mea, et super vestem meam misérunt sortem. ℣. Líbera me de ore leónis : et a córnibus unicórnium humilitátem meam. ℣. Qui timétis Dóminum, laudáte eum : univérsum semen Jacob magnificáte eum. ℣. Annuntiábitur Dómino generátio ventúra ; et annuntiábunt cæli justítiam

Tract. Ps. 21

O GOD, my God, look upon me : why hast thou forsaken me? ℣. Far from my salvation are the words of my sins. ℣. O my God, I shall cry by day, and thou wilt not hear : and by night, and it shall not be reputed as folly in me. ℣. But thou dwellest in the holy place, the praise of Israël. ℣. In thee have our fathers hoped : they have hoped, and thou hast delivered them. ℣. They cried to thee, and they were saved : they trusted in thee, and were not confounded. ℣. But I am a worm and no man : the reproach of men, and the outcast of the people. ℣. All they that saw me have laughed me to scorn : they have spoken with the lips, and wagged the head. ℣. He hoped in the Lord, let him deliver him : let him save him, seeing he delighteth in him. ℣. But they have looked and stared upon me : they parted my garments amongst them, and upon my vesture they cast lots. ℣. Deliver me from the lion's mouth, and my lowness from the horns of the unicorns. ℣. Ye that fear the Lord, praise him : all ye the seed of Jacob, glorify him. ℣. There shall be declared to the Lord a generation to come, and the heavens shall show forth his justice. ℣. To a people that

ejus. ℣. Pópulo qui nascétur, quem fecit Dóminus.

shall be born, which the Lord hath made.

The Passion is read without lights or incense; the deacon does not ask the priest's blessing, nor say Dóminus vobíscum, *nor is* Glória tibi Dómine *sung after the title. The same is observed on the other days on which the Passion is read.*

Pássio Dómini nostri Jesu Christi secúndum Matthæum, c. 26 & 27.

IN illo témpore : Dixit Jesus discipulis suis : ✠ Scítis quia post bíduum Pascha fiet : et Fílius hóminis tradétur, ut crucifigátur. Tunc congregáti sunt príncipes sacerdótum et senióres pópuli in átrium princípis sacerdótum, qui dicebátur Cáiphas : et consílium fecérunt, ut Jesum dolo tenérent, et occíderent. Dicébant autem : Non in die festo ne forte tumúltus fíeret in pópulo. Cum autem Jesus esset in Bethánia, in domo Simónis leprósi, accéssit ad eum múlier habens alabástrum unguénti pretiósi ; et effúdit super caput ipsíus recumbéntis. Vidéntes autem discípuli, indignáti sunt, dicéntes : Ut quid perdítio hæc? Pótuit enim istud venúmdari multo, et dari paupéribus. Sciens autem Jesus, ait illis : ✠ Quid molésti estis huic mulíeri? Opus enim bonum operáta est in me. Nam semper páuperes habétis

The Passion of our Lord Jesus Christ according to St. Matthew, c. 26 & 27.

AT that time : Jesus said to his disciples : You know that after two days shall be the pasch, and the Son of man shall be delivered up to be crucified. Then there were gathered together the chief priests and ancients of the people, into the court of the high priest, who was called Caiphas ; and they consulted together that by subtilty they might apprehend Jesus, and put him to death. But they said : Not on the festival day, lest perhaps there should be a tumult among the people. And when Jesus was in Bethania, in the house of Simon the leper, there came to him a woman having an alabaster box of precious ointment, and poured it on his head, as he was at table. And the disciples, seeing it, had indignation, saying : To what purpose is this waste? for this might have been sold for much, and given to the poor. And Jesus, knowing it, said to them : Why

vobíscum : me autem non semper habétis. Mittens enim hæc unguéntum hoc in corpus meum, ad sepeliéndum me fecit. Amen dico vobis, ubicúmque prædicátum fúerit hoc Evangélium in toto mundo, dicétur et quod hæc fecit in memóriam ejus. Tunc ábiit unus de duódecim, qui dicebátur Judas Iscariótes, ad príncipes sacerdótum : et ait illis : Quid vultis mihi dare, et ego vobis eum tradam? At illi constituérunt ei trigínta argénteos. Et exínde quærébat opportunitátem, ut eum tráderet. Prima autem die azymórum accessérunt discípuli ad Jesum, dicéntes : Ubi vis parémus tibi comédere Pascha? At Jesus dixit : ✠ Ite in civitátem ad quemdam, et dícite ei : Magister dicit : Tempus meum prope est; apud te fácio Pascha cum discípulis meis. Et fecérunt discípuli, sicut constítuit illis Jesus, et paravérunt Pascha. Véspere autem facto, discumbébat cum duódecim discípulis suis. Et edéntibus illis, dixit : ✠ Amen dico vobis, quia unus vestrum me tradilúrus est. Et contristáti valde, cœpérunt sínguli dícere : Num-

do you trouble this woman? for she hath wrought a good work upon me. For the poor you have always with you ; but me you have not always. For she, in pouring this ointment upon my body, hath done it for my burial. Amen I say to you, wheresoever this Gospel shall be preached in the whole world, that also which she hath done shall be told, for a memory of her. Then went one of the twelve, who was called Judas Iscariot, to the chief priests, and said to them : What will you give me, and I will deliver him unto you? but they appointed him thirty pieces of silver. And from thenceforth he sought opportunity to betray him. And on the first day of the azymes the disciples came to Jesus, saying : Where wilt thou that we prepare for thee to eat the pasch? But Jesus said : Go ye into the city to a certain man, and say to him : The master saith : My time is near at hand, I will keep the pasch at thy house with my disciples. And the disciples did as Jesus appointed to them ; and they prepared the pasch. Now, when it was evening, he sat down with his twelve disciples : and whilst they were eating, he said : Amen I say to

quid ego sum, Dómine? At ipse respóndens, ait : ✠ Qui intíngit mecum manum in parópside, hic me tradet. Fílius quidem hóminis vadit, sicut scriptum est de illo : væ autem hómini illi, per quem Fílius hóminis tradétur : bonum erat ei, si natus non fuísset homo ille. Respóndens autem Judas, qui trádidit eum, dixit : Numquid ego sum, Rabbi? Ait illi : ✠ Tu dixísti. Cœnántibus autem eis, accépit Jesus panem, et benedíxit, ac fregit, deditque discípulis suis, et ait : ✠ Accípite, et comédite : Hoc est corpus meum. Et accípiens cálicem, grátias egit : et dedit illis, dicens : ✠ Bibite ex hoc omnes. Hic est enim sanguis meus novi testaménti, qui pro multis effundétur in remissiónem peccatórum. Dico autem vobis : non bibam ámodo de hoc genímine vitis, usque in diem illum, cum illud bibam vobíscum novum in regno Patris mei. Et hymno dicto, exiérunt in montem Olivéti. Tunc dicit illis Jesus : ✠ Omnes vos scándalum patiémini in me, in ista nocte. Scriptum est enim : Percútiam pastórem, et dispergéntur oves gregis.

you, that one of you is about to betray me. And they, being very much troubled, began every one to say : Is it I, Lord? But he answering, said : He that dippeth his hand with me in the dish, he shall betray me. The Son of man indeed goeth, as it is written of him ; but woe to that man by whom the Son of man shall be betrayed : it were better for him, if that man had not been born. And Judas that betrayed him, answering, said : Is it I, Rabbi? He saith to him : Thou hast said it. And whilst they were at supper, Jesus took bread, and blessed, and broke ; and gave to his disciples, and said : Take ye, and eat : this is my body. And taking the chalice, he gave thanks : and gave to them, saying : Drink ye all of this. For this is my blood of the new testament, which shall be shed for many unto remission of sins. And I say unto you, I will not drink from henceforth of this fruit of the vine, until that day when I shall drink it with you new in the kingdom of my Father. And a hymn being said, they went out unto mount Olivet. Then Jesus saith to them : All you shall be scandalized in me this night. For it is written :

Postquam autem resurréxero, præcédam vos in Galilǽam. Respóndens autem Petrus, ait illi : Et si omnes scandalizáti fúerint in te, ego numquam scandalizábor. Ait illi Jesus : ✠ Amen dico tibi, quia in hac nocte, ántequam gallus cantet, ter me negábis. Ait illi Petrus : Étiam si oportúerit me mori tecum, non te negábo. Simíliter et omnes discípuli dixérunt. Tunc venit Jesus cum illis in villam, quæ dícitur Gethsémani, et dixit discípulis suis : ✠ Sedéte hic, donec vadam illuc, et orem. Et assúmpto Petro, et duóbus fíliis Zebedǽi, cœpit contristári et mœstus esse. Tunc ait illis : ✠ Tristis est ánima mea usque ad mortem : sustinéte hic, et vigiláte mecum. Et progréssus pusíllum, prócidit in fáciem suam, orans et dicens : ✠ Pater mi, si possíbile est, tránseat a me calix iste. Verúmtamen non sicut ego volo, sed sicut tu. Et venit ad discípulos suos, et invénit eos dormiéntes : et dicit Petro : ✠ Sic, non potuístis una hora vigiláre mecum? Vigiláte et oráte, ut non intrétis in tentatiónem. Spíritus quidem promptus est, caro autem infírma. Ite-

I will strike the shepherd : and the sheep of the flock shall be dispersed. But after I shall be risen again, I will go before you into Galilee. And Peter answering, said to him : Although all shall be scandalized in thee, I will never be scandalized. Jesus said to him : Amen I say to thee, that in this night, before the cock crow, thou wilt deny me thrice. Peter saith to him : Yea, though I should die with thee, I will not deny thee : and in like manner said all the disciples. Then Jesus came with them into a country place which is called Gethsemani ; and he said to his disciples : Sit you here, till I go yonder and pray. And taking with him Peter and the two sons of Zebedee, he began to grow sorrowful and to be sad. Then he saith to them : My soul is sorrowful even unto death ; stay you here and watch with me. And going a little farther, he fell upon his face, praying, and saying : My Father, if it be possible, let this chalice pass from me : nevertheless, not as I will, but as thou wilt. And he cometh to his disciples, and findeth them asleep : and he saith to Peter : What ! could you not watch one hour with me? Watch ye, and pray, that

rum secúndo ábiit, et orávit dicens : ✠ Pater mi, si non potest hic calix transíre, nisi bibam illum, fiat volúntas tua. Et venit íterum, et invénit eos dormiéntes : erant enim óculi eórum graváti. Et relíctis illis, íterum ábiit : et orávit tértio, eúmdem sermónem dicens. Tunc venit ad discípulos suos, et dicit illis : ✠ Dormíte jam, et requiéscite. Ecce appropinquávit hora : et Fílius hóminis tradétur in manus peccatórum. Súrgite, eámus : ecce appropinquávit qui me tradet. Adhuc eo loquénte, ecce Judas unus de duódecim venit, et cum eo turba multa cum gládiis, et fústibus, missi a princípibus sacerdótum, et senióribus pópuli. Qui autem trádidit eum, dedit illis signum, dicens : Quemcúmque osculátus fúero, ipse est, tenéte eum. Et conféstim accédens ad Jesum, dixit : Ave, Rabbi. Et osculátus est, eum. Dixítque illi Jesus : ✠ Amíce, ad quid venísti? Tunc accessérunt, et manus injecérunt in Jesum, et tenuérunt eum. Et ecce, unus ex his qui erant cum Jesu, exténdens manum, exémit gládium suum et percútiens servum

ye enter not into temptation. The spirit indeed is willing, but the flesh is weak. Again the second time, he went, and prayed, saying : My Father, if this chalice may not pass away, but I must drink it, thy will be done. And he cometh again, and findeth them sleeping ; for their eyes were heavy. And leaving them, he went again : and he prayed the third time, saying the selfsame word. Then he cometh to his disciples, and saith to them : Sleep ye now, and take your rest ; behold, the hour is at hand, and the Son of man shall be betrayed into the hands of sinners. Rise, let us go ; behold, he is at hand that will betray me. As he yet spoke, behold Judas, one of the twelve, came ; and with him a great multitude with swords and clubs, sent from the chief priests and the ancients of the people. And he that betrayed him gave them a sign, saying : Whomsoever I shall kiss, that is he ; hold him fast. And forthwith coming to Jesus, he said : Hail, Rabbi. And he kissed him. And Jesus said to him : Friend, whereto art thou come? Then they came up, and laid hands on Jesus, and held him. And behold, one of them that were with Jesus,

príncipis sacerdótum, amputávit aurículam ejus. Tunc ait illi Jesus : ✠ Convérte gládium tuum in locum suum. Omnes enim, qui accéperint gládium, gládio períbunt. An putas, quia non possum rogáre Patrem meum, et exhibébit mihi modo plus quam duódecim legiónes angelórum? Quómodo ergo implebúntur Scriptúræ, quia sic opórtet fíeri? In illa hora dixit Jesus turbis : ✠ Tamquam ad latrónem exístis cum gládiis et fústibus comprehéndere me : quotídie apud vos sedébam docens in templo, et non me tenuístis. Hoc autem totum factum est, ut adimpleréntur Scriptúræ Prophetárum. Tunc discípuli omnes, relícto eo, fugérunt. At illi tenéntes Jesum, duxérunt ad Cáipham príncipem sacerdótum, ubi scribæ et senióres convénerant. Petrus autem sequebátur eum a longe, usque in átrium príncipis sacerdótum. Et ingréssus intro, sedébat cum minístris, ut vidéret finem. Príncipes autem sacerdótum, et omne concílium, quærébant falsum testimónium contra Jesum, ut eum morti tráderent : et non invenérunt, cum multi falsi

stretching forth his hand, drew out his sword, and, striking the servant of the high priest, cut off his ear. Then Jesus saith to him : Put up again thy sword into its place ; for all that take the sword shall perish by the sword. Thinkest thou that I cannot ask my Father, and he will give me presently more than twelve legions of angels? How then shall the Scriptures be fulfilled, that so it must be done? In that same hour Jesus said to the multitudes : You are come out, as it were to a robber, with swords and clubs, to apprehend me. I sat daily with you teaching in the temple, and you laid not hands on me. Now all this was done, that the Scriptures of the prophets might be fulfilled. Then the disciples, all leaving him, fled. But they holding Jesus, led him to Caiphas the high priest, where the scribes, and ancients were assembled. And Peter followed him afar off, even to the court of the high priest. And going in, he sat with the servants, that he might see the end. And the chief priests and the whole council sought false witness against Jesus that they might put him to death. And they found not ; whereas many false

testes accessíssent. Novíssime autem venérunt duo falsi testes, et dixérunt : Hic dixit : Possum destrúere templum Dei, et post tríduum reædificáre illud. Et surgens princeps sacerdótum, ait illi : Nihil respóndes ad ea, quæ isti advérsum te testificántur? Jesus autem tacébat. Et princeps sacerdótum ait illi : Adjúro te per Deum vivum : ut dicas nobis, si tu es Christus Fílius Dei. Dicit illi Jesus : ✠ Tu dixísti. Verúmtamen dico vobis, ámodo vidébitis Fílium hóminis sedéntem a dextris virtútis Dei, et veniéntem in núbibus cæli. Tunc princeps sacerdótum scidit vestiménta sua, dicens : Blasphemávit. Quid adhuc egémus téstibus? Ecce : nunc audístis blasphémiam. Quid vobis vidétur? At illi respondéntes, dixérunt : Reus est mortis. Tunc exspuérunt in fáciem ejus : et cólaphis eum cecidérunt. Alii autem palmas in fáciem ejus dedérunt, dicéntes : Prophetíza nobis, Christe, quis est, qui te percússit? Petrus vero sedébat foris in átrio. Et accéssit ad eum una ancílla, dicens : Et tu cum Jesu Galilæo eras. At ille negávit coram ómni-

witnesses had come in. And last of all, there came two false witnesses. And they said : This man said : I am able to destroy the temple of God, and in three days to rebuild it. And the high priest, rising up, said to him : Answerest thou nothing to the things which these witness against thee? But Jesus held his peace. And the high priest said to him : I adjure thee by the living God, that thou tell us if thou be the Christ the Son of God. Jesus saith to him : Thou hast said it. Nevertheless I say to you, hereafter you shall see the Son of man sitting on the right hand of the power of God, and coming in the clouds of heaven. Then the high priest rent his garments, saying : He hath blasphemed ; what further need have we of witnesses? Behold, now you have heard the blasphemy. What think you? But they answering, said : He his guilty of death. Then did they spit in his face and buffeted him ; and others struck his face with the palms of their hands, saying : Prophesy unto us. O Christ, who is he that struck thee? But Peter sat without in the court, and there came to him a servant-maid, saying : Thou also wast with Jesus the Gali-

bus, dicens : Néscio quid dicis. Exeúnte autem illo jánuam, vidit eum ália ancílla : et ait his qui erant ibi : Et hic erat cum Jesu Nazaréno. Et íterum negávit cum juraménto : Quia non novi hóminem. Et post pusíllum accessérunt qui stabant, et dixérunt Petro : Vere et tu ex illis es : nam et loquéla tua maniféstum te facit. Tunc cœpit detestári et juráre quia non novísset hóminem. Et contínuo gallus cantávit. Et recordátus est Petrus verbi Jesu quod díxerat : Priúsquam gallus cantet, ter me negábis. Et egréssus foras, flevit amáre. Mane autem facto, consílium iniérunt omnes príncipes sacerdótum, et senióres pópuli advérsus Jesum, ut eum morti tráderent. Et vinctum adduxérunt eum, et tradidérunt Póntio Piláto, præsidi. Tunc videns Judas, qui eum trádidit, quod damnátus esset, pœniténtia ductus, rétulit trigínta argénteos princípibus sacerdótum, et senióribus, dicens : Peccávi, tradens sánguinem justum. At illi dixérunt : Quid ad nos? tu víderis. Et projéctis argénteis in templo, recéssit : et ábiens, láqueo se suspén-

lean. But he denied before them all, saying : I know not what thou sayest. And as he went out of the gate, another maid saw him, and she saith to them that were there : This man also was with Jesus of Nazareth. And again he denied with an oath : I know not the man. And after a little while they came that stood by, and said to Peter : Surely thou also art one of them ; for even thy speech doth discover thee. Then he began to curse and to swear that he knew not the man ; and immediately the cock crew. And Peter remembered the word of Jesus which he had said : Before the cock crow, thou wilt deny me thrice. And going forth, he wept bitterly. And when morning was come, all the chief priests and ancients of the people took counsel against Jesus, to put him to death. And they brought him bound, and delivered him to Pontius Pilate, the governor. Then Judas, who betrayed him seeing that he was condemned, repenting himself, brought back the thirty pieces of silver to the chief priests and ancients, saying : I have sinned, in betraying innocent blood. But they said : What is that to us? look thou to it. And casting down the pieces of silver

dit. Príncipes autem sacerdótum, accéptis argénteis, dixérunt : Non licet eos míttere in córbonam : quia prétium sánguinis est. Consílio autem ínito, emérunt ex illis agrum fíguli, in sepultúram peregrinórum. Propter hoc vocátus est ager ille, Hacéldama, hoc est, ager sánguinis, usque in hodiérnum diem. Tunc implétum est quod dictum est per Jeremíam Prophétam, dicéntem : Et accepérunt trigínta argénteos prétium appretiáti, quem appretiavérunt a fíliis Israël : et dedérunt eos in agrum fíguli, sicut constítuit mihi Dóminus. Jesus autem stetit ante præsídem, et interrogávit eum præses, dicens : Tu es Rex Judæórum? Dicit illi Jesus : ✠ Tu dicis. Et cum accusarétur a princípibus sacerdótum, et senióribus, nihil respóndit. Tunc dicit illi Pilátus : Non audis quanta advérsum te dicunt testimónia? Et non respóndit ei ad ullum verbum, ita ut mirarétur præses veheménter. Per diem autem solémnem consuéverat præses pópulo dimíttere unum vínctum, quem voluíssent. Habébat autem tunc vínctum insígnem, qui dicebátur Barábbas.

in the temple, he departed ; and went, and hanged himself with an halter. But the chief priests, having taken the pieces of silver, said : It is not lawful to put them into the corbona, because it is the price of blood. And after they had consulted together, they bought with them the potter's field, to be a buryingplace for strangers. Wherefore that field was called Haceldama, that is, the field of blood, even to this day. Then was fulfilled that which was spoken by Jeremias the prophet, saying : And they took the thirty pieces of silver, the price of him that was prized, whom they prized of the children of Israel ; and they gave them unto the potter's field, as the Lord appointed to me. And Jesus stood before the governor, and the governor asked him, saying : Art thou the king of the Jews? Jesus saith to him : Thou sayest it. And when he was accused by the chief priests and ancients, he answered nothing. Then Pilate saith to him : Dost not thou hear how great testimonies they allege against thee? And he answered to him never a word, so that the governor wondered exceedingly. Now upon the solemn day the governor was accustomed to release

Congregátis ergo illis, dixit Pilátus : Quem vultis dimíttam vobis : Barábbam, an Jesum, qui dícitur Christus? Sciébat enim quod per invídiam tradidíssent eum. Sedénte autem illo pro tribunáli, misit ad eum uxor ejus, dicens : Nihil tibi, et justo illi : multa enim passa sum hódie per visum propter eum. Príncipes autem sacerdótum et senióres persuasérunt pópulis ut péterent Barábbam, Jesum vero pérderent. Respóndens autem præses, ait illis : Quem vultis vobis de duóbus dimítti? At illi dixérunt : Barábbam. Dicit illis Pilátus : Quid ígitur fáciam de Jesu, qui dícitur Christus? Dicunt omnes: Crucifigátur. Ait illis præses : Quid enim mali fecit? At illi magis clamábant, dicéntes : Crucifigátur. Videns autem Pilátus quia nihil profíceret, sed magis tumúltus fíeret : accépta aqua, lavit manus coram pópulo, dícens : Innocens ego sum a sánguine justi hujus : vos vidéritis. Et respóndens univérsus pópulus, dixit : Sanguis ejus super nos, et super fílios nostros. Tunc dimísit illis Barábbam : Jesum autem flagellátum trádidit eis ut cru-

to the people one prisoner, whom they would ; and he had then a notorious prisoner, that was called Barabbas. They therefore being gathered together, Pilate said : Whom will you that I release to you, Barrabas, or Jesus that is called Christ? For he knew that for envy they had delivered him. And as he was sitting in the place of judgement, his wife sent to him, saying : Have thou nothing to do with that just man, for I have suffered many things this day in a dream because of him. But the chief priests and ancients persuaded the people that they should ask Barabbas, and make Jesus away. And the governor answering, said to them : Whether will you of the two to be released unto you? But they said : Barrabas. Pilate saith to them : What shall I do then with Jesus that is called Christ? They say all : Let him be crucified. The governor said to them : Why, what evil hath he done? But they cried out the more, saying : Let him be crucified. And Pilate seeing that he prevailed nothing, but that rather a tumult was made, taking water, washed his hands before the people, saying : I am innocent of the blood of

cifigerétur. Tunc mílites præsidis suscipiéntes Jesum in prætórium, congregavérunt ad eum univérsam cohórtem. Et exuéntes eum, chlámydem coccíneam circumdedérunt ei. Et plecténtes corónam de spínis, posuérunt super caput ejus, et arúndinem in déxtera ejus. Et genufléxo ante eum, illudébant ei, dicéntes : Ave Rex Judæórum ! Et exspuéntes in eum, accepérunt arúndinem, et percutiébant caput ejus. Et postquam illusérunt ei, exuérunt eum chlámyde : et induérunt eum vestiméntis ejus, et duxérunt eum ut crucifígerent. Exeúntes autem, invenérunt hóminem Cyrenǽum, nómine Simónem. Hunc angariavérunt ut tólleret crucem ejus. Et venérunt in locum, qui dícitur Gólgotha : quod est, Calváriæ locus. Et dedérunt ei vinum bíbere cum felle mixtum. Et cum gustásset, nóluit bíbere. Postquam autem crucifixérunt eum, divisérunt vestiménta ejus, sortem mitténtes : ut implerétur quod dictum est per Prophétam dicéntem : Divisérunt sibi vestiménta mea, et super vestem meam misérunt sortem. Et sedéntes,

this just man ; look you to it. And the whole people answering, said : His blood be upon us, and upon our children. Then he released to them Barrabas, and having scourged Jesus, delivered him unto them to be crucified. Then the soldiers of the governor, taking Jesus into the hall, gathered together unto him the whole band, and stripping him, they put a scarlet cloak about him. And platting a crown of thorns, they put it upon his head, and a reed in his right hand. And bowing the knee before him, they mocked him, saying : Hail, King of the Jews. And spitting upon him, they took the reed and struck his head. And after they had mocked him, they took off the cloak from him, and put on him his own garments, and led him away to crucify him. And going out, they found a man of Cyrene, named Simon ; him they forced to take up his cross. And they came to the place that is called Golgotha, which is, the place of Calvary. And they gave him wine to drink mingled with gall. And when he had tasted, he would not drink. And after they had crucified him, they divided his garments, casting lots ; that it might be fulfilled which was spoken by the

servábant eum. Et imposuérunt super caput ejus causam ipsíus scriptam : Hic est Jesus Rex Judæórum. Tunc crucifíxi sunt cum eo duo latrónes, unus a dextris, et unus a sinístris. Prætereúntes autem blasphemábant eum, movéntes cápita sua, et dicéntes : Vah! qui déstruis templum Dei, et in tríduo illud reædíficas : salva temetípsum. Si Fílius Dei es, descénde de cruce. Simíliter et príncipes sacerdótum illudéntes cum scribis et senióribus, dicébant : Alios salvos fecit : seípsum non potest salvum fácere. Si Rex Israël est, descéndat nunc de cruce, et crédimus ei. Confídit in Deo : líberet nunc si vult eum : dixit enim : Quia Fílius Dei sum. Idípsum autem et latrónes, qui crucifíxi erant cum eo, improperábant ei. A sexta autem hora, ténebræ factæ sunt super univérsam terram, usque ad horam nonam. Et circa horam nonam clamávit Jesus voce magna, dicens : ✠ Eli, Eli, lamma sabactháni? Hoc est : ✠ Deus meus, Deus meus, ut quid dereliquísti me ? Quidam autem illic stantes, et audiéntes, dicébant : E-

prophet, saying : They divided my garments among them, and upon my vesture they cast lots. And they sat, and watched him. And they put over his head his cause written : This is Jesus the King of the Jews. Then were crucified with him two thieves, one on the right hand, and one on the left. And they that passed by, blasphemed him, wagging their heads, and saying : Vah, thou that destroyest the temple of God, and in three days dost rebuild it, save thy own self; if thou be the Son of God, come down from the cross. In like manner also the chief priests with the scribes and ancients mocking, said : He saved others, himself he cannot save : if he be the King of Israel, let him now come down from the cross, and we will believe him. He trusted in God, let him now deliver him if he will have him ; for he said : I am the Son of God. And the selfsame thing the thieves also, that were crucified with him, reproached him with. Now from the sixth hour there was darkness over the whole earth, until the ninth hour. And about the ninth hour, Jesus cried with a loud voice, saying : Eli, Eli, lamma sabacthani? that is, My God, my God, why hast thou forsaken me? And some that

líam vocat iste. Et contínuo currens unus ex eis, accéptam spóngiam implévit acéto, et impósuit arúndini et dabat ei bíbere. Céteri vero dicébant : Sine videámus an véniat Elías liberans eum. Jesus autem íterum clamans voce magna, emísit spíritum.

stood there, and heard, said: This man calleth Elias. And immediately one of them running, took a sponge and filled it with vinegar, and put it on a reed, and gave him to drink. And the others said : Let be ; let us see whether Elias will come to deliver him. And Jesus, again crying with a loud voice, yielded up the ghost.

Here a pause is made, and all kneel down.

ET ecce velum templi scíssum est in duas partes, a summo usque deórsum : et terra mota est, et petræ scissæ sunt, et monuménta apérta sunt : et multa córpora Sanctórum, qui dormíerant, surrexérunt. Et exeúntes de monuméntis post resurrectiónem ejus venérunt in sanctam civitátem, et apparuérunt multis. Centúrio autem, et qui cum eo erant custodiéntes Jesum, viso terræmótu et his quæ fiébant, timuérunt valde dicéntes: Vere Fílius Dei erat iste. Erant autem ibi mulíeres multæ a longe, quæ secútæ erant Jesum a Galilǽa, ministrántes ei : inter quas erat María Magdaléne, et María Jacóbi et Joseph mater, et mater filiórum Zebedǽi. Cum autem sero factum esset, venit quidam homo di-

AND behold the veil of the temple was rent in two, from the top even to the bottom ; and the earth quaked, and the rocks were rent ; and the graves were opened, and many bodies of the saints that had slept arose, and coming out of the tombs after his resurrection, came into the holy city, and appeared to many. Now the centurion and they that were with him watching Jesus, having seen the earthquake and the things that were done, were sore afraid, saying : Indeed this was the Son of God. And there were many women afar off, who had followed Jesus from Galilee, ministering unto him ; among whom was Mary Magdalen, and Mary the mother of James and Joseph, and the mother of the sons of Zebedee. And when it was evening, there came a certain rich man of Arimathea, named Joseph, who

ves ab Arimathæa, nómine Joseph, qui et ipse discípulus erat Jesu. Hic accéssit ad Pilátum, et pétiit corpus Jesu. Tunc Pilátus jussit reddi corpus. Et accépto córpore, Joseph invólvit illud in síndone munda. Et pósuit illud in moduménto suo novo, quod excíderat in petra. Et advólvit saxum magnum ad óstium monuménti, et ábiit. Erat autem ibi María Magdaléne, et áltera María, sedéntes contra sepúlcrum.

also himself was a disciple of Jesus. He went to Pilate, and asked the body of Jesus. Then Pilate commanded that the body should be delivered. And Joseph, taking the body, wrapt it up in a clean linen cloth, and laid it in his own new monument, which he had hewn out in a rock ; and he rolled a great stone to the door of the monument, and went his way. And there was there Mary Magdalen, and the other Mary, sitting over against the sepulchre.

Here the deacon says the prayer Munda cor meum, *and then asks the priest's blessing ; he incenses the book, but lights are nor carried.*

ALTERA autem die, quæ est post Parascéven, convenérunt príncipes sacerdótum et Pharisæi ad Pilátum, dicéntes : Dómine, recordáti sumus, quia sedúctor ille dixit adhuc vivens : Post tres dies resúrgam. Jube ergo custodíri sepúlcrum usque in diem tértium : ne forte véniant discípuli ejus, et furéntur eum : et dicant plebi : Surréxit a mórtuis : et erit novíssimus error pejor prióre. Ait illis Pilátus : Habétis custódiam, ite, custódíte sicut scitis. Illi autem abeúntes, muniérunt sepúlcrum, signántes lápidem, cum custódibus.

AND the next day, which followed the day of preparation, the chief priests and the pharisees came together to Pilate, saying : Sir, we have remembered that that seducer said, while he was yet alive : after three days, I will rise again ; command therefore the sepulchre to be guarded until the third day, lest perhaps his disciples come and steal him away, and say to the people: He is risen from the dead ; and the last error shall be worse than the first. Pilate saith to them : You have a guard ; go, guard it as you know. And they, departing, made the sepulchre sure, sealing the stone, and setting guards.

Credo.

Offertorium. Ps. 68.

IMPROPERIUM exspectávit cor meum, et misériam ; et sustínui qui simul contristarétur, et non fuit : consolántem me quæsívi, et non invéni ; et dedérunt in escam meam fel, et in siti mea potavérunt me acéto.

Secreta.

CONCEDE, quǽsumus, Dómine : ut óculis tuæ majestátis munus oblátum, et grátiam nobis devotiónis obtíneat, et efféctum beátæ perennitátis acquírat. Per Dóminum.

Creed.

Offertory. Ps. 68.

MY heart hath expected reproach and misery ; and I looked for one that would grieve together with me, and there was none : I sought for one to comfort me, and I found none ; and they gave me gall for my food, and in my thirst they gave me vinegar to drink.

Secret.

GRANT, we beseech thee, O Lord, that the gift we offer in the eyes of thy majesty may obtain for us the grace of devotion and the fruit of a blessed eternity. Through our Lord.

The Preface is that of the Cross, Qui salútem, *p.* 15.

Communio. Matth. 26.

PATER, si non potest hic calix transíre, nisi bibam illum : fiat volúntas tua.

Postcommunio.

PER hujus, Dómine, operatiónem mystérii, et vítia nostra purgéntur, et justa desidéria compleántur. Per Dóminum.

Communion. Matth. 26.

FATHER, if this chalice may not pass away, but I must drink it, thy will be done.

Postcommunion.

BY the working of this mystery, O Lord, may our vices be purged away and our just desires fulfilled. Through our Lord.

In private Masses the Gospel of the blessing of the palms, Cum appropinquásset, *p.* 37, *is read at the end instead of that of St. John.*

VESPERS

Pater noster, Ave María, *secreto*.

℣. Deus, in adjutórium meum inténde.

℞. Dómine, ad adjuvándum me festína.

Glória Patri, et Fílio, et Spirítui Sancto.

Sicut erat in princípio, et nunc et semper, et in sǽcula sæculórum. Amen.

Laus tibi, Dómine, Rex ætérnæ glóriæ.

Ana. Dixit Dóminus.

Psalm 109.

DIXIT Dóminus Dómino meo : * Sede a dextris meis :

Donec ponam inimícos tuos : * scabéllum pedum tuórum.

Virgam virtútis tuæ emíttet Dóminus ex Sion : * domináre in médio inimicórum tuórum.

Tecum princípium in die virtútis tuæ in splendóribus sanctórum : * ex útero ante lucíferum génui te.

Jurávit Dóminus et non pœnitébit eum : * tu es sacérdos in ætérnum secúndum órdinem Melchísedech.

Dóminus a dextris tuis, * confrégit in die iræ suæ reges.

Judicábit in natióni-

Our Father, Hail Mary, *said silently*.

℣. Incline unto my aid, O God.

℞. O Lord, make haste to help me.

Glory be to the Father, and to the Son, and to the Holy Ghost.

As it was in the beginning, is now, and ever shall be, world without end. Amen.

Praise be to thee, O Lord, King of eternal glory.

Ant. The Lord said to my Lord.

Psalm. 109.

THE Lord said unto my Lord : Sit thou at my right hand :

Until I make thine enemies : thy footstool.

The Lord will send forth the sceptre of thy power out of Sion : rule thou in the midst of thine enemies.

Thine shall be dominion in the day of thy power, amid the brightness of the saints : from the womb before the day-star have I begotten thee.

The Lord hath sworn, and he will not repent : thou art a priest for ever after the order of Melchisedech.

The Lord upon thy right hand : hath overthrown kings in the day of his wrath.

He shall judge among

bus, implévit ruínas : *
conquassábit cápita in
terra multórum.

De torrénte in via bi-
bet : * proptérea exal-
tábit caput.
Glória Patri.
Aña. Dixit Dóminus
Dómino meo : Sede a
dextris meis.
Aña. Magna ópera
Dómini.

Psalm 110.

CONFITEBOR tibi,
Dómine, in toto cor-
de meo : * in consílio
justórum, et congrega-
tióne.

Magna ópera Dómini :
* exquisíta in omnes vo-
luntátes ejus.

Conféssio et magnifi-
céntia opus ejus : * et
justítia ejus manet in
sǽculum sǽculi.

Memóriam fecit mira-
bílium suórum, miséri-
cors et miserátor Dómi-
nus : * escam dedit ti-
méntibus se.

Memor erit in sǽculum
testaménti sui : * virtú-
tem óperum suórum an-
nuntiábit pópulo suo :

Ut det illis hereditá-
tem géntium : * ópera
mánuum ejus véritas
et judícium.

Fidélia ómnia man-
dáta ejus : confirmáta in
sǽculum sǽculi, * facta
in veritáte et æquitáte.

the nations ; he shall fill
them with ruins ; he shall
smite in sunder the heads
in the land of many.

He shall drink of the
brook in the way : there-
fore shall he lift up his head.
Glory be.
Ant. The Lord said to
my Lord : Sit thou at my
right hand.
Ant. Great are the works
of the Lord.

Psalm. 110.

I WILL praise thee, O
Lord, with my whole
heart : in the assembly of
the just, and in the con-
gregation.

Great are the works of
the Lord : sought out are
they according unto all his
pleasure.

His work is his praise
and his honour : and his
justice endureth for ever
and ever.

A memorial hath the
merciful and gracious Lord
made of his marvellous
works : he hath given
meat unto them that fear
him.

He shall ever be mindful
of his covenant : he shall
show forth to his people
the power of his works ;

That he may give them
the heritage of the gentiles :
the works of his hands are
truth and judgment.

All his commandments
are faithful ; they stand fast
for ever and ever, they are
done in truth and equity.

Redemptiónem misit pópulo suo : * mandávit in ætérnum testaméntum suum.

Sanctum et terríbile nomen ejus : * inítium sapiéntiæ timor Dómini.

Intelléctus bonus ómnibus faciéntibus eum : * laudátio ejus manet in sǽculum sǽculi.

Glória Patri.

Aña. Magna ópera Dómini : exquisíta in omnes voluntátes ejus.

Aña. Qui timet Dóminum.

Psalm. 111.

BEATUS vir, qui timet Dóminum : * in mandátis ejus volet nimis.

Potens in terra erit semen ejus : * generátio rectórum benedicétur.

Glória et divítiæ in domo ejus : * et justítia ejus manet in sǽculum sǽculi.

Exórtum est in ténebris lumen rectis : * miséricors, et miserátor, et justus.

Jucúndus homo qui miserétur et cómmodat, dispónet sermónes suos in judício : * quia in ætérnum non commovébitur.

In memória ætérna erit justus : * ab auditióne mala non timébit.

He hath sent redemption unto his people : he hath commanded his covenant for ever.

Holy and terrible is his name : the fear of the Lord is the beginning of wisdom.

A good understanding have all they that do thereafter : his praise endureth for ever and ever.

Glory be.

Ant. Great are the works of the Lord : sought out are they according unto all his pleasure.

Ant. Blessed is the man.

Psalm 111.

BLESSED is the man that feareth the Lord : he shall delight exceedingly in his commandments.

His seed shall be mighty upon earth : the generation of the upright shall be blessed.

Glory and riches shall be in his house : and his justice endureth for ever and ever.

Unto the upright there hath risen up light in the darkness : he is merciful, and compassionate and just.

Acceptable is the man who is merciful and lendeth : he shall order his words with judgment, for he shall not be moved for ever.

The just man shall be in everlasting remembrance : he shall not be afraid for evil tidings.

Parátum cor ejus speráre in Dómino, confirmátum est cor ejus : * non commovébitur donec despíciat inimícos suos.

Dispérsit dedit paupéribus : justítia ejus manet in sǽculum sǽculi, * cornu ejus exaltábitur in glória.

Peccátor vidébit, et irascétur, déntibus suis fremet et tabéscet : * desidérium peccatórum períbit.

Glória Patri.

Aña. Qui timet Dóminum : in mandátis ejus cupit nimis.

Aña. Sit nomen Dómini.

Psalm. 112.

LAUDATE, púeri, Dóminum : * laudáte nomen Dómini.

Sit nomen Dómini benedíctum, * ex hoc nunc, et usque in sǽculum.

A solis ortu usque ad occásum, * laudábile nomen Dómini.

Excélsus super omnes gentes Dóminus, * et super cælos glória ejus.

Quis sicut Dóminus Deus noster, qui in altis hábitat, * et humília réspicit in cælo et in terra?

Súscitans a terra ínopem, * et de stércore érigens paúperem :

His heart is ready to hope in the Lord ; his heart is strengthened : he shall not be moved until he look down upon his enemies.

He hath dispersed abroad, he hath given to the poor ; his justice endureth for ever and ever : his horn shall be exalted in glory.

The wicked shall see it and shall be wroth ; he shall gnash with his teeth, and pine away : the desire of the wicked shall perish.

Glory be.

Ant. Blessed is the man that feareth the Lord : he shall delight exceedingly in his commandments.

Ant. Be the name of the Lord.

Psalm 112.

PRAISE the Lord ye children : praise ye the name of the Lord.

Blessed be the name of the Lord : from this time forth for evermore.

From the rising of the sun unto the going down of the same : the name of the Lord is worthy of praise.

The Lord is high above all nations : and his glory above the heavens.

Who is like unto the Lord our God, who dwelleth on high : and regardeth the things that are lowly in heaven and on earth?

Who raiseth up the needy from the earth : and lifteth the poor out of the dunghill ;

Ut cóllocet eum cum princípibus, * cum princípibus pópuli sui.

Qui habitáre facit stérilem in domo, matrem filiórum lætántem.

Glória Patri.

Aña. Sit nomen Dómini benedíctum in sǽcula.

Aña. Deus autem noster.

Psalm. 113.

IN éxitu Israël de Ægýpto, * domus Jacob de pópulo bárbaro.

Facta est Judǽa sanctificátio ejus, * Israël potéstas ejus.

Mare vidit et fugit : * Jordánis convérsus est retrórsum.

Montes exsultavérunt ut aríetes : * et colles sicut agni óvium.

Quid est tibi mare quod fugísti : * et tu Jordánis, quia convérsus es retrórsum?

Montes, exsultástis sicut aríetes : * et colles sicut agni óvium.

A fácie Dómini mota est terra, * a fácie Dei Jacob.

Qui convértit petram in stagna aquárum, * et rupem in fontes aquárum.

Non nobis, Dómine, non nobis : * sed nómini tuo da glóriam.

That he may set him with the princes : even with the princes of his people.

Who maketh the barren woman to dwell in her house : the joyful mother of children. Glory be.

Ant. Be the name of the Lord for ever blessed.

Ant. But our God.

Psalm 113.

WHEN Israel came out of Egypt : the house of Jacob from among a strange people :

Judea was made his sanctuary : and Israel his dominion.

The sea saw it and fled : Jordan was turned back.

The mountains skipped like rams : and the little hills like the lambs of the flock.

What aileth thee, O thou sea that thou fleddest : and thou, Jordan, that thou wast turned back?

Ye mountains, that ye skipped like rams : and ye little hills, like the lambs of the flock?

At the presence of the Lord the earth was moved : at the presence of the God of Jacob.

Who turned the rock into a standing water : and the stony hill into a floving stream.

Not unto us, O Lord, not unto us : but unto thy name give the glory.

Super misericórdia tua, et veritáte tua : * nequándo dicant gentes : Ubi est Deus eórum?

Deus autem noster in cælo : * ómnia quæcúmque vóluit fecit.

Simulácra géntium argéntum et aúrum, * ópera mánuum hóminum.

Os habent, et non loquéntur : * óculos habent, et non vidébunt.

Aures habent, et non aúdient : * nares habent et non odorábunt.

Manus habent, et non palpábunt : pedes habent, et non ambulábunt : * non clamábunt in gútture suo.

Símiles illis fiant qui fáciunt ea : * et omnes qui confídunt in eis.

Domus Israël sperávit in Dómino : * adjútor eórum et protéctor eórum est.

Domus Aaron sperávit in Dómino : * adjútor eórum et protéctor eórum est.

Qui timent Dóminum, speravérunt in Dómino : * adjútor eórum et protéctor eórum est.

Dóminus memor fuit nostri : * et benedíxit nobis.

Benedíxit dómui Israël : * benedíxit dómui Aaron.

For thy mercy, and for thy truth's sake : lest the gentiles should say : Where is their God?

But our God is in heaven : he hath done all things whatsoever he would.

The idols of the gentiles are silver and gold : the works of the hands of men.

They have mouths, and speak not : eyes have they, and see not.

They have ears, and hear not : noses have they and smell not.

They have hands, and feel not : they have feet, and walk not ; neither shall they speak through their throat.

Let them that make them become like unto them : and all such as put their trust in them.

The house of Israel hath hoped in the Lord : he is their helper and protector.

The house of Aaron hath hoped in the Lord : he is their helper and protector.

They that fear the Lord have hoped in the Lord : he is their helper and protector.

The Lord hath been minfdul of us : and hath blessed us.

He hath blessed the house of Israel : he hath blessed the house of Aaron.

Benedíxit ómnibus, qui timent Dóminum, * pusíllis cum majóribus.

Adjíciat Dóminus super vos : * super vos, et super fílios vestros.

Benedícti vos a Dómino, * qui fecit cælum et terram.

Cælum cæli Dómino : * terram autem dedit fíliis hóminum.

Non mórtui laudábunt te Dómine : * neque omnes, qui descéndunt in inférnum.

Sed nos qui vívimus, benedícimus Dómino, * ex hoc nunc et usque in sǽculum. Glória Patri.

Aña. Deus autem noster in cælo : omnia quæcúmque voluit fecit.

He hath blessed all that fear the Lord : both small and great.

May the Lord add blessings upon you : upon you, and upon your children.

Blessed be ye of the Lord : who hath made heaven and earth.

The heaven of heavens is the Lord's : but the earth he hath given to the children of men.

The dead shall not praise thee, O Lord : neither all they that go down into hell.

But we that live bless the Lord : from this time forth for evermore.

Glory be.

Ant. But our God is in heaven : he hath done all things whatsoever he would.

CAPITULUM

(*Phil.* 2.).

FRATRES : Hoc enim sentíte in vobis, quod et in Christo Jesu : qui cum in forma Dei esset, non rapínam arbitrátus est esse se æquálem Deo : sed semetipsum exinanívit, formam servi accípiens, in similitúdinem hóminum factus, et hábitu invéntus ut homo.

℟. Deo grátias.

BRETHREN : For let this mind be in you, which was also in Christ Jesus ; who being in the form of God, thought it not roberry to be equal with God, but emptied himself, taking the form of a servant, being made in the likeness of men, and in habit found as a man.

℟. Thanks be to God.

HYMN

VEXILLA Regis pródeunt ;
Fulget crucis mystérium,

FORTH comes the Standard of the King :
All hail, thou Mystery adored !

Qua Vita mortem pér-
tulit,
Et morte vitam prótulit.

Quæ vulneráta lán-
ceæ.
Mucróne diro, críminum
Ut nos laváret sórdibus,
Manávit unda et sán-
guine.

Impléta sunt quæ cón-
cinit
David fidéli cármine,
Dicéndo natiónibus :
Regnávit a ligno Deus.

Arbor decóra et fúl-
gida,
Ornáta regis púrpura,
Elécta digno stípite
Tam sancta membra
tángere.

Beáta cujus bráchiis
Prétium pepéndit sǽ-
culi,
Statéra facta córporis,
Tulítque prædam tár-
tari.

O crux, ave, spes
única.
Hoc Passiónis tempore,
Piis adáuge grátiam,
Reísque dele crímina.

Hail, Cross ! on which the
Life himself
Died, and by death our life
restored.
On which the Saviour's
holy side,
Rent open with a cruel spear,
Its stream of blood and
water pour'd,
To wash us from defile-
ment clear.
O sacred Wood ! fulfill'd
in thee
Was holy David's truthful
lay ;
Which told the world that
from a Tree
The Lord should all the
nations sway.
Most royally empurpled
o'er,
How beauteously thy stem
doth shine !
How glorious was its lot
to touch
Those limbs so holy and
divine !
Thrice blest, upon whose
arms outstretch'd
The Saviour of the world
reclined ;
Balance sublime ! upon
whose beam
Was weigh'd ransom of
mankind [1].
Hail, Cross ! thou only
hope of man,
Hail, on this glorious
triumph day,
To saints increase the grace
they have ;
From sinners purge their
guilt away.

[1] This verse is said kneeling.

Te, fons salútis, Trínitas,
Colláudet omnis spíritus ;
Quibus crucis victóriam
Largíris, adde præmium.
Amen.

℣. Eripe Dómine, ab hómine malo.

℞. A viro iníquo éripe me.

Aña. Scriptum est enim.

Salvation's Fount, blest Trinity,
Be praise to thee through earth and skies :
Thou through the Cross the victory
Dost give ; oh, give us too the prize.
Amen.

℣. Deliver me, O Lord, from the evil man.

℞. Rescue me from the unjust man.

Ant. For it is written.

OUR LADY'S CANTICLE
(*St. Luke* 1.)

MAGNIFICAT : * ánima mea Dóminum:
Et exsultávit spíritus meus : * in Deo salutári meo.

Quia respéxit humilitátem ancíllæ suæ : * ecce enim ex hoc beátam me dicent omnes generatiónes.

Quia fecit mihi magna qui potens est : * et sanctum nomen ejus.

Et misericórdia ejus a progénie in progénies : * timéntibus eum.

Fecit poténtiam in bráchio suo : * dispérsit supérbos mente cordis sui.

Depósuit poténtes de sede : * et exaltávit húmiles.

Esuriéntes implévit bonis : * et dívites dimísit inánes.

MY soul doth magnify the Lord :
And my spirit hath rejoiced in God my Saviour.

Because he hath regarded the humility of his handmaid ; for behold, from henceforth all generations shall call me blessed.

Because he that is mighty hath done great things to me : and holy is his name.

And his mercy is from generation unto generation, to them that fear him.

He hath showed might in his arm : he hath scattered the proud in the conceit of their heart.

He hath put down the mighty from their seat : and hath exalted the humble.

He hath filled the hungry with good things : and the rich he hath sent empty away.

Suscépit Israël púerum suum : * recordátus misericórdiæ suæ.

Sicut locútus est ad patres nostros : Abraham et sémini ejus in sǽcula.

Glória Patri.

Aña. Sriptum est enim : Percútiam pastórem, et dispergéntur oves gregis : postquam autem resurréxero, præcédam vos in Galilǽam : ibi me vidébitis, dicit Dóminus.

℣. Dóminus vobíscum.
℞. Et cum spíritu tuo.

Orémus.

OMNIPOTENS sempitérne Deus, qui humáno géneri ad imitándum humilitátis exémplum, Salvatórem nostrum carnem súmere et crucem subíre fecísti, concéde propítius ; ut et patiéntiæ ipsíus habére documénta, et resurrectiónis consórtia mereámur. Per eúmdem.

℣. Dóminus vobíscum.
℞. Et cum spíritu tuo.
℣. Benedicámus Dómino.
℞. Deo grátias.
℣. Fidélium ánimæ per misericórdiam Dei requiéscant in pace.

℞. Amen.

He hath received Israel his servant, being mindful of his mercy.

As he spoke to our fathers, to Abraham and to his seed for ever.

Glory be.

Ant. For it is written : I will strike the shepherd, and the sheep of the flock shall be dispersed : but after I shall be risen again, I will go before you into Galilee : there ye shall see me, saith the Lord.

℣. The Lord be with you.
℞. And with thy spirit.

Let us pray.

O ALMIGHTY and eternal God, who wouldst have our Saviour become man, and suffer on a cross, to give mankind an example of humility ; mercifully grant that we may improve by the example of his patience, and partake of his resurrection. Through the same.

℣. The Lord be with you.
℞. And with thy spirit.
℣. Let us bless the Lord.
℞. Thanks be to God.
℣. May the souls of the faithful departed, through the mercy of God, rest in peace.

℞. Amen.

Then the anthem Ave Regína, *etc.* (p. 84) *if Compline is not immediately following Vespers.*

COMPLINE

The Reader begins :

Jube, domne, bene-dícere.

Pray, father, a blessing.

NOCTEM quiétam et finem perféctum concédat nobis Dóminus omnípotens. ℟. Amen.

THE Lord almighty grant us a quiet night and a perfect end. ℟. Amen.

(1 *Peter* 5.)

FRATRES : Sóbrii estóte, et vigiláte : quia adversárius vester diábolus tamquam leo rúgiens círcuit, quærens quem dévoret : cui resístite fortes in fide. Tu autem, Dómine, miseré-re nobis. ℟. Deo grátias.
℣. Adjutórium nostrum in nómine Dómini. ℟. Qui fecit cælum et terram.

BRETHREN, be sober and watch : because your adversary the devil, as a roaring lion, goeth about, seeking whom he may devour : whom resist ye, strong in faith. But thou, O Lord, have mercy on us. ℟. Thanks be to God.
℣. Our help is in the name of the Lord. ℟. Who made heaven and earth.

The Pater *is then said silently troughout, after which the Priest says the* Confiteor :

CONFITEOR Deo omnipoténti, beá-tæ Maríæ semper Vírgini, beáto Michaéli Archángelo, beáto Joánni Baptístæ, sanctis Apóstolis Petro et Paulo, ómnibus Sanctis, et vobis, fratres : quia peccávi nimis cogitatióne, verbo, et ópere : mea culpa, mea culpa, mea máxima culpa. Ideo precor beátam Maríam semper Vírginem, beátam Michaélem Archángelum, beátum Joán-

I CONFESS to almighty God, to blessed Mary ever Virgin, to blessed Michael the Archangel, to blessed John the Baptist, to the holy Apostles Peter and Paul, to all the Saints, and to you, brethren, that I have sinned exceedingly in thought, word, and deed : through my fault, through my fault, through my most grievous fault. Therefore I beseech blessed Mary ever Virgin, blessed Michael the Archangel, blessed John the Baptist,

nem Baptístam, sanctos Apóstolos Petrum et Paulum, omnes Sanctos, et vos, fratres, oráre pro me ad Dóminum Deum nostrum.

the holy Apostles Peter and Paul, all the Saints, and you, brethren, to pray to our Lord God for me.

The Choir answers :

MISEREATUR tui omnípotens. Deus, et, dimíssis peccátis tuis, perdúcat te ad vitam ætérnam. ℟. Amen.

MAY almighty God have mercy upon thee, forgive thee thy sins, and bring thee to life everlasting. ℟. Amen.

The Choir then repeats the Confiteor :

CONFITEOR Deo omnipoténti, beátæ Maríæ semper Vírgini, beáto Michaéli Archángelo, beáto Joánni Baptístæ, sanctis Apóstolis Petro et Paulo, ómnibus Sanctis, et tibi, pater : quia peccávi nimis cogitatióne, verbo, et ópere : mea culpa, mea culpa, mea máxima culpa. Ideo precor beátam Maríam semper Vírginem, beátum Michaélem Archángelum, beátum Joánnem Baptístam, sanctos Apóstolos Petrum et Paulum, omnes Sanctos, et te, pater, oráre pro me ad Dóminum Deum nostrum.

I CONFESS to almighty God, to blessed Mary ever Virgin, to blessed Michael the Archangel, to blessed John the Baptist, to the holy Apostles Peter and Paul, to all the Saints, and to thee, father, that I have sinned exceedingly in thought, word, and deed : through my fault, through my fault, through my most grievous fault. Therefore I beseech blessed Mary ever Virgin, blessed Michael the Archangel, blessed John the Baptist, the holy Apostles Peter and Paul, all the Saints, and thee, father, to pray to our Lord God for me.

After which the Priest says :

MISEREATUR vestri omnípotens Deus, et, dimíssis peccátis vestris, perdúcat vos ad vitam ætérnam. ℟. Amen.

MAY almighty God have mercy upon you, forgive you your sins, and bring you to life everlasting. ℟. Amen.

INDULGENTIAM, absolutiónem et remissiónem peccatórum nostrórum tríbuat nobis omnípotens et miséricors Dóminus. ℟. Amen.

CONVERTE nos, Deus, salutáris noster. ℟. Et avérte iram tuam a nobis. ℣. Deus, in adjutórium meum inténde. ℟. Dómine, ad adjuvándum me festína. Glória Patri. Sicut erat, etc. Laus tibi Dómine.

Aña. Miserére.
Psalm. 4.

CUM invocárem, exaudívit me Deus justítiæ meæ : * in tribulatióne dilatásti mihi.

Miserére mei, * et exáudi oratiónem meam.

Fílii hóminum úsquequo gravi corde? * ut quid dilígitis vanitátem, et quǽritis mendácium?

Et scitóte quóniam mirificávit Dóminus sanctum suum : * Dóminus exáudiet me, cum clamávero ad eum.

Irascímini, et nolíte peccáre : * quæ dícitis in córdibus vestris, in cubílibus vestris compungímini.

Sacrificáte sacrifícium justítiæ, et speráte in Dómino : * multi dicunt : Quis osténdit nobis bona?

Signátum est super

MAY the almighty and merciful Lord grant us pardon, absolution, and remission of our sins ℟. Amen.

CONVERT us, O God our Saviour. ℟. And turn away thine anger from us. ℣. Incline unto my aid, O God. ℟. O Lord, make haste to help me. Glory be to the Father, etc. Praise be to thee, etc.

Ant. Have mercy.
Psalm 4.

WHEN I called upon him, the God of my justice heard me : when I was in straits, thou didst set me at liberty.

Have mercy on me : and hear my prayer.

O ye sons of men, how long will ye be dull of heart? why do ye love vanity, and seek after lying?

Know ye also that the Lord hath exalted his holy one : the Lord will hear me when I cry unto him.

Be ye angry, and sin not : the things ye say in your hearts, be sorry for them upon your beds.

Offer up the sacrifice of justice, and trust in the Lord : many say, Who showeth us good things?

The light of thy counte-

nos lumen vultus tui,
Dómine : * dedísti læ-
títiam in corde meo.

A fructu fruménti, vi-
ni et ólei sui * multiplicáti sunt.

In pace in idípsum *
dórmiam et requiéscam.

Quóniam tu, Dómine,
singuláriter in spe * constituísti me.

Glória Patri.

Psalm. 90.

QUI hábitat in adju-
tório Altíssimi, *
in protectióne Dei cæli
commorábitur.

Dicet Dómino : Sus-
céptor meus es tu, et re-
fúgium meum : * Deus
meus sperábo in eum.

Quóniam ipse liberá-
vit me de láqueo venán-
tium, * et a verbo áspero.

Scápulis suis obum-
brábit tibi : * et sub
pennis ejus sperábis.

Scuto circúmdabit te
véritas ejus : * non ti-
mébis a timóre noctúr-
no,

A sagítta volánte in
die, a negótio peram-
bulánte in ténebris : *
ab incúrsu, et dæmó-
nio meridiáno.

Cadent a látere tuo
mille, et decem míllia
a dextris tuis : * ad te
autem non appropin-
quábit.

Verúmtamen óculis

nance, O Lord, is signed
upon us : thou hast given
gladness in my heart.

By the fruit of their corn,
and wine, and oil : are
they multiplied.

In peace in the selfsame ;
I will sleep and will rest.

For thou, O Lord, alone :
hast established me in hope.

Glory be.

Psalm 90.

HE that dwelleth in
the help of the Most
High, shall abide under
the protection of the God
of heaven.

He shall say unto the
Lord : Thou art my up-
holder, and my refuge : my
God, in him will I hope.

For he hath delivered
me from the snare of the
hunters : and from the
sharp word.

He shall overshadow thee
with his shoulders, and
under his wings shalt thou
trust.

His truth shall compass
thee vith a shield : thou
shalt not be afraid for the
terror of the night ;

For the arrow that flieth
in the day : for the plague
that walketh in the dark-
ness : for the assault of the
evil one in the noon-day.

A thousand shall fall at
thy side, and ten thousand
at thy right hand : but it
shall not come nigh thee.

But with thine eyes shalt

tuis considerábis : * et retributiónem peccatórum vidébis.

Quóniam tu es, Dómine, spes mea : * altíssimum posuísti refúgium tuum.

Non accédet ad te malum : * et flagéllum non appropinquábit tabernáculo tuo.

Quóniam Angelis suis mandávit de te : * ut custódiant te in ómnibus viis tuis.

In mánibus portábunt te : * ne forte offéndas ad lápidem pedem tuum.

Super áspidem, et basilíscum ambulábis : * et conculcábis leónem et dracónem.

Quóniam in me sperávit, liberábo eum : * prótegam eum, quóniam cognóvit nomen meum.

Clamábit ad me, et ego exáudiam eum ; * cum ipso sum in tribulatióne : erípiam eum, et glorificábo eum.

Longitúdine diérum replébo eum : * et osténdam illi salutáre meum. Glória Patri.

Psalm. 133.

ECCE nunc benedícite Dóminum, * omnes servi Dómini :

Qui statis in domo Dómini, * in átriis domus Dei nostri.

thou behold : and shalt see the reward of the wicked.

For thou, O Lord, art my hope : thou hast made the Most High thy refuge.

There shall no evil approach unto thee : neither shall the scourge come nigh thy dwelling.

For he hath given his angels charge over thee ; to keep thee in all thy ways.

In their hands they shall bear thee up ; lest thou dash thy foot against a stone.

Thou shalt walk upon the asp and the basilisk : the lion and the dragon shalt thou trample under foot.

Because he hath hoped in me, I will deliver him : I will protect him, because he hath known my name.

He shall cry unto me, and I will hear him : I am with him in trouble : I will deliver him, and I will glorify him.

I will fill him with length of days : and will show him my salvation.

Glory be.

Psalm 133.

BEHOLD, now, bless ye the Lord : all ye servants of the Lord.

Ye that stand in the house of the Lord : in the courts of the house of our God.

In nóctibus extóllite manus vestras in sancta, * et benedícite Dóminum.

Lift up your hands by night to the holy places : and bless ye the Lord.

Benedícat te Dóminus ex Sion : * qui fecit cœlum et terram.

May the Lord bless thee out of Sion : who hath made both heaven and earth.

Glória Patri.

Glory be.

Aña. Miserére mihi, Dómine, et exáudi oratiónem meam.

Ant. Have mercy on me, O Lord, and hear my prayer.

HYMN

TE lucis ante términum,
Rerum Creátor póscimus,
Ut pro tua cleméntia
Sis præsul, et custódia.

NOW with the fast departing light,
Maker of all ; we ask of thee,
Of thy great mercy, through the night
Our guardian and defence to be.

Procul recédant sómnia,
Et nóctium phantásmata ;
Hostémque nostrum cómprine,
Ne polluántur córpora.
Præsta, Pater piíssime,
Patríque compar Unice
Cum Spíritu Paráclito
Regnans per omne sǽculum. Amen.

Far off let idle visions fly
No phantom of the night molest :
Curb thou our raging enemy,
That we in chaste repose may rest.
Father of mercies ! hear our cry ;
Hear us, o sole-begotten Son !
Who, with the Holy Ghost most high,
Reignest while endless ages run. Amen.

LITTLE CHAPTER
Jer. 14.

TU autem in nobis es, Dómine, et nomen sanctum tuum invocátum est super nos : * ne derelínquas nos, Dómine Deus noster. ℟. Deo grátias.

BUT thou, O Lord, art among us, and thy holy name is invoked upon us : forsake us not, O Lord our God. ℟. Thanks be to God.

SHORT RESPONSORY

IN manus tuas, Dómine, * Comméndo spíritum meum. In. ℣. Redemísti nos, Dómine Deus veritátis. * Comméndo. In manus tuas, Dómine. Comméndo spíritum meum.

℣. Custódi nos, Dómine, ut pupíllam óculi. ℟. Sub umbra alárum tuárum prótege nos.

Aña. Salve nos.

INTO thy hands, O Lord, * I commend my spirit. Into thy hands. ℣. For thou hast redeemed us, O Lord God of truth. * I commend my spirit. Into thy hands.

℣. Keep us, O Lord, as the apple of thy eye. ℟. Protect us under the shadow of thy wings.

Ant. Salve us.

CANTICLE OF SIMEON
Luke 2.

NUNC dimíttis servum tuum, Dómine, * secúndum verbum tuum in pace :

Quia vidérunt óculi mei * salutáre tuum,

Quod parásti * ante fáciem ómnium populórum :

Lumen ad revelatiónem géntium, * et glóriam plebis tuæ Israël.

Glória Patri.

Aña. Salva nos, Dómine, vigilántes, custódi nos dormiéntes : ut vigilémus cum Christo, et requiescámus in pace.

NOW thou dost dismiss thy servant, O Lord, according to thy word in peace.

Because my eyes have seen thy salvation.

Which thou hast prepared before the face of all peoples.

A light to the revelation of the Gentiles, and the glory of thy people Israel.

Glory be to the Father.

Ant. Save us, O Lord, while we are awake, and guard us when we sleep, that we may watch with Christ, and rest in peace.

If a feast double of rite is commemorated at Vespers, the following prayers are omitted as far as Dóminus vobíscum, *etc.*

KYRIE, éleison. Christe, eléison. Kýrie, eléison.

Pater noster, *secreto.*

℣. Et ne nos indúcas in tentatiónem. ℟. Sed líbera nos a malo.

Credo in Deum, *secreto.*

LORD, have mercy on us. Christ, have mercy on us. Lord, have mercy on us.

Our Father, *silently.*

℣. And lead us not into temptation. ℟. But deliver us from evil.

I believe in God, *silently.*

℣. Carnis resurrectiónem. ℟. Vitam ætérnam. Amen.

℣. Benedíctus es, Dómine, Deus patrum nostrórum. ℟. Et laudábilis, et gloriósus in sǽcula.

℣. Benedicámus Patrem, et Fílium cum Sancto Spíritu. ℟. Laudémus, et superexaltémus eum in sǽcula.

℣. Benedíctus es, Dómine, in firmaménto cæli. ℟. Et laudábilis, et gloriósus, et superexaltátus in sǽcula.

℣. Benedícat et custódiat nos omnípotens et miséricors Dóminus. ℟. Amen.

℣. Dignáre, Dómine, nocte ista. ℟. Sine peccáto nos custodíre.

℣. Miserére nostri, Dómine. ℟. Miserére nostri.

℣. Fiat misericórdia tua, Dómine, super nos. ℟. Quemádmodum sperávimus in te.

℣. Dómine, exáudi oratiónem meam. ℟. Et clamor meus ad te véniat.

℣. Dóminus vobíscum. ℟. Et cum spíritu tuo.

Orémus.

VISITA, quǽsumus, Dómine, habitatiónem istam, et omnes insídias inimíci ab ea

℣. The resurrection of the body. ℟. And life everlasting. Amen.

℣. Blessed art thou, O Lord God of our fathers. ℟. And worthy to be praised, and glorious for ever.

℣. Let us bless the Father and the Son with the Holy Ghost. ℟. Let us praise and exalt him above all for ever.

℣. Blessed art thou, O Lord, in the firmament of heaven. ℟. And worthy to be praised, and glorious, and exalted above all for ever.

℣. The almighty and merciful Lord bless and preserve us. ℟. Amen.

℣. Vouchsafe, O Lord, this night. ℟. To keep us without sin.

℣. Have mercy on us, O Lord. ℟. Have mercy on us.

℣. Let thy mercy, O Lord, be upon us. ℟. As we have hoped in thee.

℣. O Lord, hear my prayer. ℟. And let my cry come unto thee.

℣. The Lord be with you. ℟. And with thy spirit.

Let us pray.

VISIT, we beseech thee, O Lord, this house and family, and drive far from it all snares of the enemy;

longe repélle : Angeli tui sancti hábitent in ea, qui nos in pace custódiant, et benedíctio tua sit super nos semper. Per Dóminum.

℞. Amen.

℣. Dóminus vobíscum.
℞. Et cum spíritu tuo.
℣. Benedicámus Dómino. ℞. Deo grátias.

let thy holy Angels dwell herein, who may keep us in peace, and let thy blessing be always upon us. Through Jesus Christ thy Son our Lord, who liveth and reigneth with thee, in the unity of the Holy Ghost, God, world without end.
℞. Amen.

℣. The Lord be with you.
℞. And with thy spirit.
℣. Let us bless the Lord.
℞. Thanks be to God.

THE BLESSING

BENEDICAT, et custódiat nos omnípotens et miséricors Dóminus, Pater, et Fílius, et Spíritus Sanctus. ℞. Amen.

MAY the almighty and merciful Lord, the Father, the Son, and the Holy Ghost, bless and preserve us. ℞. Amen.

ANTHEM

AVE, Regína cælórum,
Ave, Dómina Angelórum :
Salve radix, salve porta,
Ex qua mundo lux est orta.
Gaude, Virgo gloriósa,
Super omnes speciósa,
Vale, o valde decóra,
Et pro nobis Christum exóra.

HAIL, O Queen of heaven enthroned,
Hail, by Angels Mistress own'd.
Root of Jesse, gate of morn,
Whence the world's true Light was born :
Glorious Virgin, joy to thee,
Loveliest whom in heaven they see :
Fairest thou where all are fair,
Plead with Christ our sins to spare.

℣. Dignáre me laudáre te Virgo sacráta.
℞. Da mihi virtútem contra hostes tuos.

O émus.

CONCEDE, miséricors Deus, fragilitáti nostræ præsídium ;

℣. Vouchsafe that I may praise thee, O holy Virgin.
℞. Give me strenght against thine enemies.

Let us pray.

GRANT, O merciful God, thy protection in our weakness : that we

ut qui sanctæ Dei Genetricis memóriam agimus, intercessiónis ejus auxílio a nostris iniquitátibus resurgámus. Per eúmdem Christum Dóminum nostrum.

℞. Amen.

℣. Divínum auxílium máneat semper nobíscum. ℞. Amen.

who celebrate the memory of the holy Mother of God, may, through the aid of her intercession, rise again from our sins. Through the same Christ our Lord.

℞. Amen.

℣. May the divine assistance remain always with us. ℞. Amen.

Then the Pater, Ave María *and* Credo *are said silently.*

MONDAY IN HOLY WEEK

THE MASS

The station is at the church of St. Praxedes, where the pillar of the scourging is venerated. The Mass has the same characteristic tone as that of the preceding day, but instead of Psalm 21, passages have been taken from Pss. 34 and 142, also Messianic psalms, and the Lesson from Isaias is a mirror of the Passion. The Gospel gives the account of the anointing of Our Lord's feet by St. Mary Magdalen and the reference to *ante sex dies paschæ* takes us in reality back to the preceding Saturday, but we have already explained that this Gospel was transferred to the Monday as formerly there was no proper Mass for the Saturday. The event moreover is directly connected with the Passion.

STATION AT ST. PRAXEDES

Introitus. Ps. 34.

JUDICA, Dómine, nocéntes me, expúgna impugnántes me : apprehénde arma et scutum, et exsúrge in adjutórium meum, Dómine virtus salútis meæ. *Ps.* Effúnde frámeam, et conclúde advérsus eos qui persequúntur me : dic ánimæ meæ : Salus tua ego sum. Júdica, Dómine.

Introit. Ps. 34.

JUDGE thou, O Lord, them that wrong me ; overthrow them that fight against me : take hold of arms and shield, and rise up to help me, O Lord, the strength of my salvation. *Ps.* Bring out the sword, and shut up the way against those who persecute me : say to my soul, I am thy salvation. Judge.

Oratio.

DA, quæsumus, omnípotens Deus : ut, qui in tot advérsis ex nostra infirmitáte defícimus, intercedénte unigéniti Fílii tui Passióne respirémus. Qui tecum vivit et regnat.

Collect.

GRANT, we beseech thee, almighty God, that we, who fail through our weakness under so many adversities, may take heart again through the pleading of the Passion of thy only begotten son. Who liveth and reigneth.

Contra persecutores Ecclesiæ.

ECCLESIÆ tuæ, quǽsumus, Dómine, preces placátus admítte : ut, destrúctis adversitátibus et erróribus univérsis, secúra tibi sérviat libertáte. Per Dóminum.

Vel pro Papa.

DEUS, ómnium fidélium Pastor et rector, fámulum tuum *N.* quem pastórem Ecclésiæ tuæ præésse voluísti, propítius réspice : da ei, quǽsumus, verbo et exémplo, quibus præest, profícere ; ut ad vitam, una cum grege sibi crédito, pervéniat sempitérnam. Per Dóminum.

Léctio Isaíæ Prophétæ, *c.* 50.

IN diébus illis : Dixit Isaías : Dóminus Deus apéruit mihi aurem, ego autem non contradíco : retrórsum non ábii. Corpus meum dedi percutiéntibus, et genas meas velléntibus ; fáciem meam non avérti ab increpántibus et conspuéntibus in me. Dóminus Deus auxiliátor meus, ídeo non sum confúsus, ídeo pósui fáciem meam, ut petram duríssimam, et scio quóniam non confúndar. Juxta est, qui justíficat me, quis contradícet mihi?

Against the persecutors of the Church.

RECEIVE in thy mercy, O Lord, we beseech thee, the prayers of thy Church : that overcoming all adversity and error, she may serve thee in peace and liberty. Trough our Lord.

Or for the Pope.

O GOD, the shepherd and ruler of all the faithful, graciously regard thy servant *N.*, whom thou hast been pleased to appoint as Pastor over thy Church : grant, we beseech thee, that he may profit his subjects both by word and example, and together with the flock committed to his care, may attain to eternal life. Through our Lord.

Lesson from the Prophet Isaias, *c.* 50.

IN those days : Isaias said: The Lord God hath opened my ear, and I do not resist, I have not gone back. I have given my body to the strikers, and my cheeks to them that plucked them : I have not turned away my face from them that rebuked me, and spit upon me. The Lord God is my helper, therefore, am I not confounded : therefore have I set my face as a most hard rock, and I know that I shall not be confounded. He is near that justifieth me, who will contend with me? Let us stand together, who is

Stemus simul, quis est adversárius meus? Accédat ad me. Ecce Dóminus Deus auxiliátor meus : quis est qui condémnet me? Ecce omnes quasi vestiméntum conterentur, tínea cómedet eos. Quis ex vobis timens Dóminum, áudiens vocem servi sui? Qui ambulávit in ténebris, et non est lumen ei, speret in nómine Dómini, et innitátur super Deum suum.

Graduale. Ps. 34.

EXSURGE, Dómine, et inténde judícium meum : Deus meus, et Dóminus meus, in causam meam. ℣. Effúnde frámeam, et conclúde advérsus eos qui me persequúntur.

Tractus. Ps. 102.

DOMINE, non secúndum peccáta nostra, quæ fécimus nos : neque secúndum iniquitátes nostras retríbuas nobis. ℣. *Ps.* 78. Dómine, ne memíneris iniquitátum nostrárum antiquárum : cito antícipent nos misericórdiæ tuæ, quia páuperes facti sumus nimis. ℣. (*Hic genuflectitur.*) Adjuva nos, Deus salutáris noster : et propter glóriam nóminis tui, Dómine, líbera nos, et propítius esto peccátis nostris, propter nomen tuum.

my adversary? let him come near to me. Behold the Lord God is my helper : who is he that shall condemn me? Lo, they shall all be destroyed as a garment, the moth shall eat them up. Who is there among you that feareth the Lord, that heareth the voice of his servant, that hath walked in darkness, and hath no light? Let him hope in the name of the Lord, and lean upon his God.

Gradual. Ps. 34.

ARISE, O Lord, and be attentive to my judgement, to my cause, my God and my Lord. ℣. Bring out the sword, and shut up the way against those who persecute me.

Tract. Ps. 102.

O LORD, repay us not according to the sins we have committed, nor according to our iniquities. ℣. *Ps.* 78. O Lord, remember not our former iniquities : let thy mercies speedily prevent us, for we are become exceeding poor. ℣. (*Here all kneel down.*) Help us, O God our Saviour ; and for the glory of thy name, O Lord, deliver us : and forgive us our sins for thy name's sake.

✠ Sequéntia sancti Evangélii secúndum Joánnem, *c.* 12.

ANTE sex dies Paschæ, venit Jesus Bethániam, ubi Lázarus fúerat mórtuus, quem suscitávit Jesus. Fecérunt autem ei cœnam ibi : et Martha ministrábat, Lázarus vero unus erat ex discumbéntibus cum eo. María ergo accépit libram unguénti nardi pístici pretiósi, et unxit pedes Jesu, et extérsit pedes ejus capíllis suis : et domus impléta est ex odóre unguénti. Dixit ergo unus ex discípulis ejus, Judas Iscariótes, qui erat eum traditúrus : Quare hoc unguéntum non véniit trecéntis denáriis, et datum est egénis? Dixit autem hoc, non quia de egénis pertinébat ad eum, sed quia fur erat, et lóculos habens, ea, quæ mittebántur, portábat. Dixit ergo Jesus : Sínite illam, ut in diem sepultúræ meæ servet illud. Páuperes enim semper habétis vobíscum : me autem non semper habétis. Cognóvit ergo turba multa ex Judǽis, quia illic est : et venérunt non propter Jesum tantum, sed ut Lázarum vidérent, quem suscitávit a mórtuis.

✠ Continuation of the holy Gospel according to St. John, *c.* 12.

SIX days before the pasch, Jesus came to Bethania, where Lazarus had been dead, whom Jesus raised to life. And they made him a supper there : and Martha served, but Lazarus was one of them that were at the table with him. Mary therefore took a pound of ointment of right spikenard, of great price, and anointed the feet of Jesus, and wiped his feet with her hair : and the house was filled with the odour of the ointment. Then one of his disciples, Judas Iscariot, he that was about to betray him, said : Why was not this ointment sold for three hundred pence, and given to the poor? Now he said this, not because he cared for the poor, but because he was a thief, and having the purse, carried what was put therein. But Jesus said : Let her alone, that she may keep it against the day of my burial. For the poor you have always with you : but me you have not always. A great multitude therefore of the Jews knew that he was there ; and they came, not for Jesus' sake only, but that they might see Lazarus, whom he had raised from the dead.

Offertorium. Ps. 142.

ERIPE me de inimí-
cis meis, Dómine :
ad te confúgi, doce me
fácere voluntátem tuam:
quia Deus meus es tu.

Secreta.

HÆC sacrifícia nos,
omnípotens Deus,
poténti virtúte mundá-
tos, ad suum fáciant pu-
rióres veníre princípium.
Per Dóminum.

*Contra persecutores
Ecclesiæ.*

PROTEGE nos, Dó-
mine, tuis mystériis
serviéntes : ut divínis rebus inhæréntes, et cór-
pore tibi famulémur et
mente. Per Dóminum.

Vel pro Papa.

OBLATIS, quǽsumus,
Dómine, placáre
munéribus : et fámulum
tuum N. quem pastórem
Ecclésiæ tuæ præésse
voluísti, assídua protec-
tióne gubérna. Per
Dóminum.

Communio. Ps. 34.

ERUBESCANT, et re-
vereántur simul, qui
gratulántur malis meis :
induántur pudóre et re-
veréntia, qui malígna lo-
quúntur advérsum me.

Postcommunio.

PRÆBEANT nobis,
Dómine, divínum,
tua sancta fervórem :
quo eórum páriter et
actu delectémur, et fru-
ctu. Per Dóminum.

Offertory. Ps. 142.

DELIVER me from my
enemies, O Lord : to
thee have I fled, teach me to
do thy will ; for thou art my
God.

Secret.

MAY these sacrifices, al-
mighty God, make us
approach their source with
greater purity, cleansed by
thy mighty power. Through
our Lord.

*Against the persecutors of the
Church.*

PROTECT us, O Lord,
who assist at thy mys-
teries : that we may ever
cleave to divine things, and
serve thee both in body and
mind. Through our Lord.

Or for the Pope.

FAVOURABLY accept,
we beseech thee, O
Lord, the gifts we offer : and
govern by thy continual
protection thy servant N.,
whom thou hast been
pleased to appoint as
Pastor over thy Church.
Through our Lord.

Communion. Ps. 34.

LET them blush and be
ashamed together, who
rejoice at my evils ; let them
be clothed with shame and
fear, who speak malignant
things against me.

Postcommunion.

LET thy holy mysteries,
O Lord, inspire us with
divine fervour, that we may
delight both in the act and
in the fruit thereof. Through
our Lord.

Contra persecutores Ecclesiæ.

QUÆSUMUS, Dómine Deus noster : ut, quos divína tríbuis participatióne gaudére, humánis non sinas subjacére perículis. Per Dóminum.

Vel pro Papa.

HÆC nos, quæsumus, Dómine, divíni Sacraménti percéptio prótegat : et fámulum tuum *N.* quem pastórem Ecclésiæ tuæ præésse voluísti, una cum commísso sibi grege, salvet semper et múniat. Per Dóminum.

Oratio super populum.
Orémus.

Humiliáte cápita vestra Deo.

ADJUVA nos, Deus salutáris noster : et ad benefícia recolénda, quibus nos instauráre dignátus es, tríbue veníre gaudéntes. Per Dóminum.

Against the persecutors of the Church.

WE beseech thee, O Lord our God, that thou wouldst not suffer to be exposed to human dangers those whom thou givest to rejoice in the participation of these divine mysteries. Through our Lord.

Or for the Pope.

MAY the reception of this divine Sacrament protect us, we beseech thee, O Lord, and be ever the strength and salvation of thy servant *N.*, whom thou hast been pleased to appoint as Pastor over thy Church, together with the flock committed to his care. Through our Lord.

Prayer over the people.
Let us pray.

Bow down your heads before God.

HELP us, O God our Saviour : and vouchsafe that we may draw nigh with joy to keep the memory of those mercies, whereby thou didst deign to give us new life. Through our Lord.

TUESDAY IN HOLY WEEK

THE MASS

The station is at the church of St. Prisca. Various passages are taken from Pss. 34, 68 and 139 which are Messianic psalms, and the Epistle is the famous passage from Jeremias in which the Messias is portrayed as a lamb. The Gospel is the account of the Passion according to St. Mark. The Introit is a passage from St. Paul often used in the liturgy, but as we have already pointed out in other parts of the liturgy the scriptural text has been altered.

STATION AT ST. PRISCA

Introitus. Gal. 6.

NOS autem gloriári opórtet in cruce Dómini nostri Jesu Christi : in quo est salus, vita, et resurréctio nostra : per quem salváti et liberáti sumus. *Ps.* 66. Deus misereátur nostri, et benedícat nobis : illúminet vultum suum super nos, et misereátur nostri. Nos autem.

Introit. Gal. 6.

BUT it behoves us to glory in the cross of our Lord Jesus Christ : in whom is our salvation, life, and resurrection ; by whom we are saved and delivered. *Ps.* 66. May God have mercy on us, and bless us : may he cause the light of his countenance to shine upon us, and may he have mercy on us. But it behoves.

Oratio.

OMNIPOTENS sempitérne Deus : da nobis ita dominicæ passiónis sacraménta perágere : ut indulgéntiam percípere mereámur. Per eúmdem Dóminum nostrum.

Collect.

ALMIGHTY and eternal God, grant us so to celebrate the mysteries of our Lord's Passion, that we may deserve to obtain thy forgiveness. Through the same Lord.

Second Collect, p. 87.

Léctio Jeremíæ Prophétæ, *c.* 11.

IN diébus illis : Dixit Jeremías : Dómine, demonstrásti mihi, et cognóvi : tunc ostendísti

Lesson from the Prophet Jeremias, *c.* 11.

IN those days : Jeremias said : O Lord, thou hast showed me, and I have known : then thou showedst

mihi stúdia eórum. Et ego quasi agnus mansuétus, qui portátur ad víctimam : et non cognóvi quia cogitavérunt super me consília, dicéntes : Mittámus lignum in panem ejus, et eradámus eum de terra vivéntium, et nomen ejus non memorétur ámplius. Tu autem, Dómine Sábaoth, qui júdicas juste, et probas renes et corda, vídeam ultiónem tuam ex eis : tibi enim revelávi causam meam, Dómine Deus meus.

me their doings. And I was as a meek lamb, that is carried to be a victim : and I knew not that they had devised counsels against me, saying : Let us put wood on his bread, and cut him off from the land of the living, and let his name be remembered no more. But thou, O Lord of Sabaoth, who judgest justly, and triest the reins and the hearts, let me see thy revenge on them : for to thee have I revealed my cause, O Lord my God.

Graduale. Ps. 34.

EGO autem, dum mihi molésti essent, induébam me cilício, et humiliábam in jejúnio ánimam meam : et orátio mea in sinu meo convertétur. ℣. Júdica, Dómine, nocéntes me : expúgna impugnántes me : apprehénde arma et scutum, et exsúrge in adjutórium mihi.

Gradual. Ps. 34.

BUT I, when they were troublesome to me, clothed myself with sackcloth, and humbled my soul with fasting : and my prayer shall be turned into my bosom. ℣. Do thou, Lord, judge them that wrong me ; overthrow them that fight against me : lay hold of arms and shield, and arise to my help.

Pássio Dómini nostri Jesu Christi secúndum Marcum, *c.* 14 & 15.

IN illo témpore : Erat Pascha et Azyma post bíduum : et quærébant summi sacerdótes et scribæ, quómodo Jesum dolo tenérent, et occíderent. Dicébant autem : Non in die festo,

The Passion of our Lord Jesus Christ according to St. Mark, *c.* 14 & 15.

AT that time : The feast of the pasch and of the azymes was after two days : and the chief priests, and the scribes, sought how they might by some wile lay hold on him, and kill him. But they said : Not on the fes-

ne forte tumúltus fíeret in pópulo. Et cum esset Jesus Bethániæ in domo Simónis leprósi, et recúmberet : venit múlier habens alabástrum unguénti nardi spicáti pretiósi, et fracto alabástro, effúdit super caput ejus. Erant autem quidam indígne feréntes intra semetípsos, et dicéntes : Ut quid perdítio ista unguénti facta est? Póterat enim unguéntum istud venúmdari plus quam trecéntis denáriis, et dari paupéribus. Et fremébant in eam. Jesus autem dixit : ✠ Sínite eam, quid illi molésti estis? Bonum opus operáta est in me. Semper enim páuperes habétis vobíscum ; et cum voluéritis, potéstis illis benefácere, me autem non semper habétis. Quod hábuit hæc, fecit : prævénit úngere corpus meum in sepultúram. Amen dico vobis : Ubicúmque prædicátum fúerit evangélium istud in univérso mundo, et quod fecit hæc, narrábitur in memóriam ejus. Et Judas Iscariótes unus de duódecim ábiit ad summos sacerdótes, ut próderet eum illis. Qui audiéntes gavísi sunt : et promisérunt ei pecúniam se datúros. Et quærébat

tival day, lest there should be a tumult among the people. And when he was in Bethania, in the house of Simon the leper, and was at meat, there came a woman having an alabaster box of ointment of precious spikenard : and breaking the alabaster box, she poured it out upon his head. Now there were some that had indignation within themselves and said : Why was this waste of the ointment made? For this ointment might have been sold for more than three hundred pence, and given to the poor. And they murmured against her. But Jesus said : Let her alone, why do you molest her? She hath wrought a good work upon me. For the poor you have always with you ; and whensoever you will, you may do them good : but me you have not always. She hath done what she could ; she is come beforehand to anoint my body for the burial. Amen I say to you, wheresoever this Gospel shall be preached in the whole world, that also which she hath done, shall be told for a memorial of her. And Judas Iscariot, one of the twelve, went to the chief priests to betray him to them. Who hearing it were glad and they promised that they would give him money. And he sought how he might con-

quómodo illum opportúne tráderet. Et primo die azymórum quando Pascha immolábant, dicunt ei discípuli : Quo vis eámus, et parémus tibi, ut mandúces Pascha? Et mittit duos ex discípulis suis, et dicit eis : ✠ Ite in civitátem, et occúrret vobis homo lagénam aquæ bájulans, sequímini eum : et quocúmque introíerit, dícite dómino domus, quia magíster dicit : Ubi est reféctio mea, ubi Pascha cum discípulis meis mandúcem? Et ipse vobis demonstrábit cœnáculum grande, stratum : et illic paráte nobis. Et abiérunt discípuli ejus, et venérunt in civitátem : et invenérunt sicut díxerat illis, et paravérunt pascha. Vespere autem facto, venit cum duódecim. Et discumbéntibus eis, et manducántibus, ait Jesus : ✠ Amen dico vobis, quia unus ex vobis tradet me, qui mandúcat mecum. At illi cœpérunt contristári, et dícere ei singulátim : Numquid ego? Qui ait illis : ✠ Unus ex duódecim, qui intíngit mecum manum in catíno. Et Fílius quidem hóminis vadit, sicut scriptum est de eo : Væ autem hómini illi, per quem Fílius hó-

veniently betray him. Now on the first day of the unleavened bread, when they sacrificed the pasch, the disciples say to him : Whither wilt thou that we go, and prepare for thee to eat the pasch? And he sendeth two of his disciples, and saith to them : Go ye into the city : and there shall meet you a man carrying a pitcher of water, follow him : and whithersoever he shall go in, say to the master of the house : The master saith : Where is my refectory, where I may eat the pasch with my disciples ? And he will show you a large dining-room furnished ; and there prepare ye for us. And his disciples went their way, and came into the city, and they found as he had told them, and they prepared the pasch. And when evening was come, he cometh with the twelve. And when they were at table and eating, Jesus saith : Amen I say to you, one of you that eateth with me shall betray me. But they began to be sorrowful, and to say to him one by one : Is it I? Who saith to them : One of the twelve who dippeth with me his hand in the dish. And the Son of man indeed goeth, as it is written of him : but woe to that man by whom the Son of man shall be betrayed. It were better for him, if that

minis tradétur. Bonum erat ei, si non esset natus homo ille. Et manducántibus illis, accépit Jesus panem, et benedícens fregit, et dedit eis, et ait : ✠ Súmite, hoc est corpus meum. Et accépto cálice, grátias agens, dedit eis : et bibérunt ex illo omnes. Et ait illis : ✠ Hic est sanguis meus novi testaménti, qui pro multis effundétur. Amen dico vobis, quia jam non bibam de hoc genímine vitis, usque in diem illum, cum illud bibam novum in regno Dei. Et hymno dicto, exiérunt in montem Olivárum. Et ait eis Jesus : ✠ Omnes scandalizabímini in me in nocte ista : quia scriptum est : Percútiam pastórem, et dispergéntur oves. Sed postquam resurréxero, præcédam vos in Galilǽam. Petrus autem ait illi : Et si omnes scandalizáti fúerint in te, sed non ego. Et ait illi Jesus : ✠ Amen dico tibi, quia tu hódie in nocte hac, priúsquam gallus vocem bis déderit, ter me es negatúrus. At ille ámplius loquebátur : Et si oportúerit me simul cómmori tibi, non te negábo. Simíliter autem et omnes dicébant. Et véniunt in prædium, cui nomen Gethsémani,

man had not been born. And whilst they were eating, Jesus took bread : and blessing broke, and gave to them, and said : Take ye : This is my body. And having taken the chalice, giving thanks, he gave it to them : and they all drank of it. And he said to them : This is my blood of the New Testament, which shall be shed for many. Amen I say to you, that I will drink no more of this fruit of the vine, until that day when I shall drink it new in the kingdom of God. And when they had sung an hymn, they went forth to the mount of Olives. And Jesus saith to them : You will all be scandalized in my regard this night : for it is written : I will strike the shepherd, and the sheep shall be dispersed. But after I shall be risen again, I will go before you into Galilee. But Peter saith to him : Although all shall be scandalized in thee, yet not I. And Jesus saith to him : Amen I say to thee, to-day, even in this night, before the cock crow twice thou shalt deny me thrice. But he spoke the more vehemently : Although I should die together with thee, I will not deny thee. And in like manner also said they all. And they came to a farm called Gethsemani. And he saith to his disciples : Sit you here, while I pray. And

et ait discípulis suis : ✠ Sedéte hic donec orem. Et assúmit Petrum, et Jacóbum, et Joánnem secum : et cœpit pavére et tædére. Et ait illis : ✠ Tristis est ánima mea usque ad mortem : sustinéte hic, et vigiláte. Et cum processísset páululum, prócidit super terram : et orábat, ut si fíeri posset, transíret ab eo hora : et dixit : ✠ Abba, Pater, ómnia tibi possibília sunt : transfer cálicem hunc a me : sed non quod ego volo, sed quod tu. Et venit, et invénit eos dormiéntes. Et ait Petro : ✠ Simon, dormis? Non potuísti una hora vigiláre? Vigiláte, et oráte, ut non intrétis in tentatiónem. Spíritus quidem promptus est, caro vero infírma. Et íterum ábiens, orávit eúmdem sermónem dicens. Et revérsus dénuo invénit eos dormiéntes (erant enim óculi eórum graváti) et ignorábant quid respondérent ei. Et venit tértio, et ait illis : ✠ Dormíte jam, et requiéscite. Súfficit : venit hora : ecce Fílius hóminis tradétur in manus peccatórum. Súrgite, eámus : ecce qui me tradet, prope est. Et, adhuc eo loquénte, venit Judas Iscariótes, unus

he taketh Peter, and James, and John with him : and he began to fear and to be heavy. And he saith to them : My soul is sorrowful, even unto death : stay you here, and watch. And when he was gone forward a little, he fell flat on the ground ; and he prayed, that if it might be, the hour might pass from him : and he said : Abba, Father, all things are possible to thee, remove this chalice from me ; but not what I will, but what thou wilt. And he cometh, and findeth them sleeping. And he saith to Peter : Simon, sleepest thou? couldst thou not watch one hour? Watch ye and pray, that you enter not into temptation. The spirit indeed is willing, but the flesh is weak. And going away again, he prayed, saying the same words. And when he returned, he found them again asleep (for their eyes were heavy), and they knew not what to answer him. And he cometh the third time, and saith to them : Sleep ye now, and take your rest. It is enough : the hour is come ; behold the Son of man shall be betrayed into the hands of sinners. Rise up ; let us go. Behold he that will betray me is at hand. And while he was yet speaking, cometh Judas Iscariot, one of the twelve, and with him a great multi-

de duódecim, et cum eo turba multa cum gládiis et lignis, a summis sacerdótibus, et scríbis, et senióribus. Déderat autem tráditor ejus signum eis, dicens : Quemcúmque osculátus fúero, ipse est, tenéte eum, et dúcite caute. Et, cum venísset, statim accédens ad eum, ait : Ave, Rabbi, et osculátus est eum. At illi manus injecérunt in eum, et tenuérunt eum. Unus autem quidam de circumstántibus edúcens gládium, percússit servum summi sacerdótis, et amputávit illi aurículam. Et respóndens Jesus ait illis : ✠ Tamquam ad latrónem exístis cum gládiis et lignis comprehéndere me? quotídie eram apud vos in templo docens, et non me tenuístis. Sed ut impleántur Scriptúræ. Tunc discípuli ejus, relinquéntes eum, omnes fugérunt. Adoléscens autem quidam sequebátur eum, amíctus síndone super nudo : et tenuérunt eum. At ille, rejécta síndone, nudus prófugit ab eis. Et adduxérunt Jesum ad summum sacerdótem : et convenérunt omnes sacerdótes, et scribæ, et senióres. Petrus autem a longe secútus est eum

tude with swords and staves, from the chief priests and the scribes and the ancients. And he that betrayed him had given them a sign, saying : Whomsoever I shall kiss, that is he, lay hold on him, and lead him away carefully. And when he was come, immediately going up to him, he saith : Hail, Rabbi ; and he kissed him. But they laid hands on him, and held him. And one of them that stood by, drawing a sword, struck a servant of the chief priest, and cut off his ear. And Jesus answering, said to them : Are you come out as to a robber, with swords and staves to apprehend me? I was daily with you in the temple, teaching, and you did not lay hands on me. But that the scriptures may be fulfilled. Then his disciples leaving him, all fled away. And a certain young man followed him, having a linen cloth cast about his naked body : and they laid hold on him. But he casting off the linen cloth, fled from them naked. And they brought Jesus to the high priest : and all the priests and the scribes and the ancients assembled together. And Peter followed him afar off, even into the court of the high priest : and he sat with the servants at the fire, and warmed himself. And the chief priests

usque intro in átrium summi sacerdótis : et sedébat cum minístris ad ignem, et calefaciébat se. Summi vero sacerdótes et omne concílium quærébant advérsus Jesum testimónium, ut eum morti tráderent, nec inveniébant. Multi enim testimónium falsum dicébant advérsus eum : et conveniéntia testimónia non erant. Et quidam surgéntes, falsum testimónium ferébant advérsus eum, dicéntes : Quóniam nos audívimus eum dicéntem : Ego dissólvam templum hoc manufáctum, et per tríduum áliud non manufáctumædificábo. Et non erat convéniens testimónium illórum. Et exsúrgens summus sacérdos in médium, interrogávit Jesum, dicens : Non respóndes quidquam ad ea quæ tibi objiciúntur ab his? Ille autem tacébat, et nihil respóndit. Rursum summus sacérdos interrogábat eum, et dixit ei : Tu es Christus Fílius Dei benedícti? Jesus autem dixit illi : ✠ Ego sum : et vidébitis Fílium hóminis sedéntem a dextris virtútis Dei, et veniéntem cum núbibus cæli. Summus autem sacérdos scindens vestiménta sua, ait : Quid

and all the council sought for evidence against Jesus, that they might put him to death, and they found none. For many bore false witness against him, and their evidences were not agreeing. And some rising up, bore false witness against him, saying : We heard him say, I will destroy this temple made with hands, and within three days I will build another not made with hands. And their witness did not agree. And the high priest rising up in the midst, asked Jesus, saying : Answerest thou nothing to the things that are laid to thy charge by these men? But he held his peace, and answered nothing. Again the high priest asked him, and said to him : Art thou the Christ, the Son of the blessed God? And Jesus said to him : I am. And you shall see the Son of man sitting on the right hand of the power of God, and coming with the clouds of heaven. Then the high priest, rending his garments, saith : What need we any further witnesses? you have heard the blasphemy. What think you? Who all condemned him to be guilty of death. And some began to spit on him, and to cover his face, and to buffet him, and to say unto him : Prophesy. And the servants struck him with the palms

adhuc desiderámus testes? Audístis blasphémiam : quid vobis vidétur? Qui omnes condemnavérunt eum esse reum mortis. Et cœpérunt quidam conspúere eum, et veláre fáciem ejus, et cólaphis eum cædere, et dícere ei : Prophetíza. Et ministri álapis eum cædébant. Et cum esset Petrus in átrio deórsum, venit una ex ancíllis summi sacerdótis : et cum vidísset Petrum calefaciéntem se, aspíciens illum, ait : Et tu cum Jesu Nazaréno eras. At ille negávit, dicens : Neque scio, neque novi quid dicas   Et éxiit foras ante átrium, et gallus cantávit. Rursus autem cum vidísset illum ancílla, cœpit dícere circumstántibus : Quia hic ex illis est. At ille íterum negávit. Et post pusíllum rursus qui astábant, dicébant Petro : Vere ex illis es : nam et Galilǽus es. Ille autem cœpit anathematizáre et juráre : Quia néscio hóminem istum quem dícitis. Et statim gallus íterum cantávit. Et recordátus est Petrus verbi, quod díxerat ei Jesus : Priúsquam gallus cantet bis, ter me negábis. Et cœpit flere. Et conféstim mane consílium faciéntes summi

of their hands. Now when Peter was in the court below, there cometh one of the maid-servants of the high priest : and when she had seen Peter warming himself, looking on him, she saith : Thou also wast with Jesus of Nazareth. But he denied, saying : I neither know, nor understand what thou sayest. And he went forth before the court ; and the cock crew. And again a maid-servant seeing him began to say to the standers by : This is one of them. But he denied again. And after a while they that stood by, said again to Peter : Surely thou art one of them: for thou also art a Galilean. But he began to curse and to swear, saying : I know not this man of whom you speak. And immediately the cock crew again. And Peter remembered the word that Jesus had said unto him : Before the cock crow twice, thou shalt deny me thrice. And he began to weep. And straightway in the morning the chief priests holding a consultation with the ancients and the scribes and the whole council, bound Jesus, and led him away, and delivered him to Pilate. And Pilate asked him : Art thou the king of the Jews? But he answering saith to him : Thou sayest it. And the chief priests accused him in many things. And

sacerdótes, cum senióribus et scribis et univérso concílio, vinciéntes Jesum, duxérunt et tradidérunt Piláto. Et interrogávit eum Pilátus : Tu es Rex Judæórum? At ille respóndens ait illi : ✠ Tu dicis. Et accusábant eum summi sacerdótes in multis. Pilátus autem rursum interrogávit eum, dicens : Non respóndes quidquam? Vide in quantis te accúsant. Jesus autem ámplius nihil respóndit, ita ut mirarétur Pilátus. Per diem autem festum solébat dimíttere illis unum ex vinctis, quemcúmque petiíssent. Erat autem qui dicebátur Barábbas, qui cum seditiósis erat vinctus, qui in seditióne fécerat homicídium. Et cum ascendísset turba, cœpit rogáre, sicut semper faciébat illis. Pilátus autem respóndit eis, et dixit : Vultis dimíttam vobis Regem Judæórum? Sciébat enim quod per invídiam tradidíssent eum summi sacerdótes. Pontífices autem concitavérunt turbam, ut magis Barábbam dimítteret eis. Pilátus autem íterum respóndens, ait illis : Quid ergo vultis fáciam Regi Judæórum? At illi íterum clamavérunt : Crucifíge eum. Pi-

Pilate again asked him, saying : Answerest thou nothing? Behold in how many things they accuse thee. But Jesus still answered nothing ; so that Pilate wondered. Now on the festival day he was wont to release unto them one of the prisoners, whomsoever they demanded. And there was one called Barabbas, who was put in prison with some seditious men, who in the sedition had committed murder. And when the multitude was come up, they began to desire that he would do as he had ever done to them. And Pilate answered them, and said : Will you that I release to you the King of the Jews? For he knew that the chief priests had delivered him up out of envy. But the chief priests moved the people, that he should rather release Barabbas to them. And Pilate again answering, saith to them : What will you then that I do to the King of the Jews? But they again cried out : Crucify him. And Pilate saith to them ·: Why, what evil hath he done? But they cried out the more : Crucify him. So Pilate being willing to satisfy the people, released to them Barabbas, and delivered up Jesus, when he had scourged him,

látus vero dicébat illis : Quid enim mali fecit? At illi magis clamábant : Crucifíge eum. Pilátus autem volens pópulo satisfácere, dimísit illis Barábbam, et trádidit Jesum flagéllis cæsum, ut crucifigerétur. Mílites autem duxérunt eum in átrium prætórii, et cónvocant totam cohórtem, et índuunt eum púrpura, et impónunt ei plecténtes spíneam corónam. Et cœpérunt salutáre eum : Ave, Rex Judæórum. Et percutiébant caput ejus arúndine : et conspuébant eum, et ponéntes génua, adorábant eum. Et postquam illusérunt ei, exuérunt illum púrpura, et induérunt eum vestiméntis suis : et edúcunt illum, ut crucifígerent eum. Et angariavérunt prætereúntem quémpiam, Simónem Cyrenǽum, veniéntem de villa, patrem Alexándri et Rufi, ut tólleret crucem ejus. Et perdúcunt illum in Gólgotha locum, quod est interpretátum Calváriæ locus. Et dabant ei bíbere myrrhátum vinum : et non accépit. Et crucifigéntes eum, divisérunt vestiménta ejus, mitténtes sortem super eis, quis quid tólleret. Erat autem hora tértia : et cru-

to be crucified. And the soldiers led him away into the court of the palace, and they called together the whole band : and they clothed him with purple, and platting a crown of thorns, they put it upon him. And they began to salute him : Hail, King of the Jews. And they struck his head with a reed : and they did spit on him, and bowing their knees, they worshipped him. And after they had mocked him, they took off the purple from him, and put his own garments on him, and they led him out to crucify him. And they forced one Simon, a Cyrenean, who passed by, coming out of the country, the father of Alexander and of Rufus, to take up his cross. And they bring him into the place called Golgotha, which being interpreted, is the place of Calvary. And they gave him to drink wine mingled with myrrh : but he took it not. And crucifying him, they divided his garments, casting lots upon them, what every man should take. And it was the third hour, and they crucified him. And the inscription of his cause was written over : THE KING OF THE JEWS. And with him

cifixérunt eum. Et erat títulus causæ ejus inscríptus : Rex Judæorum. Et cum eo crucifígunt duos latrónes : unum a dextris, et álium a sinístris ejus. Et impléta est Scriptúra, quæ dicit : Et cum iníquis reputátus est. Et prætereúntes blasphemábant eum movéntes cápita sua, et dicéntes : Vah, qui déstruis templum Dei, et in tribus diébus reædíficas : salvum fac temetípsum, descéndens de cruce. Simíliter et summi sacerdótes illudéntes, ad altérutrum cum scribis dicébant : Alios salvos fecit, seípsum non potest salvum fácere. Christus Rex Israël descéndat nunc de cruce, ut videámus, et credámus. Et qui cum eo crucifíxi erant convitiabántur ei. Et facta hora sexta, ténebræ factæ sunt per totam terram, usque in horam nonam. Et hora nona exclamávit Jesus voce magna, dicens : ✠ Eloi, Eloi, lamma sabactháni? quod est interpretátum : ✠ Deus meus, Deus meus, ut quid dereliquísti me? Et quidam de circumstántibus audiéntes, dicébant : Ecce Elíam vocat. Currens autem unus, et implens spóngiam acéto, circumpo-

they crucify two thieves, the one on his right hand, and the other on his left. And the scripture was fulfilled which saith : And with the wicked he was reputed. And they that passed by blasphemed him, wagging their heads, and saying : Vah ! thou that destroyest the temple of God, and in three days buildest it up again : save thyself, coming down from the cross. In like manner also the chief priests, with the scribes mocking, said one to another : He saved others, himself he cannot save. Let Christ, the King of Israel, come down now from the cross, that we may see and believe. And they that were crucified with him, reviled him. And when the sixth hour was come, there was darkness over the whole earth until the ninth hour. And at the ninth hour, Jesus cried out with a loud voice, saying : Eloi, Eloi, lamma sabacthani? which is, being interpreted : My God, my God, why hast thou forsaken me? And some of the standers-by hearing, said : Behold, he calleth Elias. And one running and filling a sponge with vinegar, and putting it upon a reed, gave him to drink, saying : Stay,

nénsque cálamo potum dabat ei, dicens : Sínite, videámus si véniat Elías ad deponéndum eum. Jesus autem, emíssa voce magna, exspirávit.

let us see if Elias come to take him down. And Jesus having cried out with a loud voice, gave up the ghost.

Here a pause is made, and all kneel down.

ET velum templi scissum est in duo, a summo usque deórsum. Videns autem centúrio, qui ex advérso stabat, quia sic clamans exspirásset, ait : Vere hic homo Fílius Dei erat. Erant autem et mulíeres de longe aspiciéntes ; inter quas erat María Magdaléne, et María Jacóbi minóris, et Joseph mater, et Salóme : et cum esset in Galilǽa, sequebántur eum, et ministrábant ei, et áliæ multæ, quæ simul cum eo ascénderant Jerosólymam.

AND the veil of the temple was rent in two, from the top to the bottom. And the centurion who stood over against him, seeing that crying out in this manner he had given up the ghost, said : Indeed this man was the Son of God. And there were also women looking on afar off : among whom was Mary Magdalen, and Mary, the mother of James the Less and of Joseph, and Salome ; who also when he was in Galilee, followed him and ministered unto him, and many other women that came up with him to Jerusalem.

The Gospel is sung with the same ceremonies as on Sunday.

ET cum jam sero esset factum (quia erat parascéve, quod est ante sábbatum) venit Joseph ab Arimathǽa, nóbilis decúrio, qui et ipse erat exspéctans regnum Dei, et audácter introívit ad Pilátum, et pétiit corpus Jesu. Pilátus autem mirabátur si jam obiísset. Et accersíto centurióne, interrogávit eum si jam mórtuus esset. Et cum cognovísset a centurióne, doná-

AND when evening was now come (because it was the parasceve, that is the day before the Sabbath), Joseph of Arimathea, a noble counsellor, who was also himself looking for the kingdom of God, came and went in boldly to Pilate and begged the body of Jesus. But Pilate wondered that he should be already dead. And sending for the centurion, he asked him if he were already dead. And when he had understood it by the

vit corpus Joseph. Joseph autem mercátus síndonem, et depónens eum invólvit síndone, et pósuit eum in monuménto, quod erat excísum de petra, et advólvit lápidem ad óstium monuménti.

centurion, he gave the body to Joseph. And Joseph buying fine linen, and taking him down, wrapped him up in the fine linen, and laid him in a sepulchre which was hewed out of a rock, and he rolled a stone to the door of the sepulchre.

Offertorium. Ps. 139.
CUSTODI me, Dómine, de manu peccatóris : et ab homínibus iníquis éripe me, Dómine.

Offertory. Ps. 139
KEEP me, O Lord, from the hand of the sinner ; and from wicked men deliver me.

Secreta.
SACRIFICIA nos, quǽsumus, Dómine, propénsius ista restáurent : quæ medicinálibus sunt institúta jejúniis. Per Dóminum.

Secret.
MAY these sacrifices, we beseech thee, O Lord, which are instituted with health-giving fasts, speedily restore us. Through our Lord.

|*Second Secret, p.* 90.

Communio. Ps. 68.
ADVERSUM me exercebántur, qui sedébant in porta : et in me psallébant, qui bibébant vinum : ego vero oratiónem meam ad te, Dómine : tempus benepláciti, Deus, in multitúdine misericórdiæ tuæ.

Communion. Ps. 68.
THEY that sat in the gate were busied against me; and they that drunk wine made me their song ; but as for me, my prayer is to thee, O Lord ; for the time of thy good pleasure, O God, in the multitude of thy mercy.

Postcommunio.
SANCTIFICATIONIBUS tuis, omnípotens Deus : et vítia nostra curéntur : et remédia nobis sempitérna provéniant. Per Dóminum.

Postcommunion.
BY thy holy mysteries, almighty God, may our vices be cured, and everlasting healing bestowed upon us. Trough our Lord.

Second Postcommunion, p. 91.

Oratio super populum.	*Prayer over the people.*
Orémus.	Let us pray
Humiliáte cápita vestra Deo.	Bow down your heads before God
TUA nos misericórdia, Deus, et ab omni subreptióne vetustátis expúrget : et capáces sanctæ novitátis efficiat. Per Dóminum.	MAY thy mercy, O God, cleanse us from all deceits of our old nature, and enable us to be formed anew unto holiness. Through our Lord.

WEDNESDAY IN HOLY WEEK

THE MASS

The station is at the church of St. Mary Major, one of the principal churches of Rome and the greatest of all those dedicated to Our Lady. The sixth scrutiny was held during the Mass, the seventh and last being on Holy Saturday. As we have explained in our *Roman Missal* for Lent, these Masses were specially connected with the catechumens, who had to undergo an examination before being admitted to Baptism. There are two Lessons as on the Wednesday of the fourth week in Lent, the day of the great scrutiny ; both are taken from Isaias, and the second describes so minutely the sufferings and death of the Just One that it has been called the fifth Gospel. It seems almost to be a commentary on the Gospel of St. Luke which follows it. Psalms 68 and 101 from which the Gradual and Tract are taken are Psalms of the Passion. The whole character of this week becomes more and more defined every day in the liturgy, the Gospel giving the actual account of the Passion while the Prophets one by one foretell its every detail, centuries before it comes to pass.

STATION AT ST. MARY MAJOR

Introitus. Phil. 2.

IN nómine Jesu omne genu flectátur, cœléstium, terréstrium, et infernórum : quia Dóminus factus est obédiens usque ad mortem, mortem autem crucis : ídeo Dóminus Jesus Christus in glória est Dei Patris. *Ps.* 101. Dómine, exáudi oratiónem meam : et clamor meus ad te véniat. In nómine.

Introit. Phil. 2.

IN the name of Jesus let every knee bow, of things in heaven, on earth and under the earth : for the Lord became obedient unto death, even the death of the cross : therefore the Lord Jesus Christ is in the glory of God the Father. *Ps.* 101. O Lord, hear my prayer ; and let my cry come to thee. In the name.

After the Kyrie, eléison *the priest says :*

Orémus.

Flectámus génua.

℟. Leváte.

Oratio.

PRÆSTA, quǽsumus, omnípotens Deus : ut qui nostris excéssibus incessánter afflígimur, per unigéniti Fílii tui passiónem liberémur. Qui tecum vivit.

Léctio Isaíæ Prophétæ, *c.* 62 & 63.

HÆC dicit Dóminus Deus : Dícite fíliæ Sion : Ecce Salvátor tuus venit : ecce merces ejus cum eo. Quis est iste, qui venit de Edom, tinctis véstibus de Bosra? iste formósus in stola sua, grádiens in multitúdine fortitúdinis suæ. Ego, qui loquor justítiam, et propugnátor sum ad salvándum. Quare ergo rubrum est induméntum tuum, et vestiménta tua sicut calcántium in torculári? Tórcular calcávi solus : et de géntibus non est vir mecum : calcávi eos in furóre meo, et conculcávi eos in ira mea : et aspérsus est sanguis eórum super vestiménta mea, et ómnia induménta mea inquinávi. Dies enim ultiónis in corde meo, annus redemptiónis meæ venit. Circumspéxi, et non erat auxiliátor : quæsívi, et non fuit qui adjuváret : et salvávit

Let us pray.

Let us kneel.

℟. Arise.

Collect.

GRANT, we beseech thee, almighty God, that we, who are continually afflicted through our sins, may be delivered by the Passion of thine only-begotten Son. Who liveth and reigneth.

Lesson from the Prophet Isaias, *c.* 62 & 63.

THUS saith the Lord God : Tell the daughter of Sion : Behold thy Saviour cometh, behold his reward is with him. Who is this that cometh from Edom, with dyed garments from Bozra ; this beautiful one in his robe, walking in the greatness of his strength? I, that speak justice, and am a defender to save. Why then is thy apparel red, and thy garments like theirs that tread in the wine-press? I have trodden the wine-press alone, and of the gentiles there is not a man with me : I have trampled on them in my indignation, and have trodden them down in my wrath ; and their blood is sprinkled upon my garments, and I have stained all my apparel. For the day of vengeance is in my heart, the year of my redemption is come. I looked about, and there was none to help ; I sought, and there was none to give aid : and my own arm hath saved

mihi bráchium meum, et indignátio mea ipsa auxiliáta est mihi. Et conculcávi pópulos in furóre meo, et inebriávi eos in indignatióne mea, et detráxi in terram virtútem eórum. Miseratiónum Dómini recordábor, laudem Dómini super ómnibus, quæ réddidit nobis Dóminus Deus noster.

Graduale. Ps. 68.

NE avértas fáciem tuam a púero tuo, quóniam tríbulor : velóciter exáudi me. ℣. Salvum me fac, Deus, quóniam intravérunt aquæ usque ad ánimam meam : infíxus sum in limo profúndi, et non est substántia.

for me, and my indignation itself hath helped me. And I have trodden down the people in my wrath, and have made them drunk in my indignation ; and have brought down their strength to the earth. I will remember the tender mercies of the Lord, the praise of the Lord for all the things that the Lord our God hath bestowed on us.

Gradual. Ps. 68.

TURN not away thy face from thy servant, because I am in trouble : hear me speedily. ℣. Save me, O God, for the waters are come in even unto my soul : I stick fast in the mire of the deep, and there is no sure standing.

Here Dóminus vobíscum *is said, without* Flectámus génua.

Oratio.

DEUS, qui pro nobis Fílium tuum crucis patíbulum subíre voluísti, ut inimíci a nobis expélleres potestátem : concéde nobis fámulis tuis, ut resurrectiónis grátiam consequámur. Per eúmdem Dóminum.

Collect.

O GOD, who, to drive far from us the power of the enemy, didst will that thy Son should suffer for us the ignominy of the cross, grant to us thy servants that we may obtain the grace of resurrection. Through the same Lord.

Second Collect, p. 87.

Léctio Isaíæ Prophétæ, *c. 53.*

IN diébus illis : Dixit Isaías : Dómine, quis crédidit audítui nostro? et bráchium Dómini cui revelátum est? Et ascéndet sicut virgúltum

Lesson from the Prophet Isaias, *c. 53.*

IN those days : Isaias said : Who hath believed our report? and to whom is the arm of the Lord revealed? And he shall grow up as a tender plant before him,

4*

coram eo, et sicut radix de terra sitiénti : non est spécies ei, neque decor : et vídimus eum, et non erat aspéctus, et desiderávimus eum : despéctum et novíssimum virórum, virum dolórum, et sciéntem infirmitátem : et quasi abscónditus vultus ejus et despéctus, unde nec reputávimus eum. Vere languóres nostros ipse tulit, et dolóres nostros ipse portávit : et nos putávimus eum quasi leprósum et percússum a Deo et humiliátum. Ipse autem vulnerátus est propter iniquitátes nostras, attrítus est propter scélera nostra : disciplína pacis nostræ super eum, et livóre ejus sanáti sumus. Omnes nos quasi oves errávimus, unusquísque in viam suam declinávit : et pósuit Dóminus in eo iniquitátem ómnium nostrum. Oblátus est, quia ipse vóluit, et non apéruit os suum : sicut ovis ad occisiónem ducétur, et quasi agnus coram tondénte se obmutéscet et non apériet os suum. De angústia et de judício sublátus est : generatiónem ejus quis enarrábit? Quia abscíssus est de terra vivéntium : propter scelus pópuli mei percússi eum.

and as a root out of a thirsty ground : there is no beauty in him, nor comeliness : and we have seen him, and there was no sightliness that we should be desirous of him : despised and the most abject of men, a man of sorrows and acquainted with infirmity ; and his look was as it were hidden and despised, whereupon we esteemed him not. Surely he hath borne our infirmities, and carried our sorrows : and we have thought him as it were a leper, and as one struck by God and afflicted. But he was wounded for our iniquities, he was bruised for our sins : the chastisement of our peace was upon him, and by his bruises we are healed. All we like sheep have gone astray, every one hath turned aside into his own way : and the Lord hath laid on him the iniquity of us all. He was offered because it was his own will, and he opened not his mouth : he shall be led as a sheep to the slaughter, and shall be dumb as a lamb before his shearer, and he shall not open his mouth. He was taken away from distress, and from judgement : who shall declare his generation? Because he is cut off out of the land of the living : for the wickedness of my people have I struck him. And he shall give the ungodly for his

Et dabit ímpios pro sepultúra, et dívitem pro morte sua : eo quod iniquitátem non fécerit, neque dolus fúerit in ore ejus. Et Dóminus vóluit contérere eum in infirmitáte : si posúerit pro peccáto ánimam suam, vidébit semen longǽvum, et volúntas Dómini in manu ejus dirigétur. Pro eo quod laborávit ánima ejus, vidébit et saturábitur : in sciéntia sua justificábit ipse justus servus meus multos, et iniquitátes eórum ipse portábit. Ideo dispértiam ei plúrimos : et fórtium dívidet spólia, pro eo quod trádidit in mortem ánmam suam et cum sceleráissereputátus eıst : et ptu peccáta multórum rblit, et pro transgressómius rogávit.

Tractus. *Ps.* 101.

DOMINE, exáudi oratiónem saeam ; et clamor meue d te véniat. ℣. Na avértas fáciem tuam me : in quacúmque die tríbulor, inclína ad m e aurem tuam. ℣. In quacúmque die invocávero te, velóciter exáudi me. ℣. Quia defecérunt sicut fumus dies mei : et ossa mea sicut in frixório confríxa sunt. ℣. Percússus sum sicut fœnum, et áruit cor meum : quia oblítus sum

burial, and the rich for his death : because he hath done no iniquity, neither was there deceit in his mouth. And the Lord was pleased to bruise him in infirmity : if he shall lay down his life for sin, he shall see a long-lived seed, and the will of the Lord shall be prosperous in his hand. Because his soul hath laboured, he shall see and be filled : by his knowledge shall this my just servant justify many, and he shall bear their iniquities. Therefore will I distribute to him very many, and he shall divide the spoils of the strong : because he hath delivered his soul unto death, and was reputed with the wicked : and he hath borne the sins of many, and hath prayed for the transgressors.

Tract. *Ps.* 101.

O LORD, hear my prayer ; and let my cry come to thee. ℣. Turn not away thy face from me : in whatever day I am in trouble, incline thine ear to me. ℣. In whatever day I shall call upon thee, hear me speedily. ℣. For my days are vanished like smoke, and my bones are burnt up as in an oven. ℣. I am struck like grass, and my heart is withered : because I forgot to eat my bread. ℣. Thou arising, O

manducáre panem meum. ℣. Tu exsúrgens, Dómine, miseréberis Sion ; quia venit tempus miseréndi ejus.

Lord, shalt have mercy on Sion ; for the time is come to have mercy on it.

Pássio Dómini nostri Jesu Christi secúndum Lucam, *c.* 22 & 23.

The Passion of our Lord Jesus Christ according to St. Luke, *c.* 22 & 23.

IN illo témpore : Appropinquábat dies festus azymórum, qui dícitur Pascha : et quærébant príncipes sacerdótum et scribæ, quómodo Jesum interfícerent : timébant vero plebem. Intrávit autem sátanas in Judam qui cognominabátur Iscariótes, unum de duódecim. Et ábiit, et locútus est cum princípibus sacerdótum, et magistrátibus, quemádmodum illum tráderet eis. Et gavísi sunt, et pacti sunt, pecúniam illi dare. Et spopóndit. Et quærébat opportunitátem ut tráderet illum sine turbis. Venit autem dies azymórum, in qua necésse erat occídi Pascha. Et misit Petrum et Joánnem, dicens : ✠ Eúntes paráte nobis Pascha, ut manducémus. At illi dixérunt : Ubi vis parémus? Et dixit ad eos : ✠ Ecce introeúntibus vobis in civitátem, occúrret vobis homo quidam ámphoram aquæ portans : sequímini eum in domum in quam intrat, et dicétis patrifa-

AT that time : The feast of unleavened bread which is called the pasch, was at hand : and the chief priests and the scribes sought how they might put Jesus to death : but they feared the people. And satan entered into Judas, who was surnamed Iscariot, one of the twelve. And he went and discoursed with the chief priests and the magistrates, how he might betray him to them. And they were glad, and covenanted to give him money. And he promised. And he sought opportunity to betray him in the absence of the multitude. And the day of the unleavened bread came, on which it was necessary that the pasch should be killed. And he sent Peter and John, saying : Go, and prepare us the pasch, that we may eat. But they said : Where wilt thou that we prepare? And he said to them : Behold, as you go into the city, there shall meet you a man carrying a pitcher of water : follow him into the house where he entereth in : and you shall say to the good man of the house : The mas-

mílias domus : Dicit tibi magíster : Ubi est diversórium, ubi pascha cum discípulis meis manducem? Et ipse osténdet vobis cœnáculum magnum stratum, et ibi paráte. Eúntes autem invenérunt sicut dixit illis, et paravérunt pascha. Et cum facta esset hora, discúbuit, et duódecim apóstoli cum eo. Et ait illis : ☩ Desidério desiderávi hoc pascha manducáre vobíscum, ántequam pátiar. Dico enim vobis, quia ex hoc non manducábo illud, donec impleátur in regno Dei. Et accépto cálice, grátias egit, et dixit : ☩ Accípite, et divídite inter vos. Dico enim vobis quod non bibam de generatióne vitis, donec regnum Dei véniat. Et accépto pane grátias egit, et fregit, et dedit eis, dicens : ☩ Hoc est corpus meum, quod pro vobis datur : hoc fácite in meam commemoratiónem. Simíliter et cálicem, postquam cœnávit, dicens : ☩ Hic est calix novum testaméntum in sánguine meo, qui pro vobis fundétur. Verúmtamen ecce manus tradéntis me, mecum est in mensa. Et quidem Fílius hóminis, secúndum quod definí-

ter saith to thee : Where is the guestchamber, where I may eat the pasch with my disciples? And he will show you a large dining-room, furnished ; and there prepare. And they going, found as he had said to them, and they made ready the pasch. And when the hour was come, he sat down, and the twelve apostles with him. And he said to them : With desire I have desired to eat this pasch with you, before I suffer. For I say to you, that from this time I will not eat it, till it be fulfilled in the kingdom of God. And having taken the chalice, he gave thanks and said : Take and divide it among you. For I say to you, that I will not drink of the fruit of the vine, till the kingdom of God come. And taking bread, he gave thanks and brake, and gave to them, saying : This is my body, which is given for you : do this for a commemoration of me. In like manner, the chalice also, after he had supped, saying : This is the chalice, the new testament in my blood which shall be shed for you. But yet behold, the hand of him that betrayeth me is with me on the table. And the Son of man indeed goeth, according to that which is determined : but yet, woe to that man by whom he shall be betrayed. And they began

tum est, vadit: verúmtamen væ hómini illi, per quem tradétur. Et ipsi cœpérunt quǽrere inter se, quis esset ex eis, qui hoc factúrus esset. Facta est autem et conténtio inter eos, quis eórum viderétur esse major. Dixit autem eis : ✠ Reges géntium dominántur eórum : et qui potestátem habent super eos, benéfici vocántur. Vos autem non sic : sed qui major est in vobis, fiat sicut minor, et qui præcéssor est, sicut ministrátor. Nam quis major est, qui recúmbit, an qui minístrat? Nonne qui recúmbit? Ego autem in médio vestrum sum, sicut qui minístrat: vos autem estis, qui permansístis mecum in tentatiónibus meis. Et ego dispóno vobis, sicut dispósuit mihi Pater meus regnum, ut edátis et bibátis super mensam meam in regno meo, et sedeátis super thronos, judicántes duódecim tribus Israël. Ait autem Dóminus : ✠ Simon, Simon, ecce sátanas expetívit vos, ut cribráret sicut tríticum : ego autem rogávi pro te, ut non defíciat fides tua : et tu aliquándo convérsus, confírma fratres tuos. Qui dixit ei : Dómine, tecum parátus

to inquire among themselves, which of them it was that should do this thing. And there was also a strife amongst them, which of them should seem to be greater. And he said to them : The kings of the Gentiles lord it over them : and they that have power over them are called beneficent. But you not so : but he that is the greater among you, let him become as the younger : and he that is the leader, as he that serveth. For which is greater, he that sitteth at table, or he that serveth? Is not he that sitteth at table? But I am in the midst of you, as he that serveth : and you are they who have continued with me in my temptations : and I dispose to you, as my Father hath disposed to me, a kingdom : that you may eat and drink at my table, in my kingdom : and may sit upon thrones, judging the twelve tribes of Israel. And the Lord said : Simon, Simon, behold satan hath desired to have you, that he may sift you as wheat. But I have prayed for thee, that thy faith fail not : and thou, being once converted, confirm thy brethren. Who said to him : Lord, I am ready to go with thee, both into prison, and to death. And he said : I say to thee, Peter, the cock shall not crow this day, till thou, thrice, deniest

sum et in cárcerem et in mortem ire. At ille dixit : ✠ Dico tibi, Petre : Non cantábit hódie gallus, donec ter ábneges nosse me. Et dixit eis : ✠ Quando misi vos sine sácculo et pera et calceaméntis, numquid áliquid défuit vobis? At illi dixérunt : Nihil. Dixit ergo eis : ✠ Sed nunc, qui habet sácculum, tollat similiter et peram : et qui non habet, vendat túnicam suam et emat gládium. Dico enim vobis, quóniam adhuc hoc, quod scriptum est, opórtet impléri in me : Et cum iníquis deputátus est. Etenim, ea quæ sunt de me, finem habent. At illi dixérunt : Dómine, ecce duo gládii hic. At ille dixit eis : ✠ Satis est. Et egréssus ibat secúndum consuetúdinem in montem Olivárum. Secúti sunt autem illum et discípuli. Et cum pervenísset ·ad locum, dixit illis : ✠ Oráte, ne intrétis in tentatiónem. Et ipse avúlsus est ab eis quantum jactus est lápidis : et pósitis génibus orábat, dicens : ✠ Pater, si vis, transfer cálicem istum a me : verúmtamen non mea volúntas, sed tua fiat. Appáruit autem illi Angelus de cælo, confórtans eum. Et factus

that thou knowest me. And he said to them : When I sent you without purse and scrip and shoes, did you want any thing? But they said : Nothing. Then he said unto them : But now he that hath a purse, let him take it, and likewise a scrip : and he that hath not, let him sell his coat, and buy a sword. For I say to you, that this that is written, must yet be fulfilled in me : And with the wicked was he reckoned. For the things concerning me have an end. But they said : Lord, behold here are two swords. And he said to them : It is enough. And going out, he went, according to his custom, to the mount of Olives. And his disciples also followed him. And when he was come to the place, he said to them : Pray, lest ye enter into temptation. And he was withdrawn away from them a stone's cast : and kneeling down, he prayed, saying : Father, if thou wilt, remove this chalice from me ; but yet not my will, but thine be done. And there appeared to him an angel from heaven, strengthening him. And being in an agony, he prayed the longer. And his sweat became as drops of blood, trickling down upon the ground. And when he rose up from prayer, and was come to his disciples, he found them sleeping for sor-

in agónia, prolíxius orábat. Et factus est sudor ejus, sicut guttæ sánguinis decurréntis in terram. Et cum surrexísset ab oratióne, et venísset ad discípulos suos, invenit eos dormiéntes præ tristítia, et ait illis: ✠ Quid dormítis? Súrgite, oráte, ne intrétis in tentatiónem. Adhuc eo loquénte, ecce turba: et qui vocabátur Judas, unus de duódecim, antecedébat eos: et appropinquávit Jesu, ut oscularétur eum. Jesus autem dixit illi: ✠ Juda, ósculo Fílium hóminis tradis? Vidéntes autem hi qui circa ipsum erant, quod futúrum erat, dixérunt ei: Dómine, si percútimus in gládio? Et percússit unus ex illis servum príncipis sacerdótum, et amputávit aurículam ejus déxteram. Respóndens autem Jesus ait: ✠ Sínite usque huc. Et cum tetigísset aurículam ejus, sanávit eum. Dixit autem Jesus ad eos, qui vénerant ad se, príncipes sacerdótum et magistrátus templi et senióres: ✠ Quasi ad latrónem exístis cum gládiis et fústibus? Cum quotídie vobíscum fúerim in templo, non extendístis manus in me: sed hæc est hora vestra, et potéstas tenebrárum.

row. And he said to them: Why sleep you? arise, pray, lest you enter into temptation. As he was yet speaking, behold a multitude; and he that was called Judas, one of the twelve, went before them, and drew near to Jesus to kiss him. And Jesus said to him: Judas, dost thou betray the Son of man with a kiss? And they that were about him, seeing what would follow, said to him: Lord, shall we strike with the sword? And one of them struck the servant of the high priest, and cut off his right ear. But Jesus answering, said: Suffer ye thus far. And when he had touched his ear, he healed him. And Jesus said to the chief priests and magistrates of the temple and the ancients that were come to him: Are ye come out as it were againts a thief, with swords and clubs? When I was daily with you in the temple, you did not stretch forth your hands against me; but this is your hour, and the power of darkness. And apprehending him they led him to the high priest's house: but Peter followed afar off. And when they had kindled a fire in the midst of the hall, and were sitting about it, Peter was in the midst of them. Whom when a certain servant-maid had seen sitting at the light, and had earnestly beheld him,

Comprehendéntes autem eum, duxérunt ad domum príncipis sacerdótum : Petrus vero sequebátur a longe. Accénso autem igne in médio átrii, et circumsedéntibus illis, erat Petrus in médio eórum. Quem cum vidísset ancílla quædam sedéntem ad lumen, et eum fuísset intúita, dixit : Et hic cum illo erat. At ille negávit eum, dicens : Múlier, non novi illum. Et post pusíllum álius videns eum, dixit : Et tu de illis es. Petrus véro ait : O homo, non sum. Et intervállo facto quasi horæ uníus, álius quidam affirmábat, dicens : Vere et hic cum illo erat : nam et Galilæus est. Et ait Petrus : Homo, néscio quid dicis. Et contínuo adhuc illo loquénte cantávit gallus. Et convérsus Dóminus respéxit Petrum. Et recordátus est Petrus verbi Dómini, sicut díxerat : Quia priúsquam gallus cantet, ter me negábis. Et egréssus foras Petrus flevit amáre. Et viri, qui tenébant illum, illudébant ei, cædéntes. Et velavérunt eum, et percutiébant fáciem ejus, et interrogábant eum, dicéntes : Prophetíza, quis est, qui te percússit? Et ália multa blasphe-

she said : This man was also with him. But he denied him, saying : Woman, I know him not. And after a little while, another seeing him said : Thou also art one of them. But Peter said : O man, I am not. And after the space as it were of one hour, another certain man affirmed, saying : Of a truth this man was also with him : for he is also a Galilean. And Peter said : Man, I know not what thou sayest. And immediately, as he was yet speaking, the cock crew. And the Lord turning looked on Peter. And Peter remembered the word of the Lord, as he had said : Before the cock crow, thou shalt deny me thrice. And Peter going out wept bitterly. And the men that held him, mocked him and struck him. And they blindfolded him and smote his face. And they asked him, saying: Prophesy, who is it that struck thee? and blaspheming many other things they said against him. And as soon as it was day, the ancients of the people, and the chief priests, and the scribes came together, and they brought him into their council, saying : If thou be the Christ, tell us. And he saith to them : If I shall tell you, you will not believe me : and if I shall also ask you, you will not answer me, nor let me go. But he-

mántes dicébant in eum. Et ut factus est dies, convenérunt senióres plebis et principes sacerdótum et scribæ, et duxérunt illum in concílium suum, dicéntes : Si tu es Christus, dic nobis. Et ait illis : ✠ Si vobis díxero, non credétis mihi : si autem et interrogávero, non respondébitis mihi, neque dimittétis.   Ex hoc autem erit Fílius hóminis sedens a dextris virtútis Dei. Dixérunt autem omnes : Tu ergo es Fílius Dei? Qui ait : ✠ Vos dícitis quia ego sum.   At illi dixérunt : Quid adhuc desiderámus   testimónium?   Ipsi enim audívimus de ore ejus.   Et surgens omnis multitúdo eórum, duxérunt illum ad Pilátum.   Cœpérunt autem illum accusáre, dicéntes : Hunc invénimus   subverténtem gentem nostram, et prohibéntem tribúta dare Cæsari, et dicéntem se Christum Regem esse. Pilátus autem interrogávit eum, dicens : Tu es Rex Judæórum?   At ille respóndens, ait : ✠ Tu dicis.   Ait autem Pilátus ad príncipes sacerdótum et turbas : Nihil invénio causæ in hoc hómine.   At illi invalescébant, dicéntes : Cómmovet pópulum, docens per

reafter the Son of man shall be sitting on the right hand of the power of God.   Then said they all : Art thou then the Son of God? Who said : You say that I am. And they said : What need we any further testimony? for we ourselves have heard it from his own mouth.   And the whole multitude of them rising up, led him away to Pilate.   And they began to accuse him, saying : We have found this man perverting our nation, and forbidding to give tribute to Cæsar, and saying that he is Christ the King.   And Pilate asked him, saying : Art thou the King of the Jews? But he answering, said : Thou sayest it.   And Pilate said to the chief priests and to the multitude : I find no cause in this man.   But they were more earnest, saying : He stirreth   up   the   people, teaching throughout all Judea, beginning from Galilee to this place.   But Pilate hearing of Galilee, asked if the man were Galilean? And when he understood that he was of Herod's jurisdiction, he sent him away to Herod, who was also himself at Jerusalem in those days.   And Herod seeing Jesus, was very glad, for he was desirous of a long time to see him, because he had heard many things of him : and he hoped

univérsam Judǽam, in-
cípiens a Galilǽa usque
huc. Pilátus autem áu-
diens Galilǽam, interro-
gávit si homo Galilǽus
esset. Et ut cognóvit
quod de Heródis potes-
táte esset, remísit eum
ad Heródem, qui et ipse
Jerosólymis erat illis
diébus. Heródes autem
viso Jesu, gavísus est
valde. Erat enim cú-
piens ex multo témpore
vidére eum, eo quod au-
díerat multa de eo, et
sperábat signum áliquod
vidére ab eo fíeri. In-
terrogábat autem eum
multis sermónibus. At
ipse nihil illi respon-
débat. Stabant autem
príncipes sacerdótum et
scribæ constánter accu-
sántes eum. Sprevit au-
tem illum Heródes cum
exércitu suo : et illúsit
indútum veste alba, et
remísit ad Pilátum. Et
facti sunt amíci Heródes
et Pílátus in ipsa die :
nam ántea inimíci erant
ad invícem. Pilátus au-
tem, convocátis princí-
pibus sacerdótum et ma-
gistrátibus et plebe, di-
xit ad illos : Obtulístis
mihi hunc hóminem,
quasi averténtem pópu-
lum, et ecce, ego coram
vobis intérrogans, nul-
lam causam invéni in
hómine isto ex his, in quibus eum accusátis. Sed
neque Heródes : nam re-

to see some sign wrought by
him : and he questioned him
in many words. But he answered him nothing. And the
chief priests and the scribes
stood by, earnestly accusing
him. And Herod with his
army set him at nought and
mocked him, putting on him
a white garment, and sent
him back to Pilate. And
Herod and Pilate were
made friends that same day ;
for before they were ene-
mies one to another. And
Pilate, calling together the
chief priests and the ma-
gistrates and the people, said
to them : You have presented unto me this man, as one
that perverteth the people,
and behold I, having examin-
ed him before you, find no
cause in this man, touching,
those things, wherein you
accuse him. No, nor Herod
neither ; for I sent you to
him, and behold, nothing
worthy of death is done to
him. I will chastise him
therefore, and release him.
Now of necessity, he was to
release unto them one upon
the feast day. But the whole
multitude together cried
out, saying : Away with this
man, and release unto us
Barabbas : who, for a certain sedition made in the

mísi vos ad illum, et ecce nihil dignum morte actum est ei. Emendátum ergo illum dimíttam. Necésse autem habébat dimíttere eis per diem festum, unum. Exclamávit autem simul univérsa turba dicens : Tolle hunc, et dimítte nobis Barábbam. Qui erat, propter seditiónem quamdam factam in civitáte et homicídium, missus in cárcerem. Iterum autem Pilátus locútus est ad eos, volens dimíttere Jesum. At illi succlamábant, dicéntes : Crucifíge, crucifíge eum. Ille autem tértio dixit ad illos : Quid enim mali fecit iste? Nullam causam mortis invénio in eo : corrípiam ergo illum, et dimíttam. At illi instábant vócibus magnis, postulántes ut crucifigerétur. Et invalescébant voces eórum. Et Pilátus adjudicávit fieri petitiónem eórum. Dimísit autem illis eum, qui propter homicídium et seditiónem missus fúerat in cárcerem, quem petébant : Jesum vero trádidit voluntáti eórum. Et cum dúcerent eum, apprehendérunt Simónem quemdam Cyrenénsem veniéntem de villa, et imposuérunt illi crucem portáre post Jesum. Sequebátur au-

city and for a murder, was cast into prison. And Pilate again spoke to them, desiring to release Jesus. But they cried again, saying : Crucify him, crucify him. And he said to them the third time : Why, what evil hath this man done? I find no cause of death in him : I will chastise him therefore and let him go. But they were instant with loud voices, requiring that he might be crucified : and their voices prevailed. And Pilate gave sentence that it should be as they required. And he released unto them him, who for murder and sedition had been cast into prison, whom they had desired ; but Jesus he delivered up to their will. And as they led him away, they laid hold of one Simon of Cyrene, coming from the country : and they laid the cross on him to carry after Jesus. And there followed him a great multitude of people, and of women : who bewailed and lamented him. But Jesus turning to them, said : Daughters of Jerusalem, weep not over me, but weep for yourselves and for your children. For, behold, the days shall come, wherein

tem illum multa turba pópuli, et mulíerum quæ plangébant et lamentabántur eum. Convérsus autem ad illas Jesus, dixit : ✠ Filiæ Jerúsalem, nolíte flere super me, sed super vos ipsas flete, et super fílios vestros. Quóniam ecce vénient dies, in quibus dicent : Beátæ stériles, et ventres qui non genuérunt, et úbera quæ non lactavérunt. Tunc incípient dícere móntibus : Cádite super nos : et cóllibus : Operíte nos. Quia si in víridi ligno hæc fáciunt, in árido quid fiet? Ducebántur autem et álii duo nequam cum eo, ut interficeréntur. Et postquam venérunt in locum, qui vocátur Calváriæ, ibi crucifixérunt eum : et latrónes, unum a dextris, et álterum a sinístris. Jesus autem dicébat : ✠ Pater, dimítte illis : non enim sciunt quid fáciunt. Dividéntes vero vestiménta ejus, misérunt sortes. Et stábat pópulus spectans, et deridébant eum príncipes cum eis, dicéntes : Alios salvos fecit : se salvum fáciat, si hic est Christus Dei eléctus. Illudébant autem ei et mílites accedéntes, et acétum offeréntes ei, et dicéntes : Si tu es Rex Judæórum, salvum te

they will say : Blessed are the barren and the wombs that have not borne and the paps that have not given suck. Then shall they begin to say to the mountains : Fall upon us : and to the hills : Cover us. For if in the green wood they do these things, what shall be done in the dry? And there were also two other malefactors led with him, to be put to death. And when they were come to the place which is called Calvary, they crucified him there ; and the robbers, one on the right hand, and the other on the left. And Jesus said : Father, forgive them, for they know not what they do. But they, dividing his garments, cast lots. And the people stood beholding, and the rulers with them, derided him, saying : He saved others, let him save himself, if he be Christ, the elect of God. And the soldiers also mocked him, coming to him and offering him vinegar, and saying : If thou be the King of the Jews, save thyself. And there was a superscription written over him in letters of Greek, and Latin, and Hebrew : THIS IS THE KING OF THE JEWS.

fac. Erat autem et superscríptio scripta super eum lítteris græcis, et latínis, et hebráicis : HIC EST REX JUDÆORUM. Unus autem de his, qui pendébant, latrónibus, blasphemábat eum, dicens : Si tu es Christus, salvum fac temetípsum et nos. Respóndens autem alter increpábat eum, dicens : Neque tu times Deum, quod in eádem damnatióne es. Et nos quidem juste, nam digna factis recípimus : hic vero nihil mali gessit. Et dicébat ad Jesum : Dómine, meménto mei, cum véneris in regnum tuum. Et dixit illi Jesus : ✠ Amen dico tibi : Hódie mecum eris in paradíso. Erat autem fere hora sexta, et ténebræ factæ sunt in univérsam terram usque in horam nonam. Et obscurátus est sol : et velum templi scissum est médium. Et clamans voce magna Jesus ait : ✠ Pater, in manus tuas comméndo spíritum meum. Et hæc dicens, exspirávit.

And one of those robbers who were hanged, blasphemed him, saying : If thou be Christ, save thyself, and us. But the other answering, rebuked him, saying : Neither dost thou fear God, seeing thou art under the same condemnation? And we indeed justly, for we receive the due reward of our deeds ; but this man hath done no evil. And he said to Jesus : Lord, remember me when thou shalt come into thy kingdom. And Jesus said to him : Amen I say to thee : This day thou shalt be with me in paradise. And it was almost the sixth hour; and there was darkness over all the earth until the ninth hour. And the sun was darkened ; and the veil of the temple was rent in the midst. And Jesus, crying with a loud voice, said : Father, into thy hands I commend my spirit. And saying this, he gave up the ghost.

Here a pause is made, and all kneel down.

VIDENS autem centúrio quod factum fúerat, glorificávit Deum, dicens : Vere hic homo justus erat. Et omnis turba eórum, qui simul áderant ad spectáculum

NOW, the centurion seeing what was done, glorified God, saying : Indeed this was a just man. And all the multitude of them that were come together to that sight, and saw the things

istud, et vidébant quæ fiébant, percutiéntes péctora sua revertebántur. Stabant autem omnes noti ejus a longe, et mulíeres, quæ secútæ eum erant a Galilǽa, hæc vidéntes.

that were done, returned, striking their breasts. And all his acquaintance, and the women, that had followed him from Galilee, stood afar off, beholding these things.

The Gospel is sung with the same ceremonies as on Sunday.

ET ecce vir nómine Joseph, qui erat decúrio, vir bonus et justus ; hic non consénserat consílio et áctibus eórum, ab Arimathǽa, civitáte Judǽæ, qui exspectábat et ipse regnum Dei. Hic accéssit ad Pilátum, et pétiit corpus Jesu : et depósitum invólvit síndone, et pósuit eum in monuménto excíso, in quo nondum quísquam pósitus fúerat.

AND behold there was a man named Joseph, who was a counsellor, a good and a just man (the same had not consented to their counsel and doings), of Arimathea, a city of Judea, who also himself looked for the kingdom of God. This man went to Pilate, and begged the body of Jesus. And taking him down, he wrapped him in fine linen and laid him in a sepulchre that was hewed in stone, wherein never yet any man had been laid.

Offertorium. Ps. 101.
DOMINE, exáudi oratiónem meam, et clamor meus ad te pervéniat : ne avértas fáciem tuam a me.

Offertory. Ps. 101.
O LORD, hear my prayer and let my cry come to thee : turn not away thy face from me.

Secreta.
SUSCIPE, quǽsumus, Dómine, munus oblátum, et dignánter operáre : ut quod passiónis Fílii tui Dómini nostri mystério gérimus, piis afféctibus consequámur. Per eúmdem Dóminum.

Secret.
RECEIVE, O Lord, we beseech thee, the gift we offer, and in thy mercy make us to obtain by loving devotion what we celebrate in the mystery of the Passion of thy Son our Lord. Through the same Lord.

Second Secret, p. 90.

Communio. Ps. 101.

POTUM meum cum fletu temperábam : quia élevans allisísti me : et ego sicut fœnum árui : tu autem, Dómine, in ætérnum pérmanes : tu exsúrgens miseréberis Sion, quia venit tempus miseréndi ejus.

Communion. Ps. 101.

I MINGLED my drink with weeping : for having lifted me up, thou hast thrown me down : and I am withered like grass : but thou, O Lord, remainest for ever : thou shalt arise and have mercy on Sion, for the time is come to have mercy on it.

Postcommunio.

LARGIRE sénsibus nostris, omnípotens Deus : ut per temporálem Fílii tui mortem, quam mystéria veneránda testántur, vitam te nobis dedísse perpétuam confidámus. Per eumdem Dóminum.

Postcommunion.

GRANT to us, almighty God, that through the temporal death of thy Son which these venerable mysteries testify, we may have assurance that thou hast given us eternal life. Through the same Lord.

Second Postcommunion, p. 91.

Oratio super populum.
Orémus.
Humiliáte cápita vestra Deo.

RESPICE, quǽsumus, Dómine, super hanc famíliam tuam, pro qua Dóminus noster Jesus Christus non dubitávit mánibus tradi nocéntium, et crucis subíre torméntum. Qui tecum vivit.

Prayer over the people.
Let us pray.
Bow down your heads before God.

LOOK down, we beseech thee, O Lord, on this thy family, for whose sake our Lord Jesus Christ hesitated not to yield himself into the hands of sinners, and to suffer the torments of the cross. Who liveth and reigneth.

As will be indicated later on, the Tenebræ Offices *for Maundy Thursday, Good Friday, and Holy Saturday, are said on Wednesday, Thursday, and Friday evenings, viz. on the eve of the day.*

MAUNDY THURSDAY

TENEBRÆ

RECITED ON WEDNESDAY EVENING

This office is recited towards sundown on Wednesday. A general description of Tenebræ is given in the Introduction to this volume.

The psalms of all three nocturns for this day were those assigned to Thursday's Matins in the ancient Roman Psalter. Many of them, and in particular Psalms 68, 69, 70, 71, 73 and 76 are Messianic psalms and apply to the Passion. According to an ancient custom the antiphons are taken from the psalms. The responsories after each lesson are proper to Holy Week. The aptness of their choice is striking ; the responsories of the fourth, fifth and eighth lessons were composed by the Church and are probably of Byzantine origin.

The first nocturn lessons of these three days are from Jeremias, lamenting the first destruction of Jerusalem, but a more terrible catastrophe awaits the deicide city a few years after the death of Our Lord. The *Lamentations* are also the voice of the Church, the true Sion, mourning the death of her Bridegroom. The second nocturn lessons for these three days are taken from St. Augustine's Commentaries on the Psalms, those passages which bear upon the Passion having been chosen. The third nocturn lessons are from the well-known chapter of the Epistle to the Corinthians in which St. Paul speaks of the institution of the Holy Eucharist, and this in order to prepare us for tomorrow's ceremony.

After the Pater, Ave, *and* Credo, *have been said secretly, the first Nocturn begins as follows.*

THE FIRST NOCTURN

Aña. Zelus domus tuæ comédit me, et oppró- | *Ant.* The zeal of thy house hath eaten me up ; and the

bria exprobrántium tibi cecidérunt super me.

Psalm 68.

SALVUM me fac, Deus : * quóniam intravérunt aquæ usque ad ánimam meam.

Infíxus sum in limo profúndi : * et non est substántia.

Veni in altitúdinem maris : * et tempéstas demérsit me.

Laborávi clamans, raucæ factæ sunt fauces meæ : * defecérunt óculi mei, dum spero in Deum meum.

Multiplicáti sunt super capíllos cápitis mei : * qui odérunt me gratis.

Confortáti sunt qui persecúti sunt me inimíci mei injúste : * quæ non rápui, tunc exsolvébam.

Deus, tu scis insipiéntiam meam : * et delícta mea a te non sunt abscóndita.

Non erubéscant in me, qui exspéctant te, Dómine : * Dómine virtútum.

Non confundántur super me : * qui quærunt te, Deus Israël.

Quóniam propter te sustínui oppróbrium : * opéruit confúsio, fáciem meam.

Extráneus factus sum

reproaches of them that reproached thee, are fallen upon me.

Psalm. 68.

SAVE me, O God : for the waters are come in even unto my soul.

I stick fast in the mire of the deep : and there is no sure standing.

I am come into the depth of the sea : and a tempest hath overwhelmed me.

I have laboured with crying : my jaws are become hoarse : my eyes have failed, whilst I hope in my God.

They are multiplied above the hairs of my head, who hate me without cause.

My enemies are grown strong, who have wrongfully persecuted me : then did I pay that which I took not away.

O God thou knowest my foolishness ; and my offences, *the offences which I have taken upon myself*, are not hidden from thee.

Let them not be ashamed for me, who look for thee, O Lord, the Lord of hosts.

Let them not be confounded on my account, who seek thee, O God of Israel.

Because for thy sake I have borne reproach : shame hath covered my face.

I am become a stranger to

frátribus meis : * et peregrínus fíliis matris meæ.

Quóniam zelus domus tuæ comédit me : * et oppróbria exprobrántium tibi cecidérunt super me.

Et opérui in jejúnio ánimam meam : * et factum est in oppróbrium mihi.

Et pósui vestiméntum meum cilícium ; * et factus sum illis in parábolam.

Advérsum me loquebántur qui sedébant in porta : * et in me psallébant qui bibébant vinum.

Ego vero oratiónem meam ad te, Dómine : * tempus beneplácíti Deus.

In multitúdine misericórdiæ tuæ exáudi me : * in veritáte salútis tuæ.

Erípe me de luto, ut non infígar : * líbera me ab iis qui odérunt me, et de profúndis aquárum.

Non me demérgat tempéstas aquæ, neque absórbeat me profúndum : * neque úrgeat super me púteus os suum.

Exáudi me, Dómine, quóniam benígna est misericórdia tua : * secúndum multitúdinem miseratiónum tuárum réspice in me.

Et ne avértas fáciem

my brethren, and an alien to the sons of my mother.

For the zeal of thy house hath eaten me up : and the reproaches of them that reproached thee, are fallen upon me.

And I covered my soul in fasting and it was made a reproach to me.

And I made hair-cloth my garment : and I became a by-word to them.

They that sat in the gate spoke against me : and they that drank wine made me their song.

But as for me, my prayer is to thee, O Lord : for the time of thy good pleasure, O God.

In the multitude of thy mercy hear me, in the truth of thy salvation.

Draw me out of the mire, that I may not stick fast : deliver me from them that hate me, and out of the deep waters.

Let not the tempest of water drown me, nor the deep swallow me up : and let not the pit shut her mouth upon me.

Hear me, O Lord, for thy mercy is kind : look upon me according to the multitude of thy tender mercies.

And turn not away thy

tuam a púero tuo : * quóniam tríbulor, velóciter exáudi me.

Inténde ánimæ meæ et líbera eam : * propter inimícos meos éripe me.

Tu scis impropérium meum, et confusiónem meam : * et reveréntiam meam.

In conspéctu tuo sunt omnes qui tríbulant me : * impropérium exspectávit cor meum et misériam.

Et sustínui qui simul contristarétur, et non fuit : * et qui consolarétur, et non invéni.

Et dedérunt in escam meam fel : * et in siti mea potavérunt me acéto.

Fiat mensa eórum coram ipsis in láqueum : * et in retributiónes, et in scándalum.

Obscuréntur óculi eórum ne vídeant : * et dorsum eórum semper incúrva.

Effúnde super eos iram tuam : * et furor iræ tuæ comprehéndat eos.

Fiat habitátio eórum desérta : * et in tabernáculis eórum non sit qui inhábitet.

Quóniam quem tu percussísti, persecúti sunt : * et super dolórem vúlnerum meórum addidérunt.

face from thy servant : for I am in trouble, hear me speedily.

Attend to my soul, and deliver it ; save me because of my enemies.

Thou knowest my reproach, and my confusion, and my shame.

In thy sight are all they that afflict me ; my heart hath experienced reproach and misery.

And I looked for one that would grieve together with me, but there was none : and for one that would comfort me, and I found none.

And they gave me gall for my food, and in my thirst, they gave me vinegar to drink.

Let their table become as a snare before them, and a recompense, and a stumbling block.

Let their eyes be darkened that they see not : and their back bow thou down always.

Pour out thy indignation upon them : and let thy wrathful anger take hold of them.

Let their habitation be made desolate : and let there be none to dwell in their tabernacles.

Because they have persecuted him whom thou hast smitten : and they have added to the grief of my wounds.

Appóne iniquitátem super iniquitátem eórum : * et non intrent in justítiam tuam.

Deleántur de líbro vivéntium : * et cum justis non scribántur.

Ego sum pauper et dolens : * salus tua, Deus, suscépit me.

Laudábo nomen Dei cum cántico : * et magnificábo eum in laude.

Et placébit Deo super vítulum novéllum : * córnua producéntem et úngulas.

Víideant páuperes et læténtur : * quǽrite Deum, et vivet ánima vestra.

Quóniam exaudívit páuperes Dóminus : * et vinctos suos non despéxit.

Laudent illum cæli et terra : * mare et ómnia reptília in eis.

Quóniam Deus salvam fáciet Sion : * et ædificabúntur civitátes Juda.

Et inhabitábunt ibi : * et hereditáte acquírent eam.

Et semen servórum ejus possidébit eam : * et qui, díligunt nomen ejus habitábunt in ea.

Aña. Zelus domus tuæ comédit me, et oppróbria exprobrán-

Add thou iniquity upon their iniquity : and let them not come into thy justice.

Let them be blotted out of the book of the living : and with the just let them not be written.

But I am poor and sorrowful : thy salvation, O God, hath set me up.

I will praise the name of God with a canticle : and I will magnify him with praise.

And it shall please God better than a young calf, that bringeth forth horns and hoofs.

Let the poor see and rejoice : Seek ye God, and your soul shall live.

For the Lord hath heard the poor, and hath not despised his prisoners.

Let the heavens and the earth praise him ; the sea, and every thing that creepeth therein.

For God will save Sion : and the cities of Juda shall be built up.

And they shall dwell there, and acquire it by inheritance.

And the seed of his servants shall possess it : and they that love his name shall dwell therein.

Ant. The zeal of thy house hath eaten me up ; and the reproaches of them that re-

tium tibi cecidérunt super me.

Aña. Avertántur retrórsum, et erubéscant, qui cógitant mihi mala.

Psalm. 69.

DEUS in adjutórium meum inténde : * Dómine, ad adjuvándum me festína.

Confundántur et revereántur : * qui quærunt ánimam meam.

Avertántur retrórsum, et erubéscant : * qui volunt mihi mala.

Avertántur statim erubéscéntes : * qui dicunt mihi : Euge, euge.

Exsúltent et læténtur in te omnes qui quærunt te : * et dicant semper : Magnificétur Dóminus, qui díligunt salutáre tuum.

Ego vero egénus et pauper sum : * Deus, ádjuva me.

Adjútor meus et liberátor meus es tu : * Dómine, ne moréris.

Aña. Avertántur retrórsum, et erubéscant, qui cógitant mihi mala.

Aña. Deus meus, éripe me de manu peccatóris.

Psalm. 70.

IN te, Dómine, sperávi, non confúndar in ætérnum : * in justítia tua líbera me, et éripe me.

proached thee, are fallen upon me.

Ant. Let them that devise evils against me be turned back, and let them blush for shame.

Psalm 69.

O GOD, come to my assistance : O Lord, make haste to help me.

Let them be confounded and ashamed that seek my soul.

Let them be turned backward, and blush for shame, that desire evils to me.

Let them presently be turned away blushing for shame, that say to me : 'Tis well, 'tis well.

Let all that seek thee rejoice and be glad in thee : and let such as love thy salvation say always : The Lord be magnified.

But I am needy and poor; O God, help me.

Thou art my helper and my deliverer : O Lord make no delay.

Ant. Let them that devise evils against me, be turned back, and let them blush for shame.

Ant. Deliver me, O my God, out of the hand of the sinner.

Psalm 70.

IN thee, O Lord, I have hoped, let me never be put to confusion : deliver me in thy justice, and rescue me.

Inclína ad me aurem tuam : * et salva me.

Esto mihi in Deum protectórem et in locum munítum : * ut salvum me fácias.

Quóniam firmaméntum meum : * et refúgium meum es tu.

Deus meus, éripe me de manu peccatóris : * et de manu contra legem agéntis et iníqui.

Quóniam tu es patiéntia mea, Dómine : * Dómine, spes mea a juventúte mea.

In te confirmátus sum ex útero : * de ventre matris meæ tu es protéctor meus.

In te cantátio mea, semper : * tamquam prodígium factus sum multis, et tu adjútor fortis.

Repleátur os meum laude, ut cantem glóriam tuam : * tota die magnitúdinem tuam.

Ne projícias me in témpore senectútis : * cum defécerit virtus mea ne derelínquas me.

Quia dixérunt inimíci mei mihi : * et qui custodiébant ánimam meam consílium fecérunt in unum.

Dicéntes : Deus derelíquit eum, persequímini et comprehéndite eum : * quia non est qui erípiat.

Deus, ne elongéris a

Incline thine ear unto me, and save me.

Be thou unto me a God, a protector, and a place of strength, that thou mayest make me safe.

For thou art my firmament and my refuge.

Deliver me, O my God, out of the hand of the sinner, and out of the hand of the transgressor of the law, and of the unjust.

For thou art my patience, O Lord : my hope, O Lord, from my youth.

By thee have I been confirmed from the womb : from my mother's womb thou art my protector.

Of thee shall I continually sing : I am become unto many as a wonder : but thou art a strong helper.

Let my mouth be filled with praise, that I may sing thy glory : thy greatness all the day long.

Cast me not off in the time of old age ; when my strength shall fail, do not thou forsake me.

For my enemies have spoken against me ; and they that watched my soul have consulted together.

Saying : God hath forsaken him : pursue and take him, for there is none to deliver him.

O God, be not thou far

me : * Deus meus, in auxílium meum réspice.

Confundántur et defíciant detrahéntes ánimæ meæ : * operiántur confusióne et pudóre, qui quærunt mala mihi.

Ego autem semper sperábo : * et adjíciam super omnem laudem tuam.

Os meum annuntiávit justítiam tuam : * tota die salutáre tuum.

Quóniam non cognóvi litteratúram, introíbo in poténtias Dómini : * Dómine, memorábor justítiæ tuæ solíus.

Deus, docuísti me a juventúte mea : * et usque nunc pronuntiábo mirabília tua.

Et usque in senéctam et sénium : * Deus, ne derelínquas me.

Donec annúntiem bráchium tuum : * generatióni omni, quæ ventúra est.

Poténtiam tuam et justítiam tuam, Deus, usque in altíssima, quæ fecísti magnália : * Deus, quis símilis tibi?

Quantas ostendísti mihi tribulatiónes multas et malas : et convérsus vivificásti me : * et de abýssis terræ íterum reduxísti me.

Multiplicásti magnificéntiam tuam : * et con-

from me : O my God, make haste to help me.

Let them be confounded and come to nothing that detract my soul : let them be covered with confusion and shame that seek my hurt.

But I will always hope : and will add to thy praise.

My mouth shall show forth thy justice : thy salvation all the day long.

Because I have not known learning, I will enter into the powers of the Lord : O Lord, I will be mindful of thy justice alone.

Thou hast taught me, O God, from my youth, and till now I will declare thy wonderful works.

And unto old age and grey hairs, O God, forsake me not.

Until I show forth thy arm to all the generation that is to come.

Thy power, and thy justice, O God, even to the highest, great things thou hast done ; O God, who is like to thee?

How great troubles hast thou showed me, many and grievous : and turning thou hast brought me to life, and hast brought me back again from the depths of the earth.

Thou hast multiplied thy magnificence ; and turning

vérsus consolátus es me.

Nam et ego confitébor tibi in vasis psalmi veritátem tuam : * Deus, psallam tibi in cíthara, sanctus Israël.

Exsultábunt lábia mea cum cantávero tibi : * et ánima mea, quam redemísti.

Sed et lingua mea tota die meditábitur justítiam tuam : * cum confúsi et revériti fúerint qui quærunt mala mihi.

Aña. Deus meus, eripe me de manu peccatóris.

℣. Avertántur retrórsum, et erubéscant.

℟. Qui cógitant mihi mala.

to me, thou hast comforted me.

Far I will also give praise to thee : I will extol thy truth with the instruments of psaltery : O God, I will sing to thee with the harp, thou holy one of Israel.

My lips shall greatly rejoice when I shall sing to thee : and my soul which thou hast redeemed.

Yea and my tongue also shall meditate on thy justice all the day : when they shall be confounded and put to shame that seek evils to me.

Ant. Deliver me, O my God, out of the hand of the sinner.

℣. Let them be turned backward, and let them blush for shame.

℟. That devise evil things against me.

Here is said the Pater *noster, but all in secret.*

FIRST LESSON

Incipit Lamentátio Jeremíæ Prophetæ.
Cap. 1.

ALEPH. Quómodo sedet sola civítas plena pópulo : facta est quasi vídua dómina géntium, princeps provínciárum facta est sub tribúto.

BETH. Plorans plorávit in nocte et lácrimæ ejus in maxíllis ejus : non est qui consolétur eam ex ómnibus charis ejus. Omnes amíci ejus

Here beginneth the Lamentation of Jeremias the Prophet. *Ch. i.*

ALEPH. How doth the city sit solitary, that was full of people ! how is the mistress of nations become as a widow : the princes of provinces made tributary !

BETH. Weeping she hath wept in the night, and her tears are on her cheeks : there is none to comfort her among them all that were dear to her : all her friends

sprevérunt eam, et facti sunt ei inimíci.

GHIMEL. Migrávit Judas propter afflictiónem, et multitúdinem servitútis : habitávit inter gentes, nec invénit réquiem. Omnes persecutóres ejus apprehendérunt eam inter angústias.

DALETH. Viæ Sion lugent, eo quod non sint qui véniant ad solemnitátem : omnes portæ ejus destrúctæ, sacerdótes ejus geméntes, vírgines ejus squálidæ, et ipsa oppréssa amaritúdine.

HE. Facti sunt hostes ejus in cápite, inimíci ejus locupletáti sunt : quia Dóminus locútus est super eam propter multitúdinem iniquitátum ejus. Párvuli ejus ducti sunt in captivitátem, ante fáciem tribulántis.

Jerúsalem, Jerúsalem, convértere ad Dóminum Deum tuum.

℟. In monte Olivéti orávit ad Patrem : Pater, si fíeri potest, tránseat a me calix iste : * spíritus quidem promptus est, caro autem infírma.

℣. Vigiláte, et oráte, ut non intrétis in tentatiónem.

* Spíritus.

have despised her, and are become her enemies.

GHIMEL. Juda hath removed her dwelling-place because of her affliction, and the greatness of her bondage : she hath dwelt among the nations, and she hath found no rest : all her persecutors have taken her in the midst of straits.

DALETH. The ways of Sion mourn, because there are none that come to the solemn feast : all her gates are broken down : her priests sigh, her virgins are in affliction, and she is oppressed with bitterness.

HE. Her adversaries are become her lords, her enemies are enriched : because the Lord hath spoken against her for the multitude of her iniquities : her children are led into captivity, before the face of the oppressor.

Jerusalem, Jerusalem, be converted to the Lord thy God.

℟. He prayed to his Father on Mount Olivet : Father, if it be possible, let this chalice pass from me : * the spirit, indeed, is willing, but the flesh is weak.

℣. Watch and pray, that ye may not enter into temptation.

* The spirit.

SECOND LESSON

VAU. Et egréssus est a fília Sion omnis decor ejus : facti sunt príncipes ejus, velut aríetes non inveniéntes páscua, et abiérunt absque fortitúdine, ante fáciem subsequéntis.

ZAIN. Recordáta est Jerúsalem diérum afflictiónis suæ, et prævaricatiónis ómnium desiderabílium suórum, quæ habúerat a diébus antíquis, cum cáderet pópulus ejus in manu hostíli, et non esset auxiliátor. Vidérunt eam hostes, et derisérunt sábbata ejus.

HETH. Peccátum peccávit Jerúsalem ; proptérea instábilis facta est. Omnes qui glorificábant eam, sprevérunt illam : quia vidérunt ignomíniam ejus. Ipsa autem, gemens convérsa est retrórsum.

TETH. Sordes ejus in pédibus ejus, nec recordáta est finis sui. Depósita est veheménter, non habens consolatórem. Vide, Dómine, afflictiónem meam : quóniam eréctus est inimícus.

Jerúsalem, Jerúsalem, convértere ad Dóminum Deum tuum.

℞. Tristis est ánima mea usque ad mortem : sustinéte hic et vigiláte mecum : nunc vidébitis

VAU. And from the daughter of Sion all her beauty is departed : her princes are become like rams that find no pastures : and they are gone away without strength before the face of the pursuer.

ZAIN. Jerusalem hath remembered the days of her affliction, and prevarication of all her desirable things, which she had from the days of old, when her people fell in the enemy's hand, and there was no helper : the enemies have seen her, and have mocked at her sabbaths.

HETH. Jerusalem hath grievously sinned, therefore is she become unstable : all that honoured her have despised her, because they have seen her shame : but she sighed and turned backward.

TETH. Her filthiness is on her feet, and she hath not remembered her end : she is wonderfully cast down, not having a comforter : behold, O Lord, my affliction, because the enemy is lifted up.

Jerusalem, Jerusalem, be converted to the Lord thy God.

℞. My soul is sorrowful even to death : stay here, and watch with me : now ye shall see a multitude, that

turbam quæ circúmdabit me : * Vos fugam capiétis, et ego vadam immolári pro vobis.

℣. Ecce appropínquat hora, et Fílius hóminis tradétur in manus peccatórum.

* Vos.

will surround me : * Ye will take to flight, and I shall go to be sacrificed for you.

℣. Behold the hour is at hand, when the Son of Man shall be delivered into the hands of sinners.

* Ye.

THIRD LESSON

JOD. Manum suam misit hostis ad ómnia desiderabília ejus : quia vidit gentes ingréssas sanctuárium suum, de quibus præcéperas ne intrárent in ecclésiam tuam.

CAPH. Omnis pópulus ejus gemens, et quærens panem, dedérunt pretiósa quæque pro cibo ad refocillándam ánimam. Vide, Dómine, et considera, quóniam facta sum vilis.

LAMED. O vos omnes qui transítis per viam, atténdite, et vidéte si est dolor sicut dolor meus : quóniam vindemiávit me, ut locútus est Dóminus in die iræ furóris sui.

MEM. De excélso misit ignem in óssibus meis, et erudívit me : expándit rete pédibus meis, convértit me retrórsum : pósuit me desolátam, tota die mœróre conféctam.

NUN. Vigilávit jugum iniquitátum meárum :

JOD. The enemy hath put out his hand to all her desirable things : for she hath seen the Gentiles enter into her sanctuary, of whom thou gavest commandment that they should not enter into thy church.

CAPH. All her people sigh, they seek bread : they have given all their precious things for food to relieve the soul. See, O Lord, and consider, for I am become vile.

LAMED. O all ye that pass by the way, attend, and see if there be any sorrow like to my sorrow : for he hath made a vintage of me, as the Lord spoke in the day of his fierce anger.

MEM. From above he hath sent fire into my bones, and hath chastised me : he hath spread a net for my feet, he hath turned me back ; he hath made me desolate, wasted with sorrow all the day long.

NUN. The yoke of my iniquities hath watched for me :

in manu ejus convolútæ sunt, et impósitæ collo meo : infirmáta est virtus mea : dedit me Dóminus in manu, de qua non pótero súrgere.

they are folded together in his hand, and put upon my neck : my strength is weakened : the Lord hath delivered me into a hand, out of which I am not able to rise.

Jerúsalem, Jerúsalem, convértere ad Dóminum Deum tuum.

Jerusalem, Jerusalem, be converted to the Lord thy God.

℞. Ecce vídimus eum non habéntem spéciem, neque decórem ; aspéctus ejus in eo non est : hic peccáta nostra portávit et pro nobis dolet : ipse autem vulnerátus est propter iniquitátes nostras : Cujus livóre sanáti sumus.

℞. Lo ! we have seen him as one not having beauty nor comeliness ; there is no sightliness in him : he hath borne our sins, and he grieves for us : and he was wounded for our iniquities : * By his wounds we have been healed.

℣. Vere languóres nostros ipse tulit, et dolóres nostros ipse portávit.

℣. Surely he hath borne our infirmities, and carried our sorrows.

* Cujus.
Here is repeated : Ecce vídimus.

* By.
Here is repeated : Lo ! we have seen.

THE SECOND NOCTURN

Aña. Liberávit Dóminus páuperem a poténte, et ínopem, cui non erat adjútor.

Ant. The Lord hath delivered the poor from the mighty ; and the needy that had no helper.

Psalm. 71.

DEUS, judícium tuum regi da : * et justítiam tuam fílio regis :

Psalm 71.

GIVE to the king thy judgment, O God ; and to the king's son thy justice :

Judicáre pópulum tuum in justítia : * et páuperes tuos in judício.

To judge thy people with justice, and thy poor with judgment.

Suscípiant montes pacem pópulo : * et colles justítiam.

Let the mountains receive peace for the people, and the hills justice.

Judicábit páuperes

He shall judge the poor of

pópuli, et salvos fáciet fílios páuperum : * et humiliábit calumniatórem.

Et permanébit cum sole, et ante lunam : * in generatióne et generatiónem.

Descéndet sicut plúvia in vellus : * et sicut stillicídia stillántia super terram.

Oriétur in diébus ejus justítia, et abundántia pacis : * donec auferátur luna.

Et dominábitur a mari usque ad mare : * et a flúmine usque ad términos orbis terrárum.

Coram illo prócident Æthíopes : * et inimíci ejus terram lingent.

Reges Tharsis et ínsulæ múnera ófferent : * reges Arabum et Saba dona addúcent.

Et adorábunt eum omnes reges terræ : * omnes gentes sérvient ei.

Quia liberábit páuperem a poténte : * et páuperem cui non erat adjútor.

Parcet páuperi et ínopi : * et ánimas páuperum salvas fáciet.

Ex usúris et iniquitáte rédimet ánimas eórum : * et honorábile nomen eórum coram illo.

the people, and he shall save the children of the poor, and he shall humble the oppressor.

And *his kingdom on earth* shall continue with the sun ; and before the moon, throughout all generations.

He shall come down like rain upon the fleece : and as showers falling gently upon the earth.

In his days justice shall spring up, and abundance of peace : till the moon be taken away.

And he shall rule from sea to sea : and from the river *Jordan* to the ends of the earth.

Before him the Ethiopians shall fall down : and his enemies shall lick the ground.

The kings of Tharsis and the islands shall offer presents : the kings of the Arabians and of Saba shall bring gifts.

And all kings of the earth shall adore him ; all nations shall serve him.

For he shall deliver the poor from the mighty : and the needy that had no helper.

He shall spare the *human race which is* poor and needy : and he shall save the souls of the poor.

He shall redeem their souls from the usuries and iniquity of *Satan :* and their name shall be honourable in his sight.

Et vivet, et dábitur ei de aura Arábiæ, et adorábunt de ipso semper : * tota die benedícent ei.

Et erit firmaméntum in terra in summis móntium, superextollétur super Líbanum fructus ejus : * et florébunt de civitáte sicut fœnum terræ.

Sit nomen ejus benedíctum in sǽcula : * ante solem pérmanet nomen ejus.

Et benedicéntur in ipso omnes tribus terræ : * omnes gentes magnificábunt eum.

Benedíctus Dóminus Deus Israël : * qui facit mirabília solus.

Et benedíctum nomen majestátis ejus in ætérnum : * et replébitur majestáte ejus omnis terra : fiat, fiat.

Aña. Liberávit Dóminus páuperem a poténte, et ínopem cui non erat adjútor.

Aña. Cogitavérunt ímpii, et locúti sunt nequítiam : iniquitátem in excélso locúti sunt.

Psalm. 72.

QUAM bonus Israël Deus : * his qui recto sunt corde !

Mei autem pene moti sunt pedes : * pene effúsi sunt gressus mei :

And he shall live, and to him shall be given of the gold of Arabia : for him they shall always adore : they shall bless him all the day.

He is the Bread of life ; therefore, under his reign there shall be a firmament on the earth, on the tops of mountains : above Libanus shall the fruit thereof be exalted : and they of the city shall flourish like the grass of the earth.

Let his name be blessed for evermore : his name continueth before the sun.

And in him shall all the tribes of the earth be blessed : all nations shall magnify him.

Blessed be the Lord the God of Israel, who alone doth wonderful things.

And blessed be the name of his majesty for ever : and the whole earth shall be filled with his majesty. So be it. So be it.

Ant. The Lord hath delivered the poor from the mighty ; and the needy that had no helper.

Ant. The ungodly have thought and spoken wickedness : they have spoken iniquity on high.

Psalm 72.

HOW good is God to Israel, to them that are of a right heart !

But my feet were almost moved ; my steps had well nigh slipt :

Quia zelávi super iníquos : * pacem peccatórum videns.

Because I had a zeal on occasion of the wicked, seeing the prosperity of sinners.

Quia non est respéctus morti eórum : * et firmaméntum in plaga eórum.

For there is no regard to their death ; nor is there strength in their stripes.

In labóre hóminum non sunt : * et cum homínibus non flagellabúntur.

They are not in the labour of men : neither shall they be scourged like other men.

Ideo ténuit eos supérbia : * opérti sunt iniquitáte et impietáte sua.

Therefore pride hath held them fast : they are covered with their iniquity and their wickedness.

Pródiit quasi ex ádipe iníquitas eórum : * transiérunt in afféctum cordis.

Their iniquity hath come forth, as it were from fatness : they have passed intó the affection of the heart.

Cogitavérunt et locúti sunt nequítiam : * iniquitátem in excélso locúti sunt.

They have thought and spoken wickedness : they have spoken iniquity on high.

Posuérunt in cælum os suum : * et lingua eórum transívit in terra.

They have set their mouth against heaven : and their tongue hath passed through the earth.

Ideo convertétur pópulus meus, hic : * et dies pleni inveniéntur in eis.

Therefore will my people return here : and full days shall be found in them.

Et dixérunt : Quómodo scit Deus : * et si est sciéntia in Excélso?

And they said : How doth God know, and is there knowledge in the Most High?

Ecce ipsi peccatóres, et abundántes in sǽculo : * obtinuérunt divítias.

Behold these are sinners ; and yet abounding in the world, they have obtained riches.

Et dixit : Ergo sine causa justificávi cor meum : * et lavi inter innocéntes manus meas.

And I said : Then have I in vain justified my heart, and washed my hands among the innocent.

Et fui flagellátus tota

And I have been scourged

die : * et castigátio mea in matutínis.

Si dicébam : Narrábo sic : * ecce natiónem filiórum tuórum reprobávi.

Existimábam ut cognóscerem hoc : * labor est ante me :

Donec intrem in sanctuárium Dei : * et intélligam in novíssimis eórum.

Verúmtamen propter dolos posuísti eis : * dejecísti eos dum allevaréntur.

Quómodo facti sunt in desolatiónem, súbito defecérunt : * periérunt propter iniquitátem suam.

Velut sómnium surgéntium, Dómine : * in civitáte tua imáginem ipsórum ad níhilum rédiges.

Quia inflammátum est cor meum, et renes mei commutáti sunt : * et ego ad níhilum redáctus sum, et nescívi.

Ut juméntum factus sum apud te : * et ego semper tecum.

Tenuísti manum déxteram meam : et in voluntáte tua deduxísti me : * et cum glória suscepísti me.

Quid enim mihi est in cælo : * et a te quid vólui super terram?

all the day, and my chastisement hath been in the mornings.

If I said : I will speak thus : behold I should condemn the generation of thy children.

I studied that I might know this thing : it is as labour in my sight :

Until I go into the sanctuary of God, and understand concerning their last ends.

But indeed for deceits thou hast put it to them : when they were lifted up thou hast cast them down.

How are they brought to desolation? they have suddenly ceased to be : they have perished by reason of their iniquity.

As the dream of them that awake, O Lord, so in thy city thou shalt bring their image to nothing.

For my heart hath been inflamed, and my reins have been changed : I am brought to nothing, and I knew not.

I am become as a beast before thee : and I am always with thee.

Thou hast held me by my right hand : and by thy will thou hast conducted me : and with glory thou hast received me.

For what have I in heaven? and besides thee, what do I desire upon earth?

5*

Defécit caro mea, et cor meum : * Deus cordis mei et pars mea Deus in ætérnum.

For thee my flesh and my heart hath fainted away : thou art the God of my heart, and the God that is my portion for ever.

Quia ecce, qui elóngant se a te, períbunt : * perdidísti omnes qui fornicántur abs te.

For behold, they that go far from thee shall perish : thou hast destroyed all them that are disloyal to thee.

Mihi autem adhærére Deo bonum est : * pónere in Dómino Deo spem meam.

But it is good for me to stick close to my God, to put my hope in the Lord God.

Ut annúntiem omnes prædicatiónes tuas : * in portis fíliæ Sion.

That I may declare all thy praises in the gates of the daughter of Sion.

Aña. Cogitavérunt ímpii, et locúti sunt nequítiam : iniquitátem in excélso locúti sunt.

Ant. The ungodly have thought and spoken wickedness : they have spoken iniquity on high.

Aña. Exsúrge, Dómine, et júdica causam meam.

Ant. Arise, O Lord, and judge my cause.

Psalm. 73.

UT quid, Deus, repulísti in finem : * irátus est furor tuus super oves páscuæ tuæ?

Psalm 73.

O GOD, why hast thou cast us off unto the end? why is thy wrath enkindled against the sheep of thy pasture?

Memor esto congregatiónis tuæ : * quam possedísti ab inítio.

Remember thy congregation, which thou hast possessed from the beginning.

Redemísti virgam hereditátis tuæ : * mons Sion, in quo habitásti in eo.

The sceptre of thy inheritance, which thou hast redeemed : Mount Sion, in which thou hast dwelt.

Leva manus tuas in supérbias eórum in finem : * quanta malignátus est inimícus in sancto !

Lift up thy hands against their pride unto the end : see what things the enemy hath done wickedly in the sanctuary.

Et gloriáti sunt qui odérunt te : * in médio solemnitátis tuæ.

And they that hate thee have made their boasts, in the midst of thy solemnity.

Posuérunt signa sua, signa : * et non cognovérunt sicut in éxitu super summum.

Quasi in silva lignórum secúribus excidérunt jánuas ejus in idípsum : * in secúri et áscia dejecérunt eam.

Incendérunt igni sanctuárium tuum : * in terra polluérunt tabernáculum nóminis tui.

Dixérunt in corde suo cognátio eórum simul : * Quiéscere faciámus omnes dies festos Dei a terra.

Signa nostra non vídimus, jam non est prophéta : * et nos non cognóscet ámplius.

Usquequo Deus improperábit inimícus : * irrítat adversárius nomen tuum in finem ?

Ut quid avértis manum tuam, et déxteram tuam : * de médio sinu tuo in finem ?

Deus autem rex noster ante sǽcula : * operátus est salútem in médio terræ.

Tu confirmásti in virtúte tua mare : * contribulásti cápita dracónum in aquis.

Tu confregísti cápita dracónis : * dedísti eum escam pópulis Æthíopum.

Tu dirupísti fontes et

They have set up their ensigns for signs : and they knew not : both in the going out and on the highest top.

As with axes in a wood of trees, they have cut down at once the gates thereof : with axe and hatchet they have brought it down.

They have set fire to thy sanctuary : they have defiled the dwelling-place of thy name on the earth.

They said in their heart, the whole kindred of them together : Let us abolish all the festival days of God from the land.

Our signs we have not seen, there is now no prophet : and he will know us no more.

How long, O God, shall the enemy reproach? Is the adversary to provoke thy name for ever?

Why dost thou turn away thy hand ; and thy right hand out of the midst of thy bosom for ever?

But God is our king before ages : he hath wrought salvation in the midst of the eartn.

Thou by thy strength didst make the sea firm : thou didst crush the heads of the dragons in the waters.

Thou hast broken the heads of the dragon : thou hast given him to be meat for the Ethiopian people.

Thou hast broken up the

torréntes : * tu siccásti flúvios Ethan.

fountains, and the torrents : thou hast dried up the Ethan rivers.

Tuus est dies, et tua est nox : * tu fabricátus es auróram et solem.

Thine is the day, and thine is the night : thou hast made the dawn and the sun.

Tu fecísti omnes términos terræ : * æstátem et ver tu plasmásti ea.

Thou hast made all the borders of the earth : the summer and the spring were formed by thee.

Memor esto hujus, inimícus improperávit Dómino : * et pópulus insípiens incitávit nomen tuum.

Remember this, the enemy hath reproached the Lord : and a foolish people hath provoked thy name.

Ne tradas béstiis ánimas confiténtes tibi : * et ánimas páuperum tuórum ne obliviscáris in finem.

Deliver not up to beasts the souls that confess to thee : and forget not to the end the souls of thy poor.

Réspice in testaméntum tuum : * quia repléti sunt qui obscuráti sunt terræ, dómibus iniquitátum.

Have regard to thy covenant : for they that are the obscure of the earth have been filled with the dwellings of iniquity.

Ne avertátur húmilis factus confúsus : * pauper et inops laudábunt nomen tuum.

Let not the humble be turned away with confusion : the poor and the needy shall praise thy name.

Exsúrge, Deus, júdica causam tuam : * memor esto improperiórum tuórum, eórum quæ ab insipiénte sunt tota die.

Arise, O God, judge thy own cause : remember the reproaches with which the foolish man hath reproached thee all the day.

Ne obliviscáris voces inimicórum tuórum : * supérbia eórum qui te odérunt, ascéndit semper.

Forget not the voices of thy enemies : the pride of them that hate thee ascendeth continually.

Aña. Exsúrge, Dómine, et júdica causam meam.

Ant. Arise, O Lord, and judge my cause.

℣. Deus meus, éripe me de manu peccatóris.

℣. O my God, deliver me out of the hand of the sinner.

℟. Et de manu contra legem agéntis et iníqui.

℣. And out of the hand of the transgressor of the law, and of the unjust.

Here is said, in secret, the Pater noster.

FOURTH LESSON

Ex tractátu Sancti Augustíni Epíscopi super Psalmos.

Psalm. 54.

EXAUDI, Deus, oratiónem meam, et ne despéxeris deprecatiónem meam : inténde mihi et exáudi me. Satagéntis, sollíciti, in tribulatióne pósiti verba sunt ista. Orat multa pátiens, de malo liberári desíderans. Súperest ut videámus in quo malo sit ; et cum dícere cœperit, agnoscámus ibi nos esse : ut communicáta tribulatióne, conjungámus oratiónem. Contristátus sum, inquit in exercitatióne mea, et conturbátus sum. Ubi contristátus? ubi conturbátus? In exercitatióne mea, inquit. Hómines malos, quos pátitur, commemorátus est : eamdémque passiónem malórum hóminum, exercitatiónem suam dixit. Ne putétis gratis esse malos in hoc mundo, et nihil boni de illis ágere Deum. Omnis malus, aut ídeo vivit, ut corrigátur : aut ídeo vivit, ut per illum bonus exerceátur.

From the treatise of Saint Augustine, Bishop, upon the Psalms.

Psalm 54.

HEAR my prayer, O God, and despise not my petition : attend to me and hear me. These are the words of a man in trouble, solicitude, and affliction. He prays in his great sufferings, desiring to be freed from some evil. Let us now see what evil he lies under : and when he has told it to us, let us acknowledge ourselves in it : that by partaking of the affliction, we may join in his prayer. *I am become sorrowful in my exercise,* says he, *and I am troubled.* Where is he become sorrowful? Where is he troubled? He says : *In my exercise.* He speaks of the wicked men whom he suffers, and calls such sufferings of wicked men his exercise. Think not that the wicked are in the world for nothing, and that God works no good with them. Every wicked man lives, either to amend his life, or to exercise the good man.

℟. Amícus meus ósculi me trádidit signo : quem osculátus fúero, ipse est, tenéte eum : hoc malum fecit signum, qui per ósculum adimplévit homicídium. * Infélix prætermísit prétium sánguinis, et in fine láqueo se suspéndit.

℣. Bonum erat ei, si natus non fuísset homo ille. * Infélix.

℟. My friend hath betrayed me by the sign of a kiss : Whom I shall kiss, that is he ; hold him fast : this was the wicked sign given by him, who committed murder by a kiss. * The unhappy wretch returned the price of Blood, and, in the end, hanged himself.

℣. It had been well for that man, had he never been born. * The unhappy.

FIFTH LESSON

UTINAM ergo qui nos modo exércent, convertántur, et nobíscum exerceántur ; tamen quámdiu ita sunt, ut exérceant, non eos odérimus : quia in eo quod malus est quis eórum, utrum usque in finem perseveratúrus sit, ignorámus. Et plerúmque cum tibi vidéris odísse inimícum, fratrem odisti, et nescis. Diábolus, et ángeli ejus in Scriptúris sanctis manifestáti sunt nobis, quod ad ignem ætérnum sint destináti : ipsórum tantum desperánda est corréctio, contra quos habémus occúltam luctam : ad quam luctam nos armat apóstolus, dicens : non est nobis colluctátio advérsus carnem et sánguinem : id est, non advérsus hómines, quos vidétis, sed advérsus prín-

WOULD to God, then, they that now exercise us were converted and exercised with us ; but let us not hate them, though they continue to exercise us ; for we know not whether they will persevere to the end in their wickedness. And many times, when you imagine that you hate your enemy, it is your brother you hate, though you are ignorant of it. The holy Scriptures plainly show us, that the devil and his angels are doomed to eternal fire. It is only their amendment we may despair of, with whom we wage an invisible war ; for which the apostle arms us, saying : *Our conflict is not with flesh and blood*, that is, not with the men you see before your eyes, *but with the princes, and powers, and rulers of the world of this darkness.* And lest by his saying, *of the*

cipes, et potestátes, et rectóres mundi, tenebrárum harum. Ne forte cum dixísset, mundi, intellígeres dǽmones esse rectóres cæli et terræ : mundi dixit, tenebrárum harum : mundi dixit, amatórum mundi : mundi dixit, impiórum et iniquórum : mundi dixit, de quo dicit Evangélium : Et mundus eum non cognóvit.

℟. Judas mercátor péssimus ósculo pétiit Dóminum : ille ut agnus ínnocens non negávit Judæ ósculum : * Denariórum número Christum Judǽis trádidit.

℣. Mélius illi erat, si natus non fuísset.

* Denariórum.

world, you might think perhaps, that the devils are rulers of heaven and earth, he added, *of this darkness.* By the world, then, he meant the lovers of the world : by the world, he meant the impious and the wicked : by the world, he meant that which the Gospel speaks of : *And the world knew him not.*

℟. Judas, the impious trader, betrayed his Lord with a kiss : He, as an innocent Lamb, refused not the kiss to Judas : * Who, for a few pence, delivered Christ up to the Jews.

℣. It would have been better for him, had he not been born.

* Who.

SIXTH LESSON

QUONIAM vidi iniquitátem et contradictiónem in civitáte. Atténde glóriam crucis ipsíus. Jam in fronte regum crux illa fixa est, cui inimíci insultavérunt. Efféctus probávit virtútem : dómuit orbem non ferro, sed ligno. Lignum crucis contuméliis dignum visum est inimícis, et ante ipsum lignum stantes caput agitábant, et dicébant : Si Fílius Dei est, descéndat de cruce. Extendébat ille manus suas

FOR I have seen injustice and strife in the city. See the glory of the cross! That cross, which was an object of derision to his enemies, is now placed on the foreheads of kings. The effect is a proof of his power : he conquered the world not by the sword, but by the wood. The wood of the cross was thought a subject of scorn by his enemies, who, as they stood before it, shook their heads and said : *If he be the Son of God, let him come down from the*

ad pópulum non credén-
tem, et contradicéntem.
Si enim justus est qui ex
fide vivit, iníquus est
qui non habet fidem.
Quod ergo hic ait, iniquitátem, perfídiam intél-
lige.   Vidébat ergo Dó-
minus in civitáte iniqui-
tátem et contradictió-
nem, et extendébat ma-
nus suas ad pópulum
non credéntem et con-
tradicéntem : et tamen
et ipsos exspéctans di-
cébat : Pater, ignósce illis, quia nésciunt quid
fáciunt.

℞. Unus ex discípulis
meis tradet me hódie :
væ illi, per quem tradar
ego ! * Mélius illi erat, si
natus non fuísset.

℣. Qui intíngit mecum
manum in parópside,
hic me traditúrus est in
manus peccatórum.
    * Mélius.
    Here is repeated : Unus
ex discípulis meis.

cross.   He stretched forth his
hands to an unbelieving and
seditious people.   For if he is
just that lives by faith, he is
unjust that has not faith.
By *injustice* then, here you
must understand infidelity.
Our Lord, therefore, *saw
injustice and strife in the
city*, and stretched forth his
hands to an unbelieving and
seditious people : and yet
he waited for them, saying :
*Father, forgive them, for
they know not what they do.*

℞. One of my disciples
will this day betray me :
woe to him, by whom I shall
be betrayed ! * It had been
better for him, if he had
not been born.
    ℣. He that dips his hand
with me in the dish, he it is
that is about to betray me
into the hands of sinners.
    * It had.
    Here is repeated : One of
my disciples.

THE THIRD NOCTURN

Aña. Dixi iníquis :
Nolíte loqui advérsus
Deum iniquitátem.
    Psalm. 74.
CONFITEBIMUR ti-
    bi, Deus : * confité-
bimur, et invocábimus
nomen tuum.
    Narrábimus mirabília
tua : * cum accépero
tempus, ego justítias ju-
dicábo.

Ant. I said to the wicked : Speak not iniquity
against God.
    Psalm 74.
WE will praise thee, O
    God : we will praise,
and we will call upon thy
name.
    We will relate thy won-
drous works : when, *says the
Lord*, I shall take a time, I
will judge justice.

Liquefácta est terra, et omnes qui hábitant in ea : * ego confirmávi colúmnas ejus.

The earth is melted and all that dwell therein : I have established the pillars thereof.

Dixi iníquis : Nolíte iníque ágere : * et delinquéntibus : Nolíte exaltáre cornu.

I said to the wieked : Do not act wickedly : and to the sinners : Lift not up the horn.

Nolíte extóllere in altum cornu vestrum : * Nolíte loqui advérsus Deum iniquitátem.

Lift not up your horn on high : speak not iniquity against God.

Quia neque ab oriénte, neque ab occidénte, neque a desértis móntibus : * quóniam Deus judex est.

For neither from the east, nor from the west, nor from the desert hills : for God is the judge.

Hunc humíliat, et hunc exáltat : * quia calix in manu Domini vini meri plenus misto.

One he putteth down, and another he lifteth up. For in the hand of the Lord there is a cup of stong wine full of mixture.

Et inclinávit ex hoc in hoc : verúmtamen fæx ejus non est exinaníta : * bibent omnes peccatóres terræ.

And he hath poured it out from this to that : but the dregs thereof are not emptied : all the sinners of the earth shall drink.

Ego autem annuntiábo in sǽculum : * cantábo Deo Jacob.

But I will declare for ever: I will sing to the God of Jacob.

Et ómnia córnua peccatórum confríngam : * et exaltabúntur córnua justi.

And I will break all the horns of sinners : but the horns of the just shall be exalted.

Aña. Dixi iníquis : Nolíte loqui advérsus Deum iniquitátem.

Ant. I said to the wicked : Speak not iniquity against God.

Aña. Terra trémuit et quiévit, dum exsúrgeret in judício Deus.

Ant. The earth trembled, and was still, when God arose in judgment.

Psalm. 75.

NOTUS in Judǽa Deus : * in Israël magnum nomen ejus.

Psalm 75.

IN Judea God is known, his name is great in Israël.

Et factus est in pace

And his place is in

locus ejus : * et habitátio ejus in Sion.

Ibi confrégit poténtias árcuum : * scutum, gládium, et bellum.

Illúminans tu mirabíliter a móntibus ætérnis : * turbáti sunt omnes insipiéntes corde.

Dormiérunt somnum suum : * et nihil invenérunt omnes viri divitiárum in mánibus suis.

Ab increpatióne tua Deus Jacob : * dormitavérunt qui ascendérunt equos.

Tu terríbilis es, et quis resístet tibi ? : * ex tunc ira tua.

De cælo audítum fecísti judícium : * terra trémuit et quiévit.

Cum exsúrgeret in judícium Deus : * ut salvos fáceret omnes mansuétos terræ.

Quóniam cogitátio hóminis confitébitur tibi : * et relíquiæ cogitatiónis diem festum agent tibi.

Vovéte et réddite Dómino Deo vestro : * omnes qui in circúitu ejus affértis múnera.

Terríbili et ei qui aufert spíritum príncipum : * terríbili apud reges terræ.

Aña. Terra trémuit et quiévit, dum exsúrgeret in judício Deus.

peace, and his abode in Sion.

There hath he broken the power of bows, the shield, the sword, and the battle.

Thou enlightenest wonderfully from the everlasting hills : all the foolish of heart were troubled.

They have slept their sleep : and all the men of riches have found nothing in their hands.

At thy rebuke, O God of Jacob, they have all slumbered that mounted on horseback.

Thou art terrible, and who shall resist thee? from that time thy wrath.

Thou hast caused judgment to be heard from heaven : the earth trembled and was still.

When God arose in judgment, to save all the meek of the earth.

For the thought of man shall give praise to thee : and the remainders of the thought shall keep holyday to thee.

Vow ye, and pay to the Lord your God : all you that round about him bring presents.

To him that is terrible, even to him who taketh away the spirit of princes ; to the terrible with the kings of the earth.

Ant. The earth trembled, and was still, when God arose in judgment.

Aña. In die tribula-
tiónis meæ Deum exqui-
sivi mánibus meis.

Psalm. 76.

VOCE mea ad Dómi-
num clamávi : *
voce mea ad Deum, et
inténdit mihi.

In die tribulatiónis
meæ Deum exquisívi,
mánibus meis nocte con-
tra eum : * et non sum
decéptus.

Rénuit consolári áni-
ma mea : memor fui
Dei, et delectátus sum,
et exercitátus sum, * et
defécit spíritus meus.

Anticipavérunt vigi-
lias óculi mei : * turbá-
tus sum, et non sum lo-
cútus.

Cogitávi dies antíquos
* et annos ætérnos in
mente hábui.

Et meditátus sum no-
cte cum corde meo : * et
exercitábar, et scopé-
bam spíritum meum.

Numquid in ætérnum
projíciet Deus : * aut
non appónet ut compla-
cítior sit adhuc?

Aut in finem miseri-
córdiam suam abscíndet:
* a generatióne in gene-
ratiónem?

Aut obliviscétur mi-
seréri Deus : * aut con-
tinébit in ira sua misé-
ricórdias suas?

Et dixi : Nunc cœpi :
* hæc mutátio déxteræ
excélsi.

Ant. In the day of my tribulation, I sought God with
my hands *raised up in
prayer.*

Psalm 76.

I CRIED to the Lord with
my voice ; to God with
my voice and he gave ear to
me.

In the day of my trouble
I sought God : with my
hands lifted up to him in the
night, and I was not de-
ceived.

My soul refused to be
comforted ; I remembered
God, and was delighted, and
was exercised, and my spirit
swooned away.

My eyes prevented the
watches : I was troubled,
and I spoke not.

I thought upon the days
of old : and I had in my
mind the eternal years.

And I meditated in the
night with my own heart,
and I was exercised, and I
swept my spirit.

Will God then cast off for
ever? or will he never be
more favorable again?

Or will he cut off his mercy for ever, from generation
to generation?

Or will God forget to show
mercy? or will he in his anger shut up his mercies?

And I said : Now have I begun : this the change of the
right hand of the Most High.

Memor fui óperum Dómini : * quia memor ero ab inítio mirabílium tuórum.

I remembered the works of the Lord ; for I will be mindful of thy wonders from the beginning.

Et meditábor in ómnibus opéribus tuis : * et in adinventiónibus tuis exercébor.

And I will meditate on all thy works ; and will be employed in thy inventions.

Deus in sancto via tua quis Deus magnus sicut Deus noster? * Tu es Deus, qui facis mirabília.

Thy way, O God, is in the holy place : who is the great God like our God? Thou art the God that dost wonders.

Notam fecísti in pópulis virtútem tuam : * redemísti in bráchio tuo pópulum tuum, fílios Jacob et Joseph.

Thou hast made thy power known among the nations : with thy arm thou hast redeemed thy people, the children of Jacob and Joseph.

Vidérunt te aquæ, Deus, vidérunt te aquæ : * et timuérunt, et turbátæ sunt abýssi.

The waters saw thee, O God, the waters saw thee ; and they were afraid, and the depths were troubled.

Multitúdo sónitus aquárum : * vocem dedérunt nubes.

Great was the noise of the waters : the clouds sent out a sound.

Etenim sagíttæ tuæ tránseunt : * vox tonítrui tui in rota.

For thy arrows pass : the voice of thy thunder in a wheel.

Illuxérunt coruscatiónes tuæ orbi terræ : * commóta est et contrémuit terra.

Thy lightnings enlightened the world, the earth shook and trembled,

In mari via tua, et sémitæ tuæ in aquis multis : * et vestígia tua non cognoscéntur.

Thy way is in the sea, and thy paths in many waters ; and thy footsteps shall not be known.

Deduxísti sicut oves pópulum tuum : * in manu Móysi et Aaron.

Thou hast conducted thy people like sheep, by the hand of Moses and Aaron.

Aña. In die tribulatiónis meæ Deum exquisívi mánibus meis.

Ant. In the day of my tribulation, I sought God with my hands *raised up in prayer*.

℣. Exsúrge, Dómine.
℟. Et júdica causam meam.

℣. Arise, O Lord.
℟. And judge my cause.

Here is said the Pater noster *in secret.*

SEVENTH LESSON

De Epístola prima Beati Pauli Apóstoli ad Corínthios.

Cap. 11.

HOC autem præcípio: non laudans quod non in mélius, sed in detérius convenítis. Primum quidem conveniéntibus vobis in ecclésiam, áudio scissúras esse inter vos, et ex parte credo. Nam opórtet et hǽreses esse, ut et qui probáti sunt, manifésti fiant in vobis. Conveniéntibus ergo vobis in unum jam non est Domínicam Cœnam manducáre. Unusquísque enim suam cœnam præsúmit ad manducándum. Et álius quidem ésurit, álius autem ébrius est. Numquid domos non habétis ad manducándum et bibéndum? Aut Ecclésiam Dei contémnitis, et confúnditis eos qui non habent? Quid dicam vobis? Laudo vos? In hoc non laudo.

℟. Eram quasi agnus ínnocens : ductus sum ad immolándum, et nesciébam : consílium fecérunt inimíci mei advérsum me, dicéntes : * Veníte, mittámus lignum

From the first Epistle of Saint Paul, the Apostle, to the Corinthians.

Ch. 11.

NOW this I ordain : not praising you that you come together, not for the better, but for the worse. For first of all I hear that when you come together in the church, there are schisms among you, and in part I believe it. For there must be, also, heresies ; that they also, who are approved, may be made manifest among you. When you therefore come together into one place, it is not now to eat the Lord's Supper. For every one taketh before his own supper to eat. And one indeed is hungry, and another is drunk. What, have you not houses to eat and drink in? Or despise ye the Church of God, and put them to shame that have not? What shall I say to you? Do I praise you? In this I praise you not.

℟. I was like an innocent lamb ; I was led to be sacrificed, and I knew it not : my enemies conspired against me, saying : * Come, let us put wood into his bread, and root

in panem ejus, et eradámus eum de terra vivéntium.

℣. Omnes inimíci mei advérsum me cogitábant mala mihi : verbum iníquum mandavérunt advérsum me, dicéntes :

* Veníte.

him out of the land of the living.

℣. All my enemies devised evil things against me : they uttered a wicked speech against me, saying :

* Come.

EIGHTH LESSON

EGO enim accépi a Dómino, quod et trádidi vobis, quóniam Dóminus Jesus, in qua nocte tradebátur accépit panem, et grátias agens fregit et dixit : Accípite et manducáte : hoc est Corpus meum, quod pro vobis tradétur : hoc fácite in meam commemoratiónem. Simíliter et cálicem postquam cœnávit dicens : Hic calix novum testaméntum est in meo Sánguine. Hoc fácite quotiescúmque bibétis, in meam commemoratiónem. Quotiescúmque enim manducábitis panem hunc, et cálicem bibétis mortem Dómini annuntiábitis donec véniat.

℟. Una hora non potuístis vigiláre mecum, qui exhortabámini mori pro me? * Vel Judam non vidétis, quómodo non dormit, sed festínat trádere me Judæis?

℣. Quid dormítis? Súrgite, et oráte, ne intrétis in tentatiónem.

* Vel Judam.

FOR I have received of the Lord that which also I delivered to you, that the Lord Jesus, the same night in which he was betrayed, took bread, and giving thanks, broke, and said : Take ye and eat : this is my Body which shall be delivered for you : this do for the commemoration of me. In like manner also the chalice, after he had supped, saying : This chalice is the new testament in my Blood: this do ye, as often as you shall drink it, for the commemoration of me. For as often as you shall eat this bread, and drink the chalice, you shall show the death of the Lord, until he come.

℟. Could ye not watch one hour with me, ye that exhorted each other to die for me? * Or see ye not how Judas sleepeth not, but maketh speed to deliver me up to the Jews?

℣. Why sleep ye? Arise and pray, lest ye enter into temptation.

* Or see.

NINTH LESSON

ITAQUE quicúmque manducáverit, panem hunc, vel bíberit cálicem Dómini indígne, reus erit Córporis et Sánguinis Dómini. Probet autem seípsum homo ; et sic de pane illo edat, et de cálice bibat. Qui enim mandúcat et bibit indígne, judícium sibi mandúcat et bibit, non dijúdicans Corpus Dómini. Ideo inter vos multi, infírmi et imbecílles, et dórmiunt multi. Quod, si nosmetípsos dijudicarémus, non útique judicarémur. Dum judicámur autem, a Dómino corrípimur, ut non cum hoc mundo damnémur. Itaque, fratres mei, cum convenítis ad manducándum, ínvicem exspectáte. Si quis ésurit, domi mandúcet : ut non in judícium conveniátis. Cǽtera autem, cum vénero, dispónam.

THEREFORE whosoever shall eat this bread, or drink the chalice of the Lord unworthily, shall be guilty of the Body and of the Blood of the Lord. But let a man prove himself : and so let him eat of that bread, and drink of that chalice. For he that eateth and drinketh unworthily, eateth and drinketh judgment to himself, not discerning the Body of the Lord. Therefore are there many infirm and weak among you, and many sleep. But if we would judge ourselves, we should not be judged. But whilst we are judged, we are chastised by the Lord, that we be not condemned with this world. Wherefore, my brethren, when you come together to eat, wait for one another. If any man be hungry, let him eat at home ; that you come not together unto judgment. And the rest I will set in order when I come.

℟. Senióres pópuli consílium fecérunt, * Ut Jesum dolo tenérent, et occíderent : cum gládiis et fústibus exiérunt tamquam ad latrónem.

℟. The ancients of the people consulted together, * How they might, by craft, apprehend Jesus, and kill him : they went forth with swords and clubs, as to a thief.

℣. Colligérunt pontífices et pharisǽi concílium. * Ut Jesum.

℣. The priests and pharisees held a council. * How they.

Here is repeated : Senióres pópuli.

Here is repeated : The ancients.

LAUDS

The psalms are those assigned to Thursday in the ferial office of the new Psalter, Psalms 50, 89, 35 and 146. The canticle of Moses *Cantemus Domino* is that proper to Thursday in the old Roman cursus.

Aña. Justificéris, Dómine, in sermónibus tuis, et vincas cum judicáris.

Ant. Be thou justified, O Lord, in thy words, and overcome, when thou art judged.

Psalm. 50.

MISERERE mei, Deus : * secúndum magnam misericórdiam tuam.

Et secúndum multitúdinem miseratiónum tuárum : * dele iniquitátem meam.

Amplius lava me ab iniquitáte mea : * et a peccáto meo munda me.

Quóniam iniquitátem meam ego cognósco : * et peccátum meum contra me est semper.

Tibi soli peccávi, et malum coram te feci : * ut justificéris in sermónibus tuis, et vincas cum judicáris.

Ecce enim in iniquitátibus concéptus sum : * et in peccátis concépit me mater mea.

Ecce enim veritátem dilexísti : * incérta et occúlta sapiéntiæ tuæ manifestásti mihi.

Aspérges me hyssópo, et mundábor : * lavábis

Psalm 50.

HAVE mercy on me, O God, according to thy great mercy.

And according to the multitude of thy tender mercies, blot out my iniquities.

Wash me yet more from my iniquity : and cleanse me from my sin.

For I know my iniquity : and my sin is always before me.

To thee only have I sinned, and have done evil before thee : *I confess it : do thou pardon me*, that thou mayest be justified in thy words, and mayest overcome when thou art judged.

For behold I was conceived in iniquities : and in sins did my mother conceive me.

For behold thou hast loved truth : the uncertain and hidden things of thy wisdom thou hast made manifest to me.

Thou shalt sprinkle me with hyssop, *as a leper*, and

me, et super nivem de-
albábor.

Audítui meo dabis
gáudium et lætítiam : *
et exsultábunt ossa hu-
miliáta.

Avérte fáciem tuam a
peccátis meis : * et om-
nes iniquitátes meas
dele.

Cor mundum crea in
me, Deus : * et spíritum
rectum ínnova in viscé-
ribus meis.

Ne projícias me a fá-
cie tua : * et spíritum
sanctum tuum ne áufe-
ras a me.

Redde mihi lætítiam
salutáris tui : * et spíritu
principáli confírma me.

Docébo iníquos vias
tuas : * et ímpii ad te
converténtur.

Líbera me de sanguí-
nibus, Deus, Deus salútis
meæ : et exsultábit lin-
gua mea justítiam tuam.

Dómine, lábia mea
apéries : * et os meum
annuntiábit laudem tu-
am.

Quóniam si voluísses
sacrifícium dedíssem úti-
que : * holocáustis non
delectáberis.

Sacrifícium Deo spí-
ritus contribulátus : *
cor contrítum et humi-
liátum, Deus, non de-
spícies.

Benígne fac, Dómine,

I shall be cleansed : thou
shalt wash me, and I shall
be made whiter than snow.

To my hearing thou shalt
give joy and gladness : and
the bones that have been
humbled shall rejoice.

Turn away thy face from
my sins : and blot out all my
iniquities.

Create a clean heart in
me, O God : and renew a
right spirit within my bowels.

Cast me not away from
thy face : and take not thy
holy Spirit from me.

Restore unto me the joy
of thy salvation : and
strengthen me with a per-
fect spirit.

I will teach the unjust
thy ways : and the wicked
shall be converted to thee.

Deliver me from blood, O
God, the God of my salva-
tion : and my tongue shall
extol thy justice.

O Lord, thou wilt open
my lips : and my mouth
shall declare thy praise.

For if thou hadst desired
sacrifice, I would indeed
have given it : with burnt-
offerings thou wilt not be
delighted.

A sacrifice to God is an
afflicted spirit : a contrite
and humble heart, O God,
thou wilt not despise.

Deal favourably, O Lord,

in bona voluntáte tua Sion : * ut ædificéntur muri Jerúsalem.

Tunc acceptábis sacrifícium justítiæ, oblatiónes, et holocáusta : * tunc impónent super altáre tuum vítulos.

Aña. Justificéris, Dómine, in sermónibus tuis, et vincas cum judicáris.

Aña. Dóminus tamquam ovis ad víctimam ductus est, et non apéruit os suum.

Psalm. 89.

DOMINE, refúgium factus es nobis : * a generatióne in generatiónem.

Priúsquam montes fíerent, aut formarétur terra et orbis : * a sǽculo et usque in sǽculum tu es Deus.

Ne avértas hóminem in humilitátem : * et dixísti : Convertímini, fílii hóminum.

Quóniam mille anni ante óculos tuos : * tamquam dies hestérna quæ prætériit.

Et custódia in nocte, * quæ pro níhilo habéntur, eórum anni erunt.

Mane sicut herba tránseat, mane flóreat, et tránseat : * véspere décidat, indúret, et aréscat.

Quia defécimus in ira

in thy good-will with Sion : that the walls of Jerusalem may be built up.

Then shalt thou accept the sacrifice of justice, oblations and whole-burnt offerings : then shall they lay calves upon thine altar.

Ant. Be thou justified, O Lord, in thy words, and overcome when thou art judged.

Ant. The Lord was led as a sheep to the slaughter, and he opened not his mouth.

Psalm 89.

LORD, thou hast been our refuge : from generation to generation.

Before the mountains were made, or the earth and the world was formed : from eternity, and to eternity thou art God.

Turn not man away to be brought low ; and thou hast said : Be converted, O ye sons of men.

For a thousand years, in thy sight, are but as yesterday which is past and gone.

And as a watch in the night : as things that are counted nothing, so shall their years be.

In the morning, man shall grow up like grass, in the morning he shall flourish and pass away : in the evening he shall fall, grow dry, and wither.

For in thy wrath we are

tua : * et in furóre tuo turbáti sumus.

Posuísti iniquitátes nostras in conspéctu tuo : * sǽculum nostrum in illuminatióne vultus tui.

Quóniam omnes dies nostri defecérunt : * et in ira tua defécimus.

Anni nostri sicut aránea meditabúntur : * dies annórum nostrórum in ipsis septuagínta anni.

Si autem in potentátibus, octogínta anni : * et ámplius eórum labor et dolor.

Quóniam supervénit mansuetúdo : * et corripiémur.

Quis novit potestátem iræ tuæ : * et præ timóre tuo iram tuam dinumeráre?

Déxteram tuam sic notam fac : * et erudítos corde in sapiéntia.

Convértere, Dómine, úsquequo : * et deprecábilis esto super servos tuos.

Repléti sumus mane misericórdia tua : * et exsultávimus, et delectáti sumus ómnibus diébus nostris.

Lætáti sumus pro diébus quibus nos humiliásti : * annis, quibus vídimus mala.

Réspice in servos tuos, et in ópera tua : * et dírige fílios eórum.

Et sit splendor Dómini Dei nostri super

quickly consumed : and are troubled in thy indignation.

Thou hast set our iniquities before thy eyes : our life in the light of thy countenance.

For all our days are spent: and in thy wrath we have fainted away.

Our years shall be considered as a spider : the days of our years in them are threescore and ten years.

But if in the strong, they be fourscore years : and what is more of them is labour and sorrow.

For mildness is come upon us : and we shall be corrected.

Who knoweth the power of thy anger : and, for thy fear, can number thy wrath?

So make thy right hand known : and make us learned in heart in wisdom.

Return, O Lord, how long? and be entreated in favour of thy servants.

We are filled in the morning with thy mercy : and we have rejoiced and are delighted all our days.

We have rejoiced for the days in which thou hast humbled us : for the years in which we have seen evils.

Look upon thy servants, and upon their works : and direct their children.

And let the brightness of the Lord our God be upon

nos, et ópera mánuum nostrárum dírige super nos : * et opus mánuum nostrárum dírige.

Aña. Dóminus tanquam ovis ad víctimam ductus est, et non apéruit os suum.

Aña. Contrítum est cor meum in médio mei, contremuérunt ómnia ossa mea.

Psalm. 35.

DIXIT injústus ut delínquat in semetípso : * non est timor Dei ante óculos ejus.

Quóniam dolóse egit in conspéctu ejus : * ut inveniátur iníquitas ejus ad ódium.

Verba oris ejus iníquitas, et dolus : * nóluit intellígere ut bene ágeret.

Iniquitátem meditátus est in cubíli suo : * ástitit omni viæ non bonæ, malítiam autem non odívit.

Dómine, in cælo misericórdia tua : * et véritas tua usque ad nubes.

Justítia tua sicut montes Dei : * judícia tua abýssus multa.

Hómines et juménta salvábis, Dómine, * quemádmodum multiplicásti misericórdiam tuam, Deus.

Fílii autem hóminum * in tégmine alárum tuárum sperábunt.

us, and direct thou the works of our hands over us : yea, the work of our hands do thou direct.

Ant. The Lord was led as a sheep to the slaughter, and he opened not his mouth.

Ant. My heart is broken within me ; all my bones have trembled.

Psalm 35.

THE unjust hath said within himself, that he would sin : there is no fear of God before his eyes.

For in his sight he hath done deceitfully : that his iniquity may be found unto hatred.

The words of his mouth are iniquity and guile : he would not understand that he might do well.

He hath devised iniquity on his bed : he hath set himself on every way that is not good ; but evil he hath not hated.

O Lord, thy mercy is in the heavens : and thy truth reacheth even unto the clouds.

Thy justice is as the mountains of God : thy judgments are a great deep.

Men and beasts thou wilt preserve, O Lord : O how hast thou multiplied thy mercy, O God !

But the children of men shall put their trust : under the covert of thy wings.

Inebriabúntur ab u-
bertáte domus tuæ : * et
torrénte voluptátis tuæ
potábis eos.

They shall be inebriated
with the plenteousness of
thy house : and thou shalt
make them drink of the
torrent of thy pleasure.

Quóniam apud te est
fons vitæ : * et in lúmine
tuo vidébimus lumen.

For with thee is the well
of life : and in thy light we
shall see light.

Præténde misericór-
diam tuam sciéntibus
te : * et justítiam tuam
his, qui recto sunt corde.

Stretch forth thy mercy
unto them that know thee :
and thy justice unto them
that are right of heart.

Non véniat mihi pes
supérbiæ : * et manus
peccatóris non móveat
me.

Let not the foot of pride
come unto me : and let not
the hand of the sinner move
me.

Ibi cecidérunt qui ope-
rántur iniquitátem : *
expúlsi sunt, nec potu-
érunt stare.

There are the workers of
iniquity fallen : they are
cast out, and they could not
stand.

Aña. Contrítum est
cor meum in médio mei,
contremuérunt ómnia
ossa mea.

Ant. My heart is broken
within me ; all my bones
have trembled.

Aña. Exhortátus es
in virtúte tua, et in re-
fectióne sancta tua, Dó-
mine.

Ant. Thou hast encou-
raged us by thy power, and
by thy holy refreshment, O
Lord !

CANTICLE OF MOSES
(*Exod.* 15.)

CANTEMUS Dómino:
glorióse enim ma-
gnificátus est : * equum
et ascensórem dejécit in
mare.

LET us sing to the Lord :
for he is gloriously ma-
gnified : the horse and the
rider he hath thrown into
the sea.

Fortitúdo mea et laus
mea Dóminus : * et fa-
ctus est mihi in salútem.

The Lord is my strength
and my praise : and he is become salvation to me.

Iste Deus, meus, et
glorificábo eum : * Deus
patris mei, et exaltábo
eum.

He is my God, and I will
glorify him : the God of my
father, and I will exalt him.

Dóminus   quasi   vir

The Lord is as a man of

pugnátor. Omnípotens nomen ejus : * currus Pharaónis, et exércitum ejus projécit in mare.

Elécti principes ejus submérsi sunt in Mari Rubro : * abýssi operuérunt eos, descendérunt in profúndum quasi lapis.

Déxtera tua, Dómine, magnificáta est in fortitúdine : déxtera tua, Dómine, percússit inimícum : * et in multitúdine glóriæ tuæ deposuísti adversários tuos.

Misísti iram tuam, quæ devorávit eos sicut stípulam : * et in spíritu furóris tui congregátæ sunt aquæ.

Stetit unda fluens : * congregátæ sunt abýssi in médio mari.

Dixit inimícus : pérsequar et comprehéndam : * dívidam spólia, implébitur ánima mea.

Evaginábo gládium meum : * interfíciet eos manus mea.

Flávit spíritus tuus, et opéruit eos mare : * submérsi sunt quasi plumbum in aquis veheméntibus.

Quis símilis tui in fórtibus, Dómine ? * quis símilis tui, magníficus in sanctitáte, terríbilis atque laudábilis, fáciens mirabília?

Extendísti manum tu-

war, Almighty is his name. Pharaoh's chariots and his army he hath cast into the sea.

His chosen captains are drowned in the Red Sea. The depths have covered them, they are sunk to the bottom like a stone.

Thy right hand, O Lord, is magnified in strength ; thy right hand, O Lord, hath slain the enemy. And in the multitude of thy power thou hast put down thy adversaries.

Thou hast sent thy wrath, which hath devoured them like stubble. And with the blast of thy anger the waters were gathered together.

The flowing waters stood, the depths were gathered together in the midst of the sea.

The enemy said : I will pursue and overtake, I will divide the spoils, my soul shall have its fill.

I will draw my sword, my hand shall slay them.

Thy wind blew, and the sea covered them : they sank as lead in the mighty waters.

Who is like to thee among the strong, O Lord? who is like to thee, glorious in holiness, terrible and praiseworthy, doing wonders?

Thou stretchedst forth

am, et devorávit eos terra : * dux fuísti in misericórdia tua pópulo quem redemísti.

Et portásti eum in fortitúdine tua : * ad habitáculum sanctum tuum.

Ascendérunt pópuli et iráti sunt : * dolóres obtinuérunt habitatóres Philísthiim.

Tunc conturbáti sunt príncipes Edom, robústos Moab obtínuit tremor : * obriguérunt omnes habitatóres Chánaan.

Irruat super eos formído et pavor : * in magnitúdine bráchii tui.

Fiant immóbiles quasi lapis, donec pertránseat pópulus tuus, Dómine : * donec pertránseat pópulus tuus iste, quem possedísti.

Introdúces eos, et plantábis, in monte hereditátis tuæ : * firmíssimo habitáculo tuo, quod operátus es, Dómine.

Sanctuárium tuum, Dómine, quod firmavérunt manus tuæ : * Dóminus regnábit in ætérnum, et ultra.

Ingréssus est enim eques Phárao cum cúrribus et equítibus ejus in mare : * et redúxit super eos Dóminus aquas maris.

Fílii autem Israël am-

thy hand, and the earth swallowed them. In thy mercy thou hast been a leader to the people whom thou hast redeemed :

And in thy strength thou hast carried them to thy holy habitation.

Nations rose up and were angry : sorrows took hold of the inhabitants of Philisthiim.

Then were the princes of Edom troubled, trembling seized on the stout men of Moab : all the inhabitants of Canaan became stiff.

Let fear and dread fall upon them in the greatness of thy arm.

Let them become immovable as a stone, until thy people, O Lord, pass by ; until this thy people pass by, which thou hast possessed.

Thou shalt bring them in and plant them in the mountain of thy inheritance, in thy most firm habitation, which thou hast made, O Lord :

Thy sanctuary, O Lord, which thy hands have established. The Lord shall reign for ever and ever.

For Pharaoh went in on horseback with his chariots and horsemen into the sea : and the Lord brought back upon them the waters of the sea.

But the children of Israel

bulavérunt per siccum : * in médio ejus.

Aña. Exhortátus es in virtúte tua, et in refectióne sancta tua, Dómine.

Aña. Oblátus est quia ipse vóluit ; et peccáta nostra ipse portávit.

Psalm. 146.

LAUDATE Dóminum quóniam bonus est psalmus : * Deo nostro sit jucúnda, decóraque laudátio.

Ædíficans Jerúsalem Dóminus : * dispersiónes Israélis congregábit.

Qui sanat contrítos corde : * et álligat contritiónes eórum.

Qui númerat multitúdinem stellárum : * et ómnibus eis nómina vocat.

Magnus Dóminus noster, et magna virtus ejus : * et sapiéntiæ ejus non est númerus.

Suscípiens mansuétos Dóminus : * humílians autem peccatóres usque ad terram.

Præcínite Dómino in confessióne : * psállite Deo nostro in cíthara.

Qui óperit cælum núbibus : * et parat terræ plúviam.

Qui prodúcit in móntibus fœnum : * et herbam servitúti hóminum.

Qui dat juméntis es-

walked on dry ground in the midst thereof.

Ant. Thou hast encouraged us by thy power, and by thy holy refreshment, O Lord !

Ant. He was offered because it was his own will, and he himself bore our sins.

Psalm 146.

PRAISE ye the Lord, for it is good to sing praises : let the praise of our God be joyful and comely.

The Lord buildeth up Jerusalem : he will gather together the dispersed of Israel.

Who healeth the broken of heart : and bindeth up their bruises.

Who telleth the number of the stars : and calleth them all by their names.

Great is our Lord, and great is his power : and of his widsom there is no measure.

The Lord lifteth up the meek : and bringeth the wicked down even to the ground.

Sing ye to the Lord with praise : sing unto our God upon the harp.

Who covereth the heaven with clouds : and prepareth rain for the earth.

Who maketh grass to grow on the mountains : and herbs for the service of men.

cam ipsórum : * et pullis corvórum invocántibus eum.

Non in fortitúdine equi voluntátem habébit : * nec in tíbiis viri beneplácitum erit ei.

Beneplácitum est Dómino super timéntes eum : * et in eis, qui sperant super misericórdia ejus.

Aña. Oblátus est quia ipse vóluit, et peccáta nostra ipse portávit.

℣. Homo pacis meæ, in quo sperávi.

℞. Qui edébat panes meos, ampliávit advérsum me supplantatiónem.

Aña. Tráditor autem dedit eis signum dicens : Quem osculátus fúero, ipse est, tenéte eum.

Who giveth to beats their food : and to the young ravens that call upon him.

He shall not delight in the strength of the horse : nor take pleasure in the legs of a man.

The Lord taketh pleasure in them that fear him : and in them that hope in his mercy.

Ant. He was offered because it was his own will, and he himself bore our sins.

℣. The man of my peace, in whom I trusted ;

℞. Who ate my bread, hath greatly supplanted me.

Ant. But the traitor gave them a sign, saying : He whom I shall kiss, that is he ; hold him fast.

CANTICLE OF ZACHARY
(*St. Luke*, 1.)

BENEDICTUS Dóminus Deus Israël : * quia visitávit, et fecit redemptiónem plebis suæ :

Et eréxit cornu salútis nobis : * in domo David púeri sui.

Sicut locútus est per os sanctórum : * qui a sǽculo sunt prophetárum ejus :

Salútem ex inimícis nostris : * et de manu ómnium qui odérunt nos.

BLESSED be the Lord God of Israel, because he hath visited and wrought the redemption of his people :

And hath raised up a horn of salvation to us, in the house of David his servant.

As he spoke by the mouth of his holy prophets, who are from the beginning :

Salvation from our enemies, and from the hand of all that hate us.

Ad faciéndam miseri-córdiam cum pátribus nostris : * et memorári testaménti sui sancti.

To perform mercy to our fathers ; and to remember his holy covenant.

Jusjurándum, quod jurávit ad Abraham patrem nostrum : * datútum se nobis.

The oath which he swore to Abraham our father, that he would grant to us.

Ut sine timóre de manu inimicórum nostrórum liberáti : * serviámus illi.

That being delivered from the hands of our enemies, we may serve him without fear.

In sanctitáte et justítia coram ipso : * ómnibus diébus nostris.

In holiness and justice before him, all our days.

Et tu, puer, prophéta Altíssimi vocáberis : * præíbis enim ante fáciem Dómini paráre vias ejus.

And thou, child, shalt be called the prophet of the Highest : for thou shalt go before the face of the Lord to prepare his ways.

Ad dandam sciéntiam salútis plebi ejus : * in remissiónem peccatórum eórum.

To give knowledge of salvation to his people, unto the remission of their sins.

Per víscera misericórdiæ Dei nostri : * in quibus visitávit nos Oriens ex alto.

Through the bowels of the mercy of our God : in which the Orient from on high hath visited us.

Illumináre his, qui in ténebris et in umbra mortis sedent : * ad dirigéndos pedes nostros in viam pacis.

To enlighten them that sit in darkness, and in the shadow of death : to direct our feet in the way of peace.

Aña. Tráditor autem dedit eis signum, dicens : Quem osculátus fúero, ipse est, tenéte eum.

Ant. But the traitor gave them a sign, saying : He whom I shall kiss, that is he ; hold him fast.

As soon as the antiphon is finished, the choir sings :

℣. Christus factus est pro nobis obédiens usque ad mortem.

℣. Christ became, for our sake, obedient unto death.

Immediately after this the Pater noster *is said in secret, which is followed by the Psalm* Miserére *(page* 156*); it is recited with a suppressed voice, by alternate choirs. Finally the first in dignity says the following prayer :*

RESPICE, quǽsumus, Dómine, super hanc famíliam tuam : pro qua Dóminus noster Jesus Christus non dubitávit mánibus tradi nocéntium, et crucis subíre torméntum :

LOOK down, O Lord, we beseech thee, upon this thy family, for which our Lord Jesus Christ hesitated not to be delivered into the hands of wicked men, and to undergo the punishment of the cross :

(then the rest in secret :)

Qui tecum vivit et regnat, in unitáte Spíritus Sancti, Deus, per ómnia sǽcula sæculórum. Amen.

Who liveth and reigneth with thee, in the unity of the Holy Ghost, God, world without end. Amen.

THE MASS

The stational church is St. John Lateran, but the ceremony now takes place at St. Peter's.

St. Paul's account of the institution of the Holy Eucharist in his Epistle to the Corinthians which was read as the third nocturn lessons at Matines, is continued to-day in the Mass as the Epistle. The institution of the Holy Eucharist and the Passion of Our Lord are intimately connected, and the Proper of the Mass of to-day commemorates both these events, Collect, Gradual, Offertory and *Communicantes* having reference to the Passion, whilst the institution of the Holy Eucharist is commemorated in the Epistle, *Hanc igitur* and *Quam oblationem*. The Collect, which is the same for Maundy Thursday and Good Friday, is an ancient prayer. Liturgically speaking these two days are one in the same way that they were historically one, for in the swift-moving drama of the Passion each event was inevitably followed by the next, with a logic that was as inexorable as it was rapid.

The second Host consecrated at the Mass is destined for the Mass of the Presanctified on Good Friday.

In the Passion according to St. John which is read on Good Friday only the events of these two days are given, whereas the reading of the narrative of St. Matthew and St. Mark begins at the anointing of Our Lord's feet, and that of St. Luke at the betrayal of Judas. The second Lesson of the Mass on Good Friday has reference to the institution of the Holy Eucharist. We have already treated of Maundy

Thursday as being the feast of the Blessed Sacrament, and
there only remains to note that the Gospel of St. John gives
the account of the washing of the feet.   This evangelist
does not usually repeat facts mentioned by the synoptic
writers and omits the institution of the Holy Eucharist.   The
sixth chapter of his Gospel is however an admirable commentary on the Holy Eucharist.   The Gospel of to-day is
nevertheless closely connected with this Sacrament.   It
is a lesson in humility and shows the mutual charity and
equality effected by Holy Communion amongst Christians.
Also it is very probable that Our Lord wished by this to impress upon his disciples with what purity of conscience
they should approach Holy Communion.   It is not surprising therefore that this rite was adopted by the primitive
Christians and frequently practised.   It was kept up for
centuries but in these days has become rare, except in ca-
thedrals and monasteries where the Mandatum, or washing
of the feet, takes place as a solemn rite, which will be described later.

After Vespers comes the stripping of the altars.   The
reconciliation of the public penitents is of very rare occurrence
and is to be found in the Pontifical [1].

The blessing of the holy oils is of very ancient origin and
the ceremony is most solemn and impressive.   The frame-
work of this ceremony can be seen in the Apostolic Traditions of Hippolytus and in various other canonical docu-
ments of the third and fourth centuries.   Three phials are
prepared, one for the oil of the sick, another for the oil of
catechumens and a third for the holy Chrism.   This latter
is larger than the others and more ornate.   The blessing of
the holy oils can be performed only by a bishop, and in
addition to the ordinary number of ministers he is attended
by twelve priests, seven deacons and seven subdeacons.
The blessing takes place at the pontifical Mass, after the
commemoration of the dead and immediately before the
words : *Per quem haec omnia, Domine, semper bona creas*, etc.,
The oil of the sick, which is the matter of the Sacrament of
Extreme Unction, is blessed first.   This rite is very simple,
consisting of an exorcism and a prayer.   The blessing of
the holy chrism takes place after the Communion.   Only
one of the subdeacons brought the oil of the sick, whereas
now the twelve priests, seven deacons and seven subdeacons
go in procession to the sacristy to bring the other two phials,

---

1 See *Liturgical Year*, p. 353.

singing on their way back the hymn *O Redemptor, sume carmen* until they reach the choir, when it is interrupted and taken up again when the holy oils are carried back to the sacristy after the blessing. This hymn is a panegyric, singing the praises of the oil of the olive tree, and full of allusions to the Sacraments of Baptism and Confirmation. It was composed by Venantius Fortunatus, Bishop of Poitiers in the sixth century, who borrowed extensively from Prudentius, a poet of the fourth century.

STATION AT ST JOHN LATERAN

Introitus. Gal. 6.

NOS autem gloriári opórtet in cruce Dómini nostri Jesu Christi : in quo est salus, vita et resurréctio nostra : per quem salváti et liberáti sumus. *Ps.* 66. Deus misereátur nostri, et benedícat nobis : illúminet vultum suum super nos, et misereátur nostri. Nos autem.

Introit. Gal. 6.

BUT it behoves us to glory in the cross of our Lord Jesus Christ : in whom is our salvation, life, and resurrection ; by whom we are saved and delivered. *Ps.* 66. May God have mercy on us, and bless us ; may he cause the light of his countenance to shine upon us, and may he have mercy on us. But it behoves.

During the singing of the Glória in excélsis *the bells are rung and the organ played, after which they are not heard again until the same time on Holy Saturday.*

Oratio.

DEUS, a quo et Judas reátus sui pœnam, et confessiónis suæ latro præmium sumpsit : concéde nobis tuæ propitiatiónis efféctum ; ut sicut in passióne sua Jesus Christus Dóminus noster divérsa utrísque íntulit stipéndia meritórum ; ita nobis, abláto vetustátis erróre, resurrectiónis suæ grátiam largiátur. Qui tecum vivit.

Collect.

O GOD, from whom Judas received the punishment of his guilt and the thief the reward of his confession, grant us the fruit of thy clemency : that, as our Lord Jesus Christ in his Passion gave recompense to each according to his merits, so he may deliver us from our old sins and bestow on us the grace of his resurrection. Who liveth.

No other Collect is said.

Léctio Epístolæ beáti Pauli Apóstoli ad Corínthios, *I*, *c*. 11.

FRATRES : Conveniéntibus vobis in unum, jam non est Domínicam cœnam manducáre. Unusquísque enim suam cœnam præsúmit ad manducándum. Et álius quidem ésurit, álius autem ébrius est. Numquid domos non habétis ad manducándum et bibéndum? Aut ecclésiam Dei contémnitis, et confúnditis eos, qui non habent? quid dicam vobis? laudo vos? in hoc non laudo. Ego enim accépi a Dómino, quod et trádidi vobis, quóniam Dóminus Jesus, in qua nocte tradebátur, accépit panem, et grátias agens fregit, et dixit : Accípite, et manducáte ; hoc est corpus meum, quod pro vobis tradétur : hoc fácite in meam commemoratiónem. Simíliter et cálicem, postquam cœnávit, dicens : Hic calix novum testaméntum est in meo sánguine : hoc fácite quotiescúmque bibétis, in meam commemoratiónem. Quotiescúmque enim manducábitis panem hunc, et cálicem bibétis, mortem Dómini annuntiábitis donec véniat. Itaque quicúmque manducáve-

Lesson from the Epistle of St. Paul the Apostle to the Corinthians, *I*, *c*. 11.

BRETHREN : When you come therefore together into one place, it is not now to eat the Lord's supper. For every one taketh before his own supper to eat. And one indeed is hungry, and another is drunk. What, have you not houses to eat and to drink in? Or despise ye the church of God, and put them to shame that have not? What shall I say to you? Do I praise you? In this I praise you not. For I have received of the Lord that which also I delivered unto you, that the Lord Jesus, the same night in which he was betrayed, took bread, and giving thanks, broke, and said : Take ye and eat ; this is my body, which shall be delivered for you : this do for the commemoration of me. In like manner also the chalice, after he had supped, saying : This chalice is the new testament in my blood : this do ye, as often as ye shall drink it, for the commemoration of me. For as often as you shall eat this bread and drink this chalice, you shall show the death of the Lord until he come. Therefore, whosoever shall eat this bread, or drink the chalice of the Lord unworthily, shall be guilty of the body and of

rit panem hunc, vel biberit cálicem **Dómini** indígne, reus erit córporis et sánguinis Dómini. Probet autem seípsum homo, et sic de pane illo edat, et de cálice bibat. Qui enim mandúcat et bibit indigne, judícium sibi mandúcat et bibit : non dijúdicans corpus Dómini. Ideo inter vos multi infirmi et imbecílles, et dórmiunt multi. Quod si nosmetípsos dijudicarémus, non útique judicarémur. Dum judicámur autem, a Dómino corrípimur : ut non cum hoc mundo damnémur.

the blood of the Lord : but let a man prove himself ; and so let him eat of that bread, and drink of the chalice. For he that eateth and drinketh unworthily, eateth and drinketh judgement to himself, not discerning the body of the Lord. Therefore are there many infirm and weak among you, and many sleep. But if we would judge ourselves, we should not be judged. But whilst we are judged, we are chastised by the Lord : that we be not condemned with this world.

Graduale. Phil. 2.

CHRISTUS factus est pro nobis obédiens usque ad mortem, mortem autem crucis. ℣. Propter quod et Deus exaltávit illum, et dedit illi nomen, quod est super omne nomen.

Gradual. Phil. 2.

CHRIST became obedient for us unto death, even the death of the cross. ℣. Wherefore God also hath exalted him, and hath given him a name which is above every name.

✠ Sequéntia sancti Evangélii secúndum Joánnem, *c.* 13.

ANTE diem festum Paschæ, sciens Jesus quia venit hora ejus ut tránseat ex hoc mundo ad Patrem : cum dilexísset suos, qui erant in mundo, in finem diléxit eos. Et cœna facta, cum diábolus jam misísset in cor, ut tráderet eum Judas Simónis Iscariótæ : sciens quia

✠ Continuation of the holy Gospel according to St. John, *c.* 13.

BEFORE the festival day of the pasch, Jesus knowing that his hour was come, that he should pass out of this world to the Father : having loved his own who were in the world, he loved them unto the end. And when supper was done (the devil having now put into the heart of Judas Iscariot, the son of Simon,

ómnia dedit ei Pater in
manus, et quia a Deo
exívit, et ad Deum va-
dit : surgit a cœna, et po-
nit vestiménta sua : et
cum accepísset línteum,
præcínxit se.   Deinde
mittit aquam in pelvim,
et cœpit laváre pedes
discipulórum, et extér-
gere línteo quo erat præ-
cínctus. Venit ergo ad
Simónem Petrum. Et
dicit ei Petrus : Dómine,
tu mihi lavas pedes? Re-
spóndit Jesus, et dixit
ei : Quod ego fácio, tu
nescis modo, scies autem
póstea. Dicit ei Pe-
trus : Non lavábis mihi
pedes in ætérnum. Re-
spóndit ei Jesus : Si non
lávero te, non habébis
partem mecum. Dicit
ei Simon Petrus : Dó-
mine, non tantum pe-
des meos, sed et manus,
et caput. Dicit ei Je-
sus : Qui lotus est, non
índiget nisi ut pedes la-
vet, sed est mundus to-
tus. Et vos mundi estis,
sed non omnes. Sciébat
enim quisnam esset qui
tráderet eum : proptér-
ea dixit : Non estis mun-
di omnes. Postquam er-
go lavit pedes eórum, et
accépit vestiménta sua,
cum recubuísset íterum,
dixit eis : Scitis quid
fécerim vobis? vos vocá-
tis me, Magíster, et Dó-
mine : et bene dícitis :
sum étenim. Si ergo

to betray him), knowing
that the Father had given
him all things into his
hands, and that he came
from God, and goeth to
God : he riseth from supper,
and layeth aside his gar-
ments : and having taken
a towel, he girded himself.
After that, he poureth water into a basin, and began
to wash the feet of the disciples, and to wipe them
with the towel, wherewith
he was girded. He cometh
therefore to Simon Peter.
And Peter saith to him :
Lord, dost thou wash my
feet? Jesus answered and
said to him : What I do, thou
knowest not now, but thou
shalt know hereafter. Peter
saith to him : Thou shalt
never wash my feet. Jesus
answered him : If I wash
thee not, thou shalt have
no part with me. Simon
Peter saith to him : Lord,
not only my feet, but also
my hands, and my head.
Jesus saith to him : He that
is washed, needeth not but
to wash his feet, but is clean
wholly. And you are clean,
but not all : for he knew
who he was that would be-
tray him : therefore he said :
You are not all clean. Then
after he had washed their
feet and taken his garments,
being sat down again, he
said to them : Know you
what I have done to you?
You call me Master and
Lord : and you say well,

ego lavi pedes vestros, Dóminus et Magíster : et vos debétis alter altérius laváre pedes. Exémplum enim dedi vobis, ut quemádmodum ego feci vobis, ita et vos faciátis.

Credo.

Offertorium. Ps. 117.

DEXTERA Dómini fecit virtútem, déxtera Dómini exaltávit me : non móriar, sed vivam, et narrábo ópera Dómini.

Secreta.

IPSE tibi, quǽsumus Dómine sancte, Pater omnípotens, ætérne Deus, sacrifícium nostrum reddat accéptum, qui discípulis suis in sui commemoratiónem hoc fíeri hodiérna traditióne monstrávit, Jesus Christus Fílius tuus Dóminus noster : Qui tecum vivit.

for so I am. If then I, being your Lord and Master, have washed your feet, you also ought to wash one another's feet. For I have given you an example, that as I have done to you, so you do also.

Creed.

Offertory. Ps. 117.

THE right hand of the Lord hath wrought strength, the right hand of the Lord hath exalted me : I shall not die, but live, and shall declare the works of the Lord.

Secret.

WE beseech thee, O holy Lord, Father almighty, eternal God, that our sacrifice may be made pleasing to thee through him who on this day taught his disciples to do this in commemoration of him, even Jesus Christ thy Son our Lord : who liveth and reigneth.

The Preface is that of the Cross, Qui salútem, *p.* 15.
In the Canon of the Mass the following variations are used :

COMMUNICANTES, et diem sacratíssimum celebrántes, quo Dóminus noster Jesus Christus pro nobis est tráditus : sed et memóriam venerántes, in primis gloriósæ semper Vírginis Maríæ, Genitrícis ejúsdem Dei et Dómini nostri Jesu Christi : sed et beatórum Apostolórum ac Mártyrum tuó-

COMMUNICATING and celebrating this most sacred day, in which our Lord Jesus Christ was betrayed for us : and also honouring in the first place the memory of the glorious ever Virgin Mary, Mother of the same our God and Lord Jesus Christ : as also of thy blessed apostles and martyrs, Peter and Paul.

6*

rum, Petri et Pauli, An-
dréæ, Jacóbi, Joánnis,
Thomæ, Jacóbi, Philíppi,
Bartholomǽi, Matthǽi,
Simónis et Thaddǽi : Li-
ni, Cleti, Cleméntis, Xy-
sti, Cornélii, Cypriáni,
Lauréntii, Chrysógoni,
Joánnis et Pauli, Cos-
mæ et Damiáni, et óm-
nium Sanctórum tuó-
rum : quorum méritis
precibúsque concédas, ut
in ómnibus protectiónis
tuæ muniámur auxílio.
Per eúmdem Christum
Dóminum nostrum. A-
men.

H ANC ígitur oblatió-
nem servitútis no-
stræ, sed et cunctæ fa-
míliæ tuæ, quam tibi of-
férimus ob diem, in qua
Dóminus noster Jesus
Christus trádidit discí-
pulis suis córporis et sánguinis sui mystéria cele-
bránda, quǽsumus, Dó-
mine, ut placátus accí-
pias : diésque nostros in
tua pace dispónas : at-
que ab ætérna damna-
tióne nos éripi, et in electórum tuórum júbeas
grege numerári. Per
eúmdem Christum Dó-
minum nostrum. Amen.

Q UAM oblatiónem
tu, Deus, in ómni-
bus, quǽsumus, bene ✠
díctam, adscrí ✠ ptam,
ra ✠ tam, rationábilem,
acceptabilémque fácere
dignéris : ut nobis cor ✠
pus, et san ✠ guis fiat di-

Andrew, James John, Tho-
mas, James, Philip, Bartholomew, Matthew, Simon,
and Thaddeus : Linus, Cletus, Clement, Xystus, Cornelius, Cyprian, Laurence,
Chrysogonus, John and
Paul, Cosmas and Damian,
and of all thy saints : by
whose merits and prayers,
grant that we may in all
things be defended by the
help of thy protection.
Through the same Christ
our Lord. Amen.

W E therefore beseech
thee, O Lord, to be
appeased and to receive this
offering which we, thy servants, and thy whole household, do make to thee in
memory of the day in which
our Lord Jesus Christ commanded his disciples to
celebrate the mysteries of
his body and blood : order
also our days in thy peace,
and command us to be pre-
served from eternal damnation, and to be numbered in
the fold of thine elect.
Through the same Christ
our Lord. Amen.

W HICH offering do
thou, O God, we be-
seech thee, render in al-
things ✠ blessed, ✠ apl
proved, ✠ ratified, reasonable, and acceptable : that
it may be made to us the
✠ body and ✠ blood of thy

lectíssimi Fílii tui Dómini nostri Jesu Christi.

QUI prídie, quam pro nostra omniúmque salúte paterétur, hoc est, hódie, accépit panem, *et reliqua ut in Canone.*

most beloved Son our Lord Jesus Christ.

WHO, the day before he suffered for the salvation of us, and all men, that is, on this day, took bread, &c., *as in the Canon.*

The Pax, or kiss of peace, is not given on this and the two following days.

To-day the priest consecrates two hosts, one of which he receives, the other he places in a separate chalice, which the deacon covers with the pall and paten and a white veil ; he then places it in the middle of the altar. Holy Communion is given to the clergy and people, and the Mass is concluded in the usual manner.

Communio. Joan. 13.

DOMINUS Jesus, postquam cœnávit cum discípulis suis, lavit pedes eórum, et ait illis : Scitis quid fécerim vobis, ego Dóminus et Magíster? Exémplum dedi vobis, ut et vos ita faciátis.

Communion. John 13.

THE Lord Jesus, after he had supped with his disciples, washed their feet, and saith to them : Do you know what I, your Lord and Master, have done for you? I have given you an example, that so you do also.

Postcommunio.

REFECTI vitálibus aliméntis, quæsumus, Dómine Deus noster, ut quod témpore nostræ mortalitátis exséquimur, immortalitátis tuæ múnere consequámur. Per Dóminum.

Postcommunion.

WE who have received the food of life, beseech thee, O Lord our God, that by thy gift of immortality we may attain to the possession of that which we celebrate even in this mortal life. Through our Lord.

After Mass the priest takes off his chasuble and vests in a white cope ; then returning to the altar he offers incense to the blessed Sacrament reserved in the chalice. Preceded by cross and torch-bearers and the clergy, he carries it to the altar of repose prepared in a side chapel, where it will remain until the Mass of the Presanctified on Good Friday, when no consecration takes place. During this procession the hymn Pange lingua is sung.

PANGE lingua gloriósi Córporis mystérium,

NOW, my tongue, the mystery telling Of the glorious body, sing,

Sanguinísque pretiósi,
Quem in mundi prétium
Fructus ventris gene-
rósi
Rex effúdit géntium.

And the blood, all price
excelling,
Which the Gentiles' Lord
and King,
In a Virgin's womb once
dwelling,
Shed for this world's ran-
soming.

Nobis datus, nobis na-
tus
Ex intácta Vírgine,
Et in mundo conversá-
tus
Sparso verbi sémine,
Sui moras incolátus
Miro clausit órdine.

Given for us, and con-
descending
To be born for us below,
He, with men in converse
blending,
Dwelt, the seed of truth to
sow,
Till he closed with wondrous
ending
His most patient life of
woe.

In suprémæ nocte cœ-
næ,
Recúmbens cum frátri-
bus,
Observáta lege plene
Cibis in legálibus,
Cibum turbæ duodénæ
Se dat suis mánibus.

That last night, at supper
lying,
'Mid the twelve, his chosen
band,
Jesus, with the law com-
plying,
Keeps the feast its rites de-
mand ;
Then, more precious food
supplying,
Gives himself with his own
hand.

Verbum caro panem ve-
rum
Verbo carnem éfficit :
Fitque Sanguis Christi
merum :
Et si sensus déficit,
Ad firmándum cor sin-
cérum.
Sola fides súfficit.

Word made flesh, true
bread he maketh
By his word his flesh to
be ;
Wine his blood ; which who
so taketh
Not with eyes of flesh will
see :
Faith alone, since sight for-
saketh,
Shows true hearts the mystery.

Tantum ergo Sacramén-
tum

Therefore we,before it bend-
ing,

Venerémur cérnui :
Et antíquum documén-
tum
Novo cedat rítui :
Præstet fides supplemén-
tum
Sénsuum deféctui.

This great Sacrament re-
vere :
Types and shadows have
their ending,
For the newer rite is here ;
Faith, our outward sense
befriending,
Makes our inward vision
clear.

Genitóri, Genitóque
Laus et jubilátio.
Salus, honor, virtus quo-
que
Sit et benedíctio :
Procedénti ab utróque
Compar sit laudátio.
Amen.

Gory let us give, and bless-
ing
To the Father and the Son,
Honour, might, and praise
addressing,
While eternal ages run :
Ever too his love confes-
sing,
Who from Both, with Both
is One. Amen.

*On reaching the altar of repose the priest again incenses the blessed
Sacrament, and then places it in the tabernacle. Vespers are then
said in the choir ; on this day and on Good Friday they are not sung,
but merely recited on a monotone. The* Our Father *and* Hail Mary
are said in secret at the beginning.

VESPERS

Aña. Cálicem salutá-
ris accípiam, et nomen
Dómini invocábo.

Ant. I will take the chalice of salvation, and call
upon the name of the Lord.

Psalm. 115.

Psalm 115.

CREDIDI, propter
quod locútus sum :
* ego autem humiliátus
sum nimis.

I HAVE believed, there-
fore have I spoken :
but I have been humbled
exceedingly.

Ego dixi in excéssu
meo : * Omnis homo
mendax.

I said in my excess : Every man is a liar.

Quid retríbuam Dómi-
no, * pro ómnibus quæ
retríbuit mihi ?

What shall I render to the
Lord for all the things that
he hath rendered to me?

Cálicem salutáris accí-
piam : * et nomen Dó-
mini invocábo.

I will take the chalice of
salvation : and I will call
upon the name of the Lord.

Vota mea Dómino red-
dam coram omni pópulo
ejus : * pretiósa in con-

I will pay my vows to the
Lord before all his people :
precious in the sight of the

spéctu Dómini mors sanctórum ejus.

O Dómine, quia ego servus tuus : * ego servus tuus, et fílius ancíllæ tuæ.

Dirupísti víncula mea: * tibi sacrificábo hóstiam laudis, et nomen Dómini invocábo.

Vota mea Dómino reddam in conspéctu omnis pópuli ejus : * in átriis domus Dómini, in médio tui Jerúsalem.

Aña. Cálicem salutáris accípiam, et nomen Dómini invocábo.

Aña. Cum his qui odérunt pacem, eram pacíficus : dum loquébar illis, impugnábant me grátis.

Psalm. 119.

AD Dóminum, cum tribulárer, clamávi : * et exaudívit me.

Dómine, líbera ánimam meam a lábiis iníquis, * et a lingua dolósa?

Quid detur tibi, aut quid apponátur tibi, * ad linguam dolósam?

Sagíttæ poténtis acútæ, * cum carbónibus desolatóriis.

Heu mihi, quia incolátus meus prolongátus est : habitávi cum habitántibus Cedar : * multum íncola fuit ánima mea.

Lord is the death of his saints.

O Lord, for I am thy servant ; I am thy servant, and the son of thy handmaid.

Thou hast broken my bonds : I will sacrifice to thee the sacrifice of praise, and I will call upon the name of the Lord.

I will pay my vows to the Lord in the sight of all his people : in the courts of the house of the Lord, in the midst of thee, O Jerusalem.

Ant. I will take the chalice of salvation, and call upon the name of the Lord.

Ant. With them that hated peace, I was peaceable : when I spoke to them, they fought against me without cause.

Psalm 119.

IN my trouble, I cried to the Lord, and he heard me.

O Lord, deliver my soul from wicked lips, and a deceitful tongue.

What shall be given to thee, or what shall be added to thee, to a deceitful tongue?

The sharp arrows of the mighty, with coals that lay waste.

Woe is me that my sojourning is prolonged : I have dwelt with the inhabitants of Cedar : my soul hath been long a sojourner.

Cum his qui odérunt pacem, eram pacíficus : * cum loquébar illis, impugnábant me gratis.

Aña. Cum his qui odérunt pacem, eram pacíficus : dum loquébar illis, impugnábant me gratis.

Aña. Ab homínibus iníquis líbera me, Dómine.

Psalm. 139.

ERIPE me, Dómine, ab hómine malo : * a viro iníquo éripe me.

Qui cogitavérunt iniquitátes in corde : * tota die constituébant prǽlia.

Acuérunt linguas suas sicut serpéntis : * venénum áspidum sub lábiis eórum.

Custódi me, Dómine, de manu peccatóris : * et ab homínibus iníquis éripe me.

Qui cogitavérunt supplantáre gressus meos : * abscondérunt supérbi láqueum mihi.

Et funes extendérunt in láqueum : * juxta iter scándalum posuérunt mihi.

Dixi Dómino : Deus meus es tu : * exáudi, Dómine, vocem deprecatiónis meæ.

Dómine, Dómine, virtus salútis meæ : * ob-

With them that hated peace, I was peaceable : when I spoke to them, they fought against me without cause.

Ant. With them that hated peace, I was peaceable : when I spoke to them, they fought against me without cause.

Ant. From unjust men deliver me, O Lord.

Psalm 139.

DELIVER me, O Lord, from the evil man : rescue me from the unjust man.

Who have devised iniquities in their hearts : all the day long they designed battles.

They have sharpened their tongues like a serpent : the venom of asps is under their lips.

Keep me, O Lord, from the hands of the wicked : and from unjust men deliver me.

Who have proposed to supplant my steps : the proud have hidden a net for me.

And they have stretched out cords for a snare : they have laid for me a stumbling-block by the wayside.

I said to the Lord : Thou art my God : hear, O Lord, the voice of my supplication.

O Lord, Lord, the strength of my salvation :

umbrásti super caput meum in die belli.

Ne tradas me, Dómine, a desidério meo peccatóri : * cogitavérunt contra me ; ne derelínquas me, ne forte exalténtur.
Caput circúitus eórum : * labor labiórum ipsórum opériet eos.

Cadent super eos carbónes, in ignem dejícies eos ; * in misériis non subsístent.

Vir linguósus non dirigétur in terra : * virum injústum mala cápient in intéritu.

Cognóvi quia fáciet Dóminus judícium ínopis, * et vindíctam páuperum.
Verúmtamen justi confitebúntur nómini tuo : * et habitábunt recti cum vultu tuo.

Aña. Ab homínibus iníquis líbera me, Dómine.
Aña. Custódi me a láqueo quem statuérunt mihi, et a scándalis operántium iniquitátem.

Psalm. 140.

DOMINE, clamávi ad te, exáudi me : * inténde voci meæ cum clamávero ad te.

thou hast overshadowed my head in the day of battle.

Give me not up, O Lord, from my desire to the wicked : they have plotted against me ; do not thou forsake me, lest they should triumph.
The head of them compassing me about : the labour of their lips shall overwhelm them.
Burning coals shall fall upon them ; thou wilt cast them down into the fire : in miseries they shall not be able to stand.
A man full of tongue shall not be established in the earth ; evils shall catch the unjust man unto destruction.
I know that the Lord will do justice to the needy, and will revenge the poor.

But as for the just, they shall give glory to thy name: and the upright shall dwell with thy countenance.
Ant. From unjust men deliver me, O Lord.

Ant. Keep me from the snare which they have laid for me, and from the stumbling-blocks of those that work iniquity.

Psalm 140.

I HAVE cried out to thee, O Lord, hear me : hearken to my voice when I cry to thee.

Dirigátur orátio mea sicut incénsum in conspéctu tuo : * elevátio mánuum meárum, sacrifícium vespertínum.

Pone, Dómine, custódiam óri meo : * et óstium circumstántiæ lábiis meis.

Non declínes cor meum in verba malítiæ : * ad excusándas excusatiónes in peccátis.

Cum homínibus operántibus iniquitátem : * et non communicábo cum eléctis eórum.

Corrípiet me justus in misericórdia, et increpábit me : * óleum autem peccatóris non impínguet caput meum.

Quóniam adhuc et orátio mea in beneplácitis eórum : * absórpti sunt juncti petræ júdices eórum.

Audient verba mea quóniam potuérunt : * sicut crassitúdo terræ erúpta est super terram.

Dissipáta sunt ossa nostra secus inférnum : * quia ad te Dómine, Dómine, óculi mei : in te sperávi, non áuferas ánimam meam.

Custódi me a láqueo quem statuérunt mihi : * et a scándalis operántium iniquitátem.

Cadent in retiáculo

Let my prayer be directed as incense in thy sight : the lifting up of my hands as evening sacrifice.

Set a watch, O Lord, before my mouth : and a door round about my lips.

Incline not my heart to evil words : to make excuses in sins.

With men that work iniquity : and I will not communicate with the choicest of them.

The just man shall correct me in mercy, and shall reprove me : but let not the oil of the sinner fatten my head.

For my prayer also shall still be against the things with which they are well pleased : their judges falling upon the rock have been swallowed up.

They shall hear my words, for they have prevailed : as when the thickness of the earth is broken up upon the ground.

Our bones are scattered by the side of hell : but on thee, O Lord, Lord, are my eyes : in thee have I put my trust, take not away my soul.

Keep me from the snare, which they have laid for me: and from the stumbling-blocks of them that work iniquity.

The wicked shall fall in

ejus peccatóres : * singuláriter sum ego, donec tránseam.

Aña. Custódi me a láqueo quem statuérunt mihi : et a scándalis operántium iniquitátem.

Aña. Considerábam ad déxteram, et vidébam : et non erat qui cognósceret me.

Psalm. 141.

VOCE mea ad Dóminum clamávi : * voce mea ad Dóminum deprecátus sum.

Effúndo in conspéctu ejus oratiónem meam : * et tribulatiónem meam ante ipsum pronúntio.

In deficiéndo ex me spíritum meum : * et tu cognovísti sémitas meas.

In via hac qua ambulábam : * abscondérunt láqueum mihi.

Considerábam ad déxteram et vidébam : * et non erat qui cognósceret me.

Périit fuga a me : * et non est qui requírat ánimam meam.

Clamávi ad te, Dómine, * dixi : Tu es spes mea, pórtio mea in terra vivéntium.

Inténde ad deprecatiónem meam : * quia humiliátus sum nimis.

Líbera me a persequéntibus me : * quia confortáti sunt super me.

Educ de custódia áni-

his net : I am alone, until I pass.

Ant. Keep me from the snare, which they have laid for me : and from the stumbling-blocks of them that work iniquity.

Ant. I looked on my right hand, and beheld : and there was no one that would know me.

Psalm 141.

I CRIED to the Lord with my voice : with my voice I made supplication to the Lord.

In his sight I pour out my prayer : and before him I declare my trouble.

When my spirit failed me: then thou knewest my paths.

In this way wherein I walked : they have hid a snare for me.

I looked on my right hand, and beheld : and there was no one that would know me.

Flight hath perished from me : and there is no one that hath regard to my soul.

I cried to thee, O Lord ; I said : Thou art my hope, my portion in the land of the living.

Attend to my supplication : for I am brought very low.

Deliver me from my persecutors: for they are stronger than I.

Bring my soul out of pri-

mam meam ad confiténdum nómini tuo : * me exspéctant justi, donec retríbuas mihi.

Aña. Considerábam ad déxteram, et vidébam : et non erat qui cognósceret me.

son, that I may praise thy name : the just wait for me until thou reward me.

Ant. I looked on my right hand, and beheld : and there was no one that would know me.

Antiphon of the Magnificat.

CŒNANTIBUS autem illis, accépit Jesus panem, et benedíxit, ac fregit, dedítque discípulis suis.

WHILE they were at supper, Jesus took bread, and blessed, and broke, and gave to his disciples.

On Good Friday the following Antiphon is said instead of the above :

CUM accepísset acétum, dixit : Consummátum est : et inclináto cápite, emísit spíritum.

WHEN he had taken the vinegar, he said : It is consummated : and bowing his head, he gave up the ghost.

Here is said the Magnificat, *See, at* Vespers, *p.* 74.

Aña. Cœnántibus autem illis, accépit Jesus panem, et benedíxit, ac fregit, dedítque discípulis suis.

Ant. While they were at supper, Jesus took bread, and blessed, and broke, and gave to his disciples.

vel

Aña. Cum accepísset acétum, dixit : Consummátum est ; et inclináto cápite, emísit spíritum.

or

Ant. When he had taken the vinegar, he said : It is consummated ; and bowing his head, he gave up the ghost.

Then is said kneeling :

℣. Christus factus est pro nobis obédiens usque ad mortem.

℣. Christ became for our sake obedient unto death.

On Good Friday this ℣. *is as follows :*

℣. Christus factus est pro nobis obédiens usque ad mortem, mortem autem crucis.

Pater noster, *sub silentio.*

℣. Christ became for our sake obedient unto death, even to the death of the cross.

Our Father, *silently.*

Here is said the Miserere. *See above, p.* 156.

Oratio.

RESPICE, quǽsumus, Dómine, super hanc famíliam tuam, pro qua Dóminus noster Jesus Christus non dubitávit mánibus tradi nocéntium, et crucis subíre torméntum. (Qui tecum vivit, *etc., sub silentio.*)

Collect.

LOOK down, we beseech thee, O Lord, on this thy family, for whose sake our Lord Jesus Christ hesitated not to yield himself into the hands of sinners, and to suffer the torments of the cross. (Who liveth and reigneth, &c., *silently.*)

THE STRIPPING OF THE ALTARS

At the conclusion of Vespers the priest and his ministers strip the altars, reciting meanwhile the following Antiphon and Psalm :

Aña. Divisérunt sibi vestiménta mea, et super vestem meam misérunt sortem.

Ant. They parted my garments among them, and upon my vesture they cast lots.

Psalm. 21.

DEUS, Deus meus, réspice in me : quare me dereliquísti? * Longe a salúte mea verba delictórum meórum.

Deus meus, clamábo per diem et non exáudies : * et nocte, et non ad insipiéntiam mihi.

Tu autem in sancto hábitas, * Laus Israël.

In te speravérunt patres nostri : * speravérunt, et liberásti eos.

Ad te clamavérunt, et salvi facti sunt : * in te speravérunt, et non sunt confúsi.

Ego autem sum vermis, et non homo : * oppróbrium hóminum, et abjéctio plebis.

Omnes vidéntes me derisérunt me : * locúti

Psalm 21.

O GOD, my God, look upon me : why hast thou forsaken me? Far from my salvation are the words of my sins.

O my God, I shall cry by day, and thou wilt not hear: and by night, and it shall not be reputed as folly in me.

But thou dwellest in the holy place, the praise of Israel.

In thee have our fathers hoped : they have hoped and thou hast delivered them.

They cried to thee, and they were saved : they trusted in thee, and were not confounded.

But I am a worm, and no man : the reproach of men, and the outcast of the people.

All they that saw me have laughed me to scorn : they

sunt lábiis et movérunt caput.

Sperávit in Dómino, erípiat eum : * salvum fáciat eum, quóniam vult eum.

Quóniam tu es qui extraxísti me de ventre : * spes mea ab ubéribus matris meæ. In te projéctus sum ex útero.

De ventre matris meæ Deus meus es tu : * ne discésseris a me.

Quóniam tribulátio próxima est : * quóniam non est qui ádjuvet.

Circumdedérunt me vítuli multi : * tauri pingues obsedérunt me.

Aperuérunt super me os suum, * sicut leo rápiens et rúgiens.

Sicut aqua effúsus sum : * et dispérsa sunt ómnia ossa mea.

Factum est cor meum tamquam cera liquéscens * in médio ventris mei.

Aruit tamquam testa virtus mea, et lingua mea adhæsit fáucibus meis : * et in púlverem mortis deduxísti me.

Quóniam circumdedérunt me canes multi : * concílium malignántium obsédit me.

Fodérunt manus meas et pedes meos : * dinumeravérunt ómnia ossa mea.

Ipsi vero consideravé-

have spoken with the lips, and wagged the head.

He hoped in the Lord, let him deliver him : let him save him, seeing he delighted in him.

For thou art he that hast drawn me out of the womb: my hope from the breasts of my mother. I was cast upon thee from the womb.

From my mother's womb thou art my God : depart not from me.

For tribulation is very near : for there is none to help me.

Many calves have surrounded me : fat bulls have besieged me.

They have opened their mouths against me as a lion ravening and roaring.

I am poured out like water : and all my bones are scattered.

My heart is become like wax melting in the midst of my bowels.

My strength is dried up like a potsherd, and my tongue hath cleaven to my jaws : and thou hast brought me down into the dust of death.

For many dogs have encompassed me : the council of the malignant hath besieged me.

They have dug my hands and feet : they have numbered all my bones.

And they have looked and

runt et inspexérunt me : * divisérunt sibi vestiménta mea et super vestem meam misérunt sortem.

Tu autem, Dómine, ne elongáveris auxílium tuum a me : * ad defensiónem meam cónspice.

Erue a frámea, Deus, ánimam meam : * et de manu canis únicam meam.

Salva me ex ore leónis : * et a córnibus unicórnium humilitátem meam.

Narrábo nomen tuum frátribus meis : * in médio ecclésiæ laudábo te.

Qui timétis Dóminum, laudáte eum : * univérsum semen Jacob, glorificáte eum.

Tímeat eum omne semen Israël : * quóniam non sprevit, neque despéxit deprecatiónem páuperis.

Nec avértit fáciem suam a me : * et cum clamárem ad eum, exaudívit me.

Apud te laus mea in ecclésia magna : * vota mea reddam in conspéctu timéntium eum.

Edent páuperes et saturabúntur : et laudábunt Dóminum qui requírunt eum : * vivent corda eórum in sǽculum sǽculi.

Reminiscéntur et con-

stared upon me : they parted my garments among them, and upon my vesture they cast lots.

But thou, O Lord, remove not thy help to a distance from me : look towards my defence.

Deliver, O God, my soul from the sword : my only one from the hand of the dog.

Save me from the lion's mouth : and my lowness from the horns of the unicorns.

I will declare thy name to my brethren : in the midst of the church will I praise thee.

Ye that fear the Lord praise him : all ye the seed of Jacob, glorify him.

Let all the seed of Israel fear him : because he hath not slighted nor despised the supplication of the poor man.

Neither hath he turned away his face from me : and when I cried to him he heard me.

With thee is my praise in the great church : I will pay my vows in the sight of them that fear him.

The poor shall eat and shall be filled : and they shall praise the Lord that seek him : their hearts shall live for ever and ever.

All the ends of the earth

verténtur ad Dóminum * univérsi fines terræ.

Et adorábunt in conspéctu ejus * univérsæ famíliæ Géntium.

Quóniam Dómini est regnum : * et ipse dominábitur Géntium.

Manducavérunt et adoravérunt omnes pingues terræ : * in conspéctu ejus cadent omnes qui descéndunt in terram.

Et ánima mea illi vivet : * et semen meum sérviet ipsi.

Annuntiábitur Dómino generátio ventúra : * et annuntiábunt cæli justítiam ejus pópulo qui nascétur, quem fecit Dóminus.

Aña. Divisérunt sibi vestiménta mea, et super vestem meam misérunt sortem.

shall remember, and shall be converted to the Lord.

And all the kindreds of the Gentiles shall adore in his sight.

For the kingdom is the Lord's : and he shall have dominion over the nations.

All the fat ones of the earth have eaten and have adored : all they that go down to the earth shall fall before him.

And to him my soul shall live : and my seed shall serve him.

There shall be declared to the Lord a generation to come : and the heavens shall show forth his justice to a people that shall be born, which the Lord hath made.

Ant. They parted my garments among them, and upon my vesture they cast lots.

THE MAUNDY OR WASHING OF THE FEET

At a convenient hour, after the stripping of the altars, the clergy assemble for the washing of the feet. The Prelate or Superior comes to the appointed place vested in alb, purple stole and cope, with deacon and subdeacon vested in white dalmatics. The deacon first sings the Gospel of the Mass, Ante diem festum Paschæ, with the usual ceremonies. After the Gospel the Prelate takes off the cope and girds himself with a linen cloth ; he then approaches the persons whose feet are to be washed. Kneeling before each one in turn, he washes the right foot, wipes it, and kisses it, the deacon and subdeacon assisting him on either side. Meanwhile the following chants are sung by the choir.

Antiphona.

MANDATUM novum do vobis : ut diligátis ínvicem, sicut di-

Antiphon.

A NEW commandment I give you : that you love one another, as I have loved

léxi vos, dicit Dóminus.
Ps. Beáti immaculáti in
via : * qui ámbulant in lege Dómini.

you, saith the Lord.   Ps.
Blessed are the undefiled in
the way : who walk in the
law of the Lord.

The antiphon Mandátum novum *is immediately repeated. For
the following antiphons, after each psalm or versicle, the antiphon is
repeated. One verse only of each psalm is said.*

Aña. Postquam sur-
réxit Dóminus a cœna,
misit aquam in pelvim,
et cœpit laváre pedes di-
scipulórum suórum : hoc
exémplum relíquit eis.
Ps. Magnus Dóminus, et
laudábilis nimis :* in civitáte Dei nostri, in monte
sancto ejus. Postquam.

Ant. After the Lord was
risen from supper, he put
water into a basin, and began to wash the feet of his
disciples : this was the
example he gave unto them.
Ps. Great is the Lord, and
exceedingly to be praised :
in the city of our God, in his
holy mountain. After,

Aña. Dóminus Jesus
postquam cœnávit cum
discípulis suis, lavit pedes eórum, et ait illis :
Scitis quid fécerim vo-
bis, ego Dóminus et Ma-
gíster? Exémplum de-
di vobis, ut et vos ita faciátis. Ps. Benedixísti,
Dómine, terram tuam : *
avertísti captivitátem
Jacob.   Dómine Jesus.

Ant. The Lord Jesus, af-
ter he had supped with his
disciples, washed their feet,
and said unto them : Know
you what I being your Lord
and Master have done unto
you? I have given you an
example, that ye also may
do the same. Ps. Thou hast
blessed, O Lord, thy land :
thou hast delivered Jacob
from captivity. The Lord
Jesus.

Aña. Dómine, tu mihi
lavas pedes? Respóndit
Jesus, et dixit ei : Si non
lávero tibi pedes, non habébis partem mecum.
℣. Venit ergo * ad Simó-
nem Petrum, et dixit ei
Petrus.   ℣. Quod ego
fácio, tu nescis modo : *
scies autem póstea.   Dó-
mine.

Ant. Lord, dost thou
wash my feet? Jesus an-
swered and said to him : If
I shall not wash thy feet,
thou shalt have no part
with me.   ℣. He came to
Simon Peter, and Peter
said to him.   ℣. What I do,
thou knowest not now :
but thou shalt know here-
after. Lord.

Aña. Si ego Dóminus
et Magíster vester lavi
vobis pedes : quanto ma-
gis debétis alter altérius

Ant. If I being your Lord
and Master have washed
your feet : how much more
ought you to wash the feet

laváre pedes? *Ps.* Audíte hæc, omnes gentes : * áuribus percípite qui habitátis orbem. **Si ego.**

Aña. In hoc cognóscent omnes quia mei estis discípuli, si dilectiónem habuéritis ad ínvicem. ℣. Dixit Jesus discípulis suis. **In hoc.**

Aña. Máneant in vobis fides, spes, cáritas, tria hæc ; major autem horum est cáritas. ℣. Nunc autem manent fides, spes, cáritas, tria hæc : * major horum est cáritas. **Máneant.**

Aña. Benedícta sit sancta Trínitas atque indivísa Únitas : confitébimur ei, quia fecit nobíscum misericórdiam suam. ℣. Benedicámus Patrem et Fílium, * cum Sancto Spíritu. *Ps.* Quam dilécta tabernácula tua, Dómine virtútum : * concupíscit et déficit ánima mea in átria Dómini. **Benedícta.**

Aña. Ubi cáritas et amor, Deus ibi est. ℣. Congregávit nos in unum Christi amor. ℣. Exsultémus, et in ipso jucundémur. ℣. Timeámus, et amémus Deum vivum. ℣. Et ex corde diligámus nos sincéro. **Ubi cáritas.**

℣. Simul ergo cum in unum congregámur. ℣. Ne nos mente dividámur, caveámus. ℣. Ces-

of one another? *Ps.* Hear these things, all ye nations : hearken to them all ye inhabitants of the world. **If I.**

Ant. In this all shall know that ye are my disciples, if ye have love one for another. ℣. Said Jesus to his disciples. **In this.**

Ant. Let these three, faith, hope, and charity, remain in you : but the greatest of them is charity. ℣. But now remain faith, hope, and charity, these three : but the greatest of them is charity. **Let these.**

Ant. Blessed be the holy Trinity and undivided Unity : we will praise him because he has shown us his mercy. ℣. Let us bless the Father and the Son with the Holy Ghost. *Ps.* How lovely are thy tabernacles, O Lord of Hosts : my soul longeth and fainteth for the courts of the Lord. **Blessed be.**

Ant. Where charity and love are, there is God. ℣. The love of Christ has gathered us together. ℣. Let us rejoice in him and be glad. ℣. Let us fear and love the living God. ℣. And let us love one another with a sincere heart. **Where charity.**

℣. When therefore we are assembled together. ℣. Let us take heed, we be not divided in mind. ℣. Let mali-

sent júrgia malígna, cessent lites. ℣. Et in médio nostri sit Christus Deus.

cious quarrels and contentions cease. ℣. And let Christ our God dwell among us.

The ant. Ubi cáritas *is repeated here only.*

℣. Simul quoque cum beátis videámus. ℟.Gloriánter vultum tuum, Christe Deus. ℣. Gáudium quod est imménsum, atque probum. ℣. Sǽcula per infiníta sæculórum.   Amen.

℣. Let us also with the blessed see. ℟. Thy face in glory, O Christ our God. ℣. There to possess an immense and happy joy. ℣. For infinite ages of ages. Amen.

After the washing of the feet, the Superior washes and wipes his hands. Then putting on his cope, he stands with his head uncovered, and says :

Pater noster, *secreto.*

Our Father, *silently.*

℣. Et ne nos indúcas in tentatiónem.

℣. And lead us not into temptation.

℟. Sed líbera nos a malo.

℟. But deliver us from evil.

℣. Tu mandásti mandáta tua, Dómine.

℣. Thou hast commanded, O Lord, that thy commandments.

℟. Custodíri nimis.

℟. Should be exactly observed.

℣. Tu lavásti pedes discipulórum tuórum.

℣. Thou hast washed the feet of thy disciples.

℟. Opera mánuum tuárum ne despícias.

℟. Despise not the work of thy hands.

℣. Dómine, exáudi oratiónem meam.

℣. O Lord, hear my prayer.

℟. Et clamor meus ad te véniat.

℟. And let my cry come to thee.

℣. Dóminus vobíscum.

℣. The Lord be with you.

℟. Et cum spíritu tuo.

℟. And with thy spirit.

Orémus.

Let us pray.

ADESTO, Dómine, quǽsumus, offício servitútis nostræ, et quia tu discípulis tuis pedes laváre dignátus es, ne despícias ópera mánuum tuárum, quæ nobis retinénda mandásti : ut sic-

ATTEND, O Lord, we beseech thee, to the performance of our service : and since thou didst vouchsafe to wash the feet of thy disciples, despise not the work of thy hands, which thou hast commanded us

ut hic nobis, et a nobis exterióra abluúntur inquinaménta, sic a te ómnium nostrum interióra lavéntur peccáta. Quod ipse præstáre dignéris, qui vivis et regnas Deus per ómnia sǽcula sæculórum. ℟. Amen.

to imitate : that as here the outward stains are washed away for us and by us, so the inward sins of us all may be blotted out by thee. Which be thou pleased to grant, who livest and reignest God for ever and ever. ℟. Amen.

THE BLESSING OF THE HOLY OILS

The Blessing of the Oil of Catechumens, the Oil of Unction for the sick, and the Consecration of the Holy Chrism take place on Maundy Thursday in Cathedral Churches.

The Bishop, with his attendants, enters the church and he vests for Mass. There are also twelve priests, seven deacons, seven subdeacons, and acolytes. A procession is formed to the altar, and the Bishop begins Mass. When the Bishop comes to the words of the Canon : Per quem hæc ómnia, Dómine, semper bona creas, " *By whom, O Lord, thou dost always create* ", *he goes to the Epistle side of the altar, and washes his hands. Then descending the first step of the altar, and receiving his mitre and crosier, he goes to the foldstool, where a table has been prepared, and sits down, the twelve priests and others in attendance standing round.*

The assistant priest then says : Oleum infirmórum, " *The Oil for the Sick* ". *This is brought from the sacristy by one of the subdeacons accompanied by two acolytes and given to [the assistant priest with the words :* Oleum infirmórum.

Repeating the same words, the assistant priest presents it to be blessed by the Bishop and puts it on the table. The Bishop, standing, with his mitre on, says in a low voice :

BLESSING OF THE OIL FOR THE SICK

EXORCIZO te, immundíssime spíritus, omnísque incúrsio Sátanæ, et omne phantásma, in nómine Pa✠tris, et Fi✠lii, et Spíritus ✠ Sancti ; ut recédas ab hoc Oleo, ut possit éffici únctio spiritális ad corroborándum templum Dei vivi : ut in eo possit Spíritus Sanctus habitáre, per nomen Dei

I EXORCISE thee, O unclean spirit, and every assault of Satan, and every illusion in the name of the Fa✠ther, and of the ✠ Son, and of the Holy ✠ Ghost ; that thou depart from this Oil, that it may be made a spiritual unction to fortify the temple of the living God ; that in it the Holy Ghost may dwell through the name of God the Father

Patris omnipoténtis, et per nomen dilectíssimi Fílii ejus Dómini nostri Jesu Christi, qui ventúrus est judicáre vivos et mórtuos, et sǽculum per ignem. ℟. Amen.

Almighty, and through the name of his most beloved Son, our Lord Jesus Christ who will come to judge the living and the dead and the world by fire. ℟. Amen.

Then his mitre being removed, the Bishop blesses the Oil.

℣. Dóminus vobíscum.
℟. Et cum spíritu tuo.
Orémus.

℣. The Lord be with you.
℟. And with thy spirit.
Let us pray.

EMITTE, quǽsumus, Dómine, Spíritum Sanctum tuum Paráclitum de cælis in hanc pinguédinem olívæ, quam de víridi ligno prodúcere dignátus es, ad refectiónem mentis et córporis : ut tua sancta bene✠dictióne, sit omni hoc unguénto cæléstis medicínæ perúncto tutámen méntis et córporis, ad evacuándos omnes dolóres, omnes infirmitátes, omnémque ægritúdinem mentis et córporis, unde unxísti Sacerdótes, Reges, Prophétas et Mártyres ; sit Chrisma tuum perféctum, Dómine, nobis a te benedíctum, pérmanens in viscéribus nostris. In nómine Dómini nostri Jesu Christi.

SEND forth, we beseech Thee, O Lord, thy Holy Ghost the Paraclete from Heaven upon this rich juice of the olive, which thou hast vouchsafed to bring forth out of a green wood, for the solace of soul and body : that by thy holy bene✠diction whosoever is anointed with this ointment of heavenly virtue, wherewith thou didst anoint Priests, Kings, Prophets, and Martyrs, may receive protection of soul and body, for deliverance from all pains, all infirmities, and all sickness of soul and body ; may it be thy perfect Chrism, O Lord, blessed by thee for us, abiding in our whole being : in the name of our Lord Jesus Christ.

One of the seven subdeacons then carries the Oleum Infirmorum back to the sacristy to be kept, and the Bishop returns to the altar and continues the Mass. After he has given holy Communion to the clergy, he returns to the table prepared for the ceremony and sits down. The assistant priest then says in a loud voice : Oleum ad sanctum Chrisma, " the Oil for the Holy Chrism " and then Oleum Catechumenorum, " the Oil for the Catechumens ". The Bishop blesses incense and places it in the thurible and the priests, deacons and subdeacons go in procession to the sacristy to

bring the Oil for the Chrism and the Oil of Catechumens which are carried by two deacons preceded by a subdeacon, carrying a vase of balm, and followed by the remaining priests, deacons and sub-deacons.

Meanwhile two cantors chant the following Verses :

O Redémptor, sume carmen temet con-cinéntium.

O Redeemer of mankind! receive the hymn of them that sing thy praise.

The choir repeat the same chant, and the cantors then sing :

Audi, judex mortuó-rum, una spes mortá-lium, audi voces profe-réntum donum pacis prævium.

O Judge of the dead ! thou only hope of men ! hear the prayers of them that carry the emblem of the gift of peace.

Chorus. O Redémptor.

Choir. O Redeemer.

Cantores. Arbor fœta alma luce hoc sacrán-dum prótulit : fert hoc prona præsens turba Salvatóri sǽculi.

A tree made fruitful by the fostering sun, produced this oil which is now to be bless-ed, which we, the adorers of his holy name, bring to the Saviour of the world.

Chorus. O Redémptor.

Choir. O Redeemer.

Cantores. Stans ad aram immo supplex in-fulátus Póntifex, débi-tum persólvit omne, consecráto Chrìsmate.

The mitred pontiff, too, standing humbly before the altar, is about to pay his debt, by consecrating the chrism.

Chorus. O Redémptor.

Choir. O Redeemer.

Cantores. Consecráre tu dignáre, Rex perén-nis pátriæ, hoc olívum, signum vivum, jura con-tra dǽmonum.

O King of the everlasting Kingdom ! deign to conse-crate this oil, this instru-ment of life that breaks the demons power.

Chorus. O Redémptor.

Choir. O Redeemer.

When all have reached the choir, the deacon who carries the Oil for the Chrism comes before the Bishop ; and the assistant priest, receiving it, places it on the table before the Bishop. Then the subdeacon, carrying the balm, gives it to the assistant priest, who places it upon the table. The Bishop then rises, without his mitre, and blesses the balm :

℣. Dóminus vobíscum.

The Lord be with you.

℟. Et cum spíritu tuo.

And with thy spirit.

Orémus.

Let us pray.

DEUS, mysteriórum cæléstium et virtú-tum ómnium præpará-

O God, the author of hea-venly mysteries, and of all virtues, we beseech Thee

tor, nostras, quǽsumus, preces exáudi, hanc odoríferam sicci córticis lácrymam (quæ felícis virgæ profluéndo sudórem, sacerdotáli nos opímat unguénto) acceptábilem tuis præsta mystériis, et concéssa benedictióne sanctí✠fica. Per Dóminum nostrum Jesum Christum Fílium tuum, qui tecum vivit et regnat in unitáte Spíritus Sancti Deus, per ómnia sǽcula sæculórum.

℟. Amen.

Orémus.

CREATURARUM ómnium, Dómine, procreátor, qui per Móysen fámulum tuum permístis herbis arómatum fieri præcepísti sanctificatiónem unguénti; cleméntiam tuam supplíciter depóscimus, ut huic unguénto, quod radix prodúxit stírpea, spirituálem grátiam largiéndo, plenitúdinem sancti✠ficatiónis infúndas. Sit nobis, Dómine, fídei hilaritáte condítum; sit sacerdotális unguénti Chrisma perpétuum; sit ad cæléstis vexílli impressiónem digníssimum; ut quicúmque Baptísmate sacro renáti isto fúerint liquóre perúncti, córporum atque animárum benedictiónem pleníssimam consequántur, et beátæ fídei col-

to hear our prayers : that these fragrant tears of the dry bark (which trickling down from a fruitful branch supply us with a rich ointment for the anointing of the priesthood) may be made acceptable to thee for thy Sacraments, and sancti✠fy them by giving thy blessing. Through Jesus Christ, thy Son, our Lord ; who liveth and reigneth with thee, in the unity of the Holy Ghost, world without end.

Amen.

Let us pray.

O Lord, the Creator of all things, who by thy servant Moses didst command the hallowing of ointment made with the mixture of aromatic herbs, we suppliantly beseech thy clemency to bestow the grace of thy Spirit, and the fulness of conse✠cration on this ointment, drawn from a growing plant. Make it savour to us, O Lord, of the joy of faith ; make it a lasting Chrism for the anointing of the priesthood ; make it worthy to be used in impressing the sign of thy heavenly banner ; that whosœver after having been born again by Holy Baptism shall be anointed with this ointment, may gain the fulness of thy blessing in

láto múnere perénniter ampliéntur. Per Dóminum nostrum Jesum Christum Fílium tuum, qui tecum vivit et regnat in unitáte Spíritus Sancti Deus, per ómnia sæcula sæculórum.

℞. Amen.

Then the Bishop, resuming his mitre, mixes in a paten the balm with a little of the Oil from the phial containing the Oil for the Chrism, saying :

OREMUS Dóminum Deum nostrum omnipoténtem, qui incomprehensíbilem unigéniti Fílii sui sibíque coætérni divinitátem mirábili dispositióne veræ humanitáti inseparabíliter conjúnxit, et cooperánte grátia Spíritus Sancti, óleo exsultatiónis præ particípibus suis linívit, ut homo, fraude diáboli pérditus, gémina et síngulári constans matéria, perénni redderétur, de qua excíderat, hereditáti : quátenus hos ex divérsis creaturárum speciébus liquóres creátos Sanctæ Trinitátis perfectióne bene ✠ dícat, et benedicéndo sancti ✠ ficet, concedátque, ut simul permísti unum fiant ; et quicúmque extérius inde perúnctus fúerit, ita intérius liniátur, quod ómnibus sórdibus corporális matériæ carens, se partícipem regni cæléstis éffici gra-

body and soul, and be ever enriched by the blessed faith given to them. Through Jesus Christ our Lord, *etc.*

Amen.

LET us beg our Lord God Almighty, who inseparably united the incomprehensible Godhead of his only-begotten and co-eternal Son unto a true humanity, and by the grace of the Holy Ghost anointed Him with the oil of gladness above his fellows, in order that man who is made of two substances united in one, and who had been undone by the fraud of the devil, might be restored to the everlasting inheritance from which he had fallen ; that He may bless ✠ with the fulness of the blessing of the Holy Trinity these liquids which are derived from different species of creatures, and that He will sancti ✠ fy them by his blessing, and grant that being mingled together they may become one ; and that whosoever shall be outwardly anointed therewith, may

tulétur. Per eúmdem Dóminum nostrum Jesum Christum Fílium suum, qui cum eo vivit et regnat in unitáte ejúsdem Spíritus Sancti Deus, per ómnia sǽcula sæculórum.

℞. Amen.

The Bishop then sitting breathes three times over the Chrism.

After which the twelve priests in order approach the table, and each breathes over the Chrism. After which the Bishop stands, and exorcises the Chrism, saying :

be so inwardly anointed that being freed from all contamination of bodily matter, he may rejoice in being made partaker of the kingdom of heaven. Through the same Jesus Christ, *etc.*

Amen.

THE BLESSING OF THE CHRISM

EXORCIZO te, creatúra ólei, per Deum Patrem omnipoténtem, qui fecit cælum et terram, mare, et ómnia quæ in eis sunt, ut omnis virtus adversárii, omnis exércitus diáboli, omnísque incúrsio, et omne phantásma Sátanæ eradicétur, et effugétur a te; ut fias ómnibus qui ex te ungéndi sunt, in adoptiónem filiórum, per Spíritum Sanctum. In nómine Dei Pa✠tris omnipoténtis, et Jesu ✠ Christi Fílii ejus Dómini nostri, qui cum eo vivit et regnat Deus, in unitáte ejúsdem Spíritus ✠ Sancti.

I EXORCISE thee, O creature of Oil, by God the Father Almighty, who made heaven and earth and sea, and all therein, that all the power of the enemy, all the host of Satan, and all the assaults and illusions of the devil may be rooted out and chased away from thee ; that thou mayest be, to all who shall be anointed with thee, the means of their adoption as sons through the Holy Ghost ; in the name of God the Fa✠ther Almighty, and of Jesus ✠ Christ, his Son, our Lord who liveth and reigneth, one God, in the unity of the same Holy ✠ Ghost.

His mitre being removed, the Bishop, extending his hands, says :

PER ómnia sǽcula sæculórum.

℞. Amen.

℣. Dóminus vobíscum.

℞. Et cum spíritu tuo.

℣. Sursum corda.

WORLD without end.

Amen.

The Lord be with you.

And with thy spirit.

Lift up your hearts.

℟. Habémus ad Dóminum.

℣. Grátias agámus Dómino Deo nostro.

℟. Dignum et justum est.

VERE dignum et justum est, æquum et salutáre, nos tibi semper, et ubíque grátias ágere, Dómine sancte, Pater omnípotens, ætérne Deus. Qui in princípio, inter cétera bonitátis tuæ múnera, terram prodúcere fructífera ligna jussísti, inter quæ hujus pinguíssimi liquóris ministræ olivæ nasceréntur, quarum fructus sacro Chrísmati desevíret. Nam et David prophético spíritu grátiæ tuæ Sacraménta prænóscens, vultus nostros in óleo exhilarándos esse cantávit. Et cum mundi crímina dilúvio quondam expiaréntur effúso, similitúdinem futúri múneris colúmba demónstrans per olívæ ramum, pacem terris rédditam nuntiávit. Quod in novíssimis tempóribus maniféstis est efféctibus declarátum, cum Baptísmatis aquis ómnium críminum commíssa deléntibus, hæc ólei únctio vultus nostros jucúndos éfficit, ac serénos. Inde étiam Móysi fámulo tuo mandátum dedísti, ut Aaron

We have lifted them up unto the Lord.

Let us give thanks to the Lord our God.

It is meet and just.

IT is truly meet and just, right and available to salvation, that we should always, and in all places, give thanks to thee, O holy Lord, almighty Father, eternal God : who in the beginning, among the rest of thy bounteous gifts, didst command the earth to yield fruitbearing trees, among which should be the olive, which produces this most rich liquour, and whose fruit was to serve for making holy chrism. Hence it was that David, foreknowing by a prophetic spirit the Sacraments of thy grace, sang that our faces were to be made glad with oil : and when the sins of the world were expiated of old by the deluge, a dove announced that peace was restored to the earth, by bearing an olive branch, the type of the gift to come, which has been manifested in these latter ages ; for after the waters of Baptism have washed away the sins of men, this anointing of oil gives us joy and calm. Hence, too, thou didst command thy servant Moses to ordain his brother Aaron priest by pouring oil upon him, after he had been

fratrem suum prius aqua lotum per infusiónem hujus unguénti constitúeret sacerdótem. Accéssit ad hoc ámplior honor, cum Fílius tuus Jesus Christus Dóminus noster lavári se a Joánne undis Jordánicis exegísset, ut Spíritu Sancto in colúmbæ similitúdine désuper misso, Unigénitum tuum, in quo tibi óptime complacuísse, testimónio subsequéntis vocis osténderes, et hoc illud esse manifestíssime comprobáres, quod cum óleo lætítiæ, præ consórtibus suis ungéndum David Prophéta cecinísset. Te ígitur deprecámur, Dómine sancte, Pater omnípotens, ætérne Deus, per eúmdem Jesum Christum Fílium tuum Dóminum nostrum, ut hujus creatúræ pinguédinem sancti✠ficáre tua bene✠dictióne dignéris, et Sancti ✠ Spíritus ei admiscére virtútem cooperánte Christi Fílii tui poténtia, a cujus nómine sancto Chrisma nomen accépit, unde unxísti Sacerdótes, Reges, Prophétas, et Mártyres ; ut spirituáli lavácri Baptísmo renovándis, creatúram Chrísmatis in Sacraméntum perféctæ salútis vitǽque confírmes ; ut sanctificatióne

cleansed with water. A greater honour still was, that when thy Son, our Lord Jesus Christ, bade John baptize him in the waters of the Jordan, thou didst send upon him the Holy Ghost in the form of a dove ; that thus by a voice that bore testimony, thou mightest designate thine only-begotten Son, in whom thou wast well pleased, and mightest prove, beyond all doubt, that this was the fulfilment of what the prophet David had foretold, when he sang, that he was to be anointed with the oil of gladness above his fellows. We, therefore, beseech thee, O holy Lord, almighty Father, eternal God, through the same Jesus Christ, thy Son, our Lord, that thou wouchsafe to ✠ sanctify, by thy ✠ blessing, this thy creature oil, and infuse into it the virtue of the ✠ Holy Ghost, through the co-operating power of Christ, thy Son, from whose name it hath borrowed its own of *chrism*, and wherewith thou didst anoint the priests, kings, prophets, and martyrs. Raise this chrism into a Sacrament of perfect salvation and life, to them that are to be renewed by the spiritual laver of Baptism. That thus, the corruption of their first birth being absorbed by the infusion of this holy anointing

unctiónis infúsa, corruptióne primæ nativitátis absórpta, sanctum uniuscujúsque templum acceptábilis vitæ innocéntiæ ódore redoléscat ; ut secúndum constitutiónis tuæ Sacraméntum, regio, et sacerdotáli, propheticóque honóre perfúsi, vestiménto incorrúpti múneris induántur ; ut sit his qui renáti fúerint ex aqua et Spíritu Sancto, Chrima salútis, eósque ætérnæ vitæ partícipes, et cæléstis glóriæ fáciat esse consórtes.

they may become a holy temple, redolent with the fragrance of the innocence of holy living. According to what thou hast appointed in this mystery, bestow upon them the honour of kings, priests, and prophets, by vesting them in the robe of incorruption. May this oil be to them, that are born again from water and the Holy Ghost, a chrism of salvation making them partakers of life everlasting, and coheirs of heavenly glory.

What follows is not sung but read in such way as to be heard by those around the Bishop.

Per eúmdem Dóminum nostrum Jesum Christum Fílium tuum, qui tecum vivit et regnat in unitáte ejúsdem Spíritus Sancti Deus, per ómnia sæcula sæculórum.

℟. Amen.

Through the same Jesus Christ, thy son our Lord, who with thee liveth and reigneth in the unity of the same Holy Spirit, one God, world without end. Amen.

The Bishop then pours the balm and oil which he had previously mixed into the vessel containing the Holy Chrism, saying :

Hæc commíxtio liquórum fiat ómnibus ex ea perúnctis propitiátio, et custódia salutáris in sǽcula sæculórum.

℟. Amen.

Let this mixture of liquids bring to all anointed therewith mercy and safe protection for ever and ever. Amen.

The deacon then removes the veil which had previously covered the phial, and the Bishop salutes the Chrism, saying :

Ave, Sanctum Chrisma.

Hail, Holy Chrism !

This he does a second and a third time, saying it louder each time : and after the third time, he kisses the lip of the phial. Afterwards priests in order make the same salutation, thrice repeating :

Ave, Sanctum Chrisma. | Hail, Holy Chrism!

and each, having kissed the lip of the phial, returns to his place. The deacon next approaches with the other phial containing the Oil of catechumens, which he presents to the assistant priest, who places it on the table. The Bishop and the priests breathe over it, as was done previoulsy in the case of the Chrism. Which done, the Bishop rises, and, in a low tone, says the following :

THE BLESSING OF THE OIL OF CATECHUMENS

EXORCIZO te, creatúra ólei, in nómine Dei Pa✠tris omnipoténtis, et in nómine Jesu ✠ Christi, et Spíritus✠Sancti, ut in hac invocatióne indivíduæ Trinitátis atque únius virtúte Deitátis, omnis nequíssima virtus adversárii, omnis inveteráta malítia diáboli, omnis violénta incúrsio, omne confúsum et cæcum phantásma eradicétur, et effugétur, et discédat a te : ut divínis Sacraméntis purificáta fias in adoptiónem carnis et spíritus, eis qui ex te ungéndi sunt, in remissiónem ómnium peccatórum ; ut efficiántur eórum córpora ad omnem grátiam spirituálem accipiéndam sanctificáta. Per eúmdem Dóminum nostrum Jesum Christum, qui ventúrus est judicáre vivos et mórtuos, et sǽculum per ignem.

℟. Amen.

I EXORCISE thee, O creature of Oil, in the name of God the Fa✠ther Almighty, and in the name of Jesus ✠ Christ, and of the Holy ✠ Ghost, that by this invocation of the undivided Trinity, and by the power of the one Godhead, all the most wicked powers of the enemy, all the inveterate malice of the devil, every violent assault, every disorderly and dark illusion may be rooted out and chased away, and dispelled from thee : that hallowed by divine mysteries, thou mayest be for the adoption both of the flesh and the spirit of those who shall be anointed with thee, for the forgiveness of all sins : that their bodies may be sanctified for receiving all spiritual grace. Through the same Jesus Christ our Lord, who shall come to judge the living and the dead, and the world by fire.

Amen.

Then the Bishop, his mitre being removed, blesses the Oil of Catechumens, saying :

This blessing is as simple as that used for the Oil of the Sick, consisting only of an exorcism and a blessing.

℣. Dóminus vobíscum.
℟. Et cum spíritu tuo.
Orémus.

DEUS, incrementórum ómnium et proféctuum spirituálium remunerátor, qui virtúte Sancti Spíritus imbecillárum méntium rudiménta confirmas; te orámus, Dómine, ut emíttere dignéris tuam bene-✠dictiónem super hoc Oleum, et ventúris ad beatæ regeneratiónis lavácrum tríbuas, per unctiónem hujus creatúræ, purgatiónem mentis et córporis; ut si quæ illis adversántium spirituum inhæsére máculæ, ad tactum sanctificáti Olei hujus abscédant; nullus spirituálibus nequítiis locus, nulla réfugis virtútibus sit facúltas, nulla insidiántibus malis laténdi licéntia relinquátur. Sed veniéntibus ad fidem servis tuis, et Sancti Spíritus tui operatióne mundándis, sit unctiónis hujus præparátio útilis ad salútem, quam étiam cæléstis regeneratiónis nativitáte in Sacraménto sunt Baptísmatis adeptúri. Per Dóminum nostrum Jesum Christum Fílium tuum, qui venturus est judicáre vivos et mórtuos, et sæculum per ignem.
℟. Amen.

The Lord be with you.
And with thy spirit.
Let us pray.

O GOD the rewarder of all spiritual growth and progress, who by the power of the Holy Ghost dost strengthen the first beginnings of feeble minds, deign, O Lord, we beseech thee, to send down thy bles✠sing upon this Oil, and grant that all who come to the laver of Regeneration, may, through the unction of this thy creature, be cleansed in mind and body; that if any pollution of their spiritual enemies have adhered to them, it may depart at the touch of this hallowed Oil; let there be no place for the wickedness of evil spirits, no occasion for the apostate angels, no power of concealment left to the snares of sin; but to thy servants, who come to the Faith, and are to be cleansed by the operation of thy Holy Spirit, let the preparation of this unction be serviceable for that salvation, which they are to gain when born by heavenly generation in the Sacrament of Baptism. Through Jesus Christ our Lord, thy Son, who shall come to judge the living and the dead, and the world by fire.
Amen.

Then the Bishop and priests in order salute the Oil of Cate-chumens, saying thrice :

Ave, Sanctum Oleum. | Hail, Holy Oil !

After the third time, each kisses the mouth of the phial. After this the two vessels are carried in procession to the sacristy by the two deacons, in the same order as before : the two cantors chanting the following verses :

Ut novétur sexus om-nis unctióne Chrísmatis, ut sanétur sauciáta di-gnitátis glória.

That by this most sacred unction, either sex may be renewed. And our wounded glory rescued through the Spirit's plentitude.

Chorus. O Redémptor, sume carmen temet con-cinéntium.

Choir. Hear our hymn, Redeemer, Lord : thee we praise with one accord.

Cantores. Lota mente sacro fonte aufugántur crímina, uncta fronte sacrosáncta ínfluunt cha-rísmata.

Cantors. First the hallow-ed fountain's waters cleanse the soul from taint of sin. Then with oil the brows anointed, and all graces flow within.

Chorus. O Redémptor.

Choir. Hear our hymn.

Cantores. Corde natus ex Paréntis, alvum im-plens Vírginis, præsta lucem, claude mortem Chrísmatis consórtibus.

Cantors. Son of the Eternal Father, Virgin-born, afford us light : Who receive this holy unction ; save us from Death's gloomy night.

Chorus. O Redémptor.

Choir. Hear our hymn.

Cantores. Sit hæc dies festa nobis sæculórum sæculis : sit sacráta di-gna laude, nec senéscat témpore.

Cantors. May this day of festal gladness, keep its holy joys in store. Dignified with joyful praises, blooming now and evermore.

Chorus. O Redémptor.

Choir. Hear our hymn.

During the singing of the verses the Bishop, wearing his mitre, washes his hands ; then returning to the altar, he proceeds with the Mass for Maundy Thursday, and after the Ite Missa est, *gives the Blessing.*

As we have already observed, these rites are of ancient origin. Formerly on Maundy Thursday there was a special Mass for the blessing of the holy oils, another for the reconciliation of the public penitents, and a third in the evening in memory of the Last Supper [1].

In the evening the Tenebræ *of Good Friday are said.*

---

[1] For further information on this subject see article on " huile " in our *Dictionnaire d'archéologie chrétienne et de liturgie.*

GOOD FRIDAY
TENEBRÆ

RECITED ON THURSDAY EVENING

Unlike the psalms of Maundy Thursday, those of to-day do not belong to the weekly *cursus* but are specially chosen on account of their reference to the Passion. Psalm 2 speaks of the final triumph of the Messias when he shall reign over all the peoples of the earth ; Psalm 21 is the psalm of the Crucifixion ; Psalmas 37, 39 and 53 foretell the sufferings of Christ, and Psalms 58, 87 and 93 are the cry of our Lord in agony, appealing to the divine Justice. As on the preceding days, the first nocturn lessons are from Jeremias, and those of the second nocturn from St. Augustine's eloquent commentary on the Psalms of the Passion, but those of the third nocturn introduce a new element. They are taken from St. Paul's Epistle to the Hebrews and expound the theology of the priesthood of Christ. The responsories have been most appropriately chosen from both the Old and the New Testaments, and their accompanying melodies voice the deep sorrow expressed by the texte.

Pater noster, Ave, *and* Credo, *in secret.*

THE FIRST NOCTURN

Aña. Astitérunt reges terræ, et príncipes convenérunt in unum, advérsus Dóminum, et advérsus Christum ejus.

Ant. The kings of the earth stood up, and the princes met together against the Lord, and against his Christ.

Psalmus 2.

QUARE fremuérunt gentes : * et pópuli meditáti sunt inánia?

Psalm 2.

WHY have the Gentiles raged, and the people devised vain things?

Astitérunt reges terræ, et príncipes convenérunt in unum : * advérsus Dóminum et advérsus Christum ejus.

Dirumpámus víncula eórum : * et projiciámus a nobis jugum ipsórum.

Qui hábitat in cælis irridébit, eos : * et Dóminus subsannábit eos.

Tunc loquétur ad eos in ira sua : * et in furóre suo conturbábit eos.

Ego autem constitútus sum rex ab eo super Sion montem sanctum ejus : * prǽdicans præcéptum ejus.

Dóminus dixit ad me : * Fílius meus es tu, ego hódie génui te.

Póstula a me, et dabo tibi Gentes hereditátem tuam : * et possessiónem tuam términos terræ.

Reges eos in virga férrea : * et tamquam vas fíguli confrínges eos.

Et nunc, reges, intellígite : * erudímini, qui judicátis terram.

Servíte Dómino in timóre : * et exsultáte ei cum tremóre.

Apprehéndite disciplínam, nequándo irascátur Dóminus : * et pereátis de via justa.

Cum exárserit in brevi

The kings of the earth stood up, and the princes met together, against the Lord, and against his Christ.

They said : Let us break their bonds asunder : and let us cast away their yoke from us.

He that dwelleth in heaven shall laugh at them : and the Lord shall deride them.

Then shall he speak to them in his anger : and trouble them in his rage.

But I am appointed king by him over Sion his holy mountain, preaching his commandment.

The Lord hath said to me : Thou art my Son, this day have I begotten thee.

Ask of me, and I will give thee the Gentiles for thy inheritance : and the utmost parts of the earth for thy possession.

Thou shalt rule them with a rod of iron : and shalt break them in pieces like a potter's vessel.

And now, O ye kings, understand : receive instruction, you that judge the earth.

Serve ye the Lord with fear : and rejoice unto him with trembling.

Embrace discipline, lest at any time the Lord be angry : and you perish from the just way.

When his wrath shall be

ira ejus : * beáti omnes qui confídunt in eo.

Aña. Astitérunt reges terræ, et príncipes convenérunt in unum, advérsus Dóminum, et advérsus Christum ejus.

Aña. Divisérunt sibi vestiménta mea, et super vestem meam misérunt sortem.

Psalm. 21.

DEUS, Deus meus, réspice in me : quare me dereliquísti : * longe a salúte mea verba delictórum meórum.

Deus meus, clamábo per diem, et non exáudies : * et nocte, et non ad insipiéntiam mihi.

Tu autem in sancto habitas : * laus Israël.

In te speravérunt patres nostri : * speravérunt, et liberásti eos.

Ad te clamavérunt, et salvi facti sunt : * in te speravérunt, et non sunt confúsi.

Ego autem sum vermis, et non homo : * oppróbrium hóminum, et abjéctio plebis.

Omnes vidéntes me derisérunt me : * locúti sunt lábiis, et movérunt caput.

Sperávit in Dómino, erípiat eum : * salvum fáciat eum, quóniam vult eum,

kindled in a short time, blessed are all they that trust in him.

Ant. The kings of the earth stood up, and the princes met together, against the Lord and against his Christ.

Ant. They parted my garments among them, and upon my vesture they cast lots.

Psalm 21.

O GOD, my God, look upon me : why hast thou forsaken me : Far from my salvation are the words of my sins.

O my God, I shall cry by day, and thou wilt not hear : and by night, and it shall not be reputed as folly in me.

But thou dwellest in the holy place, the praise of Israel.

In thee have our fathers hoped : they have hoped and thou hast delivered them.

They cried to thee, and they were saved : they trusted in thee, and were not confounded.

But I am a worm, and no man : the reproach of men, and the outcast of the people.

All they that saw me have laughed me to scorn : they have spoken with the lips, and wagged the head.

He hoped in the Lord, let him deliver him : let him save him, seeing he delighted in him.

Quóniam tu es, qui extraxísti me de ventre : * spes mea ab ubéribus matris meæ. In te projéctus sum ex útero :

De ventre matris meæ Deus meus es tu : * ne discésseris a me.

Quóniam tribulátio próxima est : * quóniam non est qui ádjuvet.

Circumdedérunt me vítuli multi : * tauri pingues obsedérunt me.

Aperuérunt super me os suum : * sicut leo rápiens et rúgiens.

Sicut aqua effúsus sum: * et dispérsa sunt ómnia ossa mea.

Factum est cor meum tamquam cera liquéscens : * in médio ventris mei.

Aruit tamquam testa virtus mea, et lingua mea adhǽsit fáucibus meis : * et in púlverem mortis deduxísti me.

Quóniam circumdedérunt me canes multi : * concílium malignántium obsédit me.

Fodérunt manus meas et pedes meos : * dinumeravérunt ómnia ossa mea.

Ipsi vero consideravérunt et inspexérunt me : * divisérunt sibi vestiménta mea, et super vestem meam misérunt sortem.

Tu autem, Dómine,

For thou art he that hast drawn me out of the womb : my hope from the breasts of my mother. I was cast upon thee from the womb :

From my mother's womb thou art my God, depart not from me.

For tribulation is very near : for there is none to help me.

Many calves have surrounded me : fat bulls have besieged me.

They have opened their mouths against me, as a lion ravening and roaring.

I am poured out like water : and all my bones are scáttered.

My heart is become like wax melting in the midst of my bowels.

My strength is dried up like a potsherd, and my tongue hath cleaved to my jaws : and thou hast brought me down into the dust of death.

For many dogs have encompassed me : the council of the malignant hath besieged me.

They have dug my hands and feet : they have numbered all my bones.

And they have looked and stared upon me : they parted my garments amongst them, and upon my vesture they cast lots.

But thou, O Lord, remove

ne elongáveris auxílium tuum a me, * ad defensiónem meam cónspice.

Erue a frámea, Deus, ánimam meam : * et de manu canis únicam meam.

Salva me ex ore leónis: et a córnibus unicórnium humilitátem meam.

Narrábo nomen tuum frátribus meis : * in médio ecclésiæ laudábo te.

Qui timétis Dóminum, laudáte eum : * univérsum semen Jacob, glorificáte eum.

Tímeat eum omne semen Israël : * quóniam non sprevit, neque despéxit deprecatiónem páuperis.

Nec avértit fáciem suam a me : * et cum clamárem ad eum, exaudívit me.

Apud te laus mea in ecclésia magna : * vota mea reddam in conspéctu timéntium eum.

Edent páuperes, et saturabúntur, et laudábunt Dóminum qui requírunt eum : * vivent corda eórum in sǽculum sǽculi.

Reminiscéntur et converténtur ad Dóminum * univérsi fines terræ.

Et adorábunt in conspéctu ejus * univérsæ famíliæ géntium.

Quóniam Dómini est

not thy help to a distance from me : look towards my defence.

Deliver, O God, my soul from the sword : my only one from the hand of the dog.

Save me from the lion's mouth : and my lowness from the horns of the unicorns.

I will declare thy name to my brethren : in the midst of the church will I praise thee.

Ye that fear the Lord, praise him : all ye the seed of Jacob, glorify him.

Let all the seed of Israel fear him : because he hath not slighted nor despised the supplication of the poor man.

Neither hath he turned away his face from me : and when I cried to him he heard me.

With thee is my praise in the great church : I will pay my vows in the sight of them that fear him.

The poor shall eat and shall be filled, and they shall praise the Lord that seek him : their hearts shall live for ever and ever.

All the ends of the earth shall remember, and shall be converted to the Lord.

And all the kindreds of the Gentiles shall adore in his sight.

For the kingdom is the

regnum : * et ipse domi-
nábitur géntium.

Manducavérunt, et ad-
oravérunt omnes pin-
gues terræ : * in conspe-
ctu ejus cadent omnes,
qui descéndunt in ter-
ram.

Et ánima mea illi vi-
vet : * et semen meum
sérviet ipsi.

Annuntiábitur Dómi-
no generátio ventúra : *
et annuntiábunt cæli ju-
stítiam ejus, pópulo qui
nascétur, quem fecit Dó-
minus.

Aña. Divisérunt sibi
vestiménta mea, et su-
per vestem meam misé-
runt sortem.

Aña. Insurrexérunt in
me testes iníqui, et men-
títa est iníquitas sibi.

Psalm. 26.

DOMINUS illuminátio
mea, et salus mea :
* quem timébo?

Dóminus protéctor vi-
tæ meæ : * a quo trepi-
dábo?

Dum apprópiant su-
per me nocéntes : * ut
edant carnes meas.

Qui tríbulant me ini-
míci mei : * ipsi infirmáti
sunt et cecidérunt.

Si consístant advér-
sum me castra : * non
timébit cor meum.

Si exsúrgat advérsum
me prǽlium : * in hoc
ego sperábo.

Unam pétii a Dómino,

Lord's : and he shall have
dominion over the nations.

All the fat ones of the
earth have eaten and have
adored : all they that go
down to the earth shall fall
before him.

And to him my soul shall
live : and my seed shall
serve him.

There shall be declared to
the Lord a generation to
come : and the heavens shall
show forth his justice to a
people that shall be born,
which the Lord hath made.

Ant. They parted my garments among them, and
upon my vesture they cast
lots.

Ant. Unjust witnesses
have risen up against me,
and iniquity hath belied
itself.

Psalm 26.

THE Lord is my light and
my salvation, whom
shall I fear?

The Lord is the protector
of my life, of whom shall I
be afraid ?

Whilst the wicked draw
near against me, to eat my
flesh.

My enemies that troubled
me have been weakened,
and have fallen.

If armies in camp should
stand together against me,
my heart shall not fear.

If a battle should rise up
against me, in this will I be
confident.

One thing have I asked of

hanc requíram : * ut in-hábitem in domo Dómini ómnibus diébus vitæ meæ.

Ut vídeam voluptátem Dómini : * et vísitem templum ejus.

Quóniam abscóndit me in tabernáculo suo : * in die malórum protéxit me in abscóndito tabernáculi sui.

In petra exaltávit me : * et nunc exaltávit caput meum super inimícos meos.

Circuívi, et immolávi in tabernáculo ejus hóstiam vociferatiónis : * cantábo, et psalmum dicam Dómino.

Exáudi, Dómine, vocem meam, qua clamávi ad te : * miserére mei, et exáudi me.

Tibi dixit cor meum, exquisívit te fácies mea: * fáciem tuam, Dómine, requíram.

Ne avértas fáciem tuam a me : * ne declínes in ira a servo tuo.

Adjútor meus esto : * ne derelínquas me, neque despícias me, Deus salutáris meus.

Quóniam pater meus et mater mea dereliquérunt me : * Dóminus autem assúmpsit me.

Legem pone mihi, Dómine, in via tua : * et dírige me in sémitam rectam propter inimícos meos.

the Lord, this will I seek after, that I may dwell in the house of the Lord all the days of my life.

That I may see the delight of the Lord, and may visit his temple.

For he hath hidden me in his tabernacle ; in the day of evils he hath protected me in the secret place of his tabernacle.

He hath exalted me upon a rock : and now he hath lifted up my head above my enemies.

I have gone round, and have offered up in his tabernacle a sacrifice of jubilation : I will sing, and recite a psalm to the Lord.

Hear, O Lord, my voice, with which I have cried to thee : have mercy on me, and hear me.

My heart hath said to thee, my face hath sought thee : thy face, O Lord, will I still seek.

Turn not away thy face from me : decline not in thy wrath from thy servant.

Be thou my helper : forsake me not, do not thou despise me, O God my Saviour.

For my father and my mother have left me : but the Lord hath taken me up.

Set me, O Lord, a law in thy way : and guide me in the right path, because of my enemies.

Ne tradíderis me in ánimas tribulántium me : * quóniam insurrexérunt in me testes iníqui, et mentíta est iníquitas sibi.

Credo vidére bona Dómini : * in terra vivéntium.

Exspécta Dóminum, viríliter age : * et confortétur cor tuum, et sustíne Dóminum.

Aña. Insurrexérunt in me testes iníqui, et mentíta est iníquitas sibi.

℣. Divisérunt sibi vestiménta mea.

℟. Et super vestem meam misérunt sortem.

Deliver me not over to the will of them that trouble me : for unjust witnesses have risen up against me, and iniquity hath belied itself.

I believe to see the good things of the Lord in the land of the living.

Expect the Lord, do manfully : and let thy heart take courage, and wait thou for the Lord.

Ant. Unjust witnesses have risen up against me, and iniquity hath belied itself.

℣. They parted my garments among them.

℟. And upon my vesture they cast lots.

Here is said, in secret, the Pater noster.

FIRST LESSON

De Lamentatióne Jeremíæ Prophétæ. *Cap.* 2

From the Lamentation of Jeremias the Prophet.
Ch. 2.

HETH. Cogitávit Dóminus dissipáre murum fíliæ Sion : teténdit funículum suum, et non avértit manum suam a perditióne : luxítque antemurále, et murus páriter dissipátus est.

TETH. Defíxæ sunt in terra portæ ejus, pérdidit et contrívit vectes ejus : regem ejus et príncipes ejus in géntibus. Non est lex : et prophétæ ejus non invenérunt visiónem a Dómino.

HETH. The Lord hath purposed to destroy the wall of the daughter of Sion: he hath stretched out his line, and hath not withdrawn his hand from destroying : and the bulwark hath mourned, and the wall hath been destroyed together.

TETH. Her gates are sunk into the ground : he hath destroyed and broken her bars : her king and her princes are among the Gentiles. The law is no more, and her prophets have found no vision from the Lord.

JOD. Sedérunt in terra, conticuérunt senes fíliæ Sion : conspersérunt cínere cápita sua, accíncti sunt cilíciis ; abjecérunt in terram cápita sua vírgines Jerúsalem.

CAPH. Defecérunt præ lácrymis óculi mei, conturbáta sunt víscera mea. Effúsum est in terra jecur meum super contritióne fíliæ pópuli mei, cum defíceret párvulus et lactens in platéis óppidi.

Jerúsalem, Jerúsalem, convertére ad Dóminum Deum tuum.

℟. Omnes amíci mei dereliquérunt me, et prævaluérunt insidiántes mihi : trádidit me quem diligébam. * Et terribílibus óculis plaga crudéli percutiéntes, acéto potábant me.

℣. Inter iníquos projecérunt me : et non pepercérunt ánimæ meæ. * Et terribílibus.

JOD. The ancients of the daughter of Sion sit upon the ground, they have held their peace ; they have sprinkled their heads with dust, they are girded with hair-cloth, the virgins of Jerusalem hang down their heads to the ground.

CAPH. My eyes have failed with weeping, my bowels are troubled. My liver is poured out upon the earth, for the destruction of the daughter of my people, when the children and the sucklings fainted away in the streets of the city.

Jerusalem, Jerusalem, be converted to the Lord thy God.

℟. All my friends have forsaken me, and they that lay in ambush for me prevailed : he whom I loved has betrayed me. * And they, with terrible looks, striking me with a cruel wound, gave me vinegar to drink.

℣. They cast me out among the wicked, and spared not my life. * And they.

SECOND LESSON

LAMED. Mátribus suis dixérunt : Ubi est tríticum et vinum? cum defícerent quasi vulneráti in platéis civitátis, cum exhalárent ánimas suas in sinu matrum suárum.

MEM. Cui comparábo

LAMED. They said to their mothers : Where is corn and wine? when they fainted away as the wounded in the streets of the city : when they breathed out their souls in the bosoms of their mothers.

MEM. To what shall I

te? vel cui assimilábo te fília Jerúsalem? cui exæquábo te, et consolábor te, virgo fília Sion? Magna est enim velut mare contrítio tua : quis medébitur tui?

NUN. Prophétæ tui vidérunt tibi falsa et stulta : nec aperiébant iniquitátem tuam, ut te ad pœniténtiam provocárent. Vidérunt autem tibi assumptiónes falsas, et ejectiónes.

SAMECH. Plausérunt super te mánibus omnes transeúntes per viam : sibilavérunt, et movérunt caput suum super fíliam Jerúsalem : Hǽccine est urbs, dicéntes, perfécti decóris, gáudium univérsæ terræ?

Jerúsalem, Jerúsalem, convértere ad Dóminum Deum tuum.

℞. Velum templi scissum est, * Et omnis terra trémuit : latro de cruce clamábat, dicens : Meménto mei, Dómine, dum véneris in regnum tuum.

℣. Petræ scissæ sunt, et monuménta apérta sunt, et multa córpora sanctórum, qui dormíerant, surrexérunt.
* Et omnis.

compare thee, or to what shall I liken thee, O daughter of Jerusalem? to what shall I equal thee, that I may comfort thee, O virgin daughter of Sion? For great as the sea is thy destruction : who shall heal thee?

NUN. Thy prophets have seen false and foolish things for thee ; and they have not laid open thy iniquity, to excite thee to penance, but they have seen for thee false revelations and banishments.

SAMECH. All they that passed by the way, have clapped their hands at thee : they have hissed and wagged their heads at the daughter of Jerusalem, saying : Is this the city of perfect beauty, the joy of all the earth?

Jerusalem, Jerusalem, be converted to the Lord thy God.

℞. The veil of the temple was rent, * And all the earth shook : the thief cried out from the cross, saying : Remember me, O Lord, when thou shalt come into thy kingdom.

℣. The rocks were spilt, and the monuments opened, and many bodies of the saints that were dead rose out of them.
* And all.

THIRD LESSON

ALEPH. Ego vir videns paupertátem meam, in virga indignatiónis ejus.

ALEPH. Me minávit et addúxit in ténebras, et non in lucem.

ALEPH. Tantum in me vertit, et convértit manum suam tota die.

BETH. Vetústam fecit pellem meam et carnem meam : contrívit ossa mea.

BETH. Ædificávit in gyro meo, et circúmdedit me felle et labóre.

BETH. In tenebrósis collocávit me, quasi mórtuos sempitérnos.

GHIMEL. Circumædificávit advérsum me, ut non egrédiar : aggravávit cómpedem meum.

GHIMEL. Sed et cum clamávero et rogávero, exclúsit oratiónem meam.

GHIMEL. Conclúsit vias meas lapídibus quadris, sémitas meas subvértit.

Jerúsalem, Jerúsalem, convértere ad Dóminum Deum tuum.

℟. Vínea mea * elécta ego te plantávi :

* Quómodo convérsa es in amaritúdinem, ut me crucifígeres, et Barábbam dimítteres? ℣.

ALEPH. I am the man that see my poverty by the rod of his indignation.

ALEPH. He hath led me, and brought me into darkness, and not into light.

ALEPH. Only against me he hath turned, and turned again his hand all the day.

BETH. My skin and my flesh he hath made old, he hath broken my bones.

BETH. He hath built round about me, and he hath compassed me with gall and labour.

BETH. He hath set me in dark places as those that are dead for ever.

GHIMEL. He hath built against me round about, that I may not get out : he hath made my fetters heavy.

GHIMEL. Yea, and when I cry and entreat, he hath shut out my prayer.

GHIMEL. He hath shut up my ways with square stones, he hath turned my paths upside down.

Jerusalem, Jerusalem, be converted to the Lord thy God.

℟. O my chosen vineyard, it is I that have planted thee :

* How art thou become so bitter, that thou shouldst crucify me, and release Barabbas? ℣. I have hedged

Sepívi te et lapídes elégi ex te, et ædificávi turrim.

* Quómodo.

Here is repeated : Vínea mea.

thee in, and picked the stones out of thee, and have built a tower.

* How art thou.

Here is repeated : O my chosen.

THE SECOND NOCTURN

Aña. Vim faciébant, qui quærébant ánimam meam.

Ant. They used violence that sought my soul.

Psalm. 37.

DOMINE, ne in furóre tuo árguas me : * neque in ira tua corrípias me.

Quóniam sagíttæ tuæ infíxæ sunt mihi : * et confirmásti super me manum tuam.

Non est sánitas in carne mea a fácie iræ tuæ : * non est pax óssibus meis a fácie peccatórum meórum.

Quóniam iniquitátes meæ supergréssæ sunt caput meum : * et sicut onus grave gravátæ sunt super me.

Putruérunt, et corrúptæ sunt cicatríces meæ : * a fácie insipiéntiæ meæ.

Miser factus sum, et curvátus sum usque in finem : * tota die contristátus ingrediébar.

Quóniam lumbi mei impléti sunt illusiónibus : * et non est sánitas in carne mea.

Afflíctus sum et humiliátus sum nimis : * rugiébam a gémitu cordis mei.

Psalm 37.

REBUKE me not, O Lord, in thy indignation : nor chastise me in thy wrath.

For thy arrows are fastened in me : and thy hand hath been strong upon me.

There is no health in my flesh, because of thy wrath : there is no peace for my bones, because of my sins.

For my iniquities are gone over my head : and as a heavy burden are become heavy upon me.

My sores are putrefied and corrupted, because of my foolishness.

I am become miserable, and am bowed down even to the end : I walked sorrowful all the day long.

For my loins are filled with illusions : and there is no health in my flesh.

I am afflicted and humbled exceedingly : I roared with the groaning of my heart.

Dómine, ante te omne desidérium meum : * et gémitus meus a te non est abscónditus.

Lord, all my desire is before thee : and my groaning is not hidden from thee.

Cor meum conturbátum est, derelíquit me virtus mea : * et lumen oculórum meórum, et ipsum non est mecum.

My heart is troubled, my strength hath left me : and the light of my eyes itself is not with me.

Amíci mei et próximi mei : * advérsum me appropinquavérunt et stetérunt.

My friends and my neighbours have drawn near, and stood against me.

Et qui juxta me erant, de longe stetérunt : * et vim faciébant qui quærébant ánimam meam.

And they that were near me stood afar off : and they that sought my soul used violence.

Et qui inquirébant mala mihi, locúti sunt vanitátes : * et dolos tota die meditabántur.

And they that sought evils to me spoke vain things : and studied deceits all the day long.

Ego autem tamquam surdus non audiébam : * et sicut mutus non apériens os suum.

But I, as a deaf man, heard not : and was as a dumb man not opening his mouth.

Et factus sum sicut homo non áudiens : * et non habens in ore suo redargutiónes.

And I became as a man that heareth not : and, that hath no reproofs in his mouth.

Quóniam in te Dómine, sperávi : * tu exáudies me, Dómine Deus meus.

For in thee, O Lord, have I hoped : thou wilt hear me, O Lord my God.

Quia dixi : Nequándo supergáudeant mihi inimíci mei : * et dum commovéntur pedes mei super me magna locúti sunt.

For I said : Lest at any time my enemies rejoice over me : and whilst my feet are moved, they speak great things against me.

Quóniam ego in flagélla parátus sum : * et dolor meus in conspéctu meo semper.

For I am ready for scourges : and my sorrow is continually before me.

Quóniam iniquitátem

For I will declare my ini-

meam annuntiábo : * et cogitábo pro peccáto meo.

Inimíci autem mei vivunt, et confirmáti sunt super me : * et multiplicáti sunt qui odérunt me iníque.

Qui retríbuunt mala pro bonis detrahébant mihi : * quóniam sequébar bonitátem.

Ne derelínquas me, Dómine Deus meus : * ne discésseris a me.

Inténde in adjutórium meum : * Dómine, Deus salútis meæ.

Aña. Vim faciébant qui quærébant ánimam meam.

Aña. Confundántur et revereántur, qui quærunt ánimam meam, ut áuferant eam.

Psalm. 39.

EXSPECTANS expectávi Dóminum: * et inténdit mihi.

Et exaudívit preces meas : * et edúxit me de lacu misériæ et de luto fæcis.

Et státuit super petram pedes meos : * et diréxit gressus meos.

Et immísit in os meum cánticum novum : * carmen Deo nostro.

Vidébunt multi, et timébunt : * et sperábunt in Dómino.

Beátus vir, cujus est nomen Dómini spes ejus:

quity : and I will think for my sin.

But my enemies live, and are stronger than I : and they that hate me wrongfully are multiplied.

They that render evil for good have detracted me, because I followed goodness.

Forsake me not, O Lord my God : do not thou depart from me.

Attend unto my help, O Lord, the God of my salvation.

Ant. They used violence that sought my soul.

Ant. Let them be confounded and ashamed that seek after my soul, to take it away.

Psalm 39.

WITH expectation I have waited for the Lord, and he was attentive to me.

And he heard my prayers and he brought me out of the pit of misery, and the mire of dregs.

And he set my feet upon a rock, and directed my steps.

And he put a new canticle into my mouth, a song to our God.

Many shall see this, and shall fear : and they shall hope in the Lord.

Blessed is the man whose trust is in the name of the

* et non respéxit in vanitátes et insánias falsas.

Multa fecísti tu, Dómine Deus meus, mirabília tua : * et cogitatiónibus tuis non est qui símilis sit tibi.

Annuntiávi et locútus sum : * multiplicáti sunt super númerum.

Sacrifícium et oblatiónem noluísti : * aures autem perfecísti mihi.

Holocáustum et pro peccáto non postulásti : * tunc dixi : Ecce vénio.

In cápite libri scriptum est de me, ut fácerem voluntátem tuam : * Deus meus, vólui, et legem tuam in médio cordis mei.

Annuntiávi justítiam tuam in ecclésia magna: * ecce lábia mea non prohibébo : Dómine, tu scisti.

Justítiam tuam non abscóndi in corde meo : * veritátem tuam et salutáre tuum dixi.

Non abscóndi misericórdiam tuam, et veritátem tuam : * a concílio multo.

Tu autem Dómine, ne longe fácias miseratiónes tuas a me : * misericórdia tua et véritas tua semper suscepérunt me.

Quóniam circumdedé-

Lord : and who hath not had regard to vanities and lying follies.

Thou hast multiplied thy wonderful works, O Lord my God : and in thy thoughts there is no one like to thee.

I have declared, and I have spoken : they are multiplied above number.

Sacrifice and oblation thou didst not desire : but thou hast pierced ears for me.

Burnt-offerings and sin-offerings thou didst not require : then said I : Behold I come.

In the head of the book it was written of me, that I should do thy will : O my God, I have desired it, and thy law in the midst of my heart.

I have declared thy justice in the great Church : lo ! I will not restrain my lips : O Lord, thou knowest it.

I have not hid thy justice within my heart. I have declared thy truth and thy salvation.

I have not concealed thy mercy and thy truth from the great council.

Withhold not thou, O Lord, thy tender mercies from me : thy mercy and thy truth have always upheld me.

For evils without number

runt me mala, quorum non est númerus : * comprehendérunt me iniquitátes meæ, et non pótui ut vidérem.

Multiplicátæ sunt super capíllos cápitis mei : * et cor meum derelíquit me.

Compláceat tibi Dómine, et éruas me : * Dómine, ad adjuvándum me réspice.

Confundántur et revereántur simul, qui quærunt ánimam meam: * ut áuferant eam.

Convertántur retrórsum et revereántur : * qui volunt mihi mala.

Ferant conféstim confusiónem suam : * qui dicunt mihi : Euge, euge.

Exsúltent et læténtur super te omnes quæréntes te : * et dicant semper : Magnificétur Dóminus, qui díligunt salutáre tuum.

Ego autem mendícus sum, et pauper : * Dóminus sollícitus est mei.

Adjútor meus et protéctor meus tu es : * Deus meus, ne tardáveris.

Aña. Confundántur et revereántur qui quærunt ánimam, ut áuferant eam.

Aña. Aliéni insurrexérunt in me, et fortes quæsiérunt ánimam meam.

have surrounded me : my iniquities have overtaken me, and I was not able to see.

They are multiplied above the hairs of my head : and my heart hath forsaken me.

Be pleased, O Lord, to deliver me : look down, O Lord, to help me.

Let them be confounded and ashamed together, that seek after my soul, to take it away.

Let them be turned backward, and be ashamed, that desire evils to me.

Let them immediately bear their confusion that say to me : 'Tis well, 'tis well.

Let all that seek thee rejoice and be glad in thee : and let such as love thy salvation, say always, The Lord be magnified.

But I am a beggar and poor : the Lord is careful for me.

Thou art my helper and my protector : O my God, be not slack.

Ant. Let them be confounded and ashamed that seek after my soul, to take it away.

Ant. Strangers have risen up against me, and the mighty have sought after my soul.

Psalm. 53.

DEUS, in nómine tuo salvum me fac : * et in virtúte tua júdica me.

Deus, exáudi oratiónem meam : * áuribus pércipe verba oris mei.

Quóniam aliéni insurrexérunt advérsum me, et fortes quæsiérunt ánimam meam : * et non proposuérunt Deum ante conspéctum suum.

Ecce enim Deus ádjuvat me : * et Dóminus suscéptor est ánimæ meæ.

Avérte mala inimícis meis : * et in veritáte tua dispérde illos.

Voluntárie sacrificábo tibi : * et confitébor nómini tuo, Dómine, quóniam bonum est.

Quóniam ex omni tribulatióne eripuísti me : * et super inimícos meos despéxit oculus meus.

Aña. Aliéni insurrexérunt in me, et fortes quæsiérunt ánimam meam

℣. Insurrexérunt in me testes iníqui.

℟. Et mentita est iníquitas sibi.

Psalm 53.

SAVE me, O God, by thy name, and judge me in thy strength.

O God, hear my prayer : give ear to the words of my mouth.

For strangers have risen up against me : and the mighty have sought after my soul : and they have not set God before their eyes.

For behold God is my helper : and the Lord is the protector of my soul.

Turn back the evils upon my enemies : and cut them off in thy truth.

I will freely sacrifice to thee, and will give praise, O God, to thy name : because it is good.

For thou hast delivered me out of all trouble : and my eye hath looked down upon my enemies.

Ant. Strangers have risen up against me, and the mighty have sought after my soul.

℣. Unjust witnesses have risen up against me.

℟. And iniquity hath belied itself.

Here is said, in secret, the Pater noster.

FOURTH LESSON

Ex tractátu Sancti Augustíni Epíscopi, super Psalmos.

Psalm. 63.

PROTEXISTI me, Deus, a convéntu malignántium, a multi-

From the treatise of Saint Augustine, Bishop, upon the Psalms.

Psalm 63.

THOU hast protected me, O God, from the assembly of the malignant, from

túdine operántium iniquitátem. Jam ipsum caput nostrum intueámur. Multi mártyres tália passi sunt sed nihil sic elúcet, quómodo caput mártyrum : ibi mélius intuémur, quod illi expérti sunt. Protéctus est a multitúdine malignántium : protegénte se Deo, protegénte carnem suam ipso Filio et hómine quem gerébat, quia Fílius hóminis est, et Fílius Dei est : Fílius Dei propter formamDei : Fílius hóminis, propter formam servi, habens in potestáte pónere ánimam suam, et recípere eam. Quid ei potuérunt fácere inimíci? Occidérunt corpus, ánimam non occidérunt. Inténdite. Parum ergo erat Dóminum hortári mártyres verbo, nisi firmáret exémplo.

℞. Tamquam ad latrónem exístis cum gládiis et fústibus comprehéndere me. * Quotídie apud vos eram in templo docens, et non me tenuístis : et ecce flagellátum dúcitis ad crucifigéndum.
℣. Cumque injecíssent manus in Jesum, et tenuíssent eum, dixit ad eos :
    * Quotídie.

the multitude of the workers of iniquity. Now let us behold our head himself. Many martyrs have suffered such torments, but nothing is so conspicuous as the head of the martyrs ; there we see better what they endured. He was *protected from the multitude of the malignant :* that is, God protected himself ; the Son, and the Man assumed by the Son, protected his own flesh. For he is the Son of Man, and the Son of God : the Son of God because of the form of God : the Son of Man because of the form of a servant, having it in his power to lay down his life, and take it up again. What could his enemies do against him? They killed his body, but they did not kill his soul. Take notice, then. It signified little, for our Lord to exhort the martyrs by word, if he had not fortified them by his example.

℞. Ye are come out to take me, as a thief, with swords and clubs. * I was daily with you in the temple teaching, and ye did not apprehend me : and lo ! ye scourge me, and lead me to be crucified.
℣. And when they had laid hands on Jesus, and taken him, he said to them :

    * I was daily.

FIFTH LESSON

NOSTIS qui convéntus erat malignántium Judæórum, et quæ multitúdo erat operántium iniquitátem. Quam iniquitátem? Quia voluérunt occídere Dóminum Jesum Christum. Tanta ópera bona, inquit, osténdi vobis ; propter quod horum me vultis occídere? Pértulit omnes infírmos eórum, curávit omnes lánguidos eórum, prædicávit regnum cælórum, non tácuit vítia eórum, ut ipsa pótius eis displicérent, non médicus a quo sanabántur. His ómnibus curatiónibus ejus ingráti, tamquam multa febre phrenétici, insaniéntes in médicum qui vénerat curáre eos, excogitavérunt consílium perdéndi eum ; tamquam ibi voléntes probáre, utrum vere homo sit qui mori possit, an áliquid super hómines sit, et mori se non permíttat. Verbum ipsórum agnóscimus in Sapiéntia Salomónis. Morte turpíssima, ínquiunt condemnémus eum : interrogémus eum : erit enim respéctus in sermónibus illíus. Si enim vere Fílius Dei est, líberet eum.

℟. Ténebræ factæ sunt, dum crucifixíssent Jesum Judǽi : et circa

YOU know what was the *assembly of the wicked* Jews, and what the *multitude of those that work iniquity*. But what was that iniquity? It was that they intended to kill our Lord Jesus Christ. 'I have done,' saith he, 'so many good works among you : for which of them will you kill me?' He bore with all their weaknesses, he cured all their sick, he preached the kingdom of heaven, he concealed not their crimes, that they might rather hate them, than the physician that healed them. Yet such was their ingratitude for all these cures, that, like men raving in a high fever, they raged against the physician that came to cure them, and formed a design of destroying him : as if they had a mind to try whether he was a real man that could die, or something above men, and would not die. We find their words in the Wisdom of Solomon : 'Let us condemn him,' say they, 'to a most shameful death. Let us examine him : for regard will be had to his words. If he is truly the Son of God, let him deliver him.'

℟. Darkness covered the earth, whilst the Jews crucified Jesus : and about the

horam nonam exclamá-
vit Jesus voce magna :
Deus meus, ut quid me
dereliquisti? * Et incli-
náto cápite, emísit spí-
ritum.

℣. Exclámans Jesus
voce magna ait : Pater,
in manus tuas commén-
do spíritum meum.

* Et inclináto.

ninth hour, Jesus cried out
with a loud voice : My God !
why hast thou forsaken me?
* And bowing down his
head, he gave up the ghost.

℣. Jesus crying out with
a loud voice said : Father !
into thy hands I commend
my spirit !

* And bowing.

SIXTH LESSON

EXACUERUNT tam-
quam gládium lin-
guas suas. Non dicant
Judǽi : Non occídimus
Christum. Etenim prop-
térea eum dedérunt jú-
dici Piláto, ut quasi ipsi
a morte ejus videréntur
immúnes. Nam cum
dixísset eis Pilátus : Vos
eum occídite ; respon-
dérunt : Nobis non licet
occídere quemquam. In-
iquitátem facínoris sui
in júdicem hóminem re-
fúndere volébant : sed
numquid Deum júdi-
cem fallébant? Quod fe-
cit Pilátus, in eo ipso
quod fecit, aliquántum
párticeps fuit : sed in
comparatióne illórum,
multo ipse innocéntior.
Institit enim quantum
pótuit, ut illum ex eó-
rum mánibus liberáret :
nam proptérea flagellá-
tum prodúxit ad eos.
Non persequéndo Dómi-
num flagellávit, sed eó-
rum furóri satisfácere
volens : ut vel sic jam

THEY sharpened their ton-
gues like a sword. Let
not the Jews say : 'We did
not kill Christ :' for they
delivered him up to Pilate,
the judge, that they might
seem innocent of his death.
Thus when Pilate had said
to them : ' Put him to death
yourselves :' they answered:
'It is not lawful for us to put
any man to death.' Hereby
they pretended to throw the
injustice of their crime upon
a judge that was a man :
but could they deceive a
judge that is God? What
Pilate did, made him partaker of their crime : but in
comparison with them, he
was much more innocent.
For he laboured what he
could to get him out of
their hands ; and for that
reason ordered him to be
scourged and shown to
them. This he did to our
Lord, not by way of per-
secution, but to satisfy
their rage ; that the sight
of him in that condition
might move them to pity,

mitéscerent, et desíne-
rent velle occídere, cum
flagellátum víderent. Fe-
cit et hoc.   At ubi per-
severavérunt, nostis il-
lum lavísse manus, et
dixísse quod ipse non fe-
císset, mundum se esse
a morte illíus.   Fecit tamen.   Sed si reus, quia
fecit vel invítus : illi innocéntes, qui coëgérunt
ut fáceret?   Nullo modo.
Sed ille dixit in eum sen-
téntiam, et jussit eum
crucifígi, et quasi ipse
occídit : et vos, O Judǽi,
occidístis.   Unde occi-
dístis?   Gládio linguæ ;
acuístis enim linguas ve-
stras.   Et quando per-
cussístis,   nisi   quando
clamástis : Crucifíge,
crucifíge?

℞. Animam meam di-
léctam trádidi in manus
iniquórum, et facta est
mihi heréditas mea sicut
leo in silva : dedit con-
tra me voces adversá-
rius, dicens : Congregá-
mini, et properáte ad
devorándum illum.   Po-
suérunt me in desérto
solitúdinis, et luxit su-
per me omnis terra : *
Quia non est invéntus
qui me agnósceret, et
fáceret bene.

℣. Insurrexérunt in
me viri absque miseri-
córdia, et non pepercé-
runt ánimæ meæ.

* Quia non est.

and make them desist from
desiring his death.   All this
he did.   But when they still
persisted,   you   know   that
he washed his hands, and
said that he had no hand in
it, that he was innocent of
his death.   And yet he really
put him to death.   But if he
was guilty for doing so
against his will : are they
innocent that forced him
to do it? By no means.   He
pronounced sentence upon
him, and commanded him
to be crucified, and so
might be said to kill him :
but you, O Jews, you also
killed him.   How?   With
the sword of your tongues :
for *ye sharpened your tongues.*   And when gave you
the stroke, but when you
cried out : ' Crucify him,
crucify him'?

℞. I have delivered my
beloved soul into the hands
of the wicked, and my inheritance is become to me like
a lion in the forest : my adversary gave out his words
against me, saying : Come
together, and make haste
to devour him.   They placed
me in a solitary desert, and
all the earth mourned for
me : * Because there was
none found that would
know me, and do good unto
me.

℣. Men without mercy
rose up against me, and
they spared not my life.

* Because there was.

Here is repeated : Animam meam diléctam.

Here is repeated : I have delivered.

THE THIRD NOCTURN

Aña. Ab insurgéntibus in me, líbera me, Dómine, quia occupavérunt ánimam meam.

Ant. From them that rise up against me, deliver me, O Lord : for they are in possession of my soul.

Psalm. 58.

ERIPE me de inimícis meis, Deus meus, * et ab insurgéntibus in me, líbera me.

Eripe me de operántibus iniquitátem : * et de viris sánguinum salva me.

Quia ecce cepérunt ánimam meam : * irruérunt in me fortes.

Neque iníquitas mea, neque peccátum meum, Dómine : * sine iniquitáte cucúrri, et diréxi.

Exsúrge in occúrsum meum, et vide : * et tu, Dómine, Deus virtútum, Deus Israël.

Inténde ad visitándas omnes Gentes : * non misereáris ómnibus qui operántur iniquitátem.

Converténtur ad vesperam, et famem patiéntur ut canes : * et circuíbunt civitátem.

Eccé loquéntur in ore suo, et gládius in lábiis eórum : * quóniam quis audívit?

Et tu, Dómine, deridébis eos : * ad níhilum dedúces omnes Gentes.

Psalm 58.

DELIVER me from my enemies, O my God : and defend me from them that rise up against me.

Deliver me from them that work iniquity : and save me from bloody men.

For behold they have caught my soul : the mighty have rushed in upon me.

Neither is it for my iniquity, nor for sin, O Lord : without iniquity have I run and directed my steps.

Rise up thou to meet me, and behold : even thou, O Lord, the God of hosts, the God of Israel.

Attend to visit all the nations : have no mercy on all them that work iniquity.

They shall return at evening, and shall suffer hunger like dogs : and shall go round about the city.

Behold they shall speak with their mouth, and a sword is in their lips : for who, say they, hath heard us?

But thou, O Lord, shalt laugh at them : thou shalt bring all the nations to nothing.

Fortitúdinem meam ad te custódiam, quia Deus suscéptor meus es : * Deus meus, misericórdia ejus prævéniet me.

Deus osténdit mihi super inimícos meos, ne occídas eos : * nequándo obliviscántur pópuli mei.

Dispérge illos in virtúte tua : * et depóne eos, protéctor meus, Dómine.

Delíctum oris eórum sermónem labiórum ipsórum : * et comprehendántur in supérbia sua.

Et de execratióne et mendácio annuntiabúntur in consummatióne : * in ira consummatiónis, et non erunt.

Et scient quia Deus dominábitur Jacob : * et fínium terræ.

Converténtur ad vespéram, et famem patiéntur ut canes : * et circuíbunt civitátem.

Ipsi dispergéntur ad manducándum : * si vero non fúerint saturáti, et murmurábunt.

Ego autem cantábo fortitúdinem tuam : * et exsultábo mane misericórdiam tuam.

Quia factus es suscéptor meus : * et refúgium meum, in die tribulatiónis meæ.

Adjútor meus tibi

I will keep my strength to thee, for thou art my protector : my God, his mercy shall prevent me.

God shall let me see over my enemies : slay them not, lest at any time my people forget.

Scatter them by thy power : and bring them down, O Lord, my protector.

For the sin of their mouth, and the word of their lips : and let them be taken in their pride.

And for their cursing and lying they shall be talked of, when they are consumed : when they are consumed by thy wrath, and they shall be no more.

And they shall know that God will rule Jacob : and all the ends of the earth.

They shall return at evening, and shall suffer hunger like dogs : and shall go round about the city.

They shall be scattered abroad to eat : and shall murmur if they be not filled.

But I will sing thy strength : and will extol thy mercy in the morning.

For thou art become my support and my refuge, in the day of my trouble.

Unto thee, O my helper,

psallam, quia Deus suscéptor meus es : * Deus meus, misericórdia mea.

Aña. Ab insurgéntibus in me, líbera me, Dómine, quia occupavérunt ánimam meam.

Aña. Longe fecísti notos meos a me : tráditus sum, et non egrediébar.

Psalm. 87.

DOMINE, Deus salútis meæ : * in die clamávi, et nocte coram te.

Intret in conspéctu tuo orátio mea : * inclína aurem tuam ad precem meam.

Quia repléta est malis ánima mea : * et vita mea inférno appropinquávit.

Æstimátus sum cum descendéntibus in lacum : * factus sum sicut homo sine adjutório, inter mórtuos liber.

Sicut vulneráti dormiéntes in sepúlcris, quorum non es memor ámplius : * et ipsi de manu tua repúlsi sunt.

Posuérunt me in lacu inferióri : * in tenebrósis, et in umbra mortis.

Super me confirmátus est furor tuus : * et omnes fluctus tuos induxísti super me.

Longe fecísti notos meos a me : * posuérunt me abominatiónem sibi.

will I sing, for thou art God, my defence : my God, my mercy.

Ant. From them that rise up against me, deliver me, O Lord, for they are in possession of my soul.

Ant. Thou hast put away my acquaintance far from me : I was delivered up, and I escaped not.

Psalm 87.

O GOD, the God of my salvation, I have cried in the day, and in the night before thee.

Let my prayer come in before thee : incline thy ear to my petition.

For my soul is filled with evils : and my life hath drawn nigh to hell.

I am counted among them that go down to the pit : I am become as a man without help, free among the dead.

Like the slain sleeping in the sepulchres, whom thou rememberest no more : and they are cast off from thy hand.

They have laid me in the lower pit : in the dark places and in the shadow of death.

Thy wrath is strong over me : and all thy waves thou hast brought in upon me.

Thou hast put away my acquaintance far from me : they have set me an abomination to themselves.

Tráditus sum, et non egrediébar : * óculi mei languérunt præ inópia.

Clamávi ad te, Dómine, tota die : * expándi ad te manus meas.

Numquid mórtuis fácies mirabília : * aut médici suscitábunt, et confitebúntur tibi?

Numquid narrábit áliquis in sepúlcro misericórdiam tuam : * et veritátem tuam in perditióne?

Numquid cognoscéntur in ténebris mirabília tua : * et justítia tua in terra obliviónis?

Et ego ad te, Dómine, clamávi : * et mane orátio mea prævéniet te.

Ut quid, Dómine, repéllis oratiónem meam : * avértis fáciem tuam a me?

Pauper sum ego, et in labóribus a juventúte mea : * exaltátus autem, humiliátus sum et conturbátus.

In me transiérunt iræ tuæ : * et terróres tui conturbavérunt me.

Circumdedérunt me sicut aqua tota die : * circumdedérunt me simul.

Elongásti a me amícum et próximum : * et notos meos a miséria.

Ant. Longe fecísti

I was delivered up, and came not forth : my eyes languished through poverty.

All the day I cried to thee, O Lord : I stretched out my hands to thee.

Wilt thou show wonders to the dead : or shall physicians raise to life, and give praise to thee?

Shall any one in the sepulchre declare thy mercy, and thy truth in destruction?

Shall thy wonders be known in the dark : and thy justice in the land of forgetfulness?

But I, O Lord, have cried to thee, and in the morning my prayer shall prevent thee.

Lord, why castest thou off my prayer : why turnest thou away thy face from me?

I am poor and in labours from my youth : and being exalted, have been humbled and troubled.

Thy wrath hath come upon me : and thy terrors have troubled me.

They have come round about me like water all the day : they have compassed me about together.

Friend and neighbour thou hast put far from me : and my acquaintance because of misery.

Ant. Thou hast put away

notos meos a me : tráditus sum, et non egrediébar.

Ant. Captábunt in ánimam justi, et sánguinem innocéntem condemnábunt.

Psalm. 93.

DEUS ultiónum Dóminus : * Deus ultiónum líbere egit.

Exaltáre qui júdicas terram : * redde retributiónem supérbis.

Usquequo peccatóres Dómine : * usquequo peccatóres gloriabúntur?

Effabúntur et loquéntur iniquitátem : * loquéntur omnes qui operántur injustítiam?

Pópulum tuum, Dómine, humiliavérunt : * et hereditátem tuam vexavérunt.

Víduam et ádvenam interfecérunt : * et pupíllos occidérunt.

Et dixérunt : Non vidébit Dóminus : * nec intélliget Deus Jacob.

Intellígite insipiéntes in pópulo : * et stulti aliquándo sápite.

Qui plantávit aurem, non áudiet : * aut qui finxit óculum, non consíderat?

Qui córripit gentes, non árguet : * qui docet hóminem sciéntiam?

my acquaintance far from me : I was delivered up, and I escaped not.

Ant. They will hunt after the soul of the Just ; and will condemn innocent Blood.

Psalm 93.

THE Lord is the God to whom revenge belongeth : the God of revenge acted freely.

Lift up thyself, thou that judgest the earth : render a reward to the proud.

How long shall the wicked, O Lord, how long shall the wicked make their boast?

How long shall they utter and speak wrong things : how long shall the workers of iniquity talk?

Thy people, O Lord, they have brought low : and they have afflicted thy inheritance.

They have slain the widow and the stranger : and they have murdered the fatherless.

And they have said : The Lord shall not see : neither shall the God of Jacob understand.

Understand, ye senseless among the people : and you fools be wise at last.

He that planted the ear, shall he not hear : or he that formed the eye, doth he not consider?

He that chastiseth nations, shall he not rebuke : he that teacheth man knowledge?

Dóminus scit cogitatiónes hóminum : * quóniam vanæ sunt.

Beátus homo, quem tu erudíeris, Dómine : * et de lege tua docúeris eum.

Ut mítiges ei a diébus malis : * donec fodiátur peccatóri fóvea.

Quia non repéllet Dóminus plebem suam : * et hereditátem suam non derelínquet.

Quoadúsque justítia convertátur injudícium : et qui juxta illam omnes qui recto sunt corde.

Quis consúrget mihi advérsus malignántes? * aut quis stabit mecum advérsus operántes iniquitátem?

Nisi quia Dóminus adjúvit me : * paulo minus habitásset in inférno ánima mea.

Si dicébam : Motus est pes meus : *misericórdia tua, Dómine, adjuvábat me.

Secúndum multitúdinem dolórum meórum in corde meo : * consolatiónes tuæ lætificavérunt ánimam meam.

Numquid adhǽret tibi sedes iniquitátis : * qui fingis labórem in præcépto?

Captábunt in ánimam justi : * et sánguinem innocéntem condemnábunt.

The Lord knoweth the thoughts of men, that they are vain.

Blessed is the man whom thou shalt instruct, O Lord : and shalt teach him out of thy law.

That thou mayst give him rest from the evil days : till a pit be dug for the wicked.

For the Lord will not cast off his people : neither will he forsake his own inheritance.

Until justice be turned into judgement : and they that are near it are all the upright of heart.

Who shall rise up for me against the evil doers? or who shall stand with me against the workers of iniquity?

Unless the Lord had been my helper : my soul had almost dwelt in hell.

If I said : my foot is moved : thy mercy, O Lord, assisted me.

According to the multitude of my sorrows in my heart : thy comforts have given joy to my soul

Doth the seat of iniquity stick to thee, who framest labour in commandment?

They will hunt after the soul of the just : and will condemn innocent blood.

Et factus est mihi Dóminus in refúgium : * et Deus meus in adjutórium spei meæ.

But the Lord is my refuge : and my God the help of my hope.

Et reddet illis iniquitátem ipsórum : * et in malítia eórum dispérdet eos : * dispérdet illos Dóminus Deus noster.

And he will render to them their iniquity : and in their malice he will destroy them : yea, the Lord our God will destroy them.

Aña. Captábunt in ánimam justi, et sánguinem innocéntem condemnábunt.

Ant. They will hunt after the soul of the Just : and will condemn innocent Blood.

℣. Locúti sunt advérsum me lingua dolósa.

℣. They have spoken against me with a deceitful tongue.

℟. Et sermónibus ódii circumdedérunt me, et expugnavérunt me gratis.

℟. And they have compassed me about with words of hatred, and have fought against me without cause.

Here is said the Pater noster *in secret.*

SEVENTH LESSON

De Epístola Beáti Pauli Apóstoli ad Hebrǽos.

From the Epistle of St. Paul the Apostle, to the Hebrews.

Cap. 4 et 5.

Ch. 4 and 5.

FESTINEMUS íngredi in illam réquiem : ut ne in idípsum quis íncidat incredulitátis exémplum. Vivus est enim sermo Dei, et éfficax, et penetrabílior omni gládio ancípiti : et pertíngens usque ad divisiónem ánimæ ac spíritus, compágum quoque ac medullárum, et discrétor cogitatiónum et intentiónum cordis. Et non est ulla creatúra invisíbilis in conspéctu ejus : ómnia autem nuda et apérta sunt óculis ejus, ad quem nobis ser-

LET us hasten therefore to enter into that rest : lest any man fall into the same example of unbelief. For the word of God is living and effectual, and more piercing than any twoedged sword, and reaching unto the division of the soul and the spirit, of the joints also, and the marrow, and is a discerner of the thoughts and intents of the heart. Neither is there any creature invisible in his sight : but all things are naked and open to his eyes, to whom our speech is. Having therefore a great

mo. Habéntes ergo Pontíficem magnum, qui penetrávit cælos, Jesum Fílium Dei : teneámus confessiónem. Non enim habémus Pontíficem qui non possit cómpati infirmitátibus nostris : tentátum autem per ómnia pro similitúdine absque peccáto.

℟. Tradidérunt me in manus impiórum, et inter iníquos projecérunt me, et non pepercérunt ánimæ meæ : congregáti sunt advérsum me fortes : * Et sicut gigántes stetérunt contra me.

℣. Aliéni insurrexérunt advérsum me, et fortes quæsiérunt ánimam meam.

* Et sicut.

High Priest that hath passed into the heavens, Jesus the Son of God, let us hold fast our confession. For we have not a High Priest who cannot have compassion on our infirmities : but one tempted in all things like as we are, without sin.

℣. They delivered me into the hands of the impious and cast me out among the wicked, and spared not my life : the powerful gathered together against me : * And like giants they stood against me.

℣. Strangers have risen up against me, and the mighty have sought my soul.

* And like.

EIGHTH LESSON

ADEAMUS ergo cum fidúcia ad thronum grátiæ : ut misericórdiam consequámur,· et grátiam inveniámus in auxílio opportúno. Omnis namque póntifex ex homínibus assúmptus, pro homínibus constitúitur in iis quæ sunt ad Deum, ut ófferat dona et sacrifícia pro peccátis : qui condolére possit iis qui ignórant et errant : quóniam et ipse circúmdatus est infirmitáte. Et proptérea debet, quemádmodum pro pópulo, ita étiam et pro semetípso offérre pro peccátis.

LET us go therefore with confidence to the throne of grace : that we may obtain mercy, and find grace in seasonable aid. For every high priest taken from among men, is appointed for men in the things that appertain to God, that he may offer up gifts and sacrifices for sins : who can have compassion on them that are ignorant, and that err : because he himself also is encompassed with infirmity. And therefore he ought, as for the people, so also for himself, to offer for sins.

℞. Jesum trádidit ímpius summis princípibus sacerdótum, et senióribus pópuli : * Petrus autem sequebátur eum a longe, ut vidéret finem.

℣. Adduxérunt autem eum ad Caïpham príncipem sacerdótum, ubi scribæ et pharisæi convénerant.

* Petrus.

℞. The wicked man betrayed Jesus to the chief priests and elders of the people : * But Peter followed him afar off, that he might see the end.

℣. And they led him to Caiphas the high priest, where the scribes and pharisees were met together.

* But Peter.

NINTH LESSON

NEC quisquam sumit sibi honórem sed qui vocátur a Deo, tanquam Aaron. Sic et Christus non semetípsum clarificávit ut póntifex fíeret : sed qui locútus est ad eum : Fílius meus es tu, ego hódie génui te. Quemádmodum et in álio loco dicit : Tu es sacérdos in ætérnum secúndum órdinem Melchísedech. Qui in diébus carnis suæ, preces, supplicationésque ad eum, qui possit illum salvum fácere a morte, cum clamóre válido et lácrimis, ófferens, exaudítus est pro sua reveréntia. Et quidem cum esset Fílius Dei, dídicit ex iis, quæ passus est, obediéntiam : et consummátus, factus est ómnibus obtemperántibus sibi, causa salútis ætérnæ, appellátus a Deo póntifex juxta órdinem Melchísedech.

NEITHER doth any man take the honour to himself, but he that is called by God, as Aaron was. So also Christ did not glorify himself that he might be made a high priest : but he that said unto him : Thou art my Son, this day have I begotten thee. As he saith also in another place : Thou art a priest for ever according to the order of Melchisedech. Who in the days of his flesh, with a strong cry and tears, offering up prayers and supplications to him that was able to save him from death, was heard for his reverence : and whereas indeed he was the Son of God, he learned obedience by the things which he suffered : and being consummated he became, to all that obey him, the cause of eternal salvation, called by God a highpriest according to the order of Melchisedech.

℞. Caligavérunt óculi mei a fletu meo : quia elongátus est a me, qui consolabátur me. Vidéte, omnes pópuli, * Si est dolor símilis sicut dolor meus.

℞. My eyes are darkened by my tears : for he is far from me that comforted me. See all ye people, *If there be sorrow like unto my sorrow.

℣. O vos omnes qui transítis per viam, atténdite et vidéte.

℣. O all ye that pass by the way, behold and see,

* Si est.

* If there.

Here is repeated : Caligavérunt óculi mei.

Here is repeated : My eyes are darkened.

LAUDS

Psalms 50, 142, 84 and 147 are those of the ferial office in the new Psalter. The antiphons though not taken from the psalms are most appropriate. From very early times the canticle of Habacuc has been assigned to Friday's Lauds. The style of this canticle is energetic and full of imagery, depicting in terrifying similes that great Day of the Lord, the Last Judgment, when Christ, now humiliated and put to death, will return in all the majesty of his power to judge those who despised and condemned him. The text is obscure, but it must be borne in mind that the Latin is a translation from a Greek version, itself a translation from the original Hebrew.

The first psalm of Lauds is the Miserere, *as yesterday, page* 156. *It is sung to the following antiphon :*

Ant. Próprio Fílio suo non pepércit Deus, sed pro nobis ómnibus trádidit illum.

Ant. God spared not his own Son, but delivered him up for us all.

Ant. Anxiátus est in me spíritus meus, in me turbátum est cor meum.

Ant. My spirit is in anguish within me, my heart within me is troubled.

Psalm. 142.

Psalm 142.

DOMINE, exáudi oratiónem meam : áuribus pércipe obsecratiónem meam in veritáte tua : * exáudi me in tua justítia.

HEAR, O Lord, my prayer, give ear to my supplication in thy truth : hear me in thy justice.

Et non intres in judí-

And enter not into judg-

cium cum servo tuo : * quia non justificábitur in conspéctu tuo omnis vivens.

Quia persecútus est inimícus ánimam meam: * humiliávit in terra vitam meam.

Collocávit me in obscúris sicut mórtuos sǽculi : * et anxiátus est super me spíritus meus, in me turbátum est cor meum.

Memor fui diérum antiquórum, meditátus sum in ómnibus opéribus tuis : * in factis mánuum tuárum meditábar.

Expándi manus meas ad te : * ánima mea sicut terra sine aqua tibi.

Velóciter exáudi me, Dómine : * defécit spíritus meus.

Non avértas fáciem tuam a me : * et símilis ero descendéntibus in lacum.

Audítam fac mihi mane misericórdiam tuam : * quia in te sperávi.

Notam fac mihi viam in qua ámbulém : * quia ad te levávi ánimam meam.

Eripe me de inimícis meis, Dómine, ad te confúgi : * doce me fácere voluntátem tuam, quia Deus meus es tu.

Spíritus tuus bonus

---

ment with thy servant : for in thy sight no man living shall be justified.

For the enemy hath persecuted my soul : he hath brought down my life to the earth.

He hath made me to dwell in darkness, as those that have been dead of old ; and my spirit is in anguish within me, my heart within me is troubled.

I remembered the days of old, I meditated on all thy works, I mused upon the works of thy hands.

I stretched forth my hands to thee : my soul is as earth without water unto thee.

Hear me speedily, O Lord : my spirit hath fainted away.

Turn not away thy face from me, lest I be like unto them that go down into the pit.

Cause me to hear thy mercy in the morning : for in thee have I hoped.

Make the way known to me wherein I should walk : for I have lifted up my soul to thee.

Deliver me from my enemies, O Lord, to thee have I fled : teach me to do thy will, for thou art my God.

Thy good spirit shall lead

dedúcet me, in terram rectam : * propter nomen tuum, Dómine, vivificábis me in æquitáte tua.

Edúces de tribulatióne ánimam meam : * et in misericórdia tua dispérdes inimícos meos.

Et perdes omnes qui tríbulant ánimam meam : * quóniam ego servus tuus sum.

Ant. Anxiátus est in me spíritus meus, in me turbátum est cor meum.

Ant. Ait latro ad latrónem : Nos quidem digna factis recípimus : hic autem quid fecit? Meménto mei, Dómine, dum véneris in regnum tuum.

Psalm. 84.

BENEDIXISTI, Dómine, terram tuam : * avertísti captivitátem Jacob.

Remisísti iniquitátem plebis tuæ : * operuísti ómnia peccáta eórum.

Mitigásti omnem iram tuam : * avertísti ab ira indignatiónis tuæ.

Convérte nos, Deus, salutáris noster : * et avérte iram tuam a nobis.

Numquid in ætérnum irascéris nobis? * aut exténdes iram tuam a generatióne in generatiónem?

me into the right land : for thy name's sake, O Lord, thou wilt quicken me in thy justice.

Thou wilt bring my soul out of troubles : and in thy mercy thou wilt destroy my enemies.

And thou wilt cut off all them that afflict my soul : for I am thy servant.

Ant. My spirit is in anguish within me, my heart within me is troubled.

Ant. The thief said to the thief : We, indeed, receive the due reward of our deeds; but what has this Man done? Remember me, O Lord, when thou shalt come into thy kingdom.

Psalm 84.

THOU hast blessed thy land, O Lord : thou hast turned away the captivity of Jacob.

Thou hast forgiven the iniquity of thy people : thou hast covered all their sins.

Thou hast softened all thine anger : thou hast turned away from the wrath of thine indignation.

Convert us, O God our Saviour : and turn away thine anger from us.

Wilt thou be angry with us for ever : or wilt thou stretch out thy wrath from generation to generation?

Deus, tu convérsus vivificábis nos : * et plebs tua lætábitur in te.

Thou shalt turn again, O God, and quicken us : and thy people shall rejoice in thee.

Osténde nobis, Dómine, misericórdiam tuam : * et salutáre tuum da nobis.

Show us thy mercy, O Lord ; and grant us thy salvation.

Audiam quid loquátur in me Dóminus Deus : * quóniam loquétur pacem in plebem suam.

I will hearken to what the Lord shall say within me : for he will speak peace unto his people :

Et super sanctos suos : * et in eos, qui convertúntur ad cor.

And unto his saints : and unto them that are converted in heart.

Verúmtamen prope timéntes eum salutáre ipsíus : * ut inhábitet glória in terra nostra.

Surely his salvation is nigh unto them that fear him : that glory may dwell in our land.

Misericórdia et véritas obviavérunt sibi : * justítia et pax osculátæ sunt.

Mercy and truth have met together : justice and peace have kissed each other.

Véritas de terra orta est : * et justítia de cælo prospéxit.

Truth is sprung out of the earth : and justice hath looked down from heaven.

Etenim Dóminus dabit benignitátem : * et terra nostra dabit fructum suum.

For the Lord shall give goodness : and our earth shall yield her fruit.

Justítia ante eum ambulábit : * et ponet in via gressus suos.

Justice shall walk before him ; and shall set his steps in the way.

Ant. Ait latro ad latrónem : Nos quidem digna factis recípimus : hic autem quid fecit? Meménto mei, Dómine, dum véneris in regnum tuum.

Ant. The thief said to the thief : We, indeed, receive the due reward of our deeds: but what has this Man done? Remember me, O Lord, when thou shalt come into thy kingdom.

Ant. Dum conturbáta fúerit ánima mea, Dómine, misericórdiæ memor eris.

Ant. When my soul shall be in trouble, O Lord ! thou wilt be mindful of thy mercy.

CANTICLE OF HABACUC

DOMINE, audívi audi-tiónem tuam : * et timui.

Dómine, opus tuum : * in médio annórum vivífica illud.

In médio annórum notum fácies : * cum irátus fúeris, misericórdiæ recordáberis.

Deus ab austro véniet : * et Sanctus de monte Pharan.

Opéruit cælos glória ejus : * et laudis ejus plena est terra.

Splendor ejus ut lux erit : * córnua in mánibus ejus.

Ibi abscóndita est fortitúdo ejus : * ante fáciem ejus ibit mors.

Et egrediétur diábolus ante pedes ejus : * stetit et mensus est terram.

Aspéxit et dissólvit Gentes : * et contríti sunt montes sǽculi.

Incurváti sunt colles mundi : * ab itinéribus æternitátis ejus.

Pro iniquitáte vidi tentoria Æthiópiæ : * turbabúntur pelles terræ Mádian.

Numquid in flumínibus irátus es, Dómine? * aut in flumínibus furor tuus, vel in mari indignátio tua?

Qui ascéndes super

O Lord, I heard what thou madest me hear, and was afraid.

O Lord, thy work, in the midst of the years bring it to life.

In the midst of the years thou shalt make it known : when thou art angry, thou wilt remember mercy.

God will come from the south, and the Holy One from mount Pharan.

His glory covered the heavens : and the earth is full of his praise.

His brightness shall be as the light : horns are in his hands.

There is his strength hid : death shall go before his face.

And the devil shall go forth before his feet : he stood and measured the earth.

He beheld, and melted the nations : and the ancient mountains were crushed to pieces. The hills of the world were bowed down, by the journeys of his eternity.

I saw the tents of Æthiopia for their iniquity : the curtains of the land of Madian shall be troubled.

Wast thou angry, O Lord, with the rivers? or was thy wrath upon the rivers? or thy indignation in the sea?

Who wilt ride upon thy

equos tuos : * et qua-
drígæ tuæ salvátio.

Súscitans suscitábis
arcum tuum : * jura-
ménta tríbubus, quæ
locútus es.

Flúvios scindes terræ :
vidérunt te et doluérunt
montes : * gurges aquá-
rum tránsiit.

Dedit abýssus vocem
suam : * altitúdo manus
suas levávit.

Sol et luna stetérunt
in habitáculo suo : * in
luce sagittárum tuárum,
íbunt in splendóre fulgu-
rántis hastæ tuæ.

In frémitu conculcábis
terram : * et in furóre ob-
stupefácies Gentes.

Egréssus es in salútem
pópuli tui : * in salútem
cum Christo tuo.

Perscussísti caput de
domo ímpii : * denudásti
fundaméntum ejus us-
que ad collum.

Maledixísti sceptris
ejus, cápiti bellatórum
ejus : * veniéntibus ut
turbo ad dispergéndum
me.

Exsultátio eórum : *
sicut ejus qui dévorat
páuperem in abscóndito.

Viam fecísti in mari
equis tuis : * in luto
aquárum multárum.

Audívi et conturbátus

horses : and thy chariots are
salvation.

Thou wilt surely take up
thy bow according to the
oaths which thou hast
spoken to the tribes.

Thou wilt divide the ri-
vers of the earth : the mountains saw thee and were
grieved : the great body of
waters passed away.

The deep put forth its
voice : the deep lifted up its
hands.

The sun and the moon
stood still in their habitation, in the light of thy
arrows, they shall go in the
brightness of thy glittering
spear.

In thy anger thou wilt
tread the earth under foot :
in thy wrath thou wilt as-
tonish the nations.

Thou wentest forth for
the salvation of thy people,
for salvation with thy
Christ.

Thou struckest the head
of the house of the wicked :
thou hast laid bare his
foundation even to the
neck.

Thou hast cursed his
sceptres, the head of his
warriors, them that came
out as a whirlwind to scatter
me.

Their joy was like that of
him that devoureth the poor
man in secret.

Thou madest a way in the
sea for thy horses, in the
mud of many waters.

I have heard, and my bo-

est venter meus : * a
voce contremuérunt lá-
bia mea.

Ingrediátur putrédo in
óssibus meis : * et subter
me scáteat.

Ut requiéscam in die
tribulatiónis : * ut ascén-
dam ad pópulum accín-
ctum nostrum.

Ficus enim non flo-
rébit : * et non erit germen in víneis.

Mentiétur opus olívæ :
* et arva non áfferent
cibum.

Abscindétur de ovíli
pecus : * et non erit
arméntum in præsépi-
bus.

Ego autem in Dómino
gaudébo : * et exsultábo
in Deo Jesu meo.

Deus Dóminus forti-
túdo mea : * et ponet pe-
des meos quasi cervó-
rum.

Et super excélsa mea
dedúcet me victor : * in
psalmis canéntem.

Ant. Dum conturbáta
fúerit ánima mea, Dó-
mine, misericórdiæ me-
mor eris.

Aña. Meménto mei,
Dómine Deus, dum vé-
neris in regnum tuum.

Psalm. 147.

LAUDA, Jerúsalem,
Dóminum : * Lauda
Deum tuum Sion.

Quóniam confortávit
seras portárum tuárum :
* benedíxit fíliis tuis in
te.

wels were troubled : my
lips trembled at the voice.

Let rottenness enter into
my bones, and swarm under
me.

That I may rest in the
day of tribulation : that I
may go up to our people
that are girded.

For the fig-tree shall not
blossom : and there shall be
no spring in the vines.

The labour of the olive-
tree shall fail : and the fields
shall yield no food.

The flock shall be cut off
from the fold : and there
shall be no herd in the stalls.

But I will rejoice in the
Lord : and I will rejoice in
God my Jesus.

The Lord God is my
strength : and he will make
my feet like the feet of
harts.

And he the conqueror will
lead me upon my high pla-
ces, singing psalms.

Ant. When my soul shall
be in trouble, O Lord ! thou
wilt be mindful of thy mercy.

Ant. Remember me, O
Lord, God when thou shalt
come into thy kingdom.

Psalm 147.

PRAISE the Lord, O Je-
rusalem : praise thy
God, O Sion.

For He hath strengthened
the bars of thy gates : he
hath blessed thy children
within thee.

Qui pósuit fines tuos pacem : * et ádipe fruménti sátiat te.

Qui emíttit elóquium suum terræ : * velóciter currit sermo ejus.

Qui dat nivem sicut lanam : * nébulam sicut cínerem spargit.

Mittit crystállum suam sicut buccéllas : * ante fáciem frígoris ejus quis sustinébit?

Emíttet verbum suum, et liquefáciet ea : * flabit spíritus ejus et fluent aquæ.

Qui annúntiat verbum suum Jacob : justítias et judícia sua Israël.

Non fecit táliter omni natióni : * et judícia sua non manifestávit eis.

Aña. Meménto mei, Dómine Deus, dum véneris in regnum tuum.

℣. Collocávit me in obscúris.

℟. Sicut mórtuos sǽculi.

After this versicle, is sung the canticle Benedictus *(see p. 165) with the following antiphon :*

Aña. Posuérunt super caput ejus causam ipsíus scriptam : Jesus Nazarénus Rex Judæórum.

This antiphon having been repeated after the canticle, the choir sings, to a touching melody, the following words. They are repeated at the end of all the Canonical Hours of these three days, adding to them each day. The addition for to-day is, that the death which our Saviour deigned to suffer for us was the most disgraceful and painful of all deaths—the death of the cross.

℣. Christus factus est pro nobis obédiens usque

Who hath made peace in thy borders : and filleth thee with the fat of corn.

Who sendeth forth his speech upon the earth : his word runneth very swiftly.

Who giveth snow like wool : he scattereth mists like ashes.

He sendeth his crystal like morsels : who shall stand before the face of his cold?

He shall send out his word and shall melt them : his wind shall blow, and the waters shall run.

Who declareth his word unto Jacob : his justice and judgments unto Israel.

He hath not done in like manner to every nation : and his judgments he hath not made manifest to them.

Ant. Remember me, O Lord God, when thou shalt come into thy kingdom.

℣. He hath made me to dwell in darkness.

℟. As those that have been dead of old.

Ant. They put over his head his cause written : Jesus of Nazareth, King of the Jews.

℣. Christ became, for our sake, obedient unto death,

ad mortem, mortem autem crucis.

even to the death of the cross.

Then is said, in secret, the Pater noster, *which is followed by the* Miserere (*p.* 156). *This psalm is not sung, but only recited as explained in yesterday's Tenebræ. As soon as the Miserere is finished, the following prayer is said by the first in dignity :*

Réspice, quǽsumus, Dómine, super hanc famíliam tuam : pro qua Dóminus noster Jesus Christus non dubitávit mánibus tradi nocéntium, et crucis subíre torméntum :

Look down, O Lord, we beseech thee, upon this thy family, for which our Lord Jesus Christ hesitated not to be delivered into the hands of wicked men, and to undergo the punishment of the cross :

(then the rest in secret :)

Qui tecum vivit et regnat, in unitáte Spíritus Sancti, Deus, per ómnia sǽcula sæculórum. Amen.

Who liveth and reigneth with thee, in the unity of the Holy Ghost, God, world without end. Amen.

THE MORNING OFFICE

The liturgy of this office is even richer in ancient rites than that of the preceding day, rites peculiar to Good Friday and never used during the rest of the year.

The station is at Holy Cross in Jerusalem, built by St. Helena on her Sessorian estate. The devotion of the mother of Constantine to the true Cross is well-known. After the discovery in Jerusalem of the Cross and various other instruments of the Passion, she brought back some of these relics to Rome. The church she built became the centre of the devotion to the Holy Cross, as it were a replica of the Holy Places of Jerusalem. On Good Friday and on all feasts of the Holy Cross and of the Passion, pilgrims flock to this church, which is the stational one for these days.

The first part of the Mass is reduced to its simplest and most austere form. There is first a Lesson from the Old Testament with its complementary Tract and Collect, then a second Lesson and Tract, after which follows the reading of the Passion according to St. John. Here again

the choice of these various passages is singularly appropriate. The Lesson from Osee and the Tract from Habacuc are Messianic prophecies ; moreover as we have remarked, the latter is the canticle proper to the ferial office of Friday's Lauds in the Roman liturgy. As to the Lesson from the book of Exodus, what could be more fitting than the description of the Jewish pasch on this day whereon the true Lamb is immolated? Psalm 139 is also proper to Friday's ferial office in the old Roman *cursus,* where it is the third psalm at Vespers.

The Passion according to St. John is shorter than that of the synoptic writers, because it omits the account of the Last Supper and the agony in the garden, and begins at the betrayal of Jesus. The narratives of the three synoptic writers tally with each other, except for a few minor variations, but St. John true to his plan of action throughout the whole of his Gospel aims rather at supplying little additional details than at giving a consecutive account of events. The writer of the fourth Gospel is evidently an eye-witness, the one to whose care Jesus confided his Mother, who saw his sacred side pierced by the lance, and who gave testimony of all these things. These pages complete the portrait left to us by St. John of the Messias, Son of God, Divine Word and Eternal Truth.

STATION AT THE HOLY CROSS IN JERUSALEM

After None the priest and his ministers in black vestments, and without lights or incense, proceed to the steps of the altar, where they prostrate and pray in silence. Meanwhile the acolytes spread a linen cloth upon the altar and place the book upon it. All then rise ; the priest goes up to the Epistle corner of the altar while the lector sings the first Lesson or Prophecy, without any introductory title.

Osee, c. 6.

HÆC dicit Dóminus : In tribulatióne sua mane consúrgent ad me : Veníte, et revertámur ad Dóminum : quia ipse cépit, et sanábit nos : percútiet, et curábit nos. Vivificábit nos post duos dies : in die tértia suscitábit nos, et vivémus in conspéctu

Osee, c. 6.

THUS saith the Lord : In their affliction they will rise early to me : Come, and let us return to the Lord ; for he hath taken us, and he will heal us : he will strike, and he will cure us. He will revive us after two days ; on the third day he will raise us up, and we shall live in his sight. We

ejus. Sciémus, seque-
múrque ut cognoscámus
Dóminum. Quasi dilú-
culum præparátus est
egréssus ejus, et véniet
quasi imber nobis tem-
poráneus et serótinus
terræ. Quid fáciam ti-
bi, Ephraim? Quid fá-
ciam tibi, Juda? Miseri-
córdia vestra quasi nu-
bes matutína : et quasi
ros mane pertránsiens.
Propter hoc dolávi in
prophétis, occídi eos in
verbis oris mei : et judícia tua quasi lux egre-
diéntur. Quia misericór-
diam vólui, et non sacri-
fícium : et sciéntiam Dei
plus quam holocáusta.

Tractus. Hab. 3.

DOMINE, audívi audí-
tum tuum, et tí-
mui ; considerávi ópera
tua, et expávi. ℣. In
médio duórum animá-
lium innotescéris ; dum
appropinquáverint anni,
cognoscéris ; dum advé-
nerit tempus, ostendé-
ris. ℣. In eo, dum con-
turbáta fúerit ánima
mea : in ira misericórdiæ
memor eris. ℣. Deus a
Líbano véniet, et san-
ctus de monte umbróso
et condénso. ℣. Ópe-
ruit cælos majéstas ejus ;
et laudis ejus plena est
terra.

shall know, and we shall
follow on, that we may
know the Lord. His going
forth is prepared as the
morning light, and he will
come to us as the early and
the latter rain to the earth.
What shall I do to thee, O
Ephraim? what shall I do to
thee, O Juda? your mercy is
as a morning cloud, and as
the dew that goeth away in
the morning. For this reason
have I hewed them by the
prophets, I have slain them
by the words of my mouth :
and thy judgements shall go
forth as the light. For I desired mercy, and not sacrifice ; and the knowledge of
God more than holocausts.

Tract. Hab. 3.

O LORD, I have heard
thy hearing, and was
afraid ; I considered thy
works, and trembled. ℣. In
the midst of two animals
thou shalt be made known ;
when the years shall draw
nigh, thou shalt be known ;
when the time shall come,
thou shalt be shown. ℣. In
the time when my soul shall
be troubled : in anger thou
shalt be mindful of mercy.
℣. God shall come from
Libanus, and the holy one
from the shady and thickly-
covered mountain. ℣. His
majesty hath covered the
heavens ; and the earth is
full of his praise.

After the Tract, the priest standing at the Epistle corner sings,
Orémus ; *the deacon,* Flectámus génua ; *and the subdeacon,* Leváte.

Oratio.

DEUS, a quo et Judas reátus sui pœnam, et confessiónis suæ latro præmium sumpsit : concéde nobis tuæ propitiatiónis efféctum : ut sicut in passióne sua Jesus Christus Dóminus noster divérsa utrísque íntulit stipéndia meritórum : ita nobis, abláto vetustátis erróre, resurrectiónis suæ grátiam largiátur. Qui tecum vivit et regnat.

Collect.

O GOD, from whom Judas received the punishment of his guilt and the thief the reward of his confession, grant us the fruit of thy clemency : that, as our Lord Jesus Christ in his Passion gave recompense to each according to his merits, so he may deliver us from our old sins and bestow on us the grace of his resurrection. Who liveth and reigneth.

The subdeacon sings the following Lesson without title and on the tone of the Epistle.

Exod. c. 12.

IN diébus illis : Dixit Dóminus ad Móysen et Aaron in terra Ægýpti : Mensis iste, vobis princípium ménsium : primus erit in ménsibus anni. Loquímini ad univérsum cœtum filiórum Israël, et dícite eis : Décima die mensis hujus tollat unusquísque agnum per famílias et domos suas. Sin autem minor est númerus, ut suffícere possit ad vescéndum agnum, assúmet vicínum suum, qui junctus est dómui suæ, juxta númerum animárum, quæ suffícere possunt ad esum agni. Erit autem agnus absque mácula, másculus, annículus : juxta quem ritum tollétis et hædum. Et servábitis eum usque

Exod. c. 12.

IN those days : The Lord said to Moses and Aaron in the land of Egypt : This month shall be to you the beginning of months : it shall be the first in the months of the year. Speak ye to the whole assembly of the children of Israel, and say to them : On the tenth day of this month let every man take a lamb by their families and houses. But if the number be less than may suffice to eat the lamb, he shall take unto him his neighbour that joineth to his house, according to the number of souls which may be enough to eat the lamb. And it shall be a lamb without blemish, a male of one year : according to which rite also you shall take a kid. And you shall keep it until the fourteenth day of

ad quartam décimam diem mensis hujus : immolabítque eum univérsa multitúdo filiórum Israël ad vésperam. Et sument de sánguine ejus, ac ponent super utrúmque postem, et in superlimináribus domórum, in quibus cómedent illum. Et edent carnes nocte illa assas igni, et ázymos panes, cum lactúcis agréstibus. Non comedétis ex eo crudum quid, nec coctum aqua, sed tantum assum igni : caput cum pédibus ejus et intestínis vorábitis. Nec remanébit quidquam ex eo usque mane. Si quid resíduum fúerit, igne comburétis. Sic autem comedétis illum : renes vestros accingétis et calceaménta habébitis in pédibus, tenéntes báculos in mánibus, et comedétis festinánter. Est enim *Phase* (id est tránsitus) Dómini.

Tractus. Ps. 139.

ERIPE me, Dómine, ab hómine malo : a viro iníquo líbera me. ℣. Qui cogitavérunt malítias in corde : tota die constituébant prǽlia. ℣. Acuérunt linguas suas sicut serpéntes : venénum áspidum sub lábiis eórum. ℣. Custódi me, Dómine, de manu peccatóris : et ab homínibus iníquis líbera me. ℣.

this month, and the whole multitude of the children of Israel shall sacrifice it in the evening. And they shall take of the blood thereof, and put it upon both the side-posts, and upon the upper door-posts of the houses, wherein they shall eat it. And they shall eat the flesh that night roasted at the fire, and unleavened bread, with wild lettuce. You shall not eat thereof anything raw, nor boiled in water, but only roasted at the fire. You shall eat the head with the feet and entrails thereof : neither shall there remain any thing of it until morning. If there shall be any thing left, you shall burn it with fire. And thus you shall eat it : you shall gird your reins, and you shall have shoes on your feet, holding staves in your hands, and you shall eat in haste. For it is the *Phase* (that is the passage) of the Lord.

Tract. Ps. 139.

DELIVER me, O Lord, from the evil man ; rescue me from the unjust man. ℣. Who have devised wickedness in their heart ; all the day long they designed battles. ℣. They have sharpened their tongues like a serpent ; the venom of asps is under their lips. ℣. Keep me, O Lord, from the hand of the sinner ; and from unjust men deliver me.

Qui cogitavérunt sup-plantáre gressus meos : abscondérunt supérbi láqueum mihi. ℣. Et funes extendérunt in láqueum pédibus meis : juxta iter scándalum posuérunt mihi. ℣. Dixi Dómino : Deus meus es tu : exáudi, Dómine, vocem oratiónis meæ. ℣. Dómine, Dómine, virtus salútis meæ, obúmbra caput meum in die belli. ℣. Ne tradas me a desidério meo peccatóri : cogitavérunt advérsum me : ne derelínquas me, ne umquam exalténtur. ℣. Caput circúitus eórum : labor labiórum ipsórum opériet eos. ℣. Verúmtamen justi confitebúntur nómini tuo : et habitábunt recti cum vultu tuo.

℣. Who have proposed to supplant my steps; the proud have hid a net for me. ℣. And they have stretched out cords for a snare for my feet; they have laid for me a stumbling-block by the way-side. ℣. I said to the Lord, Thou art my God; hear, O Lord, the voice of my supplication. ℣. O Lord, Lord, the strength of my salvation, overshadow my head in the day of battle. ℣. Give me not up, from my desire to the wicked : they have plotted against me; do not thou forsake me, lest at any time they should triumph. ℣. The head of them compassing me about : the labour of their lips shall overwhelm them. ℣. But the just shall give glory to thy name; and the upright shall dwell with thy countenance.

Pássio Dómini nostri Jesu Christi secúndum Joánnem, c. 18 & 19.

The Passion of our Lord Jesus Christ according to St. John, c. 18 & 19.

IN illo témpore : Egréssus est Jesus cum discípulis suis trans torréntem Cedron, ubi erat hortus, in quem introívit ipse et discípuli ejus. Sciébat autem et Judas, qui tradébat eum, locum : quia frequénter Jesus convénerat illuc cum discípulis suis. Judas ergo cum accepísset cohórtem, et a pontifícibus et pharisæis minístros, venit illuc cum

AT that time : Jesus went forth with his disciples over the brook of Cedron, where there was a garden, into which he entered with his disciples. And Judas also, who betrayed him, knew the place : because Jesus had often resorted thither, together with his disciples. Judas, therefore, having received a band of soldiers and servants from the chief priests and the pharisees, cometh thither

latérnis, et fácibus, et armis. Jesus ítaque sciens ómnia, quæ ventúra erant super eum, procéssit, et dixit eis : ✠ Quem quæritis? Respondérunt ei : Jesum Nazarénum. Dicit eis Jesus: ✠ Ego sum. Stabat autem et Judas, qui tradébat eum, cum ipsis. Ut ergo dixit eis· : Ego sum : abiérunt retrórsum, et cecidérunt in terram. Iterum ergo interrogávit eos : ✠ Quem quæritis? Illi autem dixérunt : Jesum Nazarénum. Respóndit Jesus : ✠ Dixi vobis, quia ego sum : si ergo me quæritis, sínite hos abíre. Ut implerétur sermo, quem dixit : Quia quos dedísti mihi non pérdidi ex eis quemquam. Simon ergo Petrus habens gládium, edúxit eum : et percússit pontíficis servum : et abscídit aurículam ejus déxteram. Erat autem nomen servo Malchus. Dixit ergo Jesus Petro : ✠ Mitte gládium tuum in vagínam. Cálicem, quem dedit mihi Pater, non bibam illum? Cohors ergo, et tribúnus, et minístri Judæórum comprehendérunt Jesum, et ligavérunt eum, et adduxérunt eum ad Annam primum, erat enim socer Cáiphæ, qui erat pónti-

with lanterns and torches and weapons. Jesus, therefore, knowing all things that should come upon him, went forth and said to them : Whom seek ye? They answered him : Jesus of Nazareth. Jesus said to them : I am he. And Judas, also, who betrayed him, stood with them. As soon, therefore, as he had said to them: I am he : they went backward, and fell to the ground. Again, therefore, he asked them : Whom seek ye? And they said : Jesus of Nazareth. Jesus answered : I have told you that I am he. If, therefore, you seek me, let these go their way. That the word might be fulfilled which he said : Of them whom thou hast given me, I have not lost any one. Then Simon Peter having a sword, drew it : and struck the servant of the high priest, and cut off his right ear. And the name of the servant was Malchus. Jesus therefore said to Peter : Put up thy sword into the scabbard. The chalice which my Father hath given me, shall I not drink it? Then the band, and the tribune, and the servants of the Jews took Jesus, and bound him : and they led him away to Annas first, for he was father-in-law to Caiphas, who was the high priest of that year. Now, Caiphas was he who had given counsel to

fex anni illius. Erat autem Cáiphas, qui consílium déderat Judǽis : quia éxpedit, unum hóminem mori pro pópulo. Sequebátur autem Jesum Simon Petrus, et álius discípulus. Discípulus autem ille erat notus pontífici, et introívit cum Jesu in átrium pontíficis. Petrus autem stabat ad óstium foris. Exívit ergo discípulus álius, qui erat notus pontífici, et dixit ostiáriæ : et introdúxit Petrum. Dicit ergo Petro ancílla ostiária : Numquid et tu ex discípulis es hóminis istíus? Dicit ille : Non sum. Stabant autem servi, et minístri ad prunas, quia frigus erat, et calefaciébant se. Erat autem cum eis et Petrus stans, et calefáciens se. Póntifex ergo interrogávit Jesum de discípulis suis, et de doctrína ejus. Respóndit ei Jesus : ✠ Ego palam locútus sum mundo : ego semper dócui in synagóga, et in templo, quo omnes Judǽi convéniunt : et in occúlto locútus sum nihil. Quid me intérrogas? intérroga eos, qui audiérunt quid locútus sim ipsis : ecce hi sciunt quæ díxerim ego. Hæc autem cum dixísset, unus assístens ministró-

the Jews : that it was expedient that one man should die for the people. And Simon Peter followed Jesus, and so did another disciple. And that disciple was known to the high priest, and went in with Jesus into the court of the high priest. But Peter stood at the door without. The other disciple therefore, who was known to the high priest, went out, and spoke to the portress, and brought in Peter. And the maid that was portress saith to Peter : Art not thou also one of this man's disciples? He saith : I am not. Now, the servants and officers stood at a fire of coals because it was cold, and warmed themselves. And with them was Peter also standing, and warming himself. The high priest therefore asked Jesus of his disciples, and of his doctrine. Jesus answered him : I have spoken openly to the world : I have always taught in the synagogue, and in the temple, whither all the Jews resort : and in secret I have spoken nothing. Why askest thou me? ask them who have heard what I have spoken to them : behold they know what things I have said. And when he had said these things, one of the servants standing by gave Jesus a blow, saying : Answerest thou the high priest so? Jesus answered him :

rum dedit álapam Jesu, dicens : Sic respóndes pontífici? Respóndit ei Jesus : ✠ Si male locútus sum, testimónium pérhibe de malo : si autem bene, quid me cædis? Et misit eum Annas ligátum ad Cáipham pontíficem. Erat autem Simon Petrus stans et calefáciens se. Dixérunt ergo ei : Numquid et tu ex discípulis ejus es? Negávit ille, et dixit : Non sum. Dicit ei unus ex servis pontíficis, cognátus ejus, cujus abscídit Petrus aurículam : Nonne ego te vidi in horto cum illo? Iterum ergo negávit Petrus : et statim gallus cantávit. Addúcunt ergo Jesum a Cáipha in prætórium. Erat autem mane ; et ipsi non introiérunt in prætórium, ut non contaminaréntur, sed ut manducárent Pascha. Exívit ergo Pilátus ad eos foras, et dixit : Quam accusatiónem affértis advérsus hóminem hunc? Respondérunt et dixérunt ei : Si non esset hic malefáctor, non tibi tradidissémus eum. Dixit ergo eis Pilátus : Accípite eum vos, et secúndum legem vestram judicáte eum. Dixérunt ergo ei Judǽi : Nobis non licet interfícere quemquam.

If I have spoken evil, give testimony of the evil : but if well, why strikest thou me? And Annas sent him bound to Caiphas, the high priest. And Simon Peter was standing and warming himself. They said therefore to him : Art not thou also one of his disciples? He denied it, and said : I am not. One of the servants of the high priest (a kinsman to him whose ear Peter cut off) saith to him : Did not I see thee in the garden with him? Then Peter again denied : and immediately the cock crew. Then they led Jesus from Caiphas to the governor's hall. And it was morning : and they went not into the hall, that they might not be defiled, but that they might eat the pasch. Pilate, therefore, went out to them, and said : What accusation bring you against this man? They answered and said to him : If he were not a malefactor, we would not have delivered him up to thee. Pilate therefore said to them : Take him you, and judge him according to your law. The Jews, therefore, said to him : It is not lawful for us to put any man to death. That the word of Jesus might be fulfilled, which he said, signifying what death he should die. Pilate, therefore, went into the hall again, and called Jesus, and said to him :

Ut sermo Jesu impleré-tur, quem dixit, signí-ficans qua morte es-set moritúrus. Introívit ergo íterum in prætó-rium Pilátus, et vocávit Jesum, et dixit ei : Tu es Rex Judæórum? Re-spóndit Jesus : ✠ A te-metípso hoc dicis, an álii dixérunt tibi de me? Respóndit Pilátus : Numquid ego Judǽus sum? Gens tua, et pon-tífices tradidérunt te mihi : quid fecísti? Re-spóndit Jesus : ✠ Re-gnum meum non est de hoc mundo. Si ex hoc mundo esset regnum meum, minístri mei úti-que decertárent ut non tráderer Judǽis. Nunc autem regnum meum non est hinc. Dixit ita-que ei Pilátus : Ergo rex es tu? Respóndit Jesus : ✠ Tu dicis quia rex sum ego. Ego in hoc natus sum, et ad hoc veni in mundum, ut testimónium perhíbeam veritáti. Omnis qui est ex veritáte, audit vocem meam. Dicit ei Pilátus: Quid est véritas? Et cum hoc dixísset, íte-rum exívit ad Judǽos, et dicit eis : Ego nullam invénio in eo causam. Est autem consuetúdo vobis ut unum dimít-tam vobis in Pascha : vultis ergo dimíttam vo-bis regem Judæórum?

Art thou the king of the Jews? Jesus answered : Sayest thou this thing of thyself, or have others told it thee of me? Pilate an-swered : Am I a Jew? Thy own nation and the chief priests have delivered thee up to me : what hast thou done? Jesus answered : My kingdom is not of this world. If my kingdom were of this world, my ser-vants would certainly strive that I should not be deli-vered to the Jews ; but now my kingdom is not from hence. Pilate, therefore, said to him : Art thou a king then? Jesus answered : Thou sayest that I am a king. For this was I born, and for this came I into the world, that I should give testimony to the truth. Eve-ry one that is of the truth, heareth my voice. Pilate saith to him : What is truth? And when he had said this, he went out again to the Jews, and saith to them : I find no cause in him. But you have a custom that I should release one unto you at the pasch : will you, therefore, that I re-lease unto you the king of the Jews? Then cried they all again, saying : Not this man, but Barabbas. Now, Barabbas was a robber. Then, therefore, Pilate took Jesus and scourged him. And the soldiers, platting a crown of thorns, put it

Clamavérunt ergo rursum omnes, dicéntes : Non hunc, sed Barábbam. Erat autem Barábbas latro. Tunc ergo apprehéndit Pilátus Jesum, et flagellávit. Et mílites plecténtes corónam de spinis, imposuérunt cápiti ejus : et veste purpúrea circumdedérunt eum. Et veniébant ad eum, et dicébant : Ave, rex Judæórum : et dabant ei álapas. Exívit ergo íterum Pilátus foras, et dicit eis : Ecce addúco vobis eum foras, ut cognoscátis quia nullam invénio in eo causam. (Exívit ergo Jesus portans corónam spíneam et purpúreum vestiméntum.) Et dicit eis : Ecce homo. Cum ergo vidíssent eum pontífices, et minístri, clamábant, dicéntes : Crucifíge, crucifíge eum. Dicit eis Pilátus : Accípite eum vos, et crucifígite : ego enim non invénio in eo causam. Respondérunt ei Judæi : Nos legem habémus, et secúndum legem debet mori, quia Fílium Dei se fecit. Cum ergo audísset Pilátus hunc sermónem, magis tímuit. Et ingréssus est prætórium íterum : et dixit ad Jesum : Unde es tu? Jesus autem respónsum non de-

upon his head : and they put on him a purple garment. And they came to him and said : Hail, king of the Jews; and they gave him blows. Pilate, therefore, went forth again, and saith to them : Behold, I bring him forth unto you, that you may know that I find no cause in him. (Jesus therefore came forth bearing the crown of thorns, and the purple garment.) And he saith to them : Behold the Man. When the chief priests, therefore, and the servants had seen him, they cried out, saying : Crucify him, crucify him. Pilate saith to them : Take him you, and crucify him : for I find no cause in him. The Jews answered him : We have a law, and, according to the law, he ought to die, because he made himself the Son of God. When Pilate, therefore, had heard this saying, he feared the more. And he entered into the hall again ; and he said to Jesus : Whence art thou? But Jesus gave him no answer. Pilate therefore saith to him : Speakest thou not to me? Knowest thou not that I have power to crucify thee, and I have power to release thee? Jesus answered : Thou shouldst not have any power against me, unless it were given thee from above. Therefore he that hath delivered me to

dit ei. Dicit ergo ei Pilátus : Mihi non lóqueris? nescis quia potestátem hábeo crucifígere te, et potestátem hábeo dimíttere te? Respóndit Jesus : ✠ Non habéres potestátem advérsum me ullam, nisi tibi datum esset désuper. Proptérea qui me trádidit tibi, majus peccátum habet. Et exínde quærébat Pilátus dimíttere eum. Judǽi autem clamábant, dicéntes : Si hunc dimíttis, non es amícus Cæsaris. Omnis enim qui se regem facit contradícit Cæsari. Pilátus autem cum audísset hos sermónes, addúxit foras Jesum : et sedit pro tribunáli, in loco qui dícitur Lithóstrotos, hebráice autem Gábbatha. Erat autem Parascéve Paschæ, hora quasi sexta, et dicit Judǽis : Ecce rex vester. Illi autem clamábant : Tolle, tolle, crucifíge eum. Dicit eis Pilátus : Regem vestrum crucifígam? Respondérunt pontífices : Non habémus regem nisi Cǽsarem. Tunc ergo trádidit eis illum ut crucifigerétur. Suscepérunt autem Jesum, et eduxérunt. Et bájulans sibi crucem, exívit in eum, qui dícitur Calváriæ, locum, hebráice autem Gólgotha,

thee hath the greater sin. And from henceforth Pilate sought to release him. But the Jews cried out, saying : If thou release this man, thou art not Cæsar's friend. For whosoever maketh himself a king, speaketh against Cæsar. Now when Pilate had heard these words, he brought Jesus forth ; and sat down in the judgement-seat, in the place that is called Lithostrotos, and in Hebrew, Gabbatha. And it was the parasceve of the pasch, about the sixth hour, and he saith to the Jews : Behold your king. But they cried out : Away with him, away with him, crucify him. Pilate saith to them : Shall I crucify your king? The chief priests answered : We have no king but Cæsar. Then, therefore, he delivered him to them to be crucified. And they took Jesus and led him forth. And bearing his own cross, he went forth to that place which is called Calvary, but in Hebrew, Golgotha, where they crucified him, and with him two others, one on each side, and Jesus in the midst. And Pilate wrote a title also : and he put it upon the cross. And the writing was : JESUS OF NA-

ubi crucifixérunt eum, et cum eo álios duos, hinc et hinc, médium autem Jesum. Scripsit autem et títulum Pilátus : et pósuit super crucem. Erat autem scriptum : JESUS NAZARÉNUS, REX JUDÆÓRUM. Hunc ergo títulum multi Judæórum legérunt, quia prope civitátem erat locus, ubi crucifíxus est Jesus. Et erat scriptum hebráice, græce, et latíne. Dicébant ergo Piláto Pontífices Judæórum : Noli scríbere : Rex Judæórum : sed quia ipse dixit : Rex sum Judæórum. Respóndit Pilátus : Quod scripsi, scripsi. Mílites ergo cum crucifixíssent eum, accepérunt vestiménta ejus (et fecérunt quátuor partes : unicuíque míliti partem) et túnicam. Erat autem túnica inconsútilis, désuper contéxta per totum. Dixérunt ergo ad ínvicem : Non scindámus eam, sed sortiámur de illa cujus sit. Ut Scriptúra implerétur, dicens : Partíti sunt vestiménta mea sibi : et in vestem meam misérunt sortem. Et mílites quidem hæc fecérunt. Stabant autem juxta crucem Jesu, mater ejus, et soror matris ejus María Cléophæ, et María Magda-

ZARETH, THE KING OF THE JEWS. This title, therefore many of the Jews did read, because the place where Jesus was crucified was nigh to the city. And it was written in Hebrew, in Greek, and in Latin. Then the chief priests of the Jews said to Pilate : Write not : The King of the Jews ; but that he said : I am the king of the Jews. Pilate answered : What I have written, I have written. The soldiers, therefore, when they had crucified him, took his garments (and they made four parts, to every soldier a part) and also his coat. Now the coat was without seam, woven from the top throughout. They said then one to another : Let us not cut it, but let us cast lots, for it whose it shall be : that the Scripture might be fulfilled, saying : They have parted my garments among them : and upon my vesture they have cast lots. And the soldiers indeed did these things. Now there stood by the cross of Jesus, his mother, and his mother's sister, Mary of Cleophas, and Mary Magdalen. When Jesus, therefore, had seen his mother and the disciple stand-

léne. Cum vidísset ergo Jesus matrem, et discípulum stantem quem diligébat, dicit matri suæ : ✠ Múlier, ecce fílius tuus . Deínde dicit discípulo : ✠ Ecce mater tua. Et ex illa hora accépit eam discípulus in sua. Póstea sciens Jesus, quia ómnia consummáta sunt, ut consummarétur Scriptúra, dixit : ✠ Sítio. Vas ergo erat pósitum acéto plenum. Illi autem spóngiam plenam acéto, hyssópo circumponéntes, obtulérunt ori ejus. Cum ergo accepísset Jesus acétum dixit : ✠ consummátum est. Et inclináto cápite, trádidit spíritum.

ing, whom he loved, he saith to his mother : Woman, behold thy son. After that, he saith to the disciple : Behold thy mother. And from that hour the disciple took her to his own. Afterwards Jesus knowing that all things were now accomplished, that the Scripture might be fulfilled, said : I thirst. Now there was a vessel set there full of vinegar. And they putting a sponge full of vinegar about hyssop, put it to his mouth. Jesus, therefore, when he had taken the vinegar, said : It is consummated. And bowing his head, he gave up the ghost.

Here a pause is made, and all kneel down.

JUDÆI ergo (quóniam Parascéve erat) ut non remanérent in cruce córpora sábbato (erat enim magnus dies ille sábbati), rogavérunt Pilátum ut frangeréntur eórum crura et tolleréntur. Venérunt ergo mílites : et primi quidem fregérunt crura, et altérius qui crucifíxus est cum eo. Ad Jesum autem cum veníssent, ut vidérunt eum jam mórtuum, non fregérunt ejus crura. Sed unus mílitum láncea latus ejus apéruit, et contínuo exívit sanguis et aqua. Et

THEN the Jews (because it was the Parasceve), that the bodies might not remain upon the cross on the sabbath-day (for that was a great sabbath-day), besought Pilate that their legs might be broken, and that they might be taken away. The soldiers, therefore, came, and they broke the legs of the first, and of the other that was crucified with him. But after they were come to Jesus, when they saw that he was already dead, they did not break his legs. But one of the soldiers with a spear opened his side, and immediately there

qui vidit, testimónium perhíbuit, et verum est testimónium ejus. Et ille scit, quia vera dicit : ut et vos credátis. Facta sunt enim hæc ut Scriptúra implerétur : Os non comminuétis ex eo. Et íterum ália Scriptúra dicit : Vidébunt in quem transfixérunt.

came out blood and water. And he that saw it hath given testimony : and his testimony is true. And he knoweth that he saith true : that you also may believe. For these things were done that the Scripture might be fulfilled : You shall not break a bone of him. And again another Scripture saith : They shall look on him whom they pierced.

Here Munda cor meum *is said, but the deacon does not ask the priest's blessing, nor does he incense the book.*

POST hæc autem rogávit Pilátum Joseph ab Arimathǽa (eo quod esset discípulus Jesu, occúltus autem propter metum Judæórum), ut tólleret corpus Jesu. Et permísit Pilátus. Venit ergo, et tulit corpus Jesu. Venit autem et Nicodémus, qui vénerat ad Jesum nocte primum, ferens mixtúram myrrhæ et áloes, quasi libras centum. Accepérunt ergo corpus Jesu et ligavérunt illud línteis cum aromátibus, sicut mos est Judǽis sepelíre. Erat autem in loco, ubi crucifíxus est, hortus : et in horto monuméntum novum, in quo nondum quisquam pósitus erat. Ibi ergo propter Parascéven Judæórum, quia juxta erat monuméntum, posuérunt Jesum.

AND after these things Joseph of Arimathea (because he was a disciple of Jesus, but secretly, for fear of the Jews) besought Pilate that he might take away the body of Jesus. And Pilate gave him leave. He came, therefore, and took away the body of Jesus. And Nicodemus also came, he who at the first came to Jesus by night, bringing a mixture of myrrh and aloes, about a hundred pounds weight. They took, therefore, the body of Jesus, and bound it in linen cloths with the spices, as the manner of the Jews is to bury. Now there was a garden in the place where he he was crucified : and in the garden a new sepulchre, wherein no man yet had been laid. There, therefore, because of the parasceve of the Jews, they laid Jesus, because the sepulchre was nigh at hand.

Then the priest, standing at the Epistle corner of the altar, sings the following Collects :

Prayers in the form of a litany.

The first part of the Mass is now over and the prayers which follow belong to a distinct liturgical group, being the ancient form of prayer or litany which preceded the Offertory.   The object of the petition is first announced by the priest, the deacon calls on the people to bend the knee and the subdeacon gives the signal to rise.   The priest then makes himself the mouth piece of all assembled in the prayer. In these prayers are included all sorts and conditions of men and all the needs of the Church.   St. Augustine, Pope St. Celestine and other writers of the fourth and fifth centuries allude to these prayers which were then universally recited, and the text of which has remained practically unchanged.

OREMUS, dilectíssimi nobis, pro Ecclésia sancta Dei : ut eam Deus et Dóminus noster pacificáre, adunáre, et custodíre dignétur toto orbe terrárum : subjíciens ei principátus, et potestátes : detque nobis quiétam et tranquíllam vitam degéntibus, glorificáre Deum Patrem omnipoténtem.
Orémus.

LET us pray, dearly beloved, for the holy Church of God : that our God and Lord would be pleased to give it peace, maintain it in union, and preserve it over the earth : subjecting to it the princes and potentates of the world: and grant us, that live in peace and tranquillity, grace to glorify God the Father almighty.
Let us pray.

The deacon says :

Flectámus génua.   Let us kneel.

The subdeacon answers :

℟. Leváte.   ℟. Arise.

OMNIPOTENS sempitérne Deus, qui glóriam tuam ómnibus in Christo géntibus revelásti : custódi ópera misericórdiæ tuæ : ut Ecclésia tua toto orbe diffúsa, stábili fide in confessióne tui nóminis per-

ALMIGHTY and eternal God, who in Christ hast revealed thy glory to all nations, preserve the works of thy mercy : that thy Church, spread over all the world, may persevere with a constant faith in the confession of thy name.

sevéret. Per eúmdem Dóminum nostrum Jesum Christum. ℟. Amen.

OREMUS et pro beatíssimo Papa nostro N. ut Deus et Dóminus noster, qui elégit eum in órdine Episcopátus, salvum atque incólumem custódiat Ecclésiæ suæ sanctæ, ad regéndum pópulum sanctum Dei.

Orémus.
Flectámus génua.
℟. Leváte.

OMNIPOTENS sempitérne Deus, cujus judício univérsa fundántur : réspice propítius ad preces nostras, et eléctum nobis Antístitem tua pietáte consérva : ut Christiána plebs, quæ te gubernátur auctóre, sub tanto Pontífice, credulitátis suæ méritis augeátur. Per Dóminum.
℟. Amen.

OREMUS, et pro ómnibus Epíscopis, Presbýteris, Diacónibus, Subdiacónibus, Acólythis, Exorcístis, Lectóribus, Ostiáriis, Confessóribus, Virgínibus, Víduis, et pro omni pópulo sancto Dei.

Orémus.
Flectámus génua.
℟. Leváte.

OMNIPOTENS sempitérne Deus, cujus spíritu totum corpus Ecclésiæ sanctificátur et régitur : exáudi nos pro

Through the same Lord Jesus Christ.
℟. Amen.

LET us pray also for our most holy Pope N. that our Lord God, who elected him to the order of the episcopate, may preserve him in health and safety for the good of his holy Church, to govern the holy people of God.

Let us pray.
Let us kneel.
℟. Arise.

ALMIGHTY and eternal God, by whose judgement all things are founded : mercifully regard our prayers, and by thy goodness preserve our chief bishop chosen for us : that the Christian people, who are governed by thine authority, may increase the merits of their faith under so great a prelate. Through our Lord. ℟. Amen.

LET us pray also for all bishops, priests, deacons, subdeacons, acolytes, exorcists, readers, doorkeepers, confessors, virgins, widows, and for all the holy people of God.

Let us pray.
Let us kneel.
℟. Arise.

ALMIGHTY and eternal God, by whose spirit the whole body of the Church is hallowed and governed : hear our prayers for all or-

univérsis ordínibus supplicántes : ut grátiæ tuæ múnere, ab ómnibus tibi grádibus fidéliter serviátur. Per Dóminum. ℞. Amen.

OREMUS et pro catechúmenis nostris : ut Deus et Dóminus noster adapériat aures præcordiórum ipsórum, januámque misericórdiæ : ut per lavácrum regeneratiónis accépta remissióne ómnium peccatórum, et ipsi inveniántur in Christo Jesu Dómino nostro.

Orémus.
Flectámus génua.
℞. Leváte.

OMNIPOTENS sempitérne Deus, qui Ecclésiam tuam nova semper prole fœcúndas : auge fidem et intelléctum catechúmenis nostris ; ut renáti fonte baptísmatis, adoptiónis tuæ filiis aggregéntur. Per Dóminum. ℞. Amen.

OREMUS, dilectíssimi nobis, Deum Patrem omnipoténtem, ut cunctis mundum purget erróribus : morbos áuferat : famem depéllat : apériat cárceres : víncula dissólvat : peregrinántibus réditum : infirmántibus sanitátem : navigántibus portum salútis indúlgeat.

ders thereof : that by the assistance of thy grace, all degrees may faithfully serve thee. Through our Lord. ℞. Amen.

LET us pray also for our catechumens : that our Lord God would open the ears of their hearts and the gate of his mercy : that having received, by the laver of regeneration, the remission of all their sins, they may also belong to our Lord Jesus Christ.

Let us pray.
Let us kneel.
℞. Arise.

ALMIGHTY and eternal God, who always makest thy Church fruitful in new children : increase the faith and understanding of our catechumens ; that being regenerated in the waters of baptism, they may be admitted into the society of thine adopted children. Through our Lord. ℞. Amen.

LET us pray, dearly beloved, to God the Father almighty, that he would purge the world of all errors : cure diseases : drive away famine : open prisons : break chains : grant a safe return to travellers, health to the sick, and a secure haven to such as are at sea.

Orémus.
Flectámus génua.
℟. Leváte.

OMNIPOTENS sempitérne Deus, mœstórum consolátio, laborántium fortitúdo : pervéniant ad te preces de quacúmque tribulatióne clamántium ; ut omnes sibi in necessitátibus suis misericórdiam tuam gáudeant affuísse. Per Dóminum.
℟. Amen.

OREMUS et pro hæréticis et schismáticis: ut Deus et Dóminus noster éruat eos ab erróribus univérsis ; et ad sanctam matrem Ecclésiam Cathólicam atque Apostólicam revocáre dignétur.

Orémus.
Flectámus génua.
℟. Leváte.

OMNIPOTENS sempitérne Deus, qui salvas omnes, et néminem vis períre : réspice ad ánimas diabólica fraude decéptas, ut omni hærética pravitáte depósita, errántium corda resipíscant : et ad veritátis tuæ rédeant unitátem. Per Dóminum.
℟. Amen.

OREMUS et pro pérfidis Judǽis : ut Deus et Dóminus noster áuferat velámen de córdibus

Let us pray.
Let us kneel.
℟. Arise.

ALMIGHTY and eternal God, the comfort of the afflicted and the strength of those that labour : let the prayers of those that call upon thee in any trouble be heard by thee ; that all may with joy find the effects of thy mercy in their necessities. Through our Lord.
℟. Amen.

LET us pray also for heretics and schismatics : that our Lord God would be pleased to deliver them from all their errors ; and recall them to our holy mother the Catholic and Apostolic Church.

Let us pray.
Let us kneel.
℟. Arise.

ALMIGHTY and eternal God, who savest all, and wilt have none to perish : look on the souls that are seduced by the deceit of the devil ; that the hearts of those that err, having laid aside all heretical malice, may repent and return to the unity of thy truth. Through our Lord.
℟. Amen.

LET us pray also for the perfidious Jews : that our Lord God would withdraw the veil from

eórum ; ut et ipsi agnó-
scant Jesum Christum
Dóminum nostrum.

their hearts : that they
also may acknowledge our
Lord Jesus Christ.

Here the Flectámus génua *is omitted, and the clergy and people do not kneel down.*

OMNIPOTENS sem-
pitérne Deus, qui
étiam Judáicam perfí-
diam a tua misericórdia
non repéllis : exáudi
preces nostras quas pro
illíus pópuli obcæcatióne
deférimus ; ut, ágnita
veritátis tuæ luce, quæ
Christus est, a suis ténebris eruántur. Pereúm-
dem Dóminum.

℞. Amen.

ALMIGHTY and eternal
God, who deniest not
thy mercy even to the perfidious Jews : hear our
prayers, which we pour
forth for the blindness of
this people : that by ack-
nowledging the light of thy
truth, which is Christ, they
may be brought out of their
darkness. Trough the same
Lord.

℞. Amen.

OREMUS et pro pagá-
nis : ut Deus omní-
potens áuferat iniquitá-
tem a córdibus eórum :
ut relíctis idólis suis,
convertántur ad Deum
vivum et verum, et
únicum Fílium ejus Je-
sum Christum Deum et
Dóminum nostrum.

Orémus.
Flectámus génua.
℞. Leváte.

LET us pray also for the
pagans : that almighty
God would take iniquity out
of their hearts : that by
quitting their idols, they
may be converted to the
true and living God, and his
only Son, Jesus Christ our
God and Lord.

Let us pray.
Let us kneel.
℞. Arise.

OMNIPOTENS sem-
pitérne Deus, qui
non mortem peccató-
rum, sed vitam semper
inquíris : súscipe propí-
tius oratiónem nostram,
et líbera eos ab idolórum
cultúra : et ággrega
Ecclésiæ tuæ sanctæ
ad laudem et glóriam nó-
minis tui. Per Dómi-
num.

℞. Amen.

ALMIGHTY and eternal
God, who seekest not
the death, but the life of
sinners : mercifully hear our
prayers, and deliver them
from the worship of idols :
and for the praise and glory
of thy name, admit them
into thy holy Church.
Through our Lord.

℞. Amen.

The Adoration of the Cross.

The Adoration of the Cross which follows these prayers is quite distinct from what has gone before, and is a rite peculiar to Good Friday. The first mention made of this ceremony occurs in a work of the fourth century. The abbess Etheria mentioned above, saw in the church of the Holy Cross at Jerusalem long files of weeping Christians coming up to kiss the Cross on which Christ had died. Rome adopted this ceremony, and other churches desirous of instituting it, made every effort to obtain relics of the Cross.

The hymn *Pange lingua gloriosi Lauream certaminis* composed by Venantius Fortunatus, is one of the most celebrated of the ancient hymnal. Despite a certain ruggedness of style, it sings with most exquisitely delicate thought of that Cross to which the Redeemer of the world was nailed. It introduces an ancient theological opinion, one that is found in the Preface of the Cross and in the works of various early writers, to wit, that the devil who had deceived our first parents by the tree, was in turn to be vanquished by a tree, that of the Cross.

The *Improperia*, also sung during this ceremony, are taken for the most part from the fourth book of Esdras, which though not in the Canon of the Old Testament enjoyed a great reputation in former times. The *Agios athanatos* is borrowed from the Greek Church, as also the *Kyrie eleison* and various other liturgical formulas. The whole ceremony is most beautiful and impressive.

The priest lays aside his chasuble and goes to the Epistle side of the altar, where at the back angle he receives from the deacon the veiled cross, which has been previously arranged on the altar. With his face to the people, he uncovers the upper portion of the cross ; and intones the verse :

Ecce lignum crucis.	Behold the wood of the cross.

Then the assistant clergy join with him as far as Venite adorémus. *When the choir says these words, all kneel except the priest. Then the priest advances to the front corner, and uncovers the right arm and elevates the crucifix a little, saying on a higher tone than before :* Ecce lignum crucis. *The clergy join, and all kneel as before. Then, at the middle of the altar, the priest uncovers the whole crucifix, and, lifting it up, begins still higher :* Ecce lignum crucis, *and the rest continue as before.*

ECCE lignum crucis, in quo salus mundi pependit.	BEHOLD the wood of the cross, on which hung the Saviour of the world.

The choir answers :

Veníte, adorémus. | Come let us adore.

The priest lays down the cross on a cushion prepared for it before the altar ; then putting off his shoes, he proceeds to adore the cross, kneeling three several times. After which, he resumes his shoes and chasuble. Then the clergy first, and afterwards the laity, proceed to adore the cross. In the meantime all or some of the following REPROACHES *are sung.*

Two cantors sing in the middle of the choir :

℣. Pópule meus, quid feci tibi? aut in quo contristávi te? respónde mihi. | ℣. O my people, what have I done to thee? or in what have I afflicted thee? answer me.

℣. Quia edúxi te de terra Ægýpti : parásti crucem Salvatóri tuo. | ℣. Because I led thee out of the land of Egypt, thou hast prepared a cross for thy Saviour.

Then one choir sings :

Agios o Theós. | O holy God.

Another choir answers :

Sanctus Deus. | O holy God.

The first choir :

Agios ischyrós. | O holy strong One.

The second choir :

Sanctus fortis. | O holy strong One.

The first choir :

Agios athánatos, eléison imas. | O holy immortal One, have mercy upon us.

The second choir :

Sanctus immortális, miserére nobis. | O holy immortal One, have mercy upon us.

Two of the second choir :

℣. Quia edúxi te per desértum quadragínta annis : et manna cibávi te, et introdúxi te in terram satis óptimam : parásti crucem Salvatóri tuo. | ℣. Because I led thee out through the desert for forty years, and fed thee with manna, and brought thee into a land exceeding good, thou hast prepared a cross for thy Saviour.

The two choirs answer in turn : Agios, &c.

Two of the first choir :

℣. Quid ultra débui fácere tibi, et non feci? | ℣. What more ought I to do for thee, and have not

Ego quidem plantávi te víneam meam speciosíssimam : et tu facta es mihi nimis amára ; acéto namque sitim meam potásti ; et láncea perforásti ; latus Salvatóri tuo.

done it? I planted thee indeed, my most beautiful vineyard : and thou art become to me exceeding bitter ; for thou hast given me vinegar in my thirst ; and with a spear thou hast pierced the side of thy Saviour.

The two choirs answer in turn : Agios, &c.

Then two of the second choir :

℣ Ego propter te flagellávi Ægýptum cum primogénitis suis : et tu me flagellátum tradidísti.

℣. For thy sake I scourged Egypt with its firstborn : and thou didst scourge me and deliver me up.

Both choirs repeat together Pópule meus, &c., *as above, as far as the* ℣. Quia edúxi.

Two of the first choir :

℣. Ego te edúxi de Ægýpto, demérso Pharaóne in Mare Rubrum : et tu me tradidísti princípibus sacerdótum.

℣. I led thee out of Egypt, drowning Pharao in the Red Sea : and thou didst deliver me to the chief priests.

Both choirs repeat Pópule meus, &c.

Two of the second choir :

℣. Ego ante te apérui mare : et tu aperuísti láncea latus meum.

℣. I opened the sea before thee ; and thou with a spear hast opened my side.

Both choirs repeat Pópule meus.

Two of the first choir :

℣. Ego ante te præívi in colúmna nubis : et tu me duxísti ad prætórium Piláti.

℣. I went before thee in a pillar of a cloud : and thou hast brought me to the palace of Pilate.

Both choirs repeat Pópule meus.

Two of the second choir :

℣. Ego te pavi manna per desértum : et tu me cecidísti álapis et flagéllis.

℣. I fed thee with manna in the desert : and thou hast beaten me with buffets and scourges.

Both choirs repeat Pópule meus.

Two of the first choir :

℣. Ego te potávi aqua

℣. I gave thee wholesome

salútis de petra : et tu me potásti felle et acéto.

water to drink out of the rock : and thou hast given me gall and vinegar.

Both choirs repeat Pópule meus.
Two of the second choir :

℣. Ego propter te Chananæórum reges percússi : et tu percussísti arúndine caput meum.

℣. For thy sake I struck the kings of the Chananites : and thou hast struck my head with a reed.

Both choirs repeat Pópule meus.
Two of the first choir :

℣. Ego dedi tibi sceptrum regále : et tu dedísti cápiti meo spíneam corónam.

℣. I gave thee a royal sceptre : and thou hast given me a crown of thorns.

Both choirs repeat Pópule meus.
Two of the second choir :

℣. Ego te exaltávi magna virtúte : et tu me suspendísti in patíbulo crucis.

℣. I have exalted thee with great strength : and thou hast hanged me on the gibbet of the cross.

Both choirs repeat Pópule meus, *and then sing the following Antiphon :*

CRUCEM tuam adorámus, Dómine : et sanctam resurrectiónem tuam laudámus, et glorificámus : ecce enim propter lignum venit gáudium in univérso mundo. *Ps.* Deus misereátur nostri, et benedícat nobis : * illúminet vultum suum super nos, et misereátur nostri. *Aña.* Crucem tuam.

WE adore thy cross, O Lord : and we praise and glorify thy holy resurrection : for by the wood of the cross the whole world is filled with joy. *Ps.* May God have mercy on us, and bless us : may he cause the light of his countenance to shine upon us : and may he have mercy on us. *Then is repeated :* We adore.

Afterwards the hymn Pange lingua *is sung in the following manner :*

CRUX fidélis, inter omnes
Arbor una nóbilis :
Nulla silva talem profert
Fronde, flore, gérmine :

FAITHFUL Cross, O Tree all beauteous,
Tree all peerless and divine :
Not a grove on earth can show us
Such a leaf and flower as thine.

Dulce lignum, dulces clavos,
Dulce pondus sústinet.

Sweet the nails and sweet the wood,
Laden with so sweet a load.

HYMN

PANGE lingua gloriósi
Láuream certáminis,
Et super Crucis trophǽo
Dic triúmphum nóbilem:
Quáliter Redémptor orbis
Immolátus vícerit.

SING, my tongue, the Saviour's glory;
Tell his triumph far and wide;
Tell aloud the famous story
Of his Body crucified;
How upon the cross a Victim,
Vanquishing in death, he died.

Here Crux fidélis *is repeated as far as* Dulce lignum.

De paréntis protoplásti
Fraude factor cóndolens,
Quando pomi noxiális
In necem morsu ruit :
Ipse lignum tunc notávit,
Damna ligni ut sólveret.

Eating of the tree forbidden,
Man had sunk in Satan's snare,
When his pitying Creator
Did this second tree prepare,
Destined, many ages later,
That first evil to repair.

Here Dulce lignum *is repeated.*

Hoc opus nostræ salútis
Ordo depopóscerat :
Multifórmis proditóris
Ars ut artem fálleret :
Et medélam ferret inde,
Hostis unde lǽserat.

Such the order God appointed
When for sin he would atone;
To the serpent thus opposing
Schemes yet deeper than his own;
Thence the remedy procuring
Whence the fatal wound had come.

Crux fidélis, &c.

Quando venit ergo sacri
Plenitúdo témporis,
Missus est ab arce Patris

So when now at length the fulness
Of the sacred time drew nigh,
Then the Son who moulded all things

Natus, orbis Cónditor :
Atque ventre virgináli
Carne amíctus pródiit.

Left his Father's throne on
high ;
From a Virgin's womb ap-
pearing,
Clothed in our mortality.

Dulce lignum, &c.

Vagit infans inter arcta
Cónditus præsépia :
Membra pannis involúta
Virgo Mater álligat ;
Et Dei manus pedésque
Stricta cingit fáscia.

All within a lowly manger,
Lo, a tender babe he lies :
See his tender Virgin-Mo-
ther
Lull to sleep his infant
cries ;
While the limbs of God In-
carnate
Round with swathing-bands
she ties.

Crux fidélis, &c.

Lustra sex qui jam per-
égit,
Tempus implens córpo-
ris,
Sponte líbera Redémp-
tor
Passióni déditus,
Agnus in Crucis levátur
Immolándus stípite.

Thus did Christ to perfect
manhood
In our mortal flesh attain;
Then of his free choice he
goeth
To a death of bitter pain ;
And as a lamb upon the
altar
Of the Cross, for us is slain.

Dulce lignum, &c.

Felle potus ecce languet:
Spina, clavi, láncea,
Mite corpus perforárunt:
Unda manat et cruor :
Terra, pontus, astra,
mundus,
Quo lavántur flúmine !

Lo, with gall his thirst he
quenches :
See the thorns upon his
brow.
Nails his tender flesh are
rending :
See, his side is opened now,
Whence to cleanse the whole
creation,
Streams of blood and water
flow.

Crux fidélis, &c.

Flecte ramos, arbor alta,
Tensa laxa víscera,
Et rigor lentéscat ille,
Quem dedit natívitas :

Lofty Tree, bend down thy
branches
To embrace thy sacred load;
Oh, relax the native tension
Of that all too rigid wood :

Et supérni membra Regis
Tende miti stípite.

Gently, gently bear the members
Of thy dying King and God.

Dulce lignum, &c.

Sola digna tu fuísti
Ferre mundi víctimam ;
Atque portum præparáre
Arca mundo naúfrago,
Quam sacer cruor perúnxit
Fusus Agni córpore.

Tree which solely was found worthy
Earth's great victim to sustain ;
Harbour from the raging tempest,
Ark that saved the world again,
Tree with sacred blood anointed,
Of the Lamb for sinners slain.

Crux fidélis, &c.

Sempitérna sit beátæ
Trinitáti glória :
Æqua Patri, Filióque,
Par decus Paráclito :
Uníus Triníque nomen
Laudet univérsitas.
  Amen.

Honour, blessing everlasting
To the immortal Deity :
To the Father, Son, and Spirit,
Praise be paid coequally :
Glory through the earth and heaven
To Trinity and Unity.
  Amen.

Dulce lignum, &c.

When the adoration of the cross is nearly completed, the candles are lighted on the altar ; and the cross having been replaced, the priest and clergy go in procession to the place where the Blessed Sacrament was deposited on the previous day. The Sacred Host is incensed, and then, being taken from the tabernacle, is solemnly borne back to the high altar. During the procession the hymn Vexílla regis *is sung.*

VEXILLA regis pródeunt,
Fulget crucis mystérium ;
Qua vita mortem pértulit,
Et morte vitam prótulit.
Quæ vulneráta lánceæ
Mucróne diro, críminum
Ut nos laváret sórdibus,

FORTH comes the standard of the King :
All hail, thou mystery ador'd :
Hail, Cross on which the Life himself
Died, and by death our life restored.
On which the Saviour's holy side,
Rent open with a cruel spear,

Manávit unda et sánguine.

Its stream of blood and water pour'd,
To wash us from defilement clear.

Impléta sunt, quæ cóncinit
David fidéli cármine,
Dicéndo natiónibus :
Regnávit a ligno Deus.

O sacred Wood fulfill'd in thee
Was holy David's truthful lay ;
Which told the world, that from a Tree
The Lord should all the nations sway.

Arbor decóra et fúlgida,
Ornáta Regis púrpura,
Elécta digno stípite
Tam sancta membra tángere.

Most royally empurpled o'er,
How beauteously thy stem doth shine,
How glorious was its lot to touch
Those limbs so holy and divine.

Béata cujus bráchiis
Prétium pepéndit sǽculi,
Statéra facta córporis,
Tulítque prædam tártari.

Thrice blest, upon whose arms outstretch'd
The Saviour of the world reclin'd ;
Balance sublime upon whose beam
Was weigh'd the ransom of mankind.

O Crux, ave, spes única,
Hoc Passiónis témpore
Piis adáuge grátiam
Reísque dele crímina.

Hail, Cross thou only hope of man,
Hail on this holy Passion day
To saints increase the grace they have ;
From sinners purge their guilt away.

Te, fons salútis, Trínitas,
Colláudet omnis spíritus:
Quibus crucis victóriam
Largíris, adde prǽmium.
Amen.

Salvation's Fount, blest Trinity,
Be praise to thee through earth and skies :
Thou through the Cross the victory
Dost give ; oh, give us too the prize.
Amen.

The Mass of the Presanctified.

The Adoration of the Cross was an interlude distinct in itself in the course of this morning's ceremony, but the procession which follows the Adoration is connected with the first part of the office. It will be remembered that on Maundy Thursday two hosts were consecrated, one being reserved in a side chapel. The stripping of the high altar would have seemed incongruous had Christ been present there in the Blessed Sacrament, and the other ceremonies would have been deprived of a great part of their meaning. After the Adoration of the Cross a procession is formed and the Sacred Host is taken from the side chapel and borne solemnly to the high altar, to the singing of the hymn *Vexilla Regis*, composed by Venantius Fortunatus. Although it is the Blessed Sacrament which is thus carried in procession, yet the hymn is one in honour of the Cross, having been composed for the occasion when a large relic of the true Cross was presented to the famous monastery of Poitiers, afterwards known as Holy Cross. All this goes to prove the intimate connection and oneness of Maundy Thursday and Good Friday in the liturgy, and how the idea of the Cross is inseparable from that of the Eucharist. The rite now to be celebrated, the Mass of the Presanctified, in the Latin Church is exclusively reserved for Good Friday, but in the Oriental liturgies and in particular the Byzantine rite it is of frequent occurrence. Strictly speaking it is not the Mass as there is no sacrifice. Bread and wine are neither offered nor consecrated, the priest communicating with the Host consecrated the previous day. The ceremony is a simple one ; the altar is incensed and the *Pater noster* is said, followed by a few short prayers of thanksgiving.

The origin of this rite is as follows. In the Eastern Church it was the custom during Lent to celebrate Mass on Sundays only, and not on the other days of the week. In order however not to deprive the faithful of Holy Communion, sufficient consecrated bread and wine were reserved on the Sunday and distributed during the week to those who wished to communicate. This ceremony was called the Mass of the Presanctified, the name itself indicating that the sacred species had been consecrated beforehand. It is to be remarked that the Holy Eucharist is reserved under both kinds in the Eastern Church, whereas in the Western Church only the consecrated Host is reserved. The fear of any possible alteration in the species of the wine may have been

the cause of this latter custom.   Christ being present whole
and entire under both kinds, he is received as completely
and wholly under one kind alone.   Another rite observed
by both Churches for many centuries was the *commixtio*,
when ordinary wine was added to the consecrated wine, and
a particle of the Sacred Host dissolved in unconsecrated
wine, as though to sanctify them.   A remainder of this
rite still survives in the Mass of Good Friday.   The deacon
pours wine and the subdeacon water into the Chalice, and
the priest after having elevated the Sacred Host divides it
into three particles, one of which is placed in the wine and
consumed, after the priest has communicated with the other
two particles.   The contact of the Sacred Host does indeed
sanctify the wine, but it is erroneous to believe that it changes
it into the most precious Blood, as was once incorrectly held.
The consecration of the bread and wine can be brought
about only by the words of consecration, and we repeat that
there is no consecration in the Mass of the Presanctified.

It has been asked recently whether the faithful might be
admitted to Holy Communion on Good Friday.   The general
custom is not in favour of this plea, but there seems to be
no valid reason against it, considering that originally the
Mass of the Presanctified was instituted solely to this end.
This is a question of discipline which still remains to be
pronounced upon by the Church.   The rubric in the Missal
foresees that the priest may have to consecrate several
additional hosts on Maundy Thursday, to be reserved for
the sick.   In spite of the custom to the contrary, Holy
Communion has been given to the faithful on Holy Saturday
in some churches, without their incurring the censure of
authority, but in no case may anyone save the sick communicate on this day outside the Mass.

*Arrived at the altar, the priest places the chalice upon it, and
again incenses it ; then, taking out the Sacred Host, he puts it upon
the paten which the deacon is holding ; and finally, receiving the
paten from the deacon, he lays the Sacred Host on the corporal.   The
deacon then pours wine into the chalice, and the subdeacon a little
water which the priest does not bless, but taking the chalice from the
deacon he places it on the altar, and the deacon covers it with the
pall.   After this the priest puts incense into the thurible, without
blessing it, and proceeds to incense the oblation and the altar in
the usual manner, but genuflecting each time he passes before the
Blessed Sacrament.   While incensing the oblation he says :*

INCENSUM istud a te
 benedíctum, ascén-
dat ad te, Dómine : et

MAY this incense, blest
 by thee, ascend unto
thee, O Lord ; and may

descéndat super nos misericórdia tua.

thy mercy descend upon us.

While incensing the altar :

DIRIGATUR, Dómine, orátio mea, sicut incénsum in conspéctu tuo : elevátio mánuum meárum sacrifícium vespertínum.   Pone, Dómine, custódiam ori meo et óstium circumstántiæ lábiis meis : ut non declínet cor meum in verba malítiæ, ad excusándas excusatiónes in peccátis.

LET my prayer, O Lord, be directed like incense in thy sight ; the lifting up of my hands as an evening sacrifice.   Set a watch, O Lord, before my mouth, and a door round about my lips : that my heart incline not to evil words, to make excuses in sins.

Giving back the thurible to the deacon :

ACCENDAT in nobis Dóminus ignem sui amóris, et flammam ætérnæ caritátis. Amen.

MAY the Lord kindle in us the fire of his love, and the flame of everlasting charity. Amen.

The priest is not incensed.

Retiring to the Epistle side of the altar, the priest washes his hands in silence ; then returning, he bows down before the middle of the altar, saying :

IN spíritu humilitátis, et in ánimo contríto suscipiámur a te, Dómine, et sic fiat sacrifícium nostrum in conspéctu tuo hódie, ut pláceat tibi, Dómine Deus.

IN the spirit of humility and with a contrite heart, let us be received by thee, O Lord ; and so let our sacrifice be made before thee this day, as to be pleasing to thee, O Lord God.

Then turning to the people, a little towards the Gospel end of the altar.

Orate, fratres, ut meum ac vestrum sacrifícium acceptábile fiat apud Deum Patrem omnipoténtem.

Berethren, pray that my sacrifice and yours may be acceptable to God the Father Almighty.

No answer is made, but the Priest continues immediataly.

Orémus.   Præcéptis salutáribus móniti, et divína institutióne formáti, audémus dícere,

Pater noster, &c.

Let us pray.   Admonished by salutary precepts, and formed by divine instruction, we presume to say,

Our Father, &c.

Having answered in secret Amen, *he continues aloud :*

LIBERA nos, quæsumus, Dómine, ab ómnibus malis, prætéritis, præséntibus et futúris : et intercedénte beáta et gloriósa semper vírgine Dei Genitríce María, cum beátis Apóstolis tuis Petro et Paulo, atque Andréa, et ómnibus sanctis, da propítius pacem in diébus nostris ; ut ope misericórdiæ tuæ adjúti, et a peccáto simus semper líberi, et ab omni perturbatióne secúri. Per eúmdem Dóminum nostrum Jesum Christum Fílium tuum, qui tecum vivit et regnat in unitáte Spíritus Sancti Deus : per ómnia sǽcula sæculórum. ℞. Amen.

DELIVER us, we beseech thee, O Lord, from all evils, past, present, and to come, and the blessed and glorious Mary ever virgin mother of God, with thy blessed apostles Peter and Paul and Andrew and all the saints interceding, grant in thy mercy peace in our days ; that, assisted by the help of thy mercy, we may both be ever free from sin, and secure from all disturbance. Through the same our Lord Jesus Christ thy Son, who liveth and reigneth with thee in the unity of the Holy Ghost God, world without end. ℞. Amen.

The priest genuflects ; then, holding the paten in his left hand, he with his right elevates the Sacred Host so that all may see and adore It. He next divides It into three portions as usual, and puts the smallest particle into the chalice without saying any thing. The Pax Dómini and Agnus Dei are omitted, and the kiss of peace is not given. Of the three Prayers before Holy Communion the last only is said :

PERCEPTIO Córporis tui, Dómine Jesu Christe, quod ego indígnus súmere præsúmo, non mihi provéniat in judícium et condemnatiónem : sed pro tua pietáte prosit mihi ad tutaméntum mentis et córporis, et ad medélam percipiéndam. Qui vivis et regnas cum Deo Patre in unitáte Spíritus Sancti Deus : per ómnia sǽcula sæculórum.

LET not this taking of thy Body, O Lord Jesus Christ, which I, all unworthy, presume to receive, turn to my judgement and condemnation : but of thy goodnes let it profit me as a safeguard and a remedy for mind and body : who livest and reignest with God the Father in the unity of the Holy Ghost, God, world without end. Amen.

Having genuflected, he takes up the paten with the Sacred Host, and says :

PANEM cæléstem accípiam, et nomen Dómini invocábo.

I WILL take bread of heaven, and call upon the name of the Lord.

And then, striking his breast, says thrice :

DOMINE, non sum dignus ut intres sub tectum meum : sed tantum dic verbo, et sanábitur ánima mea.

LORD, I am not worthy that thou shouldest enter under my roof ; say but the word, and my soul shall be healed.

He next signs himself with the Blessed Sacrament as usual, and adds :

CORPUS Dómini nostri Jesu Christi custódiat ánimam meam in vitam ætérnam. Amen.

MAY the Body of our Lord Jesus Christ keep my soul unto life everlasting. Amen.

After which he reverently receives the Body of our Lord Jesus Christ.

All the other customary prayers are omitted. The priest drinks from the chalice the wine with the consecrated particle ; purifies the chalice and his fingers as usual ; and, having received the ablution, stands at the middle of the altar with bowed head and joined hands, saying :

QUOD ore súmpsimus, Dómine, pura mente capiámus : et de múnere tempórali fiat nobis remédium sempitérnum.

WHAT with our lips we have taken, may we, O Lord, with a pure mind receive ; and from a temporal gift, may it become to us an everlasting remedy.

No blessing is given ; but the priest and his ministers, having bowed before the altar, depart in silence. Vespers are then recited in the choir, and the altar is stripped.

The Vespers are the same as on Maundy Thursday, p. 177, with the variations there notified.

In the evening the Tenebræ *of Holy Saturday are said.*

HOLY SATURDAY

TENEBRÆ

TO BE RECITED ON FRIDAY EVENING

The office of Tenebræ for to-day resembles that of the two preceding days. Psalms, antiphons, lessons and responsories are proper, and no part of the office except the actual psalms are used on any other day of the year. The psalms at Matins do not belong to the ferial office, but have been specially chosen. The first antiphon strikes the keynote of the whole office, *In pace, in idipsum, In peace… I will sleep, and I will rest.* The antiphon has been taken from Psalm 4, that exquisite psalm of eventide formerly assigned to the ferial office of Compline, and so peculiarly applicable to Christ lying in the tomb. The second antiphon explains the choice of Psalm 14, and Psalm 15 contains a special reference to the Resurrection quoted by St. Peter in his discourse to the Jews, which foretold that the Messias, the *Holy One* of God was not to see corruption. The responsories resemble in their composition and line of thought those of the two preceding days; that of the fourth lesson speaks of Christ's descent into hell. Psalm 23 of the second nocturn is the psalm of the Ascension, and plays an important part in the office of that feast. Psalm 26 is a psalm of the Resurrection, and occurred in the office of Tenebræ on Good Friday. The antiphon of Psalm 29 indicates the reason of its choice ; Psalms 53 and 87 were recited at Tenebræ of Good Friday and are, together with Psalm 75, psalms of the Resurrection. The Epistle to the Hebrews has already been treated of in the foregoing chapter.

Pater noster, Ave, *and* Credo, *in secret.*

THE FIRST NOCTURN

Aña. In pace, in idipsum, dórmiam et requiéscam. | *Ant.* In peace, in the selfsame, I will sleep, and I will take my rest.

Psalm. 4.

CUM invocárem, exaudívit me Deus justítiæ meæ : * in tribulatióne dilatásti mihi.

Miserére mei : * et exáudi oratiónem meam.

Fílii hóminum úsquequo gravi corde : * ut quid dilígitis vanitátem, et quǽritis mendácium?

Et scitóte quóniam mirificávit Dóminus sanctum suum : * Dóminus exáudiet me, cum clamávero ad eum.

Irascímini, et nolíte peccáre : * quæ dícitis in córdibus vestris in cubílibus vestris compungímini.

Sacrificáte sacrifícium justítiæ, et speráte in Dómino : * multi dicunt: Quis osténdit nobis bona?

Signátum est super nos lumen vultus tui, Dómine : * dedísti lætítiam in corde meo.

A fructu fruménti, vini et ólei sui : * multiplicáti sunt.

In pace in idípsum : * dórmiam et requiéscam.

Quóniam tu, Dómine, singuláriter in spe : * constituísti me.

Aña. In pace in idípsum dórmiam et requiéscam.

Aña. Habitábit in tabernáculo tuo : requiéscet in monte sancto tuo.

Psalm 4.

WHEN I called upon him, the God of my justice heard me : when I was in distress thou hast enlarged me.

Have mercy upon me, and hear my prayer.

O ye sons of men, how long will ye be dull of heart? why do you love vanity, and seek after lying?

Know ye also that the Lord hath made his Holy One wonderful : the Lord will hear me when I shall cry unto him.

Be ye angry and sin not : the things you say in your hearts, be sorry for them on your beds.

Offer up the sacrifice of justice, and trust in the Lord : many say : Who showeth us good things?

The light of thy countenance, O Lord, is signed upon us : thou hast given gladness in my heart.

By the fruit of their corn, their wine and oil, they are multiplied.

In peace, in the self-same, I will sleep, and I will take my rest.

For thou, O Lord, singularly hast settled me in hope.

Ant. In peace, in the selfsame, I will sleep, and I will take my rest.

Ant. He shall dwell in thy tabernacle : he shall rest in thy holy hill.

Psalm. 14.

DOMINE, quis habitábit in tabernáculo tuo : * aut quis requiéscet in monte sancto tuo?

Qui ingréditur sine mácula : * et operátur justítiam.

Qui lóquitur veritátem in corde suo : * qui non egit dolum in lingua sua.

Nec fecit próximo suo malum : * et oppróbrium non accépit advérsus próximos suos.

Ad níhilum dedúctus est in conspéctu ejus malígnus : * timéntes autem Dóminum gloríficat.

Qui jurat próximo suo, et non décipit : * qui pecúniam suam non dedit ad usúram, et múnera super innocéntem non accépit :

Qui facit hæc, * non movébitur in ætérnum.

Aña. Habitábit in tabernáculo tuo : requiéscet in monte sancto tuo.

Aña. Caro mea requiéscet in spe.

Psalm. 15.

CONSERVA me, Dómine, quóniam sperávi in te : * dixi Dómino, Deus meus es tu, quóniam bonórum meórum non eges.

Sanctis qui sunt in terra ejus : * mirificávit omnes voluntátes meas in eis.

Psalm 14.

LORD, who shall dwell in thy tabernacle? or who shall rest in thy holy hill?

He that walketh without blemish, and worketh justice.

He that speaketh truth in his heart, who hath not used deceit in his tongue.

Nor hath done evil to his neighbour, nor taken up a reproach against his neighbours.

In his sight the malignant is brought to nothing : but he glorifieth them that fear the Lord.

He that sweareth to his neighbour, and deceiveth not : he that hath not put out his money to usury, nor taken bribes against the innocent.

He that doth these things, shall not be moved for ever.

Ant. He shall dwell in thy tabernacle : he shall rest in thy holy hill.

Ant. My flesh shall rest in hope.

Psalm 15.

PRESERVE me, O Lord, for I have put my trust in thee, I have said to the Lord : thou art my God, for thou hast no need of my goods.

To the saints who are in his land, he hath made wonderful all my desires in them.

Multiplicátæ sunt infirmitátes eórum : * póstea acceleravérunt.

Non congregábo ventícula eórum de sanguínibus : * nec memor ero nóminum eórum per lábia mea.

Dóminus pars hereditátis meæ et cálicis mei : * tu es qui restítues hereditátem meam mihi.

Funes cecidérunt mihi in præcláris : * étenim heréditas mea præclára est mihi.

Benedícam Dóminum, qui tríbuit mihi intelléctum : * ínsuper et usque ad noctem increpuérunt me renes mei.

Providébam Dóminum in conspéctu meo semper : * quóniam a dextris est mihi ne commóvear.

Propter hoc lætátum est cor meum, et exsultávit lingua mea : * ínsuper et caro mea requiéscet in spe.

Quóniam non derelínques ánimam meam in inférno : * nec dabis Sanctum tuum vidére corruptiónem.

Notas mihi fecísti vias vitæ, adimplébis me lætítia cum vultu tuo : * delectatiónes in déxtera tua usque in finem.

Aña. Caro mea requiéscet in spe.

Their infirmities were multiplied : afterwards they made haste.

I will not gather together their meetings for blood-offerings : nor will I be mindful of their names by my lips.

The Lord is the portion of my inheritance and of my cup : it is thou that wilt restore my inheritance to me.

The lines are fallen unto me in goodly places : for my inheritance is goodly to me.

I will bless the Lord, who hath given me understanding : moreover my reins also have corrected me even till night.

I set the Lord always in my sight : for he is at my right hand that I be not moved.

Therefore my heart hath been glad and my tongue hath rejoiced : moreover my flesh also shall rest in hope.

Because thou wilt not leave my soul in hell : nor wilt thou give thy Holy One to see corruption.

Thou hast made known to me the ways of life, thou shalt fill me with joy with thy countenance : at thy right hand are delights even to the end.

Ant. My flesh shall rest in hope.

℣. In pace in idípsum.

℣. In peace, in the self-same.

℟. Dórmiam et requié-scam.

℟. I will sleep, and I will take my rest.

The Pater noster *is here recited in secret.*

FIRST LESSON

De Lamentatióne Jere-míæ Prophétæ.

Cap. 3.

HETH. Misericórdiæ Dómini, quia non sumus consúmpti : quia non defecérunt misera-tiónes ejus.

HETH. Novi dilúculo, multa est fides tua.

HETH. Pars mea, Dó-minus, dixit ánima mea : proptérea exspectábo eum.

TETH. Bonus est Dó-minus sperántibus in eum, ánimæ quærénti illum.

TETH. Bonum est præ-stolári cum siléntio salu-táre Dei.

TETH. Bonum est viro, cum portáverit jugum ab adolescéntia sua.

JOD. Sedébit solitá-rius, et tacébit : quia le-vávit super se.

JOD. Ponet in púlvere os suum, si forte sit spes.

JOD. Dabit percutién-ti se maxillam, saturábi-tur oppróbriis.

Jerúsalem, Jerúsalem, convértere ad Dóminum Deum tuum.

From the Lamentation of Jeremias the Prophet.

Ch. 3.

HETH. The mercies of the Lord that we are not consumed : because his ten-der mercies have not failed.

HETH. They are new eve-ry morning, great is thy faithfulness.

HETH. The Lord is my portion, said my soul : there-fore will I wait for him.

TETH. The Lord is good to them that hope in him, to the soul that seeketh him.

TETH. It is good to wait with silence for the salva-tion of God.

TETH. It is good for a man when he hath borne the yoke from his youth.

JOD. He shall sit solitary, and hold his peace : because he hath taken it up upon himself.

JOD. He shall put his mouth in the dust, if so be there may be hope.

JOD. He shall give his cheek to him that striketh him, he shall be filled with reproaches.

Jerusalem Jerusalem, be converted to the Lord thy God.

℟. Sicut ovis ad occisiónem ductus est, et dum male tractarétur, non apéruit os suum : tráditus est ad mortem : * Ut vivificáret pópulum suum.

℣. Trádidit in mortem ánimam suam, et inter scelerátos reputátus est. * Ut vivificáret.

℟. He was led like a sheep to the slaughter ; and whilst he was ill-used, he opened not his mouth : he was condemned to death : * That he might give life to his people.

℣. He delivered himself up to death, and was reckoned among the wicked. * That he.

SECOND LESSON

ALEPH. Quómodo obscurátum est aurum, mutátus est color óptimus, dispérsi sunt lápides sanctuárii in cápite ómnium plateárum?

BETH. Fílii Sion ínclyti, et amícti auro primo : quómodo reputáti sunt in vasa téstea, opus mánuum fíguli?

GHIMEL. Sed et lámiæ nudavérunt, mammam, lactavérunt cátulos suos: fília pópuli mei crudélis, quasi strúthio in desérto.

DALETH. Adhǽsit lingua lacténtis ad palátum ejus in siti : párvuli petiérunt panem, et non erat qui fángeret eis.

HE. Qui vescebántur voluptuóse interiérunt in viis ; qui nutriebántur in cróceis, amplexáti sunt stércora.

VAU. Et major effécta

ALEPH. How is the gold become dim, the finest colour is changed, the stones of the sanctuary are scattered in the top of every street?

BETH. The noble sons of Sion, and they that were clothed with the best gold : how are they esteemed as earthen vessels, the work of the potter's hands?

GHIMEL. Even the sea-monsters have drawn out the breast, they have given suck to their young : the daughter of my people is cruel, like the ostrich in the desert.

DALETH. The tongue of the suckling child hath stuck to the roof of his mouth for thirst : the little ones have asked for bread, and there was none to break it unto them.

HE. They that were fed delicately, have died in the streets : they that were brought up in scarlet, have embraced the dung.

VAU. And the iniquity of

est iníquitas fíliæ pópuli mei peccáto Sodomórum : quæ subvérsa est in moménto, et non cœpérunt in ea manus.

Jerúsalem, Jerúsalem, convértere ad Dóminum Deum tuum.

℞. Jerúsalem, surge et éxue te véstibus jucunditátis : indúere cínere et cilício : * Quia in te occísus est Salvátor Israël.

℣. Deduc quasi torréntem lácrimas per diem et noctem, et non táceat pupílla óculi tui.
* Quia.

the daughter of my people is made greater than the sin of Sodom, which was overthrown in a moment, and hands took nothing in her.

Jerusalem, Jerusalem, be converted to the Lord thy God.

℞. Arise, Jerusalem, and put off thy garments of joy : put on ashes and hair-cloth :
* For in thee was slain the Saviour of Israel.

℣. Let tears run down like a torrent day and night, and let not the apple of thine eye cease.
* For.

THIRD LESSON

Incipit Orátio Jeremíæ Prophétæ.
Cap. 5.

Here beginneth the Prayer of Jeremias the Prophet.
Ch. 5.

RECORDARE, Dómine, quid accíderit nobis : intuére, et réspice oppróbrium nostrum. Heréditas nostra versa est ad aliénos, domus nostræ ad extráneos. Pupílli facti sumus absque patre : matres nostræ quasi víduæ. Aquam nostram pecúnia bíbimus ; ligna nostra prétio comparávimus. Cervícibus nostris minabámur : lassis non dabátur réquies. Ægýpto dédimus manum, et Assýriis, ut saturarémur pane. Patres nostri peccavérunt, et non sunt : et nos iniquitátes eórum portávimus. Servi domináti

REMEMBER, O Lord, what is come upon us : consider and behold our reproach. Our inheritance is turned to aliens : our houses to strangers. We are become orphans without a father, our mothers are as widows. We have drunk our water for money : we have bought our wood. We were dragged by the necks, we were weary and no rest was given us. We have given our hand to Egypt, and to the Assyrians, that we might be satisfied with bread. Our fathers have sinned, and are not : and we have borne their iniquities. Servants have ruled over us : there was none to redeem us out

sunt nostri : non fuit qui redímeret de manu eórum. In animábus nostris afferebámus panem nobis, a fácie gládii in desérto. Pellis nostra quasi clíbanus exústa est, a fácie tempestátum famis. Mulíeres in Sion humiliavérunt, et vírgines in civitátibus Juda.

of their hand. We fetched our bread at the peril of our lives, because of the sword in the desert. Our skin was burnt as an oven, by reason of the violence of the famine. They oppressed the women in Sion, and the virgins in the cities of Juda.

Jerúsalem, Jerúsalem, convértere ad Dóminum Deum tuum.

Jerusalem, Jerusalem, be converted to the Lord thy God.

℞. Plange quasi virgo, plebs mea : ululáte, pastóres, in cínere et cilício : * Quia venit dies Dómini magna et amára valde.

℞. Mourn, O my people, as a virgin : howl, ye shepherds, in ashes and haircloth : * For the great and exceeding bitter day of the Lord is coming.

℣. Accíngite vos, sacerdótes, et plángite : minístri altáris, aspérgite vos cínere.

℣. Gird yourselves, ye priests, and mourn ; sprinkle yourselves with ashes, ye ministers of the altar.

* Quia.

* For.

Here is repeated : Plange.

Here is repeated : Mourn.

THE SECOND NOCTURN

Aña. Elevámini, portæ æternáles, et introíbit Rex glóriæ.

Ant. Be ye lifted up, O ye eternal gates, and the King of glory shall enter in.

Psalm. 23.

DOMINI est terra, et plenitúdo ejus : * orbis terrárum, et univérsi qui hábitant in eo.

Psalm 23.

THE earth is the Lord's and the fulness thereof ; the world and all they that dwell therein.

Quia ipse super mária fundávit eum : * et super flúmina præparávit eum.

For he hath founded it upon the seas : and hath prepared it upon the rivers.

Quis ascéndet in montem Dómini : * aut quis stabit in loco sancto ejus?

Who shall ascend into the mountain of the Lord? or who shall stand in his holy place?

Ínnocens mánibus et mundo corde : * qui non

The innocent in hands, and clean of heart, who hath

accépit in vano ánimam suam, nec jurávit in dolo próximo suo.

not taken his soul in vain, nor sworn deceitfully to his neighbour.

Hic accípiet benedictiónem a Dómino : * et misericórdiam a Deo salutári suo.

He shall receive a blessing from the Lord : and mercy from God his Saviour.

Hæc est generátio quæréntium eum : * quæréntium fáciem Dei Jacob.

This is the generation of them that seek him, of them that seek the face of the God of Jacob.

Attóllite portas príncipes vestras, et elevámini portæ æternáles : * et introíbit Rex glóriæ.

Lift up your gates, O ye princes, and be ye lifted up, O eternal gates : and the King of glory shall enter in.

Quis est iste Rex glóriæ? * Dóminus fortis et potens, Dóminus potens in prǽlio.

Who is this King of glory? the Lord, who is strong and mighty, the Lord mighty in battle.

Attólite portas, príncipes, vestras, et elevámini, portæ æternáles : * et introíbit Rex glóriæ.

Lift up your gates, O ye princes, and be ye lifted up, O eternal gates : and the King of glory shall enter in.

Quis est iste Rex glóriæ? * Dóminus virtútum, ipse est Rex glóriæ.

Who is this King of glory? the Lord of hosts, he is the King of glory.

Aña. Elevámini, portæ æternáles, et introíbit Rex glóriæ.

Ant. Be ye lifted up, O ye eternal gates, and the King of glory shall enter in.

Aña. Credo vidére bona Dómini in terra vivéntium.

Ant. I believe to see the good things of the Lord in the land of the living.

Psalm. 26.

DOMINUS illuminátio mea, et salus mea : * quem timébo?

Psalm 26.

THE Lord is my light and my salvation, whom shall I fear?

Dóminus protéctor vitæ meæ : * a quo trepidábo?

The Lord is the protector of my life, of whom shall I be afraid?

Dum apprópiant super me nocéntes : * ut edant carnes meas.

Whilst the wicked draw near against me, to eat my flesh.

Qui tríbulant me inimíci mei : * ipsi infirmáti sunt et cecidérunt.

My enemies that trouble me have been weakened, and have fallen.

Si consistant advérsum me castra : * non timébit cor meum.

Si exsúrgat advérsum me prǽlium : * in hoc ego sperábo.

Unam pétii a Dómino, hanc requíram : * ut inhábitem in domo Dómini ómnibus diébus vitæ meæ.

Ut vídeam voluptátem Dómini : * et vísitem templum ejus.

Quóniam abscóndit me in tabernáculo suo : * in die malórum protéxit me in abscóndito tabernáculi sui.

In petra exaltávit me: * et nunc exaltávit caput meum super inimícos meos.

Circuívi, et immolávi in tabernáculo ejus hóstiam vociferatiónis : * cantábo, et psalmum dicam Dómino.

Exáudi, Dómine, vocem meam qua clamávi ad te : * miserére mei, et exáudi me.

Tibi dixit cor meum, exquisívit te fácies mea : * fáciem tuam, Dómine, requíram.

Ne avértas fáciem tuam a me : * ne declínes in ira a servo tuo.

Adjútor meus esto : * ne derelínquas me, neque despícias me, Deus salutáris meus.

Quóniam pater meus et mater mea dereliqué-

If armies in camp should stand together against me, my heart shall not fear.

If a battle should rise up against me, in this will I be confident.

One thing have I asked of the Lord, this will I seek after, that I may dwell in the house of the Lord all the days of my life.

That I may see the delight of the Lord, and may visit his temple.

For he hath hid me in his tabernacle ; in the day of evils, he hath protected me in the secret place of his tabernacle.

He hath exalted me upon a rock : and now he hath lifted up my head above my enemies.

I have gone round, and have offered up in his tabernacle a sacrifice of jubilation : I will sing, and recite a psalm to the Lord.

Hear, O Lord, my voice, with which I have cried to thee : have mercy on me, and hear me.

My heart hath said to thee, my face hath sought thee : thy face, O Lord, will I still seek.

Turn not away thy face from me : decline not in thy wrath from thy servant.

Be thou my helper : forsake me not, do not thou despise me, O God my Saviour.

For my father and my mother have left me :

runt me : * Dóminus
autem assúmpsit me.

Legem pone mihi, Dó-
mine, in via tua : * et
dírige me in sémitam
rectam propter inimícos
meos.

Ne tradíderis me in
ánimas tribulántium me:
* quóniam insurrexé-
runt in me testes iníqui,
et mentíta est iníquitas
sibi.

Credo vidére bona Dó-
mini : * in terra vivén-
tium.

Exspécta Dóminum,
viríliter age : * et confortétur cor tuum, et sú-
stine Dóminum.

Aña. Credo vidére bo-
na Dómini in terra vi-
véntium.

Aña. Domine, abs-
traxísti ab ínferis áni-
mam meam.

Psalm. 29.

EXALTABO te, Dó-
mine, quóniam sus-
cepísti me : * nec dele-
ctásti inimícos meos su-
per me.

Dómine Deus meus,
clamávi ad te : * et sa-
násti me.

Dómine, eduxísti ab
inférno ánimam meam :
* salvásti me a descen-
déntibus in lacum.

Psallite Dómino, san-
cti ejus : * et confitémini
memóriæ   sanctitátis
ejus.

Quóniam ira in indi-

but the Lord hath taken
me up.

Set me, O Lord, a law in
thy way : and guide me in
the right path, because of
my enemies.

Deliver me not over to
the will of them that trouble me : for unjust witnesses
have risen up against me,
and iniquity hath belied itself.

I believe to see the good
things of the Lord in the
land of the living.

Expect the Lord, do man-
fully, and let thy heart take
courage, and wait thou for
the Lord.

Ant. I believe to see the
good things of the Lord in
the land of the living.

Ant. O Lord, thou hast
brought forth my soul from
hell.

Psalm 29.

I WILL extol thee, O
Lord, for thou hast
upheld me : and hast not
made my enemies to rejoice
over me.

O Lord, my God, I have
cried to thee, and thou hast
healed me.

Thou hast brought forth,
O Lord, my soul from hell :
thou hast saved me from
them that go down into the
pit.

Sing to the Lord, O you
his saints : and give praise
to the memory of his holiness.

For wrath is in his indig-

gnatióne ejus : * et vita in voluntáte ejus.

Ad vésperum demorábitur fletus : * et ad matutínum lætítia.

Ego autem dixi in abundántia mea : * Non movébor in ætérnum.

Dómine, in voluntáte tua : * præstitísti decóri meo virtútem.

Avertísti fáciem tuam a me : * et factus sum conturbátus.

Ad te, Dómine, clamábo : * et ad Deum meum deprecábor.

Quæ utílitas in sánguine meo : * dum descéndo in corruptiónem?

Numquid confitébitur tibi pulvis : * aut annuntiábit veritátem tuam?

Audívit Dóminus, et misértus est mei : * Dóminus factus est adjútor meus.

Convertísti planctum meum in gáudium mihi : * conscidísti saccum meum, et circumdedísti me lætítia.

Ut cantet tibi glória mea, et non compúngar : * Dómine Deus meus, in ætérnum confitébor tibi.

Aña. Dómine, abstraxísti ab ínferis ánimam meam.

℣. Tu autem, Dómine, miserére mei.

℟. Et resúscita me, et retríbuam eis.

nation : and life in his good will.

In the evening, weeping shall have place : and in the morning, gladness.

And in my abundance I said : I shall never be moved.

O Lord, in thy favour, thou gavest strength to my beauty.

Thou turnedst away thy face from me, and I became troubled.

To thee, O Lord, will I cry : and I will make supplication to my God.

What profit is there in my blood, whilst I go down to corruption?

Shall dust confess to thee, or declare thy truth?

The Lord hath heard, and hath had mercy on me : the Lord became my helper.

Thou hast turned for me my mourning into joy : thou hast cut my sackcloth, and hast compassed me with gladness.

To the end that my glory may sing to thee, and I may not regret. O Lord my God, I will give praise to thee for ever.

Ant. O Lord thou hast brought forth my soul from hell.

℣. But thou, O Lord, have mercy on me.

℟. And raise me up again, and I will requite them.

Here is said the Pater noster *in secret.*

FOURTH LESSON

Ex tractátu sancti Augustíni Epíscopi, super Psalmos.

Psalm. 63.

ACCEDET homo ad cor altum, et exaltábitur Deus. Illi dixérunt : Quis nos vidébit? Defecérunt scrutántes scrutatiónes, consília mala. Accéssit homo ad ipsa consília : passus est se tenéri ut homo. Non enim tenerétur nisi homo, aut viderétur nisi homo, aut cæderétur nisi homo, aut crucifigerétur, aut morerétur nisi homo. Accéssit ergo homo ad illas omnes passiónes, quæ in illo nihil valérent, nisi esset homo. Sed si ille non esset homo, non liberarétur homo. Accéssit homo ad cor altum, id est cor secrétum, objíciens aspéctibus humánis hóminem, servans intus Deum ; celans formam Dei, in qua æquális est Patri, et ófferens formam servi, qua minor est Patre.

℟. Recessit Pastor noster, fons aquæ vivæ, ad cujus tránsitum sol obscurátus est : * Nam et ille captus est, qui captívum tenébat primum hóminem : hódie portas mortis et seras páriter Salvátor noster disrúpit.

From the treatise of saint Augustine, Bishop, upon the Psalms.

Psalm 63.

MAN shall come to the deep heart, and God shall be exalted. They said : *Who will see us? They failed in making diligent search for wicked designs.* Christ, as Man, came to those designs, and suffered himself to be seized on as a Man. For he could not be seized on if he were not Man, nor seen if he were not Man, nor scourged if he were not Man, nor crucified nor die if he were not Man. As Man, therefore, he came to all these sufferings, which could have no effect on him if he were not Man. But if he had not been Man, man could not have been redeemed. *Man came to the deep heart,* that is, the secret heart, exposing his humanity to human view, but hiding his divinity : concealing the form of God, by which he is equal to the Father ; and offering the form of the servant, by which he is inferior to the Father.

℟. Our Shepherd, the fountain of living water, is gone ; at whose departure, the sun was darkened. * For he is taken who made the first man a prisoner. To-day our Saviour broke the gates and bolts of death.

℣. Destrúxit quidem claustra inférni et subvértit poténtias diáboli. * Nam et ille.

℣. He, indeed, destroyed the prisons of hell, and overthrew the powers of the devil. * For he.

FIFTH LESSON

QUO perduxérunt illas scrutatiónes suas, quas perscrutántes defecérunt, ut étiam mórtuo Dómino et sepúlto, custódes pónerent ad sepúlcrum ? Dixérunt enim Piláto : Sedúctor ille. Hoc appellabátur nómine Dóminus Jesus Christus, ad solátium servórum suórum, quando dicúntur seductóres. Ergo illi Piláto : Sedúctor ille, ínquiunt, dixit adhuc vivens : Post tres dies resúrgam. Jube ítaque custodíri sepúlcrum usque in diem tértium, ne forte véniant discípuli ejus, et furéntur eum, et dicant plebi : Surréxit a mórtuis : et erit novíssimus error pejor prióre. Ait illis Pilátus : Habétis custódiam ; ite, custodíte sicut scitis. Illi autem abeúntes, muniérunt sepúlcrum, signántes lápidem cum custódibus.

HOW far did they carry this their diligent search, in which they failed so much, that when our Lord was dead and buried, they placed guards at the sepulchre? For they said to Pilate : This seducer ; by which name our Lord Jesus Christ was called, for the comfort of his servants when they are called seducers. This seducer, say they to Pilate, while he was yet living, said : After three days I will rise again. Command therefore the sepulchre to be guarded until the third day, lest perhaps his disciples come and steal him away, and say to the people, he is risen from the dead ; and the last error will be worse than the first. Pilate saith to them : Ye have a guard, go, and guard it as ye know. And they went away and secured the sepulchre with guards, sealing up the stone.

℣. O vos omnes, qui transítis per viam, atténdite et vidéte, * Si est dolor símilis sicut dolor meus.

℟. O all ye that pass by the way, attend and see, * If there be sorrow like unto my sorrow.

℣. Atténdite univérsi pópuli, et vidéte dolórem meum.

℣. Attend all ye people, and see my sorrow.

* Si est.

* If there.

SIXTH LESSON

POSUERUNT custódes mílites ad sepúlcrum. Concússa terra Dóminus resurréxit : mirácula facta sunt tália circa sepúlcrum, ut et ipsi mílites qui custódes advénerant, testes fíerent, si vellent vera nuntiáre. Sed avarítia illa, quæ captivávit discípulum cómitem Christi, captivávit et mílitem custódem sepúlcri. Damus, ínquiunt, vobis pecúniam, et dícite, quia vobis dormiéntibus venérunt discípuli ejus, et abstulérunt eum. Vere defecérunt scrutántes scrutatiónes. Quid est quod dixísti, o infélix astútia? Tantúmne déseris lucem consílii pietátis, et in profúnda versútiæ demérgeris ut hoc dicas : Dícite, quia vobis dormiéntibus venérunt discípuli ejus, et abstulérunt eum? Dormiéntes testes ádhibes : vere tu ipse obdormísti qui scrutándo tália defecísti.

℞. Ecce quómodo móritur justus, et nemo pércipit corde : et viri justi tollúntur et nemo consíderat : a fácie iniquitátis sublátus est Justus : * Et erit in pace memória ejus.

THEY placed soldiers to guard the sepulchre. The earth shook, and the Lord rose again : such miracles were done at the sepulchre, that the very soldiers that came as guards might be witnesses of it, if they would declare the truth. But that covetousness which possessed the disciple that was the companion of Christ, blinded also the soldiers that were the guards of his sepulchre. We will give you money, said they : and say, that while ye were asleep, his disciples came and took him away. They truly failed, in making diligent search. What is it thou hast said, O wretched craft? Dost thou shut thy eyes against the light of prudence and piety, and plunge thyself so deep in cunning, as to say this : Say that while ye were asleep, his disciples came and took him away? Dost thou produce sleeping witnesses? Certainly thou thyself sleepest, that failest in making search after such things.

℞. Behold ! how the Just One dieth, and there is none that taketh it to heart : and just men are taken away and no one considereth it : the Just One is taken away because of iniquity : * And his memory shall be in peace.

℣. Tamquam agnus coram tondénte se obmútuit, et non apéruit os suum : de angústia, et de judício sublátus est.

* Et erit.

Here is repeated : Ecce.

℣. He was silent, as a lamb under his shearer, and he opened not his mouth : he was taken away from distress and judgment.

* And his.

Here is repeated : Behold !

THE THIRD NOCTURN

Aña. Deus ádjuvat me, et Dóminus suscéptor est ánimæ meæ.

Ant. God is my helper, and the Lord is the protector of my soul.

Psalm. 53.

DEUS, in nómine tuo salvum me fac : * et in virtúte tua júdica me.

Deus, exáudi oratiónem meam : * áuribus pércipe verba oris mei.

Quóniam aliéni insurrexérunt advérsum me, et fortes quæsiérunt ánimam meam : * et non proposuérunt Deum ante conspéctum suum.

Ecce enim Deus adjúvat me : * et Dóminus suscéptor est ánimæ meæ.

Avérte mala inimícis meis ; * et in veritáte tua dispérde illos.

Voluntárie sacrificábo tibi : * et confitébor nómini tuo, Dómine, quóniam bonum est.

Quóniam ex omni tribulatióne eripuísti me : * et super inimícos meos despéxit óculus meus.

Aña. Deus adjuvat me, et Dóminus suscéptor est ánimæ meæ.

Aña. In pace factus est locus ejus, et in Sion habitátio ejus.

Psalm 53.

SAVE me, O God, by thy name, and judge me in thy strength.

O God, hear my prayer : give ear to the words of my mouth.

For strangers have risen up against me : and the mighty have sought after my soul : and they have not set God before their eyes.

For behold God is my helper : and the Lord is the protector of my soul.

Turn back the evils upon my enemies : and cut them off in thy truth.

I will freely sacrifice to thee, and will give praise, O God, to thy name : because it is good.

For thou hast delivered me out of all trouble : and my eye hath looked down upon my enemies.

Ant. God is my helper, and the Lord is the protector of my soul.

Ant. His place is in peace, and his abode in Sion.

Psalm. 75.

NOTUS in Judǽa Deus : * in Israël magnum nomen ejus.

Et factus est in pace locus ejus : * et habitátio ejus in Sion.

Ibi confrégit poténtias árcuum : * scutum, gládium, et bellum.

Illúminans tu mirabíliter a móntibus ætérnis : * turbáti sunt omnes insipiéntes corde.

Dormiérunt somnum suum : * et nihil invenérunt omnes viri divitiárum in mánibus suis.

Ab increpatióne tua, Deus Jacob : * dormitavérunt qui ascendérunt equos.

Tu terríbilis es, et quis resístet tibi? * ex tunc ira tua.

De cælo audítum fecísti judícium : * terra trémuit et quiévit.

Cum exsúrgeret in judícium Deus : * ut salvos fáceret omnes mansuétos terræ.

Quóniam cogitátio hóminis confitébitur tibi : * et relíquiæ cogitatiónis diem festum agent tibi.

Vovéte et réddite Dómino Deo vestro : * omnes qui in circúitu ejus affértis múnera.

Terríbili et ei qui aufert spíritum príncipum :

Psalm 75.

IN Judea God is known, his name is great in Israel.

And his place is in peace, and his abode in Sion.

There hath he broken the power of bows, the shield, the sword, and the battle.

Thou enlightenest wonderfully from the everlasting hills : all the foolish of heart were troubled.

They have slept their sleep : and all the men of riches have found nothing in their hands.

At thy rebuke, O God of Jacob, they have all slumbered that mounted on horseback.

Thou art terrible, and who shall resist thee? from that time thy wrath.

Thou hast caused judgment to be heard from heaven : the earth trembled and was still.

When God arose in judgment, to save all the meek of the earth.

For the thought of man shall give praise to thee : and the remainders of the thought shall keep holiday to thee.

Vow ye, and pay to the Lord your God : all you that round about him bring presents.

To him that is terrible, even to him that taketh

* terríbili apud reges terræ.

away the spirit of princes; to the terrible with the kings of the earth.

Aña. In pace factus est locus ejus, et in Sion habitátio ejus.

Ant. His place is in peace, and his abode in Sion.

The ninth psalm is the Dómine, Deus salútis meæ, *repeated from yester day's Office p. 226. It is sung to the following antiphon.*

Aña. Factus sum sicut homo sine adjutório, inter mórtuos liber.

Ant. I am become as a man without help, *whose life is set* free, *and he is now numbered* among the dead.

℣. In pace factus est locus ejus.

℣. His place is in peace.

℟. Et in Sion habitátio ejus.

℟. And his abode in Sion.

The Pater noster *is here recited in secret.*

SEVENTH LESSON

De Epístola beáti Pauli Apóstoli ad Hebrǽos.

From the Epistle of St. Paul the Apostle to the Hebrews.

Cap 9.

Ch. 9.

CHRISTUS assístens Póntifex futurórum bonórum, per ámplius et perféctius tabernáculum non manufáctum, id est non hujus creatiónis; neque per sánguinem hircórum aut vitulórum, sed per próprium Sánguinem, introívit semel in sancta, ætérna redemptióne invénta. Si enim sanguis hircórum et taurórum, et cinis vítulæ aspérsus inquinátos sanctíficat ad emundatiónem carnis : quanto magis Sanguis Christi qui per Spíritum sanctum semetípsum óbtulit immaculátum Deo, emundábit consciéntiam

CHRIST being come a High Priest of the good things to come, by a greater and more perfect tabernacle not made with hands, that is, not of this creation : neither by the blood of goats, nor of calves, but by his own Blood, entered once into the holies having obtained eternal redemption. For if the blood of goats and of oxen, and the ashes of an heifer being sprinkled, sanctify such as are defiled, to the cleansing of the flesh : how much more shall the Blood of Christ, who by the Holy Ghost offered himself unspotted unto God, cleanse our conscience from

nostram ab opéribus mórtuis ad serviéndum Deo vivénti?

℟. Astitérunt reges terræ, et príncipes convenérunt in unum, * Advérsus Dóminum, et advérsus Christum ejus.

℣. Quare fremuérunt gentes, et pópuli meditáti sunt inánia?

* Advérsus.

dead works, to serve the living God?

℟. The kings of the earth stood up, and the princes met together, * Against the Lord, and against his Christ.

℣. Why have the Gentiles raged, and the people devised vain things?

* Against.

EIGHTH LESSON

ET ídeo novi testaménti mediátor est : ut morte intercedénte, in redemptiónem eárum prævaricatiónum, quæ erant sub prióri testaménto, repromissiónem accípiant, qui vocáti sunt, ætérnæ hereditátis. Ubi enim testaméntum est, mors necésse est intercédat testatóris. Testaméntum enim in mórtuis confirmátum est ; alióquin nondum valet, dum vivit qui testátus est. Unde nec primum quidem sine sánguine dedicátum est.

℟. Æstimátus sum cum descendéntibus in lacum. * Factus sum sicut homo sine adjutório, inter mórtuos liber.

℣. Posuérunt me in lacu inferióri, in tenebrósis, et in umbra mortis.

* Factus.

AND therefore he is the mediator of the new testament : that by means of his death, for the redemption of those transgressions which were under the former testament, they that are called may receive the promise of eternal inheriance. For where there is a testament, the death of a testator must of neccessity come in. For a testament is of force after men are dead : otherwise it is as yet of no strength, whilst the testator liveth. Whereupon neither was the first indeed dedicated without blood.

℟. I am counted among them that go down to the pit. * I am become as a man without help, free among the dead.

℣. They have laid me in the lower pit, in the dark places, and in the shadow of death.

* I am.

NINTH LESSON

LECTO enim omni mandáto legis a Móyse univérso pópulo, accípiens sánguinem vituló-

FOR when every commandment of the law had been read by Moses to all the people, he took the

rum et hircórum, cum aqua et lana coccínea et hyssópo : ipsum quoque librum et omnem pópulum aspérsit, dicens : Hic sanguis testaménti, quod mandávit ad vos Deus. Etiam tabernáculum, et ómnia vasa ministérii sánguine simíliter aspérsit. Et ómnia pene in sánguine secúndum legem mundántur : et sine sánguinis effusióne non fit remíssio.

℞. Sepúlto Dómino, signátum est monuméntum, volvéntes lápidem ad óstium monuménti : * Ponéntes mílites, qui custodírent illum.

℣. Accedéntes príncipes sacerdótum ad Pilátum, petiérunt illum.

* Ponéntes.

Here is repeated : Sepúlto Dómino.

blood of calves and goats, with water and scarlet wool and hyssop, and sprinkled both the book itself and all the people, saying : this is the blood of the testament, which God hath enjoined unto you. The tabernacle also, and all the vessels of the ministry, in like manner, he sprinkled with blood. And almost all things, according to the law, are cleansed with blood : and without shedding of blood there is no remission.

℞. Having buried our Lord, they sealed up the sepulchre, rolling a stone before the entrance of the sepulchre : * Placing soldiers to guard him.

℣. The chief priests went to Pilate, and sought his permission.

* Placing.

Here is repeated : Having buried.

LAUDS

The triumph of Easter Day already breaks out at Lauds, *O death, I will be thy death !* Psalms 50, 91, 63 and 150 are those assigned to Saturday's Lauds in the present Psalter. Psalm 50 the great penitential psalm, was always according to an ancient tradition recited at Lauds. Psalm 91 is a morning psalm, but psalm 63 has no particular connection with the mystery of the day ; psalm 150 is a psalm of praise, and in the ancient Psalter was always recited together with psalms 148 and 149 at Lauds. It will be remarked that the canticle, which in the Roman office took the place of the fourth psalm, is not the ferial one for Saturday *Audite cœli quœ loquor,* but the canticle of Ezechias assigned to Tuesday's Lauds, and more appropriate to the office of to-day than would have been the canticle of Moses.

The first psalm of Lauds is the Miserere (p. 156). *Its antiphon is the following :*

Aña. O mors, ero mors tua : morsus tuus ero, inférne.

Aña. Plangent eum quasi unigénitum : quia ínnocens Dóminus occísus est.

Psalm. 91.

BONUM est confitéri Dómino : * et psállere nómini tuo, Altíssime.

Ad annuntiándum mane misericórdiam tuam : * et veritátem tuam per noctem.

In decachórdo, psaltério : * cum cántico in cíthara.

Quia delectásti me, Dómine, in factúra tua : * et in opéribus mánuum tuárum exsultábo.

Quam magnificáta sunt ópera tua, Dómine ! * nimis profúndæ cogitatiónes tuæ.

Vir insípiens non cognóscet : * et stultus non intélliget hæc.

Cum exórti fúerint peccatóres sicut fœnum : * et apparúerint omnes qui operántur iniquitátem :

Ut intéreant in sǽculum sǽculi : * tu autem Altíssimus in ætérnum, Dómine.

Quóniam ecce inimíci tui, Dómine, quóniam

Ant. O death ! I will be thy death. O hell, I will be thy ruin.

Ant. They shall mourn for him as for an only son : because the innocent Lord is slain.

Psalm 91.

IT is good to give praise unto the Lord ; and to sing to thy name, O thou Most High.

To show forth thy mercy in the morning : and thy truth in the night.

Upon an instrument of ten strings, upon the psaltery : with a song upon the harp.

For thou hast given me, O Lord, delight in thy doings : and in the works of thy hands shall I rejoice.

O Lord, how great are thy works ! thy thoughts are exceeding deep.

The unwise man shall not know : nor will the fool understand these things.

When the wicked shall spring up as the grass : and all the workers of iniquity shall appear.

That they may perish for ever and ever : but thou, O Lord, art Most High for ever more.

For behold thine enemies, O Lord, for behold thine

ecce inimíci tui períbunt :
* et dispergéntur omnes,
qui operántur iniquitátem.

Et exaltábitur sicut
unicórnis cornu meum :
* et senéctus mea in misericórdia úberi.

Et despéxit óculus
meus inimícos meos : *
et in insurgéntibus in me
malignántibus áudiet auris mea.

Justus ut palma florébit : * sicut cedrus Líbani multiplicábitur.

Plantáti in domo Dómini, * in átriis domus
Dei nostri florébunt.

Adhuc multiplicabúntur in senécta úberi : *
et bene patiéntes erunt,
ut annúntient.

Quóniam rectus Dóminus Deus noster : *
et non est iníquitas in
eo.

Aña. Plangent eum
quasi unigénitum ; quia
ínnocens Dóminus occisus est.

Aña. Atténdite, univérsi pópuli, et vidéte
dolórem meum.

Psalm. 63.

EXAUDI, Deus, oratiónem meam cum
déprecor : * a timóre
inimíci éripe ánimam
meam.

Protexísti me a convéntu malignántium : *

enemies shall perish : and
all the workers of iniquity
shall be scattered.

But my horn shall be
exalted like that of the unicorn : and my old age in
plentiful mercy.

Mine eye also hath looked
down upon mine enemies :
and mine ear shall hear *of
the downfall* of the malignant that rise up against
me.

The just shall flourish
like the palm-tree : he shall
grow up like the cedar of
Libanus.

They that are planted in
the house of the Lord : shall
flourish in the courts of the
house of our God.

They shall still increase in
a fruitful old age : and it
shall be well with them.

That they may show that
the Lord our God is upright:
and there is no iniquity in
him.

Ant. They shall mourn
for him as for an only son :
because the innocent Lord is
slain.

Ant. Attend, all ye people, and see my sorrow.

Psalm 63.

HEAR my prayer, O God,
when I make supplication to thee : deliver my
soul from the fear of the
enemy.

Thou hast protected me
from the assembly of the

a multitúdine operántium iniquitátem.

Quia exacuérunt ut gládium linguas suas : * intendérunt arcum rem amáram, ut sagíttent in occúltis immaculátum.

Súbito sagittábunt eum, et non timébunt : * firmavérunt sibi sermónem nequam.

Narravérunt ut abscónderent láqueos : * dixérunt : Quis vidébit eos?

Scrutáti sunt iniquitátes : * defecérunt scrutántes scrutínio.

Accédet homo ad cor altum : * et exaltábitur Deus.

Sagíttæ parvulórum factæ sunt plagæ eórum : * et infirmátæ sunt contra eos linguæ eórum.

Conturbáti sunt omnes qui vidébant eos : * et tímuit omnis homo.

Et annuntiavérunt ópera Dei, * et facta ejus intellexérunt.

Lætábitur justus in Dómino, et sperábit in eo, * et laudabúntur omnes recti corde.

Aña. Atténdite, univérsi pópuli, et vidéte dolórem meum.

Aña. A porta ínferi érue, Dómine, ánimam meam.

malignant : from the multitude of the workers of iniquity.

For they have whetted their tongues like a sword : they have bent their bow a bitter thing, to shoot in secret the undefiled.

They will shoot at him on a sudden, and will not fear : they are resolute in words of wickedness.

They have talked of hiding snares : they have said : Who shall see them ?

They have searched after iniquities : they have failed in their search.

Man shall come to a deep heart : and God shall be exalted.

The arrows of children are their wounds : and their tongues are made weak against them.

All that saw them were troubled : and every man was afraid.

And they declared the works of God : and understood his doings.

The just shall rejoice in the Lord, and shall hope in him : and all the upright in heart shall be praised.

Ant. Attend, all ye people, and see my sorrow.

Ant. From the gate of the tomb, O Lord, deliver my soul.

CANTICLE OF EZECHIAS
(*Is.* 38).

EGO dixi : in dimídio diérum meórum : * vadam ad portas ínferi.

Quæsívi resíduum annórum meórum : * dixi : Non vidébo Dóminum Deum in terra vivéntium.

Non aspíciam hóminem ultra : * et habitatórem quiétis.

Generátio mea abláta est, et convolúta est a me : * quasi tabernáculum pastórum.

Præscísa est velut a texénte vita mea, dum adhuc ordírer succídit me : * de mane usque ad vésperam fínies me.

Sperábam usque ad mane : * quasi leo sic contrívit ómnia ossa mea.

De mane usque ad vésperam fínies me : * sicut pullus hirúndinis sic clamábo, meditábor ut colúmba.

Attenuáti sunt óculi mei : * suspiciéntes in excélsum.

Dómine, vim pátior, respónde pro me : * Quid dicam, aut quid respondébit mihi, cum ipse fécerit?

Recogitábo tibi omnes annos meos : * in amaritúdine ánimæ meæ.

Dómine, si sic vívitur,

I SAID : in the midst of my days : I shall go to the gates of hell.

I sought for the residue of my years : I said, I shall not see the Lord God in the land of the living.

I shall behold man no more, nor the inhabitant of rest.

My generation is at an end, and it is rolled away from me as a shepherd's tent.

My life is cut off as by a weaver ; whilst I was but beginning, he cut me off : from morning even till night thou wilt make an end of me.

I hoped till morning : as a lion so hath he broken my bones.

From morning even till night thou wilt make an end of me : I will cry like a young swallow, I will meditate like a dove.

My eyes are weakened with looking upward.

Lord, I suffer violence, answer thou for me. What shall I say, or what shall he answer for me, whereas he himself hath done it?

I will recount to thee all my years, in the bitterness of my soul.

O Lord, if man's life be

et in tálibus vita spíritus mei, corrípies me, et vivificábis me : * ecce in pace amaritúdo mea amaríssima.

Tu autem eruísti ánimam meam ut non períret : * projecísti post tergum tuum ómnia peccáta mea.

Quia non inférnus confitébitur tibi, neque mors laudábit te : * non exspectábunt qui descéndunt in lacum veritátem tuam.

Vivens, vivens, ipse confitébitur tibi, sicut et ego hódie : * pater fíliis notam fáciet veritátem tuam.

Dómine, salvum me fac, * et psalmos nostros cantábimus cunctis diébus vitæ nostræ in domo Dómini.

Aña. A porta ínferi, érue, Dómine, ánimam meam.

Aña. O vos omnes, qui transítis per viam, atténdite et vidéte, si est dolor sicut dolor meus.

Psalm. 150.

LAUDATE Dóminum in sanctis ejus : * laudáte eum in firmaménto virtútis ejus.

Laudáte eum in virtútibus ejus : * laudáte eum secúndum multitúdinem magnitúdinis ejus.

Laudáte eum in sono

such, and the life of my spirit be in such things as these, thou shalt correct me, and make me to live. Behold in peace is my bitterness most bitter.

But thou hast delivered my soul, that it should not perish : thou hast cast all my sins behind thy back.

For hell shall not confess to thee, neither shall death praise thee : nor shall they that go down into the pit look for thy truth.

The living, the living, he shall give praise to thee, as I do this day : the father shall make thy truth known to the children.

O Lord, save me, and we will sing our psalms all the days of our life in the house of the Lord.

Ant. From the gate of the tomb, O Lord, deliver my soul.

Ant. O all ye that pass by the way, attend and see, if there be sorrow like unto my sorrow.

Psalm 150.

PRAISE ye the Lord in his holy places : praise ye him in the firmament of his power.

Praise ye him for his mighty acts : praise ye him according to the multitude of his greatness.

Praise him with sound of

tubæ : * laudáte eum in psaltério et cíthara.

Laudáte eum in týmpano et choro : * laudáte eum in chordis et órgano.

Laudáte eum in cýmbalis benesonántibus : laudáte eum in cýmbalis jubilatiónis : * omnis spiritus laudet Dóminum.

Aña. O vos omnes, qui transítis per viam, atténdite et vidéte, si est dolor sicut dolor meus.

℣. Caro mea requiéscet in spe.

℞. Et non dabis Sanctum tuum vidére corruptiónem.

---

trumpet : praise him with psaltery and harp.

Praise him with timbrel and choir : praise him with strings and organs.

Praise him on high-sounding cymbals : praise him on cymbals of joy : let every spirit praise the Lord.

Ant. O all ye that pass by the way, attend and see, if there be sorrow like unto my sorrow.

℣. My flesh shall rest in hope.

℞. And thou wilt not suffer thy Holy One to see corruption.

After this versicle, the Benedictus (*p.* 165) *is sung, to the following antiphon :*

Aña. Mulíeres sedéntes ad monuméntum lamentabántur, flentes Dóminum.

Ant. The women, sitting near the tomb, mourned, weeping for the Lord.

The antiphon having been repeated after the canticle, the choir sings :

℣. Christus factus est pro nobis obédiens usque ad mortem, mortem autem crucis.

Propter quod et Deus exaltávit illum, et dedit illi nomen, quod est super omne nomen.

℣. Christ became, for our sake, obedient unto death, even to the death of the cross.

For which cause, God also hath exalted him, and hath given him a name, which is above all names.

Then is said, in secret, the Pater noster, *which is followed by the* Miserere (*p.* 156). *As soon as the psalm is finished, the following prayer is recited by the first in dignity :*

Réspice, quǽsumus, Dómine, super hanc famíliam tuam : pro qua Dóminus noster Jesus Christus non dubitávit

---

Look down, O Lord, we beseech thee, upon this thy family, for which our Lord Jesus Christ hesitated not to be delivered into the hands

mánibus tradi nocén- | of wicked men, and to un-
tium, et crucis subíre | dergo the punishment of the
torméntum : | cross :

(then the rest in secret :)

Qui tecum vivit et re- | Who liveth and reigneth
gnat, in unitáte Spíritus | with thee, in the unity of
Sancti, Deus, per ómnia | the Holy Ghost, God, world
sǽcula sæculórum. A- | without end. Amen.
men.

THE MORNING OFFICE

Originally Holy Saturday like the preceding Saturday
had no proper Mass, neither was there a station on these
two days. The office now celebrated in the morning is in
reality the one which formerly began on Saturday evening,
was prolonged all through the night and ended at daybreak
with Mass at the very hour at which the Resurrection took
place. Many passages occur during the course of the office
which leave no doubt on this point, such as : *O truly blessed
night, night in which Christ broke the chains of death*, and
others. To understand the full meaning of the ceremony,
this fact must be borne in mind.

To-day as on Good Friday, several successive rites not
necessarily connected with each other are performed : the
blessing of the new fire and the paschal candle, the lessons,
the blessing of the font, and the Mass. Considered separately they will be the more easily understood by the
faithful.

1. The Blessing of the New Fire.

This ceremony recalls the ancient *Lucernarium* or office
of lights held at night in certain churches, at which took
place the blessing of fire. Descriptions of it are to be found
in the *Peregrinatio Silviæ* and in other writings of the fourth
and fifth centuries. The *Lucernarium* was akin to our
office of Vespers and Compline, which have grown out of
it. On the evening of Holy Saturday the office naturally
assumed a more solemn character, the mystery itself lend-
ing a deeper meaning to the symbolism of the rites. The
Lucernarium, as it survives in the liturgy of to-day under a
modified form, consists of the blessing of the new fire, the

procession to the sanctuary and the singing of the *Exsultet*. The new fire is produced by striking a flint ; the first collect speaks of this stone which is Christ, the Corner Stone from whence proceeds that heavenly fire which burns in the hearts of the faithful. This rite is purely symbolical, and only to be understood in its mystical application. Here we see sanctified the act by which man made his first and most valuable discovery, the power to produce fire at will, fire which gives warmth and light, which purifies and consumes. The second collect invokes God, Eternal Light and Author of all light, and allusion is made to the pillar of fire which guided the Israelites by night through the desert.

Many learned liturgists have studied the question of the fourth collect, said during the blessing of the five grains of incense. The word *incensum* has now come to mean *incense*, though the original term was *thus*. The confusion of these two words may have led to the subsequent addition of this blessing. It is thought that here *incensum* really designated the paschal candle, in which case the collect would refer to the blessing of the new fire, the unity and symbolism of the ceremony thus remaining unbroken. The triple-branched candle is then lighted and the procession re-enters the church to the chant of the *Lumen Christi*, the light of Christ [1].

The *Exsultet* is considered to be the most beautiful lyric in the Roman liturgy, but it is not always fully understood. We learn from St. Augustine that the duty of composing this poem devolved upon the deacon. Certain deacons however, not feeling equal to the task, sought professional aid. St. Jerome ridicules one deacon who had applied to him for help on such an occasion. The *Exsultet* in its present form has gained in sobriety of style, having been shorn of much of its original redundancy and affectation. One of the passages rejected was an eulogy in the style of Virgil. The poet gives the first place to the bee among all the other living things

---

[1] The triple-branched candle did not figure in the original ceremony. To understand the meaning of the following rites one must suppose the paschal candle to have been brought to the threshold of the church during the blessing of the new fire, and to have been lighted during the procession. The words of the *Exsultet : qui* (cereus) *licet sit divisus in partes, mutuati tamen luminis detrimenta non novit* are quite clear when it is remembered that the paschal candle is usually so large, that the wick is made of three or more strands. If this hypothesis be accepted, the meaning of the formulas and their symbolical application become clearer.

subject to man. Though small of body, yet her industry is great ; she goes from flower to flower gathering her store of honey, whilst others are employed in building up the cells, etc.

The style of the Roman *Exsultet* is noble and inspired. It may be divided into two parts : first the prelude in which the author announces his intention of singing the praises of the paschal candle, symbol of the Light Eternal ; the second part is in the form of a preface which sings of the night in which the true Lamb was slain. The Jewish pasch with the slaying of the lamb, the flight into the desert, and the pillar of fire was but a figure of this truly blessed night in which Christ descended into the darkness of hell, rising again to liberate man whose sins are now washed away (by Baptism). This candle is to dispel the shades of night, greeting with its clear flame the bright and morning star, figure of Christ rising from the dead in the grey light of early dawn.

STATION AT ST. JOHN LATERAN

At a convenient hour the altars are prepared, and the Hours are recited in the choir ; but the candles are not lighted until the beginning of the Mass. Meanwhile fire is struck from a flint at the entrance of the church, and coals are kindled from it. Near at hand lies a vessel containing five large grains of incense to be set in the Paschal Candle. The priest, vested in purple cope, goes to the church door accompanied by his ministers and acolytes with processional cross, holy water, and incense. He first blesses the new fire :

℣. Dóminus vobíscum.
℟. Et cum spíritu tuo.

Orémus.

DEUS, qui per Fílium tuum, angulárem scílicet lápidem, claritátis tuæ ignem fidélibus contulísti : prodúctum e sílice, nostris profutúrum úsibus, novum hunc ignem sanctí✠fica : et concéde nobis, ita per hæc festa paschália cæléstibus desidériis inflammári : ut ad perpétuæ claritátis, puris méntibus, valeá-

℣. The Lord be with you.
℟. And with thy spirit.

Let us pray.

O GOD, who by thy Son, the cornerstone, hast bestowed on the faithful the fire of thy splendour ; ✠ sanctify this new fire produced from a flint for our use : and grant that, during this Paschal festival, we may be so inflamed with heavenly desires, that with pure minds we may come to the solemnity of eternal glory.

mus festa pertíngere. Per eúmdem Christum Dóminum nostrum. ℞. Amen.

Orémus.

DOMINE Deus, Pater omnípotens, lumen indefíciens, qui es cónditor ómnium lúminum : béne✠dic hoc lumen, quod a te sanctificátum atque benedíctum est, qui illuminásti omnem mundum : ut ab eo lúmine accendámur, atque illuminémur igne claritátis tuæ : et sicut illuminásti Móysen exeúntem de Ægýpto, ita illúmines corda et sensus nostros : ut ad vitam et lucem ætérnam perveníre mereámur. Per Christum Dóminum nostrum. ℞. Amen.

Orémus.

DOMINE sancte, Pater omnípotens, ætérne Deus : benedicéntibus nobis hunc ignem in nómine tuo, et unigéniti Fílii tui Dei ac Dómini nostri Jesu Christi, et Spíritus Sancti, cooperári dignéris : et ádjuva nos contra igníta tela inimíci, et illústra grátia cælésti. Qui vivis et regnas cum eódem Unigénito tuo, et Spíritu Sancto Deus : per ómnia sǽcula sæculórum. ℞. Amen.

Through the same Christ our Lord. ℞. Amen.

Let us pray.

O LORD God, almighty Father, never failing light, who art the author of all light: ✠ bless this light, that is blessed and sanctified by thee, who hast enlightened the whole world : that we may be enlightened by that light, and inflamed with the fire of thy splendour : and as thou didst give light to Moses, when he went out of Egypt, so illuminate our hearts and senses, that we may obtain light and life everlasting. Through Christ our Lord. ℞. Amen.

Let us pray.

O HOLY Lord, almighty Father, eternal God : vouchsafe to co-operate with us, who ✠ bless this fire in thy name, and in that of thine only Son Christ Jesus, our Lord and God : and of the Holy Ghost : assist us against the fiery darts of the enemy, and illumine us with thy heavenly grace. Who livest and reignest with the same only Son and Holy Ghost, one God, for ever and ever. ℞. Amen.

He next blesses the five grains of incense :

VENIAT, quǽsumus, omnípotens Deus, super hoc incénsum larga tuæ benedi✠ctiónis infúsio : et hunc noctúrnum splendórem invisíbilis regenerátor accénde : ut non solum sacrifícium, quod hac nocte litátum est, arcána lúminis tui admixtióne refúlgeat, sed in quocúmque loco ex hujus sanctificatiónis mystério áliquid fúerit deportátum, expúlsa diabólicæ fraudis nequítia, virtus tuæ majestátis assístat. Per Christum Dóminum nostrum. ℟. Amen.

POUR forth, we beseech thee, O almighty God, thy abundant ✠ blessing on this incense : and kindle, O invisible regenerator, the brightness of this night : that not only the sacrifice that is offered this night may shine by thy mysterious light ; but also into whatever place anything of this mystical sanctification shall be brought, there, by the power of thy majesty, all the malicious artifices of the devil may be defeated. Through Christ our Lord. ℟. Amen.

An acolyte taking some of the blessed coals places them in the thurible, and the priest puts incense in, blessing it in the usual manner ; then he sprinkles the grains of incense and the new fire thrice with holy water, and thrice incenses them. All the lamps in the church are extinguished, that they may afterwards be lighted from the blessed fire. The deacon now vests in a white dalmatic, and takes up a reed at the top of which is fixed a three-branched candle ; and all enter the church. First goes the thurifer with an acolyte carrying a vessel with the five grains of incense ; next the subdeacon bearing the cross ; the clergy in order : then the deacon with the reed : and lastly the priest. As soon as the deacon has entered the church he lowers the reed, and an acolyte, carrying a candle or taper lighted from the new fire, lights one of the branches of the triple candle. The deacon, raising up the reed, kneels down as do all the rest, except the subdeacon who is carrying the cross, the deacon sings :

Lumen Christi. | The light of Christ.

All answer :

Deo grátias. | Thanks be to God.

In the middle of the church the second branch of the candle is lighted, with the same ceremonies ; and the third branch in the sanctuary, the deacon each time singing Lumen Christi *on a higher tone.*

The priest now goes up to the Epistle corner of the altar ; the deacon gives the reed to an acolyte, and taking the book, asks a from the priest, who gives it in the following words :

DOMINUS sit in corde tuo, et in lábiis tuis: ut digne et competénter annúnties suum Paschále præcónium. In nómine Patris, et Fílii, ✠ et Spíritus Sancti. ℞. Amen.

THE Lord be in thy heart and on thy lips, that thou mayest worthily and fitly proclaim his paschal praise. In the name of the Father, and of the Son, ✠ and of the Holy Ghost. ℞. Amen.

Mounting the ambo, the deacon puts down the book and incenses it. At his right hand stands the subdeacon holding the cross and the thurifer; at his left two acolytes, one holding the reed, the other a vessel containing the five grains of incense. All rise and stand as at the Gospel, and the deacon proceeds to bless the paschal candle, singing:

EXSULTET jam angélica turba cælórum : exsúltent divína mystéria : et pro tanti Regis victória, tuba ínsonet salutáris. Gáudeat et tellus tantis irradiáta fulgóribus : et ætérni regis splendóre illustráta, totíus orbis se séntiat amisísse calíginem. Lætétur et mater Ecclésia tanti lúminis adornáta fulgóribus : et magnis populórum vócibus hæc aula resúltet. Quaprópter astántes vos, fratres caríssimi, ad tam miram hujus sancti lúminis claritátem, una mecum, quæso, Dei omnipoténtis misericórdiam invocáte. Ut qui me non meis méritis intra Levitárum númerum dignátus est aggregáre, lúminis sui claritátem infúndens, cérei hujus laudem implére perfíciat. Per Dóminum nostrum Jesum

LET now the heavenly hosts of angels rejoice : let the divine mysteries be joyfully celebrated : and let a sacred trumpet proclaim the victory of so great a King. Let the earth also be filled with joy, being illuminated with such resplendent rays : and let men know that the darkness which overspread the whole world is chased away by the splendour of our eternal King. Let our mother the Church be also glad, finding herself adorned with the rays of so great a light : and let this temple resound with the joyful acclamations of the people. Wherefore, beloved brethren, you who are now present at the admirable brightness of this holy light, I beseech you to invoke with me the mercy of almighty God. That he, who has been pleased above my desert to admit me into the number of his Levites, will, by an infusion of his light upon me, enable

Christum Fílium suum : qui cum eo vivit et regnat in unitáte Spíritus Sancti, Deus. Per ómnia sǽcula sæculórum. ℞. Amen.

℣. Dóminus vobíscum.
℞. Et cum spíritu tuo.
℣. Sursum corda.
℞. Habémus ad Dóminum.
℣. Grátias agámus Dómino Deo nostro.
℞. Dignum et justum est.

Vere dignum et justum est, invisíbilem Deum Patrem omnipoténtem, Filiúmque ejus unigénitum, Dóminum nostrum Jesum Christum, toto cordis ac mentis afféctu, et vocis ministério personáre. Qui pro nobis ætérno Patri, Adæ débitum solvit; et véteris piáculi cautiónem pio cruóre detérsit. Hæc sunt enim festa Paschália, in quibus verus ille Agnus occíditur, cujus sánguine postes fidélium consecrántur. Hæc nox est, in qua primum patres nostros fílios Israël edúctos de Ægýpto, Mare Rubrum sicco vestígio transíre fecísti. Hæc ígitur nox est, quæ peccatórum ténebras, colúmnæ illuminatióne purgávit. Hæc nox est, quæ hódie per univér-

me to celebrate the praises of this light. Through our Lord Jesus Christ his Son, who with him and the Holy Ghost liveth and reigneth one God for ever and ever. ℞. Amen.

℣. The Lord be with you.
℞. And with thy spirit.
℣. Lift up your hearts.
℞. We have lifted them up to the Lord.
℣. Let us give thanks to the Lord our God.
℞. It is meet and just.

It is truly meet and just to proclaim with all the affection of our heart and soul, and with the sound of our voice, the invisible God the Father almighty, and his only Son our Lord Jesus Christ. Who paid for us to his eternal Father the debt of Adam : and by his sacred blood cancelled the guilt contracted by original sin. For this is the paschal solemnity, in which the true Lamb was slain, by whose blood the doors of the faithful are consecrated. This is the night in which thou formerly broughtest forth our forefathers the children of Israel out of Egypt, leading them dry-foot through the Red Sea. This then is the night which dissipated the darkness of sin, by the light of the pillar. This is the night which now delivers all over the world those that believe in Christ from the

sum mundum, in Christo credéntes, a vítiis sǽculi, et calígine peccatórum segregátos, reddit grátiæ, sóciat sanctitáti. Hæc nox est, in qua destrúctis vínculis mortis, Christus ab ínferis victor ascéndit. Nihil enim nobis nasci prófuit, nisi rédimi profuísset. O mira circa nos tuæ pietátis dignátio! O inæstimábilis diléctio caritátis! ut servum redímeres, Fílium tradidísti. O certe necessárium Adæ peccátum, quod Christi morte delétum est! O felix culpa, quæ talem ac tantum méruit habére Redemptórem! O vere beáta nox, quæ sola méruit scire tempus et horam, in qua Christus ab ínferis resurréxit! Hæc nox est, de qua scriptum est : Et nox sicut dies illuminábitur : et nox illuminátio mea in delíciis meis. Hujus ígitur sanctificátio noctis fugat scélera, culpas lavat : et reddit innocéntiam lapsis, et mœstis lætítiam. Fugat ódia, concórdiam parat, et curvat impéria.

vices of the world and darkness of sin, restores them to grace, and clothes them with sanctity. This is the night in which Christ broke the chains of death, and ascended conqueror from hell. For it availed us nothing to be born, unless it had availed us to be redeemed. O how admirable is thy goodness towards us! O how inestimable is thy love! Thou hast delivered up thy Son to redeem a slave. O truly necessary sin of Adam, which the death of Christ has blotted out! O happy fault, that merited such and so great a Redeemer! O truly blessed night, which alone deserved to know the time and hour when Christ rose again from hell. This is the night of which it is written : And the night shall be as light as the day, and the night is my illumination in my delights. Therefore the sanctification of this night blots out crimes, washes away sins, and restores innocence to sinners, and joy to the sorrowful. It banishes enmities, produces concord, and humbles empires.

Here the deacon fixes the five grains of incense in the candle in the form of a cross.

1

4 2 5

3

In hujus ígitur noctis grátia, súscipe, sancte

Therefore on this sacred night, receive, O holy Fa-

Pater, incénsi hujus sacrifícium vespertínum : quod tibi in hac cérei oblatióne solémni, per ministrórum manus, de opéribus apum, sacrosáncta reddit Ecclésia. Sed jam colúmnæ hujus præcónia nóvimus,quam in honórem Dei rútilans ignis ascéndit.

ther, the evening sacrifice of this incense, which thy holy Church, by the hands of her ministers, presents to thee in the solemn offering of this wax candle, made out of the labour of bees. And now we know the excellence of this pillar, which the bright fire lights for the honour of God.

Here the deacon lights the candle with one of the three candles on the reed.

Qui licet sit divísus in partes, mutuáti tamen lúminis detriménta non novit. Alitur enim liquántibus ceris, quas in substántiam pretiósæ hujus lámpadis, apis mater edúxit.

Which fire, though now divided, suffers no loss from the communication of its light. Because it is fed by the melted wax, which the mother bee wrought for the substance of this precious lamp.

Here the lamps are lighted.

O vere beáta nox, quæ exspoliávit Ægyptios,ditávit Hebræos : nox, in qua terrénis cæléstia, humánis divína jungúntur. Orámus ergo te, Dómine : ut céreus iste in honórem tui nóminis consecrátus, ad noctis hujus calíginem destruéndam, indefíciens persevéret. Et in odórem suavitátis accéptus, supérnis lumináribus misceátur. Flammas ejus lúcifer matutínus invéniat. Ille, inquam, lúcifer, qui nescit occásum. Ille, qui regréssus ab ínferis, humáno géneri serénus illúxit. Precámur ergo te, Dómine : ut

O truly blessed night, which plundered the Egyptians, and enriched the Hebrews. A night, in which heaven is united to earth and God to man. We beseech thee therefore, O Lord, that this candle, consecrated to the honour of thy name, may continue burning to dissipate the darkness of this night. And being accepted as a sweet savour, may be united with the celestial lights. Let the morning star find it alight, that star which never sets. Which being returned from hell, shone with brightness on mankind. We beseech thee therefore, O Lord, to grant us peaceable times

nos fámulos tuos, omnémque clerum, et devotíssimum pópulum : una cum beatíssimo Papa nostro N. et Antístite nostro N. quiéte témporum concéssa, in his paschálibus gáudiis, assídua protectióne régere, gubernáre, et conserváre dignéris. Per eúmdem Dóminum nostrum Jesum Christum Fílium tuum : qui tecum vivit et regnat in unitáte Spíritus Sancti, Deus, per ómnia sǽcula sæculórum. ℞. Amen.

during these paschal solemnities, and with thy constant protection to rule, govern, and preserve us thy servants, all the clergy, and the devout laity, together with our holy Pope N. and our Bishop N. Through the same Lord Jesus Christ thy Son : who with thee and the Holy Ghost, liveth and reigneth one God for ever and ever.

℞. Amen.

After the blessing of the candle the deacon lays aside his white dalmatic and vests in purple ; the priest takes off the cope and puts on a purple chasuble. The prophecies are then chanted, during which in former times priests catechized those who were to be baptized and prepared them for that sacrament.

---

2. The Prophecies.

The *Lucernarium* or primitive office of Easter Eve may now be considered to have come to an end. The office is continued in a form distinct from the preceding ceremonies, consisting of Lessons, Tracts and Collects. This part of the office is similar in construction to the Mass of the catechumens and the office of Tenebræ. The Lessons are twelve in number and are either descriptions of famous events in Biblical history, such as the creation, the flood, the temptation of Abraham, the passage of the Red Sea, or same striking passage from the Prophets, the call of Isaias to all the preoples of the earth, the earnest exhortation of Baruch, the vision of Ezechiel, a prophecy of Messianic times from Isaias. These are followed by a description of the rite of the paschal lamb, the mission of Jonas to the Ninivites, the canticle of Moses, and the miracle of the three children in the fiery furnace. These Lessons serve as instructions for the catechumens about to receive Baptism, and that their teaching is mainly intended for them is evident from

the elaboration and application of each Lesson in its complementary Collect. Three of the Lessons are followed by Tracts, which continue and complete the theme of the Prophecy. Two of these are from the canticle of Moses and the third is the parable of the vineyard from Isaias.

After the fourth and fifth centuries the baptism of adult converts from judaism and paganism became rare, and Baptism was usually administered to the children of Christian parents, so that the liturgy proper to the catechumens became obsolete and much of it dropped out of the Sacramentaries. It is therefore probable that the origin of these Lessons dates back to the fifth century at least, and even earlier. Moreover the episodes themselves, the sacrifice of Abraham, the mission of Jonas, the three children in the fiery furnace etc., were favourite subjects in the mural paintings of the Catacombs. The fact that these paintings are of the third or possibly the second century is additional evidence as to the antiquity of this portion of the liturgy.

In churches which possess a font the ceremony of the blessing of the baptismal font follows immediately after the twelfth Prophecy, and Baptism is administered if any candidates are presented. All these ceremonies succeed one another in logical sequence : the *Lucernarium* with the blessing of the paschal candle during which the prophecies and types and figures of the Jewish pasch are explained ; the Lessons with their wealth of teaching on the Sacrament of Baptism, followed by the blessing of the font and the administration of Baptism, and crowning it all the Holy Sacrifice of the Mass during which the newly baptised make their first Communion.

Prophetia prima.
Gen. 1 & 2.

IN princípio creávit Deus cælum et terram. Terra autem erat inánis et vácua, et ténebræ erant super fáciem abýssi : et Spíritus Dei ferebátur super a- quas. Dixítque Deus : Fiat lux. Et facta est lux. Et vidit Deus lucem quod esset bona : et divísit lucem a téne-

The first Prophecy.
Gen. 1 & 2.

IN the beginning God created heaven and earth. And the earth was void and empty, and darkness was upon the face of the deep : and the spirit of God moved over the waters. And God said : Let there be light. And light was made. And God saw the light that it was good : and he divided the light from the darkness.

bris. Appellavítque lucem Diem, et ténebras Noctem. Factúmque est ´véspere et mane, dies uńus. Dixit quoque Deus : Fiat firmaméntum in médio aquárum, et dívidat aquas ab aquis. Et fecit Deus firmaméntum : divisítque aquas, quæ erant sub firmaménto ab his quæ erant super firmaméntum. Et factum est ita. Vocavítque Deus firmaméntum Cælum. Et factum est véspere et mane, dies secúndus. Dixit vero Deus : Congregéntur aquæ, quæ sub cælo sunt, in locum unum, et appáreat árida. Et factum est ita. Et vocávit Deus áridam Terram ; congregationésque aquárum appellávit Mária. Et vidit Deus quod esset bonum. Et ait : Gérminet terra herbam viréntem, et faciéntem semen, et lignum pomíferum fáciens fructum juxta genus suum, cujus semen in semetípso sit super terram. Et factum est ita. Et prótulit terra herbam viréntem, et faciéntem semen juxta genus suum, lignúmque fáciens fructum, et habens unumquódque seméntem secúndum spéciem suam. Et vidit Deus quod esset bonum.

And he called the light Day, and the darkness Night. And there was evening and morning one day. And God said : Let there be a firmament made amidst the waters : and let it divide the waters from the waters. And God made a firmament, and divided the waters that were under the firmament, from those that were above the firmament. And it was so. And God called the firmament Heaven. And the evening and the morning were the second day. God also said : Let the waters that are under the heaven be gathered together into one place : and let the dry land appear. And it was so done. And God called the dry land, Earth : and the gathering together of the waters he called Seas. And God saw that it was good. And he said : Let the earth bring forth the green herb, and such as may seed, and the fruit-tree yielding fruit after its kind, which may have seed in itself upon the earth. And it was so done. And the earth brought forth the green herb, and such as yieldeth seed according to its kind, and the tree that beareth fruit, having seed each one according to its kind. And God saw that it was good. And the evening and the morning were the third day. And God said : Let there be lights in the

Et factum est véspere et mane, dies tértius. Dixit autem Deus: Fiant luminária in firmaménto cæli, et dívidant diem ac noctem, et sint in signa et témpora, et dies et annos : ut lúceant in firmaménto cæli, et illúminent terram. Et factum est ita. Fecítque Deus duo luminária magna : lumináre majus, ut præésset diéi : et lumináre minus, ut præésset nocti : et stellas. Et pósuit eas in firmaménto cæli, ut lucérent super terram, et præéssent diéi ac nocti, et divíderent lucem ac ténebras. Et vidit Deus quod esset bonum. Et factum est véspere, et mane, dies quartus. Dixit étiam Deus : Prodúcant aquæ réptile ánimæ vivéntis, et volátile super terram sub firmaménto cæli. Creavítque Deus cete grándia et omnem ánimam vivéntem atque motábilem, quam prodúxerant aquæ in spécies suas, et omne volátile secúndum genus suum. Et vidit Deus quod esset bonum. Benedixítque eis, dicens : Créscite, et multiplicámini, et repléte aquas maris : avésque multiplicéntur super terram. Et factum est véspere et mane, dies quintus. Di-

firmament of heaven to divide the day and the night, and let them be for signs, and for seasons, and for days, and years : to shine in the firmament of heaven, and to give light upon the earth. And it was so done. And God made two great lights : a greater light to rule the day : and a lesser light to rule the night : and the stars. And he set them in the firmament of heaven, to shine upon the earth, and to rule the day and the night, and to divide the light and the darkness. And God saw that it was good. And the evening and the morning were the fourth day. God also said : Let the waters bring forth the creeping creature having life, and the fowl that may fly over the earth under the firmament of heaven. And God created the great whales, and every living and moving creature, which the waters brought forth according to their kinds, and every winged fowl according to its kind. And God saw that it was good. And he blessed them, saying : Increase and multiply, and fill the waters of the sea : and let the birds be multiplied upon the earth. And the evening and the morning were the fifth day. And God said : Let the earth bring forth the living creature in its kind, cattle, and creeping

xit quoque Deus : Prodúcat terra ánimam vivéntem in génere suo : juménta, et reptília, et béstias terræ secúndum spécies suas. Factúmque est ita. Et fecit Deus béstias terræ juxta spécies suas, et juménta, et omne réptile terræ in génere suo. Et vidit Deus quod esset bonum, et ait : Faciámus hóminem ad imáginem et similitúdinem nostram : et præsit píscibus maris, et volatílibus cæli, et béstiis, universæque terræ, omníque réptili quod movétur in terra. Et creávit Deus hóminem ad imáginem suam : ad imáginem Dei creávit illum, másculum et féminam creávit eos. Benedixítque illis Deus, et ait : Créscite, et multiplicámini, et repléte terram, et subjícite eam, et dominámini píscibus maris, et volatílibus cæli, et univérsis animántibus, quæ movéntur super terram. Dixítque Deus : Ecce dedi vobis omnem herbam afferéntem semen super terram, et univérsa ligna, quæ habent in semetípsis seméntem géneris sui, ut sint vobis in escam : et cunctis animántibus terræ, omníque vólucri cæli, et univérsis quæ

things, and beasts of the earth according to their kinds : and it was so done. And God made the beasts of the earth, according to their kinds, and cattle, and every thing that creepeth on the earth after its kind. And God saw that it was good. And he said : Let us make man to our image and likeness : and let him have dominion over the fishes of the sea, and the fowls of the air, and the beasts, and the whole earth, and every creeping creature that moveth upon the earth. And God created man to his own image ; to the image of God he created him, male and female he created them. And God blessed them, saying : Increase and multiply, and fill the earth, and subdue it, and rule over the fishes of the sea, and the fowls of the air, and all living creatures that move upon the earth. And God said : Behold, I have given you every herb bearing seed upon the earth, and all trees that have in themselves seed of their own kind, to be your meat : and to all beasts of the earth, and to every fowl of the air, and to all that move upon the earth, and wherein there is life that they may have to feed

movéntur in terra, et in quibus est ánima vivens, ut hábeant ad vescéndum. Et factum est ita. Vidítque Deus cunctá quæ fécerat : et erant valde bona. Et factum est véspere et mane, dies sextus. Igitur perfécti sunt cæli et terra, et omnis ornátus eórum. Complevítque Deus die séptimo opus suum,quod fécerat : et requiévit die séptimo ab univérso ópere quod patrárat.

upon. And it was so done. And God saw all the things that he had made, and they were very good. And the evening and the morning were the sixth day. So the heavens and the earth were finished, and all the furniture of them. And on the seventh day, God ended his work which he had made : and he rested on the seventh day from all his work which he had done.

The priest says :

Orémus. | Let us pray.

The deacon :

Flectámus génua. | Let us kneel.

The subdeacon :

℟. Leváte. | ℟ Arise.

Oratio.

DEUS, qui mirabíliter creásti hóminem, et mirabílius redemísti : da nobis, quǽsumus, contra oblectaménta peccáti, mentis ratióne persístere : ut mereámur ad ætérna gáudia perveníre. Per Dóminum nostrum Jesum Christum. ℟. Amen.

Collect.

O GOD, who hast wonderfully created man, and more wonderfully redeemed him : grant us, we beseech thee, such strength of mind and reason against the allurements of sin, that we may deserve to obtain eternal joys. Through our Lord Jesus Christ. ℟. Amen.

Prophetia secunda.
Gen. 5, 6, 7, 8.

NOE vero cum quingentórum esset annórum,génuitSem,Cham et Japheth. Cumque cœpíssent hómines multiplicári super terram, et fílias procreássent, vidéntes fílii Dei has fílió-

The second Prophecy.
Gen. 5, 6, 7, 8.

NOE, when he was five hundred years old, begot Sem, Cham and Japheth. And after that men began to be multiplied upon the earth, and daughters were born to them ; the sons of God seeing the daughters

minum, quod essent pulchræ, accepérunt sibi uxóres ex ómnibus quas elégerant. Dixítque Deus : Non permanébit spíritus meus in hómine in ætérnum, quia caro est. Erúntque dies illíus centum vigínti annórum. Gigántes autem erant super terram in diébus illis. Postquam enim ingréssi sunt fílii Dei ad fílias hóminum, illǽque genuérunt, isti sunt poténtes a sǽculo viri famósi. Videns autem Deus, quod multa malítia hóminum esset in terra, et cuncta cogitátio cordis inténta esset ad malum omni témpore, pœnítuit eum, quod hóminem fecísset in terra. Et tactus dolóre cordis intrínsecus : Delébo, inquit, hóminem quem creávi, a fácie terræ, ab hómine usque ad animántia, a réptili usque ad vólucres cæli : pœnitet enim me fecísse eos. Noë vero invénit grátiam coram Dómino. Hæ sunt generatiónes Noë : Noë vir justus atque perféctus fuit in generatiónibus suis, cum Deo ambulávit. Et génuit tres fílios, Sem, Cham, et Japheth. Corrúpta est autem terra coram Deo, et repléta est iniquitáte. Cumque vidísset Deus terram

of men, that they were fair, took to themselves wives of all which they chose. And God said : My spirit shall not remain in man for ever, because he is flesh : and his days shall be a hundred and twenty years. Now giants were upon the earth in those days. For after the sons of God went in to the daughters of men, and they brought forth children : these are the mighty men of old, men of renown. And God seeing that the wickedness of men was great on the earth, and that all the thought of their heart was bent upon evil at all times, it repented him that he had made man on the earth. And being touched inwardly with sorrow of heart, he said : I will destroy man, whom I have created, from the face of the earth, from man even to beasts, from the creeping thing even to the fowls of the air, for it repenteth me that I have made them. But Noe found grace before the Lord. These are the generations of Noe : Noe was a just and perfect man in his generations, he walked with God. And he begot three sons, Sem, Cham and Japheth. And the earth was corrupted before God, and was filled with iniquity. And when God had seen that the earth was corrupted (for all flesh had corrupted its way

esse corrúptam (omnis quippe caro corrúperat viam suam, super terram), dixit ad Noë : Finis univérsæ carnis venit coram me : repléta est terra iniquitáte a fácie eórum, et ego dispérdam eos cum terra. Fac tibi arcam de lignis lævigátis : mansiúnculas in arca fácies, et bitúmine línies intrínsecus et extrínsecus. Et sic fácies eam : trecentórum cubitórum erit longitúdo arcæ, quinquagínta cubitórum latitúdo, et trigínta cubitórum altitúdo illíus. Fenéstram in arca fácies, et in cúbito consummábis summitátem ejus ; óstium autem arcæ pones ex látere ; deórsum cœnácula et trístega fácies in ea. Ecce ego addúcam aquas dilúvii super terram, ut interfíciam omnem carnem, in qua spíritus vitæ est subter cælum. Univérsa quæ in terra sunt consuméntur. Ponámque fœdus meum tecum : et ingrediéris arcam tu et fílii tui, uxor tua et uxóres filiórum tuórum tecum. Et ex cunctis animántibus univérsæ carnis bina indúces in arcam, ut vivant tecum : masculíni sexus et feminíni. De volúcribus juxta genus suum, et de

upon the earth), he said to Noe : The end of all flesh is come before me, the earth is filled with iniquity through them, and I will destroy them with the earth. Make thee an ark of timber planks : thou shalt make little rooms in the ark, and thou shalt pitch it within and without. And thus shalt thou make it : the length of the ark shall be three hundred cubits : the breadth of it fifty cubits : and the height of it thirty cubits. Thou shalt make a window in the ark, and in a cubit shalt thou finish the top of it : and the door of the ark thou shalt set in the side : with lower, middle chambers, and third stories shalt thou make it. Behold, I will bring the waters of a great flood upon the earth, to destroy all flesh, wherein is the breath of life under heaven. All things that are in the earth shall be consumed. I will establish my covenant with thee ; and thou shalt enter into the ark thou and thy sons, and thy wife, and the wives of thy sons with thee. And of every living creature of all flesh, thou shalt bring two of a sort into the ark, that they may live with thee : of the male sex, and the female. Of fowls according to their kind, and of beasts in their kind, and of every thing that creepeth on the earth

juméntis in génere suo, et ex omni réptili terræ secúndum genus suum : bina de ómnibus ingrediéntur tecum, ut possint vívere. Tolles ígitur tecum ex ómnibus escis, quæ mandi possunt, et comportábis apud te : et erunt' tam tibi quam illis in cibum. Fecit ígitur Noe ómnia quæ præcéperat illi Deus. Erátque sexcentórum annórum, quando dilúvii aquæ inundavérunt super terram. Rupti sunt omnes fontes abýssi magnæ, et cataráctæ cæli apértæ sunt, et facta est plúvia super terram quadragínta diébus et quadragínta nóctibus. In artículo diéi illíus ingréssus est Noë, et Sem, et Cham, et Japheth, filii ejus : uxor illíus, et tres uxóres filiórum ejus cum eis in arcam : ipsi et omne ánimal secúndum genus suum, univérsaque juménta in génere suo, et omne quod movétur super terram in génere suo, cunctúmque volátile secúndum genus suum. Porro arca ferebátur super aquas. Et aquæ prævaluérunt nimis super terram : opertíque sunt omnes montes excélsi sub univérso cælo. Quíndecim cúbitis áltior fuit aqua super

according to its kind : two of every sort shall go in with thee, that they may live. Thou shalt take unto thee of all food that may be eaten, and thou shalt lay it up with thee : and it shall be food for thee and them. And Noe did all things which God commanded him. And he was six hundred years old when the waters of the flood overflowed the earth. All the fountains of the great deep were broken up, and the flood-gates of heaven were opened. And the rain fell upon the earth forty days and forty nights. In the self-same day, Noe, and Sem, and Cham, and Japheth, his sons : his wife, and the three wives of his sons with them, went into the ark. They and every beast according to its kind, and all the cattle in their kind, and every thing that moveth upon the earth according to its kind, and every fowl according to its kind, all birds, and all that fly. And the ark was carried upon the waters. And the waters prevailed beyond measure upon the earth : and all the high mountains under the whole heaven were covered. The water was fifteen cubits higher than the mountains, which it covered. And all flesh was destroyed that moved upon the earth, both of fowl, and of cattle, and of

montes, quos operúerat.
Consúmptaque est omnis caro quæ movebátur
super terram, vólucrum,
animántium, bestiárum,
omniúmque   reptílium
quæ reptant super terram.   Remánsit autem
solus Noë, et qui cum eo
erant in arca.   Obtinuerúntque aquæ terram
centum   quinquagínta
diébus.   Recordátus autem Deus Noë, cunctorúmque animántium, et
ómnium   jumentórum,
quæ erant cum eo in arca, addúxit spíritum super terram, et imminútæ sunt aquæ.   Et clausi
sunt fontes abýssi, et cataráctæ cæli : et prohíbitæ sunt plúviæ de cælo.   Reversǽque sunt
aquæ de terra, eúntes et
redeúntes : et cœpérunt
mínui post centum quinquagínta dies.   Cumque
transíssent quadragínta
dies, apériens Noë fenèstram arcæ, quam fécerat, dimísit corvum :
qui egrediebátur, et non
revertebátur, donec siccaréntur   aquæ   super
terram.   Emísit quoque
colúmbam post eum, ut
vidéret si jam cessássent
aquæ super fáciem terræ.   Quæ cum non invenísset ubi requiésceret
pes ejus, revérsa est ad
eum in arcam : aquæ
enim erant super univérsam terram.   Exten-

beasts, and of all creeping
things that creep upon the
earth : and Noe only remained, and they that were
with him in the ark. And the
waters prevailed upon the
earth a hundred and fifty
days. And God remembered
Noe, and all the living creatures, and all the cattle
which were with him in the
ark, and brought a wind
upon the earth, and the
waters were abated. The
fountains also of the deep,
and the flood-gates of heaven were shut up : and the
rain from heaven was restrained. And the waters returned from off the earth,
going and coming : and they
began to be abated after a
hundred and fifty days. And
after that forty days were
passed, Noe, opening the
window of the ark which he
had made, sent forth a raven : which went forth and
did not return, till the waters were dried up upon the
face of the earth. He sent
forth also a dove after him,
to see if the waters had now
ceased upon the face of the
earth. But she not finding
where her foot might rest,
returned to him into the
ark : for the waters were
upon the whole earth : and
he put forth his hand, and
caught her, and brought
her into the ark. And having

dítque manum et appre-
hénsam íntulit in arcam.
Exspectátis autem ultra
septem diébus áliis, rur-
sum dimísit colúmbam
ex arca. At illa venit ad
eum ad vésperam, por-
tans ramum olívæ virén-
tibus fóliis in ore suo.
Intelléxit ergo Noë, quod
cessássent aquæ super
terram. Exspectavítque
nihilóminus septem álios
dies : et emísit colúm-
bam, quæ non est revérsa
ultra ad eum. Locútus
est autem Deus ad Noë,
dicens : Egrédere de ar-
ca, tu, et uxor tua, fílii
tui, et uxóres filiórum
tuórum tecum. Cuncta
animántia, quæ sunt
apud te, ex omni carne
tam in volatílibus, quam
in béstiis, et univérsis
reptílibus, quæ reptant
super terram, educ te-
cum, et ingredímini super
terram : créscite, et multiplicámini super eam.
Egréssus est ergo Noë,
et fílii ejus, uxor illíus, et
uxóres filiórum ejus cum
eo. Sed et ómnia animán-
tia, juménta, et reptília
quæ reptant super ter-
ram, secúndum genus su-
um, egréssa sunt de arca.
Ædificávit autem Noë al-
táre Dómino: et tollens de
cunctis pecóribus et vo-
lúcribus mundis, óbtulit
holocáusta super altáre.
Odoratúsque est Dómi-
nus odórem suavitátis.

waited yet seven other days,
he again sent forth the dove
out of the ark. And she
came to him in the evening,
carrying a bough of an olive
tree, with green leaves in
her mouth. Noe therefore
understood that the waters
were ceased upon the earth.
And he stayed yet other
seven days and he sent forth
the dove, which returned not
any more unto him. And
God spoke to Noe, saying :
Go out of the ark, thou and
thy wife, thy sons, and the
wives of thy sons with thee.
All living things that are
with thee of all flesh, as well
in fowls as in beasts, and all
creeping things that creep
upon the earth, bring out
with thee, and go ye upon
the earth : increase and multiply upon it. So Noe went
out, he and his sons : his
wife, and the wives of his
sons with him ; and all living things, and cattle, and
creeping things that creep
upon the earth, according to
their kinds, went out of the
ark. And Noe built an altar
unto the Lord : and taking
of all cattle and fowls that
were clean, offered holo-
causts upon the altar. And
the Lord smelled a sweet
savour.

Orémus.
Flectámus génua.
℟. Leváte.
Oratio.

DEUS, incommutábilis virtus, et lumen ætérnum : réspice propítius ad totíus Ecclésiæ tuæ mirábile sacraméntum, et opus salútis humánæ, perpétuæ dispositiónis efféctu tranquíllius operáre : totúsque mundus experiátur et vídeat, dejécta érigi, inveteráta renovári, et per ipsum redíre ómnia in íntegrum a quo sumpsére princípium : Dóminum nostrum Jesum Christum Fílium tuum, qui tecum vivit et regnat.

Prophetia tertia.
Gen. 22.

IN diébus illis : Tentávit Deus Abraham et dixit ad eum : Abraham, Abraham. At ille respóndit : Adsum. Ait illi : Tolle fílium tuum unigénitum, quem díligis, Isaac, et vade in terram visiónis : atque ibi ófferes eum in holocáustum super unum móntium, quem monstrávero tibi. Igitur Abraham de nocte consúrgens, stravit ásinum suum, ducens secum duos júvenes, et Isaac fílium suum. Cumque concidísset ligna in holocáustum, ábiit ad locum,

Let us pray.
Let us kneel.
℟. Arise.
Collect.

O GOD, who art power unchangeable and light eternal : mercifully regard the wonderful mystery of thy whole Church, and by an effect of thy perpetual providence perform with tranquillity the work of human salvation : and let the whole world experience and see that what was fallen is raised up, what was old is made new, and all things are re-established, through him that gave them their first being ,our Lord Jesus Christ thy Son, who liveth and reigneth.

The third Prophecy.
Gen. 22.

IN those days : God tempted Abraham, and said to him : Abraham, Abraham. And he answered : Here I am. He said to him : Take thine only begotten son, Isaac, whom thou lovest, and go into the land of vision ; and there thou shalt offer him for an holocaust upon one of the mountains, which I will show thee. So Abraham, rising up in the night, saddled his ass: and took with him two young men, and Isaac his son. And when he had cut wood for the holocaust, he went his way to the place which God had commanded

quem præcéperat ei Deus. Die autem tértio, elevátis óculis, vidit locum procul : dixítque ad púeros suos : Exspectáte hic cum ásino : ego et puer illuc usque properántes, postquam adoravérimus, revertémur ad vos. Tulit quoque ligna holocáusti, et impósuit super Isaac fílium suum : ipse vero portábat in mánibus ignem et gládium. Cumque duo pérgerent simul, dixit Isaac patri suo : Pater mi. At ille respóndit : Quid vis, fili? Ecce, inquit, ignis et ligna : ubi est víctima holocáusti? Dixit autem Abraham : Deus providébit sibi víctimam holocáusti, fili mi. Pergébant ergo páriter : et venérunt ad locum quem osténderat ei Deus, in quo ædificávit altáre, et désuper ligna compósuit: cumque alligásset Isaac fílium suum, pósuit eum in altáre super struem lignórum : Extendítque manum, et arrípuit gládium, ut immoláret fílium suum. Et ecce Angelus Dómini de cælo clamávit, dicens : Abraham, Abraham. Qui respóndit : Adsum. Dixítque ei : Non exténdas manum tuam super púerum, neque fácias illi quidquam : nunc cognó-

him. And on the third day, lifting up his eyes, he saw the place afar off. And he said to his young men : Stay you here with the ass : I and the boy will go with speed as far as yonder, and after we have worshipped will return to you. And he took the wood for the holocaust, and laid it upon Isaac his son : and he himself carried in his hands fire and a sword. And as they two went on together, Isaac said to his father : My father. And he answered : What wilt thou, son? Behold, saith he, fire and wood : where is the victim for the holocaust? And Abrahm said : God will provide himself a victim for a holocaust, my son. So they went on together ; and they came to the place which God had showed him, where he built an altar, and laid the wood in order upon it : and when he had bound Isaac his son, he laid him on the altar upon the pile of wood. And he put forth his hand, and took the sword to sacrifice his son. And behold an Angel of the Lord from heaven called to him saying : Abraham, Abraham. And he answered : Here I am. And he said to him : Lay not thy hand upon the boy, neither do thou any thing to him : now I know that thou fearest God, and hast not spar-

vi quod times Deum, et non pepercísti unigénito fílio tuo propter me. Levávit Abraham óculos suos, vidítque post tergum aríetem inter vepres hæréntem córnibus, quem assúmens óbtulit holocáustum pro fílio. Appellavítque nomen loci illíus, Dóminus videt. Unde usque hódie dícitur : In monte Dóminus vidébit. Vocávit autem Angelus Dómini Abraham secúndo de cælo, dicens : Per memetípsum jurávi, dicit Dóminus : quia fecísti hanc rem, et non pepercísti fílio tuo unigénito propter me, benedícam tibi et multiplicábo semen tuum sicut stellas cæli, et velut arénam, quæ est in líttore maris : possidébit semen tuum portas inimicórum suórum, et benedicéntur in sémine tuo omnes gentes terræ, quia obedísti voci meæ. Revérsus est Abraham ad púeros suos, abierúntque Bersabée simul, et habitávit ibi.

Orémus.

Flectámus génua.

℞. Leváte.

Oratio.

DEUS, fidélium Pater summe, qui in toto orbe terrárum, promissiónis tuæ fílios diffúsa adoptiónis grátia multi-

ed thine only begotten son for my sake. Abraham lifted up his eyes, and saw behind his back a ram amongst the briers, sticking fast by the horns, which he took and offered for a holocaust instead of his son. And he called the name of that place : The Lord seeth. Whereupon even to this day it is said : In the mountain the Lord will see. And the Angel of the Lord called to Abraham a second time from heaven, saying : By mine own self have I sworn, saith the Lord, because thou hast done this thing, and hast not spared thine only begotten son for my sake : I will bless thee, and I will multiply thy seed as the stars of heaven, and as the sand that is by the seashore : thy seed shall possess the gates of their enemies, and in thy seed shall all the nations of the earth be blessed, because thou hast obeyed my voice. Abraham returned to his young men, and they went to Bersabee together, and he dwelt there.

Let us pray.

Let us kneel.

℞. Arise.

Collect.

O GOD, the supreme Father of all the faithful, who all over the world multipliest the children of thy promise by the grace

plicas; et per paschále sacraméntum, Abraham púerum tuum universárum, sicut jurásti, géntium éfficis patrem : da pópulis tuis digne ad grátiam tuæ vocatiónis introíre. Per Dóminum.

Prophetia quarta.
Exod. 14 *et* 15.

IN diébus illis : Factum est in vigília matutína, et ecce respíciens Dóminus super castra Ægyptiórum per colúmnam ignis et nubis, interfécit exércitum eórum : et subvértit rotas cúrruum, ferebantúrque in profúndum. Dixérunt ergo Ægýptii : Fugiámus Israélem : Dóminus enim pugnat pro eis contra nos. Et ait Dóminus ad Móysen : Exténde manum tuam super mare, ut revertántur aquæ ad Ægýptios super currus et équites eórum. Cumque extendísset Móyses manum contra mare, revérsum est primo dilúculo ad priórem locum : fugientibúsque Ægýptiis occurrérunt aquæ : et invólvit eos Dóminus in médiis flúctibus. Reversǽque sunt aquæ, et operuérunt currus et équites cuncti exércitus Pharaónis, qui sequéntes ingréssi fúerant mare : nec unus quidem su-

of thine adoption : and, according to thine oath, makest thy servant Abraham the father of all nations : by this paschal sacrament grant that thy people may worthily receive the grace of thy vocation. Through our Lord.

The fourth Prophecy.
Exod. 14 & 15.

IN those days : It came to pass in the morning watch, and behold the Lord looking upon the Egyptian army, through the pillar of fire and of the cloud, slew their host : and overthrew the wheels of the chariots, and they were carried into the deep. And the Egyptians said : Let us flee from Israel : for the Lord fighteth for them against us. And the Lord said to Moses: Stretch forth thy hand over the sea, that the waters may come again upon the Egyptians, upon their chariots and horsemen. And when Moses had stretched forth his hand towards the sea, it returned at the first break of day to the former place : and as the Egyptians were fleeing away, the waters came upon them, and the Lord shut them up in the middle of the waves. And the waters returned, and covered the chariots and the horsemen of all the army of Pharao, who had come into the sea after them, neither did there so much as one of

pérfuit ex eis. Fílii autem Israël perrexérunt per médium sicci maris, et aquæ eis erant quasi pro muro a dextris et a sinístris. Liberavítque Dóminus in die illa Israël de manu Ægyptiórum. Et vidérunt Ægýptios mórtuos super littus maris, et manum magnam quam exercúerat Dóminus contra eos : timuítque pópulus Dóminum, et credidérunt Dómino, et Móysi servo ejus. Nunc cécinit Móyses et fílii Israël carmen hoc Dómino, et dixérunt :

Tractus. Exod. 15. Cantémus Dómino, glorióse enim honorificátus est : equum et ascensórem projécit in mare : adjútor et protéctor factus est mihi in salútem. ℣. Hic Deus meus, et honorábo eum : Deus patris mei, et exaltábo eum. ℣. Dóminus cónterens bella : Dóminus nomen est illi.

Orémus.
Flectámus génua.
℟. Leváte.
Oratio.

DEUS, cujus antíqua mirácula étiam nostris sæculis coruscáre sentímus : dum quod uni pópulo a persecutióne Ægyptíaca liberándo, déxteræ tuæ poténtia contulísti, id in

---

them remain. But the children of Israel marched through the midst of the sea upon dry land, and the waters were to them as a wall on the right hand and on the left ; and the Lord delivered Israel in that day out of the hands of the Egyptians. And they saw the Egyptians dead upon the seashore, and the mighty hand that the Lord had used against them ; and the people feared the Lord, and they believed the Lord, and Moses his servant. Then Moses and the children of Israel sung this canticle to the Lord, and said :

Tract. Exod. 15. Let us sing to the Lord, for he is gloriously honoured : the horse and the rider he hath thrown into the sea : he became my helper and protector for my safety. ℣. This is my God, and I will honour him : the God of my father, and I will extol him. ℣. He is the Lord that destroys wars : the Lord is his name.

Let us pray.
Let us kneel.
℟. Arise.
Collect.

O GOD, whose ancient miracles we see renewed in our days, whilst by the water of our regeneration thou workest for the salvation of the Gentiles, that which by the power of thy right hand thou didst

salútem géntium per aquam regeneratiónis operáris : præsta, ut in Abrahæ fílios, et in Israëlíticam dignitátem, totíus mundi tránseat plenitúdo. Per Dóminum.

Prophetia quinta.
Isa. 54 et 55.

HÆC est heréditas servórum Dómini, et justítia eórum apud me, dicit Dóminus. Omnes sitiéntes veníte ad aquas : et qui non habétis argéntum, properáte, émite, et comédite : veníte, émite absque argénto, et absque ulla commutatióne, vinum et lac. Quare appénditis argéntum non in pánibus, et labórem vestrum non in saturitáte? Audíte audiéntes me, et comédite bonum, et delectábitur in crassitúdine ánima vestra. Inclináte aurem vestram, et veníte ad me : audíte, et vivet ánima vestra, et fériam vobíscum pactum sempitérnum, misericórdias David fidéles. Ecce testem pópulis dedi eum, ducem ac præceptórem géntibus. Ecce gentem, quam nesciébas, vocábis : et gentes, quæ te non cognovérunt, ad te current, propter Dóminum Deum tuum, et sanctum Israël : quia glorificávit

for the delivery of one people from the Egyptian persecution : grant that all the nations of the world may become the children of Abraham, and partake of the dignity of the people of Israel. Through our Lord.

The fifth Prophecy.
Isa. 54 & 55.

THIS is the inheritance of the servants of the Lord, and their justice with me, saith the Lord. All you that thirst, come to the waters : and you that have no money, make haste, buy and eat ; come ye, buy wine and milk without money, and without any price. Why do you spend money for that which is not bread, and your labour for that which doth not satisfy you? Hearken diligently to me, and eat that which is good, and your soul shall be delighted in fatness. Incline your ear, and come to me : hear, and your soul shall live, and I will make an everlasting covenant with you, the faithful mercies of David. Behold I have given him for a witness to the people, for a leader and a master to the Gentiles. Behold, thou shalt call a nation which thou knewest not : and the nations that knew not thee shall run to thee, because of the Lord thy God, and for the Holy One of Israel : for he hath glorified thee. Seek ye the Lord while he may be

te. Quǽrite Dóminum, dum inveníri potest, invocáte eum, dum prope est. Derelínquat ímpius viam suam, et vir iníquus cogitatiónes suas, et revertátur ad Dóminum, et miserébitur ejus, et ad Deum nostrum : quóniam multus est ad ignoscéndum. Non enim cogitatiónes meæ, cogitatiónes vestræ : neque viæ vestræ, viæ meæ : dicit Dóminus. Quia sicut exaltántur cæli a terra, sic exaltátæ sunt viæ meæ a viis vestris, et cogitatiónes meæ a cogitatiónibus vestris. Et quómodo descéndit imber et nix de cælo, et illuc ultra non revértitur, sed inébriat terram, et infúndit eam, et germináre eam facit, et dat semen serénti, et panem comedénti : sic erit verbum meum, quod egrediétur de ore meo : non revertétur ad me vácuum, sed fáciet quæcúmque vólui et prosperábitur in his, ad quæ misi illud : dicit Dóminus omnípotens.

Orémus.
Flectámus génua.
℞. Leváte.
Oratio.

OMNIPOTENS sempitérne Deus, multiplica in honórem nóminis tui, quod patrum fi-

found, call upon him while he is near. Let the wicked forsake his way, and the unjust man his thoughts, and let him return to the Lord, and he will have mercy on him, and to our God, for he is bountiful to forgive. For my thoughts are not your thoughts, nor your ways my ways, saith the Lord. For as the heavens are exalted above the earth, so are my ways exalted above your ways, and my thoughts above your thoughts. And as the rain and the snow come down from heaven, and return no more thither, but soak the earth and water it, and make it to spring, and give seed to the sower, and bread to the eater : so shall my word be which shall go forth from my mouth : it shall not return to me void, but it shall do whatsoever I please, and shall prosper in the things for which I sent it, saith the Lord Almighty.

Let us pray.
Let us kneel.
℞. Arise.
Collect.

ALMIGHTY and eternal God, multiply, for the honour of thy name, what thou didst promise to the

dei spopondísti, et promissiónis fílios sacra adoptióne diláta : ut quod prióres sancti non dubitavérunt futúrum, Ecclésia tua magna jam ex parte cognóscat implétum. Per Dóminum.

Prophetia sexta.
Baruch 3.

AUDI, Israël, mandáta vitæ : áuribus pércipe, ut scias prudéntiam. Quid est, Israël, quod in terra inimicórum es? Inveterásti in terra aliéna, coinquinátus es cum mórtuis : deputátus es cum descendéntibus in inférnum. Dereliquísti fontem sapiéntiæ. Nam si in via Dei ambulásses, habitásses útique in pace sempitérna. Disce, ubi sit prudéntia, ubi sit virtus, ubi sit intelléctus : ut scias simul, ubi sit longitúrnitas vitæ et victus, ubi sit lumen oculórum, et pax. Quis invénit locum ejus? et quis intrávit in thesáuros ejus? Ubi sunt príncipes géntium, et qui domiuántur super béstias, quæ sunt super terram? qui in ávibus cæli ludunt, qui argéntum thesaurízant, et aurum, in quo confídunt hómines, et non est finis acquisitiónis eórum? qui argéntum fábricant et sollíciti

faith of our forefathers ; and increase by thy sacred adoption the children of that promise : that what the ancient saints doubted not would come to pass, thy Church may now find in a great part accomplished. Through our Lord.

The sixth Prophecy.
Baruch 3.

HEAR, O Israel, the commandments of life : give ear, that thou mayest learn wisdom. How happeneth it, O Israel, that thou art in thine enemies' land? Thou art grown old in a strange country, thou art defiled with the dead ; thou art counted with them that go down into hell. Thou hast forsaken the fountain of wisdom. For if thou hadst walked in the way of God, thou hadst surely dwelt in peace for ever. Learn where is wisdom, where is strength, where is understanding : that thou mayest know also where is length of days and life, where is the light of the eyes and peace. Who hath found out her place? and who hath gone into her treasures? Where are the princes of the nations, and they that rule over the beasts that are upon the earth? That take their pastime with the birds of the air, that hoard up silver and gold, wherein men trust, and there is no end of their

sunt, nec est invéntio óperum illórum? Extermináti sunt, et ad ínferos descendérunt, et álii loco eórum surrexérunt. Júvenes vidérunt lumen, et habitavérunt super terram : viam autem disciplínæ ignoravérunt, neque intellexérunt sémitas ejus, neque fílii eórum suscepérunt eam : a fácie ipsórum longe facta est : non est audíta in terra Chánaan, neque visa est in Theman. Fílii quoque Agar, qui exquírunt prudéntiam quæ de terra est, negotiatóres Merrhæ et Theman, et fabulatóres, et exquisitóres prudéntiæ et intelligéntiæ : viam autem sapiéntiæ nesciérunt, neque commemoráti sunt sémitas ejus. O Israël, quam magna est domus Dei, et ingens locus possessiónis ejus ! Magnus est, et non habet finem : excélsus et imménsus. Ibi fuérunt gigántes nomináti illi, qui ab inítio fuérunt, statúra magna, sciéntes bellum. Non hos elégit Dóminus, neque viam disciplínæ invenérunt : proptérea periérunt. Et quóniam non habuérunt sapiéntiam, interiérunt propter suam insipiéntiam. Quis ascéndit in cælum, et accépit eam, et edúxit

getting? who work in silver and are solicitous, and their works are unsearchable. They are cut off, and are gone down to hell, and others are risen up in their place. Young men have seen the light, and dwelt upon the earth : but the way of knowledge they have not known, nor have they understood the paths thereof, neither have their children received it : it is far from their face : it hath not been heard of in the land of Chanaan, neither hath it been seen in Theman. The children of Agar also, that search after the wisdom that is of the earth, the merchants of Merrha, and of Theman, and the tellers of fables, and searchers of prudence and understanding : but the way of wisdom they have not known, neither have they remembered her paths. O Israel, how great is the house of God, and how vast is the place of his possession ! It is great and hath no end : it is high and immense. There were the giants, those renowned men that were from the beginning, of great stature, expert in war. The Lord chose not them, neither did they find the way of knowledge : therefore did they perish. And because they had not wisdom, they perished through their folly. Who hath gone up into hea-

eam de núbibus? Quis transfretávit máre, et invénit illam? et áttulit illam super aurum eléctum? Non est qui possit scire vias ejus, neque qui exquírat sémitas ejus : sed qui scit univérsa novit eam, et adinvénit eam prudéntia sua : qui præparávit terram in ætérno témpore, et replévit eam pecúdibus et quadrupédibus : qui emíttit lumen, et vadit : et vocávit illud, et obédit illi in tremóre. Stellæ autem dedérunt lumen in custódiis suis, et lætátæ sunt : vocátæ sunt, et dixérunt : Adsumus : et luxérunt ei cum jucunditáte, qui fecit illas. Hic est Deus noster, et non æstimábitur álius advérsus eum. Hic adinvénit omnem viam disciplínæ, et trádidit illam Jacob púero suo, et Israël dilécto suo. Post hæc in terris visus est, et cum homínibus conversátus est.

Orémus.
Flectámus génua.
℞. Leváte.
Oratio.

DEUS, qui Ecclésiam tuam semper Géntium vocatióne multíplicas : concéde propí-

ven, and taken her, and brought her down from the clouds? Who hath passed over the sea, and found her, and brought her preferably to chosen gold? There is none that is able to know her ways, nor that can search out her paths : but he that knoweth all things knoweth her, and hath found her out with his understanding. He that prepared the earth for evermore, and filled it with cattle and four-footed beasts? He that sendeth forth light, and it goeth : and hath called it, and it obeyed him with trembling. And the stars have given light in their watches, and rejoiced : they were called, and they said : Here we are : and with cheerfulness they have shined forth to him that made them. This is our God, and there shall no other be accounted of in comparison of him. He found out all the way of knowledge, and gave it to Jacob his servant, and to Israel his beloved. Afterwards he was seen upon earth, and conversed with men.

Let us pray.
Let us kneel.
℞. Arise.
Collect.

O GOD, who multipliest thy Church by the vocation of the Gentiles : mercifully grant thy perpetual

tius, ut quos aqua baptísmatis ábluis, contínua protectióne tueáris. Per Dóminum.

Prophetia septima.
Ezech. 37.

IN diébus illis : Facta est super me manus Dómini, et edúxit me in spíritu Dómini : et dimísit me in médio campi, qui erat plenus óssibus : et circumdúxit me per ea in gyro : erant autem multa valde super fáciem campi, síccaque veheménter. Et dixit ad me : Fili hóminis, putásne vivent ossa ista? Et dixi : Dómine Deus, tu nosti. Et dixit ad me : Vaticináre de óssibus istis : et dices eis : Ossa árida, audíte verbum Dómini. Hæc dicit Dóminus Deus óssibus his : Ecce ego intromíttam in vos spíritum, et vivétis. Et dabo super vos nervos, et succréscere fáciam super vos carnes, et superexténdam in vobis cutem : et dabo vobis spíritum, et vivétis, et sciétis quia ego Dóminus. Et prophetávi sicut præcéperat mihi : factus est autem sónitus, prophetánte me, et ecce commótio : et accessérunt ossa ad ossa, unumquódque ad junctúram suam. Et vidi, et ecce super ea et carnes ascendé-

protection to those whom thou washest with the water of baptism. Through our Lord.

The seventh Prophecy.
Ezech. 37.

IN those days : The hand of the Lord was upon me, and brought me forth in the spirit of the Lord : and set me down in the midst of a plain that was full of bones : and he led me about through them on every side. Now there were very many upon the face of the plain, and they were exceeding dry. And he said to me : Son of man, dost thou think these bones shall live? And I answered : O Lord God, thou knowest. And he said to me : Prophesy concerning these bones : and say to them : Ye dry bones hear the word of the Lord. Thus saith the Lord God to these bones : Behold, I will send spirit into you, and you shall live. And I will lay sinews upon you, and will cause flesh to grow over you, and will cover you with skin : and I will give you spirit, and you shall live, and you shall know that I am the Lord. And I prophesied as he had commanded me : and as I prophesied there was a noise, and behold a commotion : and the bones came together, each one to its joint. And I saw, and behold the sinews and the

runt : et exténta est in eis cutis désuper, et spíritum non habébant. Et dixit ad me : Vaticináre ad spíritum, vaticináre, fili hóminis, et dices ad spíritum : Hæc dicit Dóminus Deus : A quátuor ventis veni, spíritus, et insúffla super interféctos istos, et revivíscant. Et prophetávi sicut præcéperat mihi : et ingréssus est in ea spíritus, et vixérunt : steterúntque super pedes suos exércitus grandis nimis valde. Et dixit ad me : Fili hóminis, ossa hæc univérsa, domus Israël est : ipsi dicunt : Aruérunt ossa nostra, et périit spes nostra, et abscíssi sumus. Proptérea vaticináre, et dices ad eos : Hæc dicit Dóminus Deus : Ecce ego apériam túmulos vestros, et edúcam vos de sepúlcris vestris, pópulus meus : et indúcam vos in terram Israël. Et sciétis, quia ego Dóminus, cum aperúero sepúlcra vestra, et edúxero vos de túmulis vestris, pópule meus : et dédero spíritum meum in vobis, et vixéritis, et requiéscere vos fáciam super humum vestram : dicit Dóminus omnípotens.

Orémus.
Flectámus génua.
℟. Leváte.

flesh came upon them : and the skin was stretched out over them, but there was no spirit in them. And he said to me : Prophesy to the spirit, prophesy, O son of man, and say to the spirit : Thus saith the Lord God : Come, spirit, from the four winds, and blow upon these slain, and let them live again. And I prophesied as he had commanded me : and the spirit came into them, and they lived : and they stood up upon their feet, an exceeding great army. And he said to me : Son of man, all these bones are the house of Israel : They say : Our bones are dried up, and our hope is lost, and we are cut off. Therefore prophesy, and say to them : Thus saith the Lord God : Behold I will open your graves, and will bring you out of your sepulchres, O my people : and will bring you into the land of Israel. And you shall know that I am the Lord, when I shall have opened your sepulchres, and shall have brought you out of your graves, O my people : and shall have put my spirit in you, and you shall live, and I shall make you rest upon your own land : saith the Lord almighty.

Let us pray.
Let us kneel.
℟. Arise.

Oratio.

DEUS, qui nos ad celebrándum paschále sacraméntum, utriúsque Testaménti páginis instruis : da nobis intellígere misericórdiam tuam, ut ex perceptióne præséntium múnerum, firma sit exspectátio futurórum. Per Dóminum.

Prophetia octava.
Isa. 4.

APPREHENDENT septem mulíeres virum unum in die illa, dicéntes : Panem nostrum comedémus, et vestiméntis nostris operiémur : tantúmmodo invocétur nomen tuum super nos, aufer oppróbrium nostrum. In die illa erit germen Dómini in magnificéntia et glória, et fructus terræ sublímis, et exsultátio his qui salváti fúerint de Israël. Et erit : Omnis qui relíctus fúerit in Sion, et resíduus in Jerúsalem, sanctus vocábitur, omnis qui scriptus est in vita in Jerúsalem. Si ablúerit Dóminus sordes filiárum Sion, et sánguinem Jerúsalem láverit de médio ejus, in spíritu judícii, et spíritu ardóris. Et creábit Dóminus super omnem locum montis Sion, et ubi invocátus est, nubem per diem, et fumum et

Collect.

O GOD, who by the scriptures of both Testaments teachest us to celebrate the paschal sacrament : give us such a sense of thy mercy, that by receiving thy present graces, we may have a firm hope thy future blessings. Through our Lord.

The eighth Prophecy.
Isa. 4.

AND in that day seven women shall take hold of one man, saying : We will eat our own bread, and wear our own apparel : only let us be called by thy name, take away our reproach. In that day, the bud of the Lord shall be in magnificence and glory, and the fruit of the earth shall be high, and a great joy to them that shall have escaped of Israel. And it shall come to pass, that every one that shall be left in Sion, and that shall remain in Jerusalem shall be called holy, every one that is written in life in Jerusalem. If the Lord shall wash away the filth of the daughters of Sion, and shall wash away the blood of Jerusalem out of the midst thereof, by the spirit of judgement, and by the spirit of burning. And the Lord will create upon every place of Mount Sion, and where he is called upon, a cloud by day, and a

splendórem ignis flammántis in nocte : super omnem enim glóriam protéctio. Et tabernáculum erit in umbráculum diéi ab æstu, et in securitátem, et absconsiónem a túrbine, et a plúvia.

Tractus. Isa. 5.

VINEA facta est dilécto in cornu, in loco úberi. ℣. Et macériam circúmdedit, et circumfódit : et plantávit víneam Sorec, et ædificávit turrim in médio ejus. ℣. Et tórcular fodit in ea : vínea enim Dómini Sábaoth, domus Israël est.

Orémus.
Flectámus génua.
℞. Leváte.
Oratio.

DEUS, qui in ómnibus Ecclésiæ tuæ fíliis, sanctórum Prophetárum voce manifestásti, in omni loco dominatiónis tuæ, satórem te bonórum séminum, et electórum pálmitum esse cultórem : tríbue pópulis tuis, qui et vineárum apud te nómine censéntur et ségetum ; ut, spinárum et tribulórum squalóre resecáto, digna efficiántur fruge fœcúndi. Per Dóminum.

smoke and the brightness of a flaming fire in the night : for over all the glory shall be a protection. And there shall be a tabernacle for a shade in the day time from the heat, and for a security and covert from the whirlwind, and from rain.

Tratc. Isa. 5.

MY beloved had a vineyard on a very fruitful hill. ℣. And he enclosed it with a fence, and made a ditch round it, and planted it with the choicest vine, and built a tower in the midst thereof. ℣. And he made a wine-press in it : for the house of Israel is the vineyard of the Lord of hosts.

Let us pray.
Let us kneel.
℞. Arise.
Collect.

O GOD, who by the mouths of the holy prophets hast declared, that through the whole extent of thine empire thou sowest the good seed, and improvest the choicest branches that are found in all the children of thy Church : grant to thy people who are to thee as a vineyard and a harvest-field, that they may root out all thorns and briers, and bring forth good fruit in abundance. Through our Lord.

11*

Prophetia nona.
Exod. 12.

IN diébus illis : Dixit Dóminus ad Móysen et Aaron, &c., *ut Fer. 6 in Parasceve*, p. 244.

Orémus.

Flectámus génua.

℟. Leváte.

Oratio.

OMNIPOTENS sempitérne Deus, qui in ómnium óperum tuórum dispensatióne mirábilis es : intélligant redémpti tui, non fuísse excelléntius quod inítio factus est mundus, quam quod in fine sæculórum Pascha nostrum immolátus est Christus. Qui tecum vivit et regnat.

Prophetia decima.
Jonæ 3.

IN diébus illis : Factum est verbum Dómini ad Jonam prophétam secúndo, dicens : Surge et vade in Níniven civitátem magnam : et prædica in ea prædicatiónem, quam ego loquor ad te. Et surréxit Jonas, et ábiit in Níniven, juxta verbum Dómini. Et Nínive erat cívitas magna itínere diérum trium. Et cœpit Jonas introíre in civitátem itínere diéi uníus : et clamávit, et dixit : Adhuc quadragínta dies, et Nínive subvertétur. Et credidérunt viri Ninivítæ in Deum et prædicavé-

The ninth Prophecy.
Exod. 12.

IN those days : The Lord said to Moses and Aaron, &c., *as on Good Friday*, p. 244.

Let us pray.

Let us kneel.

℟. Arise.

Collect.

ALMIGHTY and eternal God, who art wonderful in the performance of all thy works : let thy redeemed servants understand that the creation of the world in the beginning was not more excellent than the immolation of Christ our Passover in the later ages. Who with thee liveth and reigneth.

The tenth Prophecy.
Jonas 3.

IN those days : The word of the Lord came to Jonas the second time, saying : Arise and go to Ninive, the great city : and preach in it the preaching that I bid thee. And Jonas arose and went to Ninive, according to the word of the Lord. Now, Ninive was a great city, of three days' journey. And Jonas began to enter into the city one day's journey : and he cried, and said : Yet forty days, and Ninive shall be destroyed. And the men of Ninive believed in God : and they proclaimed a fast and put on sackcloth, from the greatest to the least. And the word came to the

runt jejúnium, et vestíti sunt saccis a majóre usque ad minórem. Et pervénit verbum ad regem Nínive : et surréxit de sólio suo, et abjécit vestiméntum suum a se, et indútus est sacco, et sedit in cínere. Et clamávit, et dixit in Nínive ex ore regis et príncipum ejus, dicens : Hómines, et juménta, et boves, et pécora non gustent quidquam : nec pascántur et aquam non bibant. Et operiántur saccis hómines et juménta, et clament ad Dóminum in fortitúdine, et convertátur vir a via sua mala, et ab iniquitáte quæ est in mánibus eórum. Quis scit, si convertátur et ignóscat Deus : et revertátur a furóre iræ suæ et non períbimus? Et vidit Deus ópera eórum, quia convérsi sunt de via sua mala : et misértus est pópulo suo Dóminus Deus noster.

Orémus.
Flectámus génua.
℞. Leváte.
Oratio.

DEUS, qui diversitátem géntium in confessióne tui nóminis adunásti : da nobis et velle et posse quæ præcipis ; ut pópulo, ad æternitátem vocáto, una sit fides méntium, et píetas

king of Ninive : and he rose up out of his throne, and cast away his robe from him, and was clothed with sackcloth, and sat in ashes. And he caused it to be proclaimed and published in Ninive from the mouth of the king, and of his princes, saying : Let neither men nor beasts, oxen nor sheep, taste anything : let them not feed, nor drink water. And let men and beasts be covered with sackcloth, and cry to the Lord with all their strength, and let them turn every one from his evil way, and from the iniquity that is in their hands. Who can tell if God will turn and forgive, and will turn away from his fierce anger, and we shall not perish? And God saw their works, that they were turned from their evil way : and the Lord God had mercy on his people.

Let us pray.
Let us knell.
℞. Arise.
Collect.

O GOD who hast united the several nations of the Gentiles in the confession of thy name : give us both the will and the power to obey what thou commandest : that thy people, called to eternity, may have one

actiónum. Per Dómi-
num.

Prophetia undecima.
Deut. 31.

IN diébus illis : Scripsit
Móyses cánticum, et
dócuit fílios Israël. Præ-
cepítque Dóminus Jósue
fílio Nun, et ait : Con-
fortáre, et esto robústus :
tu enim introdúces fílios
Israël in terram, quam
pollícitus sum, et ego ero
tecum. Postquam ergo
scripsit Móyses verba le-
gis hujus in volúmine,
atque complévit : præcé-
pit Levítis, qui portá-
bant arcam fœderis Dó-
mini, dicens : Tóllite librum istum, et pónite
eum in látere arcæ fœde-
ris Dómini Dei vestri :
ut sit ibi contra te in
testimónium. Ego enim
scio contentiónem tuam,
et cervícem tuam duríss-
simam. Adhuc vivénte
me et ingrediénte vo-
bíscum, semper conten-
tióse egístis contra Dó-
minum : quanto ma-
gis cum mórtuus fúero?
Congregáte ad me omnes
majóres natu per tribus
vestras, atque doctóres,
et loquar audiéntibus
eis sermónes istos, et
invocábo contra eos cæ-
lum et terram. Novi
enim, quod post mortem
meam iníque agétis, et
declinábitis cito de via,
quam præcépi vobis : et

faith in their minds, and
show one devotion in their
actions. Through our Lord.

The eleventh Prophecy.
Deut. 31.

IN those days : Moses
wrote the canticle, and
taught it the children of
Israel. And the Lord com-
manded Josue the son of
Nun, and said : Take cou-
rage, and be valiant : for
thou shalt bring the children of Israel into the land
which I have promised, and
I will be with thee. Therefore, after Moses had wrote
the words of this law in a
volume, and finished it, he
commanded the Levites,
who carried the ark of the
covenant of the Lord, saying : Take this book and
put it in the side of the ark
of the covenant of the Lord
your God, that it may be
there for a testimony against
thee. For I know thy
obstinacy, and thy most
stiff neck. While I am yet
living, and going in with
you, you have always been
rebellious against the Lord.
How much more when I
shall be dead ? Gather unto
me all the ancients of your
tribes, and your doctors,
and I will speak these words
in their hearing, and I will
call heaven and earth to
witness against them. For I
know that after my death
you will do wickedly, and
will quickly turn aside from
the way that I have com-

occúrrent vobis mala in extrémo témpore, quando fecéritis malum in conspéctu Dómini, ut irritétis eum per ópera mánuum vestrárum. Locútus est ergo Móyses, audiénte univérso cœtu Israël, verba cárminis hujus, et ad finem usque complévit.

Tractus. Deut. 32. Atténde cælum, et loquar : et áudiat terra verba ex ore meo. ℣. Exspectétur sicut plúvia elóquium meum : et descéndant sicut ros verba mea. ℣. Sicut imber super gramen, et sicut nix super fœnum : quia nomen Dómini invocábo. ℣. Date magnitúdinem Deo nostro : Deus, vera ópera ejus, et omnes viæ ejus judícia. ℣. Deus fidélis, in quo non est iníquitas : justus et sanctus Dóminus.

Orémus.
Flectámus génua.
℟. Leváte.
Oratio.

DEUS, celsitúdo humílium, et fortitúdo rectórum, qui per sanctum Móysen puérum tuum ita erudíre pópulum tuum sacri cárminis tui decantatióne voluísti, ut illa legis iterátio fíeret étiam nostra diréctio : éxcita in omnem justificatárum géntium

manded you : and evils shall come upon you in the latter times, when you shall do evil in the sight of the Lord, to provoke him by the works of your hands. Moses therefore spoke, in the hearing of the whole assembly of Israel, the words of this canticle, and finished it even to the end.

Tract. Deut. 32. Attend, O heaven, and I will speak : and let the earth hear the words that come out of my mouth. ℣. Let my speech be expected like the rain : and let my words fall like the dew. ℣. Like the shower upon the grass, and like the snow upon the dry herb, because I will invoke the name of the Lord. ℣. Confess the greatness of our God : the works of God are perfect, and all his ways are justice. ℣. God is faithful, in whom there is no iniquity : the Lord is just and holy.

Let us pray.
Let us kneel.
℟. Arise.
Collect.

O GOD, the exaltation of the humble, and the fortitude of the righteous, who, by thy holy servant Moses, wert pleased so to instruct thy people by the singing of thy sacred canticle, that the repetition of the law should be also our guidance : show thy power to all the multitude of Gen-

plenitúdinem poténtiam tuam, et da lætítiam, mitigándo terrórem : ut ómnium peccátis tua remissióne delétis, quod denuntiátum est in ultiónem, tránseat in salútem. Per Dóminum.

Prophetia duodecima.
Dan. 3.

IN diébus illis : Nabuchodónosor rex fecit státuam áuream, altitúdine cubitórum sexagínta, latitúdine cubitórum sex, et státuit eam in campo Dura province Babylónis. Itaque Nabuchodónosor rex misit ad congregándos sátrapas, magistrátus, et júdices, duces, et tyránnos, et præféctos, omnésque príncipes regiónum, ut convenírent ad dedicatiónem státuæ, quam eréxerat Nabuchodónosor rex. Tunc congregáti sunt sátrapæ, magistrátus, et júdices, duces, et tyránni, et optimátes, qui erant in potestátibus constitúti, et univérsi príncipes regiónum, ut convenírent ad dedicatiónem státuæ, quam eréxerat Nabuchodónosor rex. Stabant autem in conspéctu státuæ, quam posúerat Nabuchodónosor rex : et præco clamábat valénter : Vobis dícitur pópulis, tríbubus, et linguis : In hora, qua audiéritis

tiles justified by thee, and by mitigating thy terror, grant them joy : that, all their sins being pardoned by thee, the threatened vengeance may give place to salvation. Through our Lord.

The twelfth Prophecy.
Dan. 3.

IN those days : King Nabuchodonosor made a statue of gold of sixty cubits high, and six cubits broad, and he set it up in the plain of Dura of the province of Babylon. Then Nabuchodonosor the king sent to call together the nobles, the magistrates, and the judges, the captains, the rulers, and governors, and all the chief men of the provinces, to come to the dedication of the statue which King Nabuchodonosor had set up. Then the nobles, the magistrates, and the judges, the captains, and rulers, and the great men that were placed in authority, and all the princes of the provinces were gathered together to come to the dedication of the statue, which King Nabuchodonosor had set up. And they stood before the statue which King Nabuchodonosor had set up. Then a herald cried with a strong voice : To you it is commanded, O nations, tribes, and languages, that in the hour that you shall hear the sound of the trumpet,

sónitum tubæ, et fístulæ, et cítharæ, sambúcæ, et psaltérii, et symphóniæ, et univérsi géneris musicórum, cadéntes adoráte státuam áuream, quam constítuit Nabuchodónosor rex. Si quis autem non prostrátus adoráverit, eádem hora mittétur in fornácem ignis ardéntis. Post hæc ígitur statim ut audiérunt omnes pópuli sónitum tubæ, fístulæ, et cítharæ, sambúcæ, et psaltérii, et symphóniæ, et omnis géneris musicórum, cadéntes omnes pópuli, tribus, et linguæ, adoravérunt státuam áuream, quam constitúerat Nabuchodónosor rex. Statímque in ipso témpore accedéntes viri Chaldǽi accusavérunt Judǽos : dixerúntque Nabuchodónosor regi : Rex in ætérnum vive : tu, rex, posuísti decrétum, ut omnis homo, qui audíerit sónitum tubæ, fístulæ, et cítharæ, sambúcæ, et psaltérii, et symphóniæ, et univérsi géneris musicórum, prostérnat se, et adóret státuam áuream : si quis autem non prócidens adoráverit, mittátur in fornácem ignis ardéntis. Sunt ergo viri Judǽi, quos constituísti super ópera regiónis Babylónis, Sidrach, Misach, et Abdénago : viri isti con-

and of the flute, and of the harp, of the sackbut, and of the psaltery, and of the symphony, and of all kinds of music, ye shall fall down and adore the golden statue which King Nabuchodonosor hath set up. But if any man shall not fall down and adore, he shall the same hour be cast into a furnace of burning fire. Upon this, therefore, at the time when all the people heard the sound of the trumpet, the flute, and the harp, of the sackbut, and psaltery, of the symphony, and of all kinds of music, all the nations, tribes, and languages fell down and adored the golden statue, which King Nabuchodonosor had set up. And presently at that very time some Chaldeans came and accused the Jews, and said to King Nabuchodonosor : O king, live for ever : thou, O king, hast made a decree, that every man that shall hear the sound of the trumpet, the flute, and the harp, of the sackbut, and the psaltery, of the symphony, and of all kinds of music, shall prostrate himself, and adore the golden statue : and that if any man shall not fall down and adore, he should be cast into a furnace of burning fire. Now there are certain Jews, whom thou hast set over the works of the province of Babylon,

tempsérunt, rex, decrétum tuum : deos tuos non colunt, et státuam áuream, quam erexisti non adórant. Tunc Nabuchodónosor, in furóre et in ira præcépit ut adducceréntur Sidrach, Misach, et Abdénago : qui conféstim addúcti sunt in conspéctu regis. Pronuntiánsque Nabuchodónosor rex, ait eis : Veréne, Sidrach, Misach, et Abdénago, deos meos non cólitis, et státuam áuream, quam constítui, non adorátis? Nunc ergo, si estis paráti, quacúmque hora audiéritis sónitum tubæ, fístulæ, cítharæ, sambúcæ, et psaltérii, et symphóniæ, omnísque géneris musicórum, prostérnite vos, et adoráte státuam quam feci : quod si non adoravéritis, eádem hora mittémini in fornácem ignis ardéntis : et quis est Deus qui erípiet vos de manu mea? Respondéntes Sidrach, Misach, et Abdénago, dixérunt regi Nabuchodónosor : Non opórtet nos de hac re respondére tibi. Ecce enim Deus noster, quem cólimus, potest erípere nos de camíno ignis ardéntis, et de mánibus tuis, o rex, liberáre. Quod si nolúerit, notum sit tibi, rex, quia deos tuos non cólimus, et

Sidrach, Misach, and Abdenago : these men, O king, have slighted thy decree : they worship not thy gods, nor do they adore the golden statue which thou hast set up. Then Nabuchodonosor, in fury and in wrath, commanded that Sidrach, Misach, and Abdenago should be brought : who immediately were brought before the king. And Nabuchodonosor the king spoke to them, and said : Is it true, O Sidrach, Misach, and Abdenago, that you do not worship my gods, nor adore the golden statue that I have set up? Now therefore, if you be ready, at what hour soever you shall hear the sound of the trumpet, flute, harp, sackbut, and psaltery, and symphony, and of all kinds of music, prostrate yourselves, and adore the statue which I have made : but if you do not adore, you shall be cast the same hour into the furnace of burning fire : and who is the cod that shall deliver you out of my hand? Sidrach, Misach and Abdenago answered, and said to the King Nabuchodonosor : We have no occasion to answer thee concerning this matter. For behold our God. whom we worship, is able to save us from the furnace of burning fire, and to deliver us out of thy hands, O king. But if he will not, be it known to thee,

státuam áuream, quam erexísti, non adorámus. Tunc Nabuchodónosor replétus est furóre : et aspéctus faciéi illíus immutátus est super Sidrach, Misach, et Abdénago, et præcépit ut succenderétur fornax séptuplum quam succéndi consuéverat. Et viris fortíssimis de exércitu suo jussit, ut ligátis pédibus Sidrach, Misach, et Abdénago, mittérent eos in fornácem ignis ardéntis. Et conféstim viri illi vincti, cum braccis suis, et tiáris, et calceaméntis, et véstibus, missi sunt in médium fornácis ignis ardéntis. Nam jússio regis urgébat : fornax autem succénsa erat nimis. Porro viros illos qui míserant Sidrach, Misach, et Abdénago, interfécit flamma ignis. Viri autem hi tres, id est, Sidrach, Misach, et Abdénago, cecidérunt in médio camíno ignis ardéntis colligáti. Et ambulábant in médio flammæ laudántes Deum, et benedicéntes Dómino.

O king, that we will not worship thy gods, nor adore the golden statue which thou hast set up. Then was Nabuchodonosor filled with fury, and the countenance of his face was changed against Sidrach, Misach, and Abdenago, and he commanded that the furnace should be heated seven times more than it had been accustomed to be heated. And he commanded the strongest men that were in his army to bind the feet of Sidrach, Misach, and Abdenago, and to cast them into the furnace of burning fire. And immediately these men were bound and were cast into the furnace of burning fire, with their coats, and their caps, and their shoes, and their garments. For the king's commandment was urgent, and the furnace was heated exceedingly. And the flame of the fire slew those men that had cast in Sidrach, Misach, and Abdenago. But these three men, that is, Sidrach, Misach and Abdenago, fell down bound in the midst of the furnace of burning fire. And they walked in the midst of the flame, praising God, and blessing the Lord.

Here Flectámus génua *is not said, but only :*

Orémus.
Oratio.

OMNIPOTENS sempitérne Deus, spes única mundi, qui Pro-

Let us pray.
Collect.

ALMIGHTY and eternal God, the only hope of the world, who by the voice

phetárum tuórum præcónio præséntium témporum declarásti mystéria : auge pópuli tui vota placátus ; quia in nullo fidélium, nisi ex tua inspiratióne, provéniunt quarúmlibet increménta virtútum. Per Dóminum.

of thy prophets, hast manifested the mysteries of this present time ; graciously increase the desires of thy people, since none of the faithful can advance in any virtue without thy inspiration. Through our Lord.

3. The Blessing of the Font.

Although reduced to its simplest elements, this ceremony is one of the most impressive and magnificent rites of the liturgy.

After the Lessons the procession leaves the sanctuary and proceeds to where the font is at the lower end of the church. In olden times the baptistery was a separate building isolated from the church, and many of these may still be seen, with the large basins into which the catechumen was plunged bodily in Baptism by immersion.

The ceremony of blessing the water destined for the Sacrament consists of a prayer and a preface or anaphora in the same lyrical strain as the *Exsultet*, but more closely allied to the ancient anaphora or Eucharistic prayer. It reproduces this ancient form of prayer even more faithfully than does the Roman Canon of the Mass. It is preceded by the dialogue *Sursum corda*, etc., and the usual introduction *Vere dignum* but instead of being interrupted by the singing of the Sanctus which ordinarily causes a temporary suspension after which the prayer of consecration is taken up, in this case the prayer of the anaphora and the *Action* form a continuous whole. The *Exsultet* sung by the deacon was a panegyric of fire and of the marvels of Easter Eve, the praise of water is the theme of the lyrical poem now sung by the priest, water which covered the face of the earth in the beginning, which flowed out of the Garden of Eden in four great rivers, which washed the earth clean of the crimes of mankind in the flood. This water upon which Christ walked, which he changed into wine, and which flowed down from his sacred side, is to become by a yet greater miracle the water of baptism, which washes away all sin. Hence the exorcisms, the frequent

signs of the Cross and the numerous invocations ; the offi-
ciating priest also breathes upon the water and dips into it
the paschal candle, blessing it by formulas resembling the
words of consecration or epiclesis.   The anaphora ends with
a doxology.

The priest sprinkles the people with the blessed water,
afterwards pouring into it oil of catechumens and chrism
and proceeds to administer the Sacrament should occasion
require, as was the custom in the primitive Church.

The ceremony over, the procession returns singing the great
Litany to the Sanctuary to proceed with the Mass.   It will
be seen that this rite though distinct in itself is yet connected
with the blessing of the paschal candle, with that of the holy
oils on Maundy Thursday and with the whole pascal ritual.

*If the church has no baptismal font, the following benediction of
the font is omitted, and the Litanies are said immediately after the
Prophecies, in the manner hereafter directed.   But where there is a
font, the priest, his ministers, and the clergy go in procession to the
font, singing :*

Tractus. Ps. 41. Sicut
cervus desíderat ad fon-
tes aquárum, ita desíde-
rat ánima mea ad te,
Deus.   ℣. Sitívit ánima
mea ad Deum vivum :
quando véniam et appa-
rébo ante fáciem Dei
mei?   ℣. Fuérunt mihi
lácrimæ meæ panes die
ac nocte, dum dícitur
mihi per síngulos dies :
Ubi est Deus tuus?

Tract. Ps. 41. As the hart
panteth after the fountains
of waters, so my soul panteth after thee, O God. ℣.
My soul hath thirsted for
the living God : when shall
I come and appear before
the face of my God?   ℣. My
tears have been my bread
day and night, whilst they
say to me every day : Where
is thy God?

Before the blessing of the font, the priest says the following prayer

℣. Dóminus vobíscum.
℟. Et cum spíritu tuo.
Orémus.
Oratio.

℣. The Lord be with you.
℟. And with thy spirit.
Let us pray.
Collect.

OMNIPOTENS sem-
pitérne Deus, réspi-
ce propítius ad devotió-
nem pópuli renascéntis,
qui, sicut cervus, aquá-
rum tuárum éxpetit fon-
tem : et concéde propí-

ALMIGHTY and eternal
God, look mercifully on
the devotion of the people
desiring a new birth, who,
like the hart, pant after
the fountain of thy waters :
so mercifully grant that the

tius ; ut fídei ipsíus sitis, baptísmatis mystério, ánimam corpúsque sanctíficet. Per Dóminum.

℟. Amen.

Then the priest begins the blessing of the font, saying :

℣. Dóminus vobíscum.

℟. Et cum spíritu tuo.

Orémus.

Oratio.

OMNIPOTENS sempitérne Deus, adésto magnæ pietátis mystériis, adésto sacraméntis : et ad recreándos novos pópulos, quos tibi fons baptísmatis párturit, spíritum adoptiónis emitte; ut quod nostræ humilitátis geréndum est ministério, virtútis tuæ impleátur efféctu. Per Dóminum nostrum Jesum Christum Fílium tuum, qui tecum vivit et regnat in unitáte ejúsdem Spíritus Sancti Deus. ℣. Per ómnia sǽcula sæculórum.

℟. Amen.

℣. Dóminus vobíscum

℟. Et cum spíritu tuo.

℣. Sursum corda.

℟. Habémus ad Dóminum.

℣. Grátias agámus Dómino Deo nostro.

℟. Dignum et justum est.

VERE dignum et justum est, æquum et salutáre, nos tibi semper et ubíque grátias ágere, Dómine sancte, Pater omnípotens, ætérne

thirst of their faith may, by the sacrament of baptism, sanctify their souls and bodies. Through our Lord.

℟. Amen.

℣. The Lord be with you.

℟. And with thy spirit.

Let us pray.

Collect.

ALMIGHTY and eternal God, be present at these mysteries, be present at these sacraments of thy great goodness : and send forth the spirit of adoption to regenerate the new people, whom the font of baptism brings forth : that what is to be done by our humble ministry may be accomplished by the effect of thy power. Through our Lord Jesus Christ thy Son, who with thee and the same Holy Spirit liveth and reigneth one God. ℣. For ever and ever.

℟. Amen.

℣. The Lord be with you.

℟. And with thy spirit.

℣. Lift up your hearts.

℟. We have lifted them up to he Lord.

℣. Let us give thanks to the Lord our God.

℟. It is meet and just.

IT is truly meet and just, right and available to salvation, to give thee thanks always and in all places, O holy Lord, almighty Father, eternal God·

Deus. Qui invisíbili poténtia, sacramentórum tuórum mirabíliter operáris efféctum : et licet nos tantis mystériis exsequéndis simus indígni : tu tamen grátiæ tuæ dona non déserens, étiam ad nostras preces, aures tuæ pietátis inclínas. Deus, cujus Spíritus super aquas, inter ipsa mundi primórdia ferebátur : ut jam tunc virtútem sanctificatiónis aquárum natúra concíperet. Deus, qui nocéntis mundi crímina per aquas ábluens, regeneratiónis spéciem in ipsa dilúvii effusióne signásti : ut uníus ejusdémque eleménti mystério, et finis esset vítiis, et orígo virtútibus. Réspice, Dómine, in fáciem Ecclésiæ tuæ, et multíplica in ea regeneratiónes tuas, qui grátiæ tuæ affluéntis ímpetu lætíficas civitátem tuam : fontémque baptísmatis áperis toto orbe terrárum, géntibus innovándis : ut tuæ majestátis império, sumat Unigéniti tui grátiam de Spíritu Sancto.

Who by thy invisible power dost wonderfully produce the effect of thy sacraments: and though we are unworthy to administer so great mysteries: yet, as thou dost not forsake the gifts of thy grace, so thou inclinest the ears of thy goodness, even to our prayers. O God, whose Spirit in the very beginning of the world moved over the waters, that even then the nature of water might receive the virtue of sanctification. O God, who by water didst wash away the crimes of the guilty world, and by the overflowing of the deluge didst give a figure of regeneration, that one and the same element might in a mystery be the end of vice and the origin of virtue. Look, O Lord, on the face of thy Church, and multiply in her thy regenerations, who by the streams of thy abundant grace fillest thy city with joy, and openest the fonts of baptism all over the world for the renovation of the Gentiles : that by the command of thy Majesty, she may receive the grace of thy only Son from the Holy Ghost.

Here the priest divides the water in the form of a cross.

Qui hanc aquam regenerándis homínibus præparátam, arcána sui Núminis admixtióne fœcúndet, ut sanctificatióne concépta, ab immaculá-

Who by a secret mixture of his divine virtue may render this water fruitful for the regeneration of men, to the end that those who have been sanctified in the im-

to divíni fontis útero, in novam renáta creatúram, progénies cæléstis emérgat : et quos aut sexus in córpore, aut ætas discérnit in témpore, omnes, in unam páriat grátia mater infántiam. Procul ergo hinc, jubénte te, Dómine, omnis spíritus immúndus abscédat : procul tota nequítia diabólicæ fraudis absístat. Nihil hic loci hábeat contráriæ virtútis admíxtio : non insidiándo circúmvolet : non laténdo subrépat : non inficiéndo corrúmpat.

maculate womb of this divine font, being born again a new creature may come forth a heavenly offspring : and that all that are distinguished either by sex in body, or by age in time, may be brought forth to the same infancy by grace, their spiritual mother. Therefore may all unclean spirits, by thy command, O Lord, depart far from hence: may the whole malice of diabolical deceit be entirely banished : may no power of the enemy prevail here : may he not fly about to lay his snares : may he not creep in by his secret artifice : may he not corrupt with his infection.

Here he touches the water with his hand.

Sit hæc sancta et ínnocens creatúra líbera ab omni impugnatóris incúrsu, et totíus nequítiæ purgáta discéssu. Sit fons vivus, aqua regénerans, unda puríficans : ut omnes hoc lavácro salutífero diluéndi, operánte in eis Spiritu Sancto, perféctæ purgatiónis indulgéntiam consequátur.

May this holy and innocent creature be free from all the assaults of the enemy, and purified by the destruction of all his malice. May it be a living fountain, a regenerating water, a purifying stream : that all those that are to be washed in this saving bath may obtain, by the operation of the Holy Ghost, the grace of a perfect purification.

Here he makes the sign of the cross thrice over the font, saying :

Unde benedíco te, creatúra aquæ, per Deum ✠ vivum, per Deum ✠ verum, per Deum ✠ sanctum : per Deum qui te in princípio, verbo separávit ab

Therefore I bless thee, O creature of water, by the living God ✠, by the true God ✠, by the holy God ✠, by that God who in the beginning separated thee by his word from the dry land,

árida ; cujus spíritus super te ferebátur.

whose spirit moved over thee.

He divides the water with his hands, and throws some of it towards the four quarters of the world, saying :

Qui te de paradísi fonte manáre fecit, et in quátuor flumínibus totam terram rigáre præcépit. Qui te in desérto amáram, suavitáte índita, fecit esse potábilem, et sitiénti pópulo de petra prodúxit. Bene✠dico te et per Jesum Christum Fílium ejus únicum, Dóminum nostrum : qui te in Cana Galilææ, signo admirábili, sua poténtia convértit in vinum. Qui pédibus super te ambulávit : et a Joánne in Jordáne in te baptizátus est. Qui te una cum sánguine de látere suo prodúxit : et discípulis suis jussit, ut credéntes baptizaréntur in te, dicens : Ite, docéte omnes gentes, baptizántes eos in nómine Patris, et Fílii, et Spíritus Sancti.

Hæc nobis præcépta servántibus, tu, Deus omnípotens, clemens adésto : tu benígnus aspíra.

Who made thee flow from the fountain of paradise and commanded thee to water the whole earth with thy four rivers. Who, changing thy bitterness in the desert into sweetness, made thee fit to drink, and produced thee out of a rock to quench the thirst of the people. I bless ✠ thee also by our Lord Jesus Christ his only Son : who in Cana of Galilee changed thee into wine, by a wonderful miracle of his power. Who walked upon thee dry foot, and was baptized in thee by John in the Jordan. Who made thee flow out of his side together with his blood, and commanded his disciples that such as believed should be baptized in thee, saying : Go teach all nations, baptizing them in the name of the Father, and of the Son, and of the Holy Ghost.

Do thou, Almighty God, mercifully assist us that observe this command : do thou graciously inspire us.

He breathes thrice upon the water in the form of a cross, saying :

Tu has símplices aquas tuo ore benedícito : ut præter naturálem emundatiónem, quam lavándis possunt adhibére corpóribus, sint etiam purificándis méntibus efficáces.

Do thou with thy mouth bless these clear waters : that besides their natural virtue of cleansing the body, they may also be effectual for the purifying of the soul.

Here the priest sinks the Paschal Candle in the water, three several times, singing each time on a higher tone :

Descéndat in hac ple-nitúdinem fontis, virtus Spíritus Sancti.

May the virtue of the Holy Ghost descend into all the water of this font.

Then breathing thrice upon the water, he goes on :

Totámque hujus aquæ substántiam, regenerándi fœcúndet efféctu.

And make the whole substance of this water fruitful, and capable of regenerating.

Here the Paschal Candle is taken out of the water, and he goes on :

Hic ómnium peccatórum máculæ deleántur : hic natúra, ad imáginem tuam cóndita, et ad honórem sui reformáta princípii, cunctis vetustátis squalóribus emundétur : ut omnis homo sacraméntum hoc regeneratiónis ingréssus, in veræ innocéntiæ novam infántiam renascátur. Per Dóminum nostrum Jesum Christum Fílium tuum : qui ventúrus est judicáre vivos et mórtuos, et sǽculum per ignem.
℞. Amen.

Here may the stains of all sins be washed out : here may human nature, created to thy image, and reformed to the honour of its author, be cleansed from all the filth of the old man : that all who receive this sacrament of regeneration, may be born again new children of true innocence. Through our Lord Jesus Christ thy Son : who shall come to judge the living and the dead, and he world by fire.
℞. Amen.

Then the people are sprinkled with the blessed water, and one of the ministers of the church reserves some of it in a vessel, to sprinkle in houses and other places. After this, the priest pours some oil of catechumens into the water, in the form of a cross, saying :

Sanctificétur, et fœcundétur fons iste Oléo salútis renascéntibus ex eo, in vitam ætérnam.
℞. Amen.

May this font be sanctified and made fruitful by the oil of salvation, for such as are regenerated therein unto life everlasting.
℞. Amen.

Then he pours chrism into it, in the same manner, saying :

Infúsio Chrísmatis Dómini nostri Jesu Christi, et Spíritus Sancti Pará-

May this infusion of the chrism of our Lord Jesus Christ, and of the Holy

cliti, fiat in nómine sanctæ Trinitátis.

℟. Amen.

Ghost the Comforter, be made in the name of the Holy Trinity.

℟. Amen.

Lastly he pours the oil and chrism both together unto the water, in the form of a cross saying :

Commíxtio Chrísmatis sanctificatiónis, et Olei unctiónis, et aquæ baptísmatis, páriter fiat in nómine Pa✠tris, et Fí✠lii, et Spíritus ✠ Sancti.

℟. Amen.

May this mixture of the chrism of sanctification, and of the oil of unction, and of the water of baptism, be made in the name of the Father ✠, and of the Son ✠, and of the Holy Ghost ✠.

℟. Amen.

Then he mingles the oil with the water, and with his hand spreads it all over the font : and if there are any to be baptized, he baptizes them with the usual manner. After the blessing of the font, he returns with his ministers to the altar steps, where they lie prostrate, and all the rest kneel, while the Litanies are sung by two cantors in the middle of the choir, both sides repeating the same.

Kyrie, eléison.

Christe, eléison.

Kyrie, eléison.

Christe, audi nos.

Christe, exáudi nos.

Pater de cælis Deus, *miserére nobis.*

Fili Redémptor mundi Deus, *miserére nobis.*

Spíritus Sancte Deus, *miserére nobis.*

Sancta Trínitas, unus Deus, *miserére nobis.*

Sancta María, *ora pro nobis.*

Sancta Dei Génitrix, *ora pro nobis.*

Sancta Virgo vírginum, *ora pro nobis.*

Sancte Míchael, *ora, &c.*

Sancte Gábriel, *ora, &c.*

Sancte Ráphael, *ora, &c.*

Omnes sancti Ángeli et Archángeli, *oráte pro nobis.*

Lord, have mercy upon us.

Christ, have mercy upon us.

Lord, have mercy upon us.

Christ, hear us.

Christ, graciously hear us.

God the Father of heaven, *have mercy upon us.*

God the Son, Redeemer of the world, *have mercy upon us.*

God the Holy Ghost, *have mercy upon us.*

Holy Trinity, one God, *have mercy upon us.*

Holy Mary, *pray for us.*

Holy Mother of God, *pray for us.*

Holy virgin of virgins, *pray for us.*

St Michael, *pray for us.*

St. Gabriel, *pray for us.*

St. Raphael, *pray for us.*

All ye holy angels and archangels, *pray for us.*

Omnes sancti beatórum Spirítuum órdines, *oráte pro nobis.* — All ye holy orders of blessed spirits, *pray for us.*

S. Joánnes Baptísta, *ora pro nobis.* — St. John the Baptist, *pray for us.*

S. Joseph, *ora pro nobis.* — St. Joseph, *pray for us.*

Omnes sancti Patriárchæ et Prophétæ, *oráte pro nobis.* — All ye holy patriarchs and prophets, *pray for us.*

S. Petre, *ora pro nobis.* — St. Peter, *pray for us.*

S. Paule, *ora pro nobis.* — St. Paul, *pray for us.*

S. Andréa, *ora pro nobis.* — St. Andrew, *pray for us.*

S. Joánnes, *ora pro nobis.* — St. John, *pray for us.*

Omnes sancti Apóstoli et Evangelístæ, *oráte pro nobis.* — All ye holy Apostles and Evangelists, *pray for us.*

Omnes sancti Discípuli Dómini, *oráte pro nobis.* — All ye holy disciples of the Lord, *pray for us.*

S. Stéphane, *ora pro nobis.* — St. Stephen, *pray for us.*

S. Laurénti, *ora pro nobis.* — St. Laurence, *pray for us.*

S. Vincénti, *ora pro nobis.* — St. Vincent, *pray for us.*

Omnes sancti Mártyres, *oráte pro nobis.* — All ye holy Martyrs, *pray for us.*

S. Silvéster, *ora pro nobis.* — St. Sylvester, *pray for us.*

S. Gregóri, *ora pro nobis.* — St. Gregory, *pray for us.*

S. Augustíne, *ora pro nobis.* — St. Augustine, *pray for us.*

Omnes sancti Pontífices et Confessóres, *oráte pro nobis.* — All ye holy Bishops and Confessors, *pray for us.*

Omnes sancti Doctóres, *oráte pro nobis.* — All ye holy Doctors, *pray for us.*

S. Antóni, *ora pro nobis.* — St. Anthony, *pray for us.*

S. Benedícte, *ora pro nobis.* — St. Benedict, *pray for us.*

S. Domínice, *ora pro nobis.* — St. Dominic, *pray for us.*

S. Francísce, *ora pro nobis.* — St. Francis, *pray for us.*

Omnes sancti Sacerdótes et Levítæ, *oráte, &c.*

All ye holy **Priests** and Levites, *pray for us.*

Omnes sancti Mónachi et Eremítæ, *oráte, &c.*

All ye holy **Monks** and Hermits, *pray for us.*

Sancta María Magdaléna, *ora pro nobis.*

St. Mary Magdalen, *pray for us.*

S. Agnes, *ora pro nobis.*

St. Agnes, *pray for us.*

S. Cæcília, *ora pro nobis.*

St. Cecily, *pray for us.*

S. Agatha, *ora pro nobis.*

St. Agatha, *pray for us.*

S. Anastásia, *ora pro nobis.*

St. Anastasia *pray for us.*

Omnes sanctæ Vírgines et Víduæ, *oráte pro nobis.*

All ye holy Virgins and Widows *pray for us.*

Omnes Sancti et Sanctæ Dei, *intercédite pro nobis.*

All ye Saints of God, both men and women, *make intercession for us.*

Propítius esto, *parce nobis, Dómine.*

Be merciful unto us, *spare us, O Lord.*

Propítius esto, *exáudi nos, Dómine.*

Be merciful unto us, *hear us, O Lord.*

Ab omni malo, *líbera nos, Dómine.*

From all evil, *O Lord, deliver us.*

Ab omni peccáto, *líbera nos, Dómine.*

From all sin, *O Lord, deliver us.*

A morte perpétua, *líbera nos, Dómine.*

From everlasting death, *O Lord, deliver us.*

Per mystérium sanctæ incarnatiónis tuæ, *líbera nos, Dómine.*

Through the mystery of thy holy incarnation, *O Lord, deliver us.*

Per advéntum tuum, *líbera nos, Dómine.*

Through thy coming, *O Lord, deliver us.*

Per nativitátem tuam, *líbera nos, Dómine.*

Through thy nativity, *O Lord, deliver us.*

Per baptísmum et sanctum jejúnium tuum, *líbera nos, Dómine.*

Through thy baptism and holy fasting, *O Lord, deliver us.*

Per crucem et passiónem tuam, *líbera nos, Dómine.*

Through thy cross and passion, *O Lord, deliver us.*

Per mortem et sepultúram tuam, *líbera nos, Dómine.*

Through thy death and burial, *O Lord, deliver us.*

Per sanctam resurrectiónem tuam, *líbera nos, Dómine.*

Through thy holy resurrection, *O Lord, deliver us.*

Per admirábilem ascen-
siónem tuam, *libera
nos, Dómine.*

Through thy admirable As-
cension, *O Lord, deliver
us.*

Per advéntum Spíritus
Sancti Parácliti, *libera
nos, Dómine.*

Through the coming of the
Holy Ghost the comfor-
ter, *O Lord, deliver us.*

In die judícii, *libera nos,
Dómine.*

In the day of judgement, *O
Lord, deliver us.*

Peccatóres, *te rogámus,
audi nos.*

We sinners, *do beseech thee
to hear us.*

*Here the priest and his ministers rise and go into the sacristy, to
vest themselves in white for the celebration of the Mass ; and whilst
the candles are being lighted upon the altar, the Litanies are continued by the choir.*

Ut nobis parcas, *te rogámus, audi nos.*

That thou spare us, *we beseech thee hear us.*

Ut Ecclésiam tuam san-
ctam régere et conser-
váre dignéris, *te roga-
mus audi nos.*

That thou vouchsafe to
govern and preserve thy
holy Church, *we beseech
thee hear us.*

Ut Domnum Apostóli-
cum, et omnes eccle-
siásticos órdines in san-
cta religióne conser-
váre dignéris, *te rogá-
mus, audi nos.*

That thou vouchsafe to
preserve our Apostolic
Prelate, and all the orders
of the Church in thy holy
religion, *we beseech thee
hear us.*

Ut inimícos sanctæ Ec-
clésiæ humiliáre digné-
ris, *te rogámus, audi
nos.*

That thou vouchsafe to
humble the enemies of
thy holy Church, *we be-
seech thee hear us.*

Ut régibus et princípibus
christiánis pacem et
veram concórdiam do-
náre dignéris, *te rogá-
mus, audi nos.*

That thou vouchsafe to
grant peace and true con-
cord to Christian kings
and princes, *we beseech
thee hear us.*

Ut nosmetípsos in tuo
sancto servítio confor-
táre et conserváre di-
gnéris, *te rogámus, au-
di nos.*

That thou vouchsafe to
strengthen and keep us in
thy holy service, *we be-
seech thee hear us.*

Ut ómnibus benefactó-
ribus nostris sempi-
térna bona retríbuas,
te rogámus, audi nos.

That thou render eternal
good things to all our be-
nefactors, *we beseech thee
hear us.*

Ut fructus terræ dare et conserváre dignéris, *te rogámus, audi nos.*	That thou vouchsafe to give and preserve the fruits of the earth, *we beseech thee hear us.*
Ut ómnibus fidélibus defúnctis réquiem ætérnam donáre dignéris, *te rogámus, audi nos.*	That thou vouchsafe to grant eternal rest to all the faithful departed, *we beseech thee hear us.*
Ut nos exaudíre dignéris, *te rogámus, audi nos.*	That thou vouchsafe graciously to hear us, *we beseech thee hear us.*
Agnus Dei, qui tollis peccáta mundi, *parce nobis, Dómine.*	Lamb of God, who takest away the sins of the world, *spare us, O Lord.*
Agnus Dei, qui tollis peccáta mundi, *exáudi nos, Dómine.*	Lamb of God, who takest away the sins of the world, *hear us, O Lord.*
Agnus Dei, qui tollis peccáta mundi, *miserére nobis.*	Lamb of God, who takest away the sins of the world, *have mercy upon us.*
Christe, audi nos.	Christ, hear us.
Christe, exáudi nos.	Christ, graciously hear us.

4. The Mass.

Although strictly speaking the Litany belongs to the procession after the blessing of the font, yet in churches where there is no font the Litany is chanted all the same, the final invocations being sung as the *Kyrie* of the Mass in order to simplify the office for the sake of the faithful. It is obvious however that in the ancient liturgy there was neither Introit nor Kyrie, the Litany serving as introduction to the Mass.

Once more we would point out that the words *hanc sacratissimam noctem* and other similar passages remind us of the fact that this Mass, and indeed the whole of the paschal office was celebrated at night. Several allusions are made to the Sacrament of Baptism just received by the catechumens. There is no Offertory, but the *Communicantes* and *Hanc igitur* are proper, the Collect and Epistle commemorate in an especial manner both the Resurrection and the newly baptised.

It would be superfluous to draw attention to the singular beauty of to-day's Mass, which ends in a striking and unusual way with an abbreviated form of Vespers, the kiss

of peace, *Agnus Dei* and Postcommunion being omitted. After the priest has communicated, the choir sing Vespers which consist of an Alleluia antiphon, a psalm, the Magnificat and a collect, after which comes the dismissal (*Ite missa est*) and the blessing.

This arrangement of the office is not ancient ; originally the Mass was said during the night and ended ad dawn, which was not a fitting time for the office of Vespers. The anticipation of the night office on the Saturday morning has entailed many changes. Vespers could not be omitted, and yet according to the Lenten observance they had to be said before the midday meal. The only solution of the difficulty was to have them immediately after the Mass in the shortest possible form, on account of the great length of the morning office.

The anticipation of the office has also necessitated the forming part of a Mass for Easter Sunday. Although not composition of the liturgy of Holy Week, this Mass will be found after Vespers of Holy Saturday. It differs only very slightly from the Mass of the preceding day. The station is at St. Mary Major's, whereas on Holy Saturday it was at St. John Lateran. The Preface, *Communicantes* and *Hanc igitur* are the same for both days and the Epistle for the Sunday is again taken from St. Paul. A fine Sequence which has escaped the general shipwreck of similar liturgical pieces follows the Gradual and Alleluia ; the Gospel gives the account of the Resurrection according to St. Mark. The Postcommunion is the same as that of Holy Saturday.

Whilst the choir sings the Kyrie *and* Christe eléison, *the priest goes to the altar, and begins Mass in the accustomed manner, reciting the Psalm* Júdica &c. *Having kissed the altar, he intones the* Glória *in excélsis* and the bells, *which have remained silent from this part of the Mass on Maundy Thursday, are now rung again. After which he turns towards the people, and says :*

℣. Dóminus vobíscum.
℞. Et cum spíritu tuo.
Orémus.
Oratio.

℣. The Lord be with you.
℞. And with thy spirit.
Let us pray.
Collect.

DEUS, qui hanc sacratíssimam noctem glória Domínicæ resurrectiónis illústras : consérva in nova famíliæ tuæ progénie adoptiónis spíritum, quem dedísti :

O GOD, who dost illumine this most holy night by the glory of our Lord's resurrection ; preserve in the new offspring of thy family the spirit of adoption which thou hast

ut córpore et mente renováti, puram tibi exhíbeant servitútem. Per eúmdem Dóminum.
℞. Amen.

Léctio Epístolæ beáti Pauli Apóstoli ad Colossénses, c. 3.

FRATRES, Si consurrexístis cum Christo, quæ sursum sunt quǽrite, ubi Christus est in déxtera Dei sedens : quæ sursum sunt sápite, non quæ super terram. Mórtui enim estis, et vita vestra est abscóndita cum Christo in Deo. Cum Christus apparúerit vita vestra : tunc et vos apparébitis cum ipso in glória.

given ; that, renewed in body and mind, they may show forth in thy sight a pure service Through the same Lord
℞ Amen.

Lesson from the Epistle of St. Paul the Apostle to the Colossians, c. 3.

BRETHREN : If you be risen with Christ, seek the things that are above where Christ is sitting at the right hand of God : mind the things that are above, not the things that are upon the earth. For you are dead, and your life is hidden with Christ in God. When Christ shall appear, who is your life, then shall you also appear with him in glory.

After the Epistle the priest solemnly intones the Allelúia, which he sings thrice, each time upon a higher tone ; the choir repeats it after him in the same manner, and after the third time adds the verse :

℣. Confitémini Dómino, quóniam bonus : quóniam in sǽculum misericórdia ejus.

Tractus. Ps. 116. Laudáte Dóminum, omnes gentes : et collaudáte eum, omnes pópuli. ℣. Quóniam confirmáta est super nos misericórdia ejus : et véritas Dómini manet in ætérnum.

℣. Praise ye the Lord, because he is good : because his mercy endureth for ever.

Tract. Ps. 116. Praise the Lord, all ye Gentiles : and praise him, all ye people. ℣. Because his mercy is confirmed upon us : and the truth of the Lord remaineth for ever.

At the Gospel, lights are not carried, but only incense.

✠ Sequéntia sancti Evangélii secúndum Matthǽum, c. 28.

VESPERE autem sábbati, quæ lucéscit in prima sábbati, venit Ma-

✠ Continuation of the holy Gospel according to St. Matthew, c. 28.

AND in the end of the sabbath, when it began to dawn towards the

ría Magdaléne et áltera María vidére sepúlcrum. Et ecce terræmótus factus est magnus. Angelus enim Dómini descéndit de cælo, et accédens revólvit lápidem, et sedébat super eum : erat autem aspéctus ejus sicut fulgur : et vestiméntum ejus sicut nix. Præ timóre autem ejus extérriti sunt custódes, et facti sunt velut mórtui. Respóndens autem Angelus, dixit muliéribus : Nolíte timére vos : scio enim quod Jesum, qui crucifíxus est, quæritis : non est hic : surréxit enim, sicut dixit. Veníte, et vidéte locum, ubi pósitus erat Dóminus. Et cito eúntes, dícite discípulis ejus quia surréxit : et ecce præcédit vos in Galilæam : ibi eum vidébitis. Ecce prædíxi vobis.

first day of the week, came Mary Magdalen, and the other Mary, to see the sepulchre. And behold there was a great earthquake. For an angel of the Lord descended from heaven, and coming, rolled back the stone, and sat upon it ; and his countenance was as lightning ; and his raiment as snow. And for fear of him, the guards were struck with terror, and became as dead men. And the angel answering, said to the women : Fear not you : for I know that you seek Jesus who was crucified. He is not here, for he is risen, as he said. Come and see the place where the Lord was laid. And going quickly, tell ye his disciples that he is risen : and behold he will go before you into Galilee : there you shall see him. Lo, I have foretold it to you.

Credo is not said ; but after Dóminus vobíscum *the priest adds* Orémus, *and proceeds to the Offertory, for which no Antiphon is said or sung.* Glória Patri *is said at the end of the Psalm* Lavábo.

Secreta.

SUSCIPE, quæsumus, Dómine, preces pópuli tui, cum oblatiónibus hostiárum : ut Paschálibus initiáta mystériis, ad æternitátis nobis medélam, te operánte, profíciant. Per Dóminum nostrum Jesum Christum Fílium tuum : qui tecum vivit et regnat in unitáte Spíritus San-

Secret.

RECEIVE, O Lord, we beseech thee, the prayers of thy people, together with the offering of sacrifices : that what we have begun at these paschal mysteries may, by thine operation, obtain for us an eternal remedy. Through our Lord Jesus Christ thy Son : who with thee and the Holy Ghost liveth and reign-

cti Deus. ℣. Per ómnia sǽcula sæculórum.

℟. Amen.

℣. Dóminus vobíscum.

℟. Et cum spíritu tuo.

℣. Sursum corda.

℟. Habémus ad Dóminum.

℣. Grátias agámus Dómino Deo nostro.

℟. Dignum et justum est.

VERE dignum et justum est, æquum et salutáre, te quidem, Dómine, omni témpore, sed in hac potíssimum nocte gloriósius prædicáre, cum Pascha nostrum immolátus est Christus. Ipse enim verus est Agnus, qui ábstulit peccáta mundi. Qui mortem nostram moriéndo destrúxit, et vitam resurgéndo reparávit. Et ídeo cum Angelis et Archángelis, cum Thronis et Dominatiónibus, cumque omni milítia cæléstis exércitus, hymnum glóriæ tuæ cánimus, sine fine dicéntes :

eth God.   ℣. For ever and ever.

℟. Amen.

℣. The Lord be with you.

℟. And with thy spirit.

℣. Lift up your hearts.

℟. We have lifted them up to the Lord.

℣. Let us give thanks to the Lord our God.

℟. It is meet and just.

IT is truly meet and just, right and available unto salvation, that at all times, but chiefly on this night, we should extol thy glory, when Christ our pasch was sacrificed. For he is the true Lamb, that hath taken away the sins of the world ; who by dying hath overcome our death, and by rising again hath restored our life. And therefore with the angels and archangels, the thrones and dominions, and with the whole host of the heavenly army, we sing a hymn to thy glory, saying again and again :

Sanctus, *and the rest, as in the Canon.*

Communicántes, et noctem sacratíssimam celebrántes resurrectiónis Dómini nostri Jesu Christi secúndum carnem : sed et memóriam venerántes in primis gloriósæ semper Vírginis Maríæ, Genitrícis ejúsdem Dei et Dómini nostri Jesu Christi, &c.

Communicating and keeping the most sacred night of the resurrection of our Lord Jesus Christ, according to the flesh : and also reverencing the memory first of the glorious Mary, ever a Virgin, mother of the same our God, and Lord Jesus Christ, &c.

12*

Hanc ígitur oblatiónem servitútis nostræ, sed et cunctæ famíliæ tuæ, quam tibi offérimus pro his quoque quos regeneráre dignátus es ex aqua et Spíritu Sancto, tríbuens eis remissiónem ómnium peccatórum, quǽsumus, Dómine, ut placátus accípias : diésque nostros in tua pace dispónas, atque ab ætérna damnatióne nos éripi, et in electórum tuórum júbeas grege numerári. Per Christum Dóminum nostrum. Amen.

We therefore beseech thee, O Lord, to be appeased and to accept this offering of our bounden duty as also of thy whole household, which we make unto thee on behalf of these too whom thou hast vouchsafed to bring to a new birth by water and the Holy Ghost, giving them remission of all their sins ; order our days in thy peace ; grant that we be rescued from everlasting damnation and counted within the fold of thine elect. Through Christ our Lord. Amen.

The rest as in the Canon, except that the kiss of peace is not given, Agnus Dei is omitted, and also the Postcommunion ; but the three prayers before Communion are said as usual. After the Communion of the priest (and of the people if any) Vespers are sung in the choir, in the following manner. The Antiphon and Psalm are intoned in the choir, but there is no Little Chapter, nor Hymn, nor Verse.

VESPERS

Aña. Allelúia, allelúia, allelúia.

Psalmus. 116.

LAUDATE Dóminum omnes gentes : * laudáte eum, omnes pópuli.

Quóniam confirmáta est super nos misericórdia ejus : * et véritas Dómini manet in ætérnum.

Glória.

Aña. Allelúia, alleluia, allelúia.

Ant. Alleluia, alleluia, alleluia.

Psalm. 116.

PRAISE the Lord, all ye nations : praise him, all ye people.

Because his mercy is confirmed in us ; and the truth of the Lord remaineth for ever.

Glory.

Ant. Alleluia, alleluia, alleluia.

Here the priest sings the first three words of the following Antiphon, which is continued by the choir :

Aña. Vespére autem sábbati, quæ lucéscit in

Ant. In the evening of the sabbath, which dawns in the

prima sábbati, venit Maria Magdaléne, et áltera María, vidére sepúlcrum. Allelúia.

first day of the week, came Mary Magdalen, and the other Mary, to see the sepulchre. Alleluia.

Afterwards the Magníficat is sung, with Glória Patri at the end, and the altar is incensed, as usual at Vespers.

Véspere autem sábbati is then repeated, and the priest at the altar turns to the people, singing :

℣. Dóminus vobíscum.
℟. Et cum spíritu tuo.
Orémus.

℣. The Lord be with you.
℟. And with thy spirit.
Let us pray.

SPIRITUM nobis, Dómine, tuæ caritátis infúnde ; ut quos sacraméntis Paschálibus satiásti, tua fácias pietáte concórdes. Per Dóminum... in unitáte Spíritus Sancti Deus.
℟. Amen.

POUR forth upon us, O Lord, the spirit of thy love, that those whom thou hast fed with the paschal sacraments may, by thy goodness, be of one mind Through our Lord in unity with the same Holy Ghost.
℟. Amen.

Then he says:

℣. Dóminus vobíscum.
℟. Et cum spíritu tuo.

℣. The Lord be with you
℟. And with thy spirit.

The deacon turns to the people and says :

Ite, missa est, allelúia, allelúia.
℟. Deo grátias, allelúia, allelúia.

Go, you are dismissed, alleluia, alleluia.
℟. Thanks be to God, alleluia, alleluia.

The blessing is given, and the Gospel of St. John is read as usual

EASTER SUNDAY

THE MASS

For this Mass we have only to refer to the Notice given p. 353 on the Mass of Holy Saturday.

For this Mass we have only to refer to the Notice given p. 353 on the Mass of Holy Saturday.

STATION AT ST. MARY MAJOR

Introitus. Ps. 138.

RESURREXI, et adhuc tecum sum, allelúia : posuísti super me manum tuam, allelúia : mirábilis facta est sciéntia tua, allelúia, allelúia. *Ps.* Dómine, probásti me, et cognovísti me : tu cognovísti sessiónem meam, et resurrectiónem meam. ℣. Glória Patri.

Introit. Ps. 138.

I AROSE, and am still with thee, alleluia : thou hast laid thy hand upon me, alleluia : thy knowledge is become wonderful, alleluia, alleluia. *Ps.* Lord, thou hast proved me, and known me : thou hast known my sitting down, and my rising up. ℣. Glory.

Oratio.

DEUS, qui hodiérna die per Unigénitum tuum, æternitátis nobis áditum, devícta morte, reserásti : vota nostra, quæ præveniéndo aspíras, étiam adjuvándo proséquere. Per eúmdem Dóminum.

Collect.

O GOD, who through thine only-begotten Son didst on this day overcome death and open unto us the gates of everlasting life, follow up with thine aid the desires which thou didst forestall with thine inspiration. Through the same Lord.

Léctio Epístolæ beáti Pauli Apóstoli ad Corínthios, *I, c.* 5.

FRATRES, Expurgáte vetus ferméntum, ut sitis nova conspérsio, sicut estis ázymi. Etenim Pascha nostrum immolátus est Christus. Itáque epulémur, non in ferménto véteri, neque in ferménto malítiæ et nequítiæ : sed in ázymis sinceritátis et veritátis.

Graduale. Ps. 117.

HÆC dies quam fecit Dóminus : exsultémus, et lætémur in ea. ℣. Confitémini Dómino, quóniam bonus : quóniam in sǽculum misericórdia ejus. Allelúia, allelúia. ℣. Pascha nostrum immolátus est Christus.

Sequentia.

VICTIMÆ pascháli laudes immolent Christiáni.

Agnus redémit oves : Christus ínnocens Patri reconciliávit peccatóres.

Mors et vita duéllo conflixére mirándo : dux vitæ mórtuus, regnat vivus.

Lesson from the Epistle of St. Paul the Apostle to the Corinthians, *I, c.* 5.

BRETHREN : Purge out the old leaven, that you may be a new paste, as you are unleavened : for Christ our Pasch is sacrificed. Therefore let us feast, not with the old leaven, nor with the leaven of malice and wickedness, but with the unleavened bread of sincerity and truth.

Gradual. Ps. 117.

THIS is the day which the Lord hath made : let us be glad and rejoice therein. ℣. Give praise to the Lord, for he is good : for his mercy endureth for ever. Alleluia, alleluia. ℣. Christ our Pasch is immolated.

Sequence.

LET Christian men their voices raise
And sing the Paschal Victim's praise
This solemn festival to keep.
Christ, innocent and undefiled,
Sinners to God hath reconciled,
The Lamb redeemed the Father's sheep.
In this great triumph death and life
Together met in wondrous strife,
The Prince of Life, once dead, doth reign.

Dic nobis, María, quid vidísti in via?

Say what thou sawest, Mary, say,
Upon thy road at break of day?

Sepúlcrum Christi vivéntis : et glóriam vidi resurgéntis :

'Christ's glory as he rose again.
'I saw the tomb where he did lie,

Angélicos testes, sudárium et vestes.

'And angel witnesses hard by,
'The winding cloths were there to see

Surréxit Christus spes mea : præcédet vos in Galilǽam.

'Christ, my hope, is risen and he
'Awaiteth you in Galilee.'

Scimus Christum surrexísse a mórtuis vere : tu nobis, victor Rex, miserére.   Amen.   Allelúia.

We know that Christ is risen indeed
And, victor king, before thee plead,
Have pity, Lord, and clemency.   Amen.   Alleluia.

✠ Sequéntia sancti Evangélii secúndum Marcum, c. 16.

✠ Continuation of the holy Gospel according to St. Mark, c. 16.

IN illo témpore : María Magdaléne, et María Jacóbi, et Salóme, emérunt arómata, ut veniéntes úngerent Jesum. Et valde mane una sabbatórum, véniunt ad monuméntum, orto jam sole.   Et dicébant ad ínvicem : Quis revólvet nobis lápidem ab óstio monuménti? Et respiciéntes vidérunt revolútum lápidem.   Erat quippe magnus valde. Et introëúntes in monuméntum, vidérunt júvenem sedéntem in dextris coopértum stola cándida, et obstupuérunt. Qui dicit illis : Nolíte expavéscere : Jesum quæ-

AT that time : Mary Magdalen, and Mary the mother of James and Salome, bought sweet spices, that, coming, they might anoint Jesus.   And very early in the morning, the first day of the week, they come to the sepulchre, the sun being now risen : and they said one to another : Who shall roll us back the stone from the door of the sepulchre? And looking, they saw the stone rolled back, for it was very great. And entering into the sepulchre, they saw a young man sitting on the right side, clothed with a white robe, and they were astonished ; who saith to them : Be not

ritis Nazarénum crucifíxum : surréxit, non est hic ; ecce locus ubi posuérunt eum. Sed ite, dícite discípulis ejus, et Petro, quia præcédit vos in Galílæam : ibi eum vidébitis, sicut dixit vobis.

affrighted ; you seek Jesus of Nazareth, who was crucified : he is risen, he is not here ; behold the place where they laid him. But go, tell his disciples and Peter, that he goeth before you into Galilee : there you shall see him, as he told you.

Credo.

Offertorium. Ps. 75.

TERRA trémuit et quiévit, dum resúrgeret in judício Deus, allelúia.

Creed.

Offertory. Ps. 75.

THE earth trembled and was still, when God aroes in judgement, alleluia.

Secreta.

SUSCIPE, quǽsumus, Dómine, preces pópuli tui cum oblatiónibus hostiárum : ut Paschálibus initiáta mystériis, ad æternitátis nobis medélam, te operánte, profíciant. Per Dóminum.

Secret.

RECEIVE, o Lord, we beseech thee, the prayers and sacrifices of thy people : and grant that what we have begun at these Paschal mysteries may by thy power avail us as a healing remedy unto everlasting life. Through our Lord.

The Preface of Easter, Te quidem Dómine (sed in hac potíssimum die), *and the proper* Communicántes *and* Hanc ígitur, *p.* 16.

Communio. 1 Cor. 5.

PASCHA nostrum immolátus est Christus, allelúia : itaque epulémur in ázymis sinceritátis et veritátis, allelúia, allelúia, allelúia.

Communion. 1 Cor. 5.

CHRIST our Pasch is immolated, alleluia : therefore let us feast with the unleavened bread of sincerity and truth, alleluia, alleluia, alleluia.

Postcommunio.

SPIRITUM nobis, Dómine, tuæ caritátis infúnde : ut quos sacraméntis Paschálibus satiásti, tua fácias pietáte concórdes. Per Dóminum.

Postcommunion.

POUR forth upon us, O Lord, the spirit of thy charity : that those whom thou hast fed with the Paschal sacraments thou, by thy loving-kindness, mayest make to be of one mind. Through our Lord.

THE RESURRECTION

A woodcut by Gustave Doré (1832–1883)